LEEDS BECKETT UNIVERSITY
LIBRARY
DISCARDED
17 0006125 7

Inequality and Development: Case Studies from the Third World

Publications of the Commonwealth Geographical Bureau

Problems of Regional Development in Eastern Africa. East African Geographical Review (special issue) No. 15, June 1977. Published jointly by Uganda Geographical Association and Makerere University.

Natural Resources in Tropical Countries. Ooi, J.B. (ed.), Singapore University Press (1983).

Remote Sensing and Tropical Land Management. Eden, M.J. and Parry, J.T. (eds), John Wiley & Sons Ltd. (1986).

Ambiguous Alternative. Tourism in Small Developing Countries. Stephen Britton and William C. Clarke, (eds), University of the South Pacific (1987).

Geographical Perspectives on Development in Southern Africa. Williams, G.J. and Wood, A.P. (eds), Commonwealth Geographical Bureau/James Cook University (1987).

Inequality and Development: Case Studies from the Third World. Swindell, K., Baba, J. and Mortimore, M. (eds), Macmillan (1989).

Energy, Development and Environment in the Tropics. Courtenay, P.P. and Abdul Samad Hadi (eds), Universiti Kebangsaan Press (in preparation).

Inequality and Development: Case Studies from the Third World

Edited by

K. Swindell
Senior Lecturer at the Department of Geography and Associate, Centre of West African Studies, University of Birmingham

J.M. Baba
Professor of Geography at the Federal University of Technology, Minna, Nigeria

and

M.J. Mortimore
formerly Professor of Geography at Bayero University, Kano, Nigeria

Published by Macmillan with a grant from the Commonwealth Foundation and the Commonwealth Geographical Bureau

First published 1989

Published by *Macmillan Publishers Ltd*
London and Basingstoke
Associated companies and representatives in Accra, Auckland, Delhi, Dublin, Gaborone, Hamburg, Harare, Hong Kong, Kuala Lumpur, Lagos, Manzini, Melbourne, Mexico City, Nairobi, New York, Singapore, Tokyo

ISBN 0-333-46543-1

Printed in Hong Kong

British Library Cataloguing in Publication Data
Inequality and development: third world perspectives.
1. Developing countries. Economic developments
I. Swindell, Kenneth, *1935–* II. Baba, J.M.
III. Mortimore, M.J.
330.9172'4

ISBN 0-333-46543-1

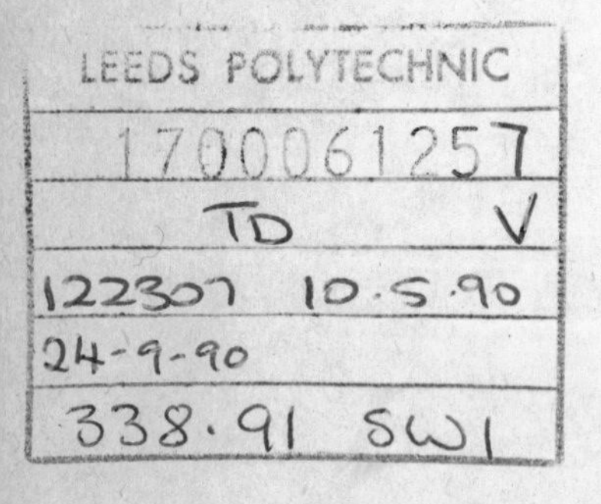

Contents

List of maps and diagrams

Editors' Preface

The papers in this volume were presented at a workshop on 'Spatial Inequalities and Development', sponsored by the Commonwealth Geographical Bureau as one of its continuing series of regionally and topically diverse workshops. The West Africa Representative of the Bureau's Committee of Management, Professor Adetoye Faniran, extended the CGB's request to Bayero University, Kano, to act as hosts for a meeting to be held in 1985, and the workshop duly took place from 16–20 September. It was made possible by a grant from the Commonwealth Foundation, which enabled seven participants from outside West Africa to contribute papers. The following countries were represented: Nigeria, Ghana, Zimbabwe, India, Canada and the United Kingdom. The CGB was represented by its Treasurer, Mr Michael Eden.

The Vice-Chancellor of Bayero University, Professor Ibrahim Umar, gave his full support from the outset and the facilities of the University were kindly put at the disposal of the organizers. The Department of Geography set up an organizing committee who made the necessary arrangements under the able chairmanship of Dr E.A. Olofin, assisted by Drs J.A. Falola and H.A.C. Main. The workshop took place at the end of one of the best growing seasons in recent years and an unforgettable field excursion was made through the resplendent farmlands of the Kano close-settled zone to the Kano River Irrigation Project, Tiga Lake and the Rano Hills.

In view of the constraints imposed by transport costs on overseas participants and the numerical strength of the geographical community in the Nigerian University system, it was inevitable that the attendance at the workshop would be weighted towards the host country. This presented the Editors, who were commissioned by the meeting to prepare a selection of papers, with an unenviable task of achieving the best possible regional balance. Several Nigerian papers had reluctantly to be omitted, while in order to broaden the scope invitations were sent to a few Commonwealth geographers who were unable to be present at the workshop. The Editors are most grateful to all those who participated, whether or not their papers appear in the present volume, for their understanding and co-operation.

The Editors would like to record their appreciation to the Treasurer Mr Michael Eden for his support at all times. Finally, it is acknowledged with gratitude that the publication of this volume of essays has been made possible by a grant from the Commonwealth Foundation, and the Commonwealth Geographical Bureau.

K. Swindell
J. Baba
M.J. Mortimore

Introduction

Ken Swindell
Department of Geography and Associate of the Centre of West African Studies, University of Birmingham, England

Developed and underdeveloped countries are commonly characterized as opposites; the former are said to be affluent, urban and industrialized while the latter are poor, rural and agrarian. This popular dichotomy was underwritten by academic debates in the 1970s when on the one hand neo-Marxists viewed the world economy as being made up of a 'core' and a 'periphery', while the new international Keynesians divided the world into the 'north' and the 'south'. A more worrying division was the one made between temperate and tropical, an approach adopted by Karmarck (1976) who argued that tropicality is the factor which underlies underdevelopment. More recently academics and observers studying underdeveloped countries have urged that they should not be seen as an undifferentiated whole, but stress should be placed on their heterogeneity. Underdeveloped countries vary in their territorial size, environments and populations as well as their economic, social and political systems. However, many have experienced colonial rule, and all of those discussed in this book with one exception were formerly part of the British Empire.

The implications of colonial rule are considerable, not only because of the impact of Europeans on local economies, cultures and political systems, but also because of the manner in which decolonization has taken place. Even so, the colonial experience (and withdrawal from it) has not been universally the same. The British presence in India extended over hundreds of years compared with the much shorter period in tropical Africa. There were also differences in colonial policies, which for example influenced the extent to which Europeans alienated land and instituted new forms of settlement. European merchant and industrial capital acted on non-capitalist systems which had substantial differences, and on groups of people and regions with widely different pre-colonial histories and levels of political organization. In some instances Europeans were dealing with princes, traditional chiefs and emirs who presided over highly centralized state systems, while in others they were dealing with people who had a less centralized system of government. Thus structural changes brought about by colonialism were refracted through prisms of indigenous experience and history, to produce regional and localized patterns of change, adaptation and resistance. And while most underdeveloped countries do lie within the tropics, tropical climates and ecologies are complex, embracing forests, savannas and deserts.

But if differences among underdeveloped countries are increasingly being recognized, then equally our attention is being focused on disparities within these countries. Within underdeveloped countries there are regional disparities in levels of well-being, as well as between town and countryside and men and women. It is true that differences in income and standards of living occur in all countries, but in underdeveloped ones they are often acute and more accentuated. Also, it has been suggested that within developing countries there is an 'internal colonialism', where one region or group dominates, controls and extracts wealth from the others (Drakakis-Smith and Williams 1983).

The development of 'development'

After World War Two the colonial authorities especially in British and French territories launched a number of initiatives which were designed to alter the direction and pace of economic development. The war effort itself had led to the setting up of marketing boards in British possessions, while afterwards an improvement in the economic performance of the colonies was required as they had to play their part in the reconstruction of post-war Britain. The entry of the United States into the world development arena occurred in the early 1960s partly prompted by their fear that decolonization of the French and British territories would leave a vacuum which would be filled by Soviet-assisted regimes.

The concern over equity issues within developing countries began to emerge after independence in the late 1960s. In 1966 a group of academics from Northwestern University USA published *Growth without development*, in which they argued that the high growth rates being experienced in Liberia as measured by indices such as GDP disguised the unequal distribution of the benefits derived from the expansion of iron-ore mining (Clower *et al.* 1966). To many observers unequal distribution seemed a novel idea. The development orthodoxy of the 1950s emphasizing production and growth was still generally accepted, and it held that mass welfare was dependent on productivity and the productive investment of the funds available. This view of economic profitability first, social improvement second, came under attack from various sources and for numerous reasons. By the 1970s it was apparent that growth in employment opportunities had been slow and explanations of poverty became increasingly linked with unemployment and underemployment. The underemployed were identified not only by the amount of work they did, but also by the limited rewards they received. The poor became those whose conditions of existence and human needs fell below a standard established either statistically or by consensus. Therefore the *basic needs* approach defining acceptable levels of food, clothing and shelter was adopted, and equity objectives were moved to the forefront of development planning (Rimmer 1984). It has been argued that the adoption of basic needs is motivated not by a 'moral' concern but out of self-interest. If the developed capitalist world is to sell its products and extend industry into Third World countries then the provision of cheap food is essential, together with attempts to stave off rural protest (Gakou 1987).

The equity issue was also influenced by the populist sentiments of the 1970s and the realization that a majority of large-scale development schemes had not produced what was expected, together with the 'discovery' of the informal manufacturing sector (see Bromley and Geery 1979). Populist notions which reiterated the importance of the peasantry, and the informal urban sector, also coincided with the nationalistic sentiments of newly independent countries because they renounced the acceptance of foreign-based technology and expertise. The case for the promotion of true development through redistribution rather than production was supported by arguments that it would not dampen growth, because improved infrastructures, health services and education would raise productivity and efficiency over wider areas. Also, patterns of demand could be reshaped as the reliance on external goods and services was reduced. But it soon became apparent that redistribution alone was not enough and equity policies became modified and couched in terms of redistribution *through*, or *with* growth.

By the mid-1970s the World Bank and other agencies began to address themselves to the problem of reaching the 'poorest of the poor' who were disproportionately located in rural areas (World Bank 1976). Efforts were redoubled to raise production levels, especially of basic foodstaples and the 'Green Revolution' based on new crop hybrids initially looked to be a breakthrough in transforming rural areas, as new seeds could be distributed to large numbers of farmers. However, the Green Revolution, which was primarily developed in India, had a poor performance in Latin America and Africa, and partly as a result of this, and the popularity of the 'basic needs' approach, 'Integrated Rural Development' became a major policy instrument in the 1970s. Integrated Rural Development is aimed at not just improving one crop or sector, but the transformation of rural life over a wide area. But even with unlimited resources the problem is one of trying to do everything at once. Simultaneous change creates problems of adjustment for villagers, while IRD like the Green Revolution appears to have benefited those already better-off peasants (Mabogunje and Gana 1979).

The equity issue has generated a large body of literature which embraces topics such as migration, the rural-urban divide, employment problems, and especially income distribution. The study of income distribution and inequality is fraught with difficulties, and as Kuznetz observed in 1955 it is primarily illuminated by speculation, rather than hard empirical information. The situation is better in India and south-east Asia than in Africa, where data are available for only one-third of the countries, and these are frequently based on cross-sectional surveys in urban areas. One of the problems of researching income distribution is whether one should attempt to measure (and correct) absolute or relative poverty. Eicher and Baker (1982) in reviewing the literature suggest that there should be a shift towards examining absolute poverty and changes in absolute income, malnutrition and employment. Also as Rimmer (1984) points out, the reduction of inequality is not a necessary condition for poverty relief. Absolute gains made by the poor can occur, at the same time as inequality is increasing.

Another major problem is the conceptual one of deciding the most appropriate unit to be studied. Although it is commonly accepted that households should be studied there is a great range in their size and complexity in Third World countries. Households can also be subdivided into sub-groups or individuals and for example recently attention has been focused on the differences between the roles of men and women. The issue is further compounded by the effects of development cycles in domestic groups, which ideally requires analysis by cohorts. It is also difficult to measure wages and income or their equivalents in households where subsistence production is a primary activity. How does one deal with unpaid family labour, and how should one value subsistence food production? These problems have plagued national account surveys in Kenya, and by 1978 Kenya's system of national accounts were of little use for making inferences about changes in the functional distribution of income.

Finally the assessment of income is made difficult on practical grounds because of the seasonality of farming, fishing and livestock grazing. The switching from one sector to another by many rural workers is symptomatic of the way in which household economies straddle both the paid and unpaid sectors. In some rural households income derived from non-farming activities is greater than from agriculture. Thus rural income data need treating with some caution. Data on income differences and on unequal access to resources such as land and labour are often well developed in small-scale studies of households or village communities; the problem however becomes acute when one needs similar information at the regional level, especially in rural areas. Frequently extrapolations are made from household surveys, or a variety of surveys are patched together to give some indication of differences in income between areas.

While evidence about income differentiation, levels of nutrition and access to resources is important, it is also necessary to think of inequality as a *process* and not just an event or a static situation. Inequalities among people and the location they occupy must be evaluated in terms of production relationships, which may be shaped by social networks such as kinship, as well as through the penetration and development of market forces leading to economic differentiation. As Eicher and Baker (1982) point out, the compilation of such things as Gini coefficients is only part of the research needed on inequality; there is also a need for research on how the changing control and ownership of assets influences income distribution.

Meaningful studies are also required of the control of resources such as land, capital and especially labour, and they should be articulated within a historical context; many researchers and development planners have a notable lack of interest in economic and social history. For example although colonial policies may have initiated inequality (through decisions to assist plantation owners, European settlers and peasant commodity producers), in pre-colonial Africa and Asia there were also existing inequalities in status and income. These inequalities are less amenable to measurement, but they were apparent in people's access to resources and power either through caste and servitude, or through descent and office.

For many observers class analysis and the relations of production are the most relevant and powerful framework for the analysis of inequality. Yet studies of production and production relations need to be complemented by analyses of distribution and exchange, as both local merchants and international markets have a powerful impact on rural producers. Arguments about production and exchange relations led to more radical interpretations of inequality and underdevelopment in the late 1960s, which have led many academics and politicians to believe that the attainment of growth with equity can only be achieved within socialist frameworks of reconstruction and by the withdrawal from political and economic clientage with former colonial powers and the world capitalist system in general.

The papers in this volume discuss several of the issues referred to above and the conference brought together not only geographers from different countries, but also those of different theoretical and methodological persuasions. Therefore it should not be surprising if the papers reflect the trends within the social sciences and geography from the 1960s onwards. Unfortunately the papers do not reflect the impact of recent events connected with the adoption of IMF policies, largely because they were written before the full effects were apparent. The organization of papers by section is one primarily of convenience and there is considerable overlap, not least in their concern with the nature and effects of state intervention in the process of social and economic development. The remainder of this Introduction considers each of the sections in turn and tries to provide a context for the papers together with comments on the issues they raise.

Measuring spatial inequalities

Spatial analysis and techniques of measurement received a good deal of attention in the mid-1960s when the quantitative revolution was running strongly in tandem with the positivist paradigm. Thus two-dimensional space was, and is, used as an explanatory variable to analyse patterns and irregularities among a whole range of socio-economic variables. However, geographical space can be used in a variety of ways (see Hinderink and Steckenburg 1978). It can be used as a means of delimiting statistical units, or as a means of collecting data, as well as a formal framework for the description and identification of intra- and inter-regional differences within a country.

Distribution patterns lend themselves to the application of techniques which investigate such things as distance-decay functions and levels of accessibility. Therefore it is hardly surprising that when the growth-pole concept emerged, it produced an almost instinctive response from geographers. Growth-poles and the 'trickle-down' effect became the stock in trade of the modernization school of development which attracted the attention of numerous geographers. The modernization school contends that the polarization of resources at particular points is a necessary short-term outcome of the distribution of limited resources. However, it is argued that in due course the concentration of resources could be diluted by the development of modern capitalism and access to social and economic resources will gradually spread ever wider within a region or country.

Growth-poles and modernization theory soon attracted a number of critiques. There were those who believed that polarization was concentrating and draining resources from less-developed into the already advantaged centres of production and exchange (Myrdal 1957). Friedmann (1966) suggested an alternative spatial framework where centres and peripheries reflect the concentration of development, or the lack of it, and the inequalities brought about by free market forces. Yet this was largely a descriptive framework, and it was the theorizing of Frank (1968; 1978) and Wallerstein (1979) which intensified the attack on the modernization school through their expositions of dependency and underdevelopment and the concept of the 'core' and 'periphery'. They argue that the 'cores' are where capitalist relations of production and exchange flourish and the means whereby 'peripheries' are permanently disadvantaged and actively underdeveloped. In the scenarios of underdevelopment considerable stress is placed on the relations of exchange and adverse terms of trade, which lead to the stagnation of peripheral regions.

Another theory with spatial undertones is that of the rural-urban divide. Lipton (1977) contends that much rural poverty in India and Africa is the result of the concentration of power and resources within urban areas, and the ability of urban classes and interest groups to manipulate producer prices to the disadvantage of the majority of rural farmers. All of these theories have had an appeal for geographers largely because of their spatial underpinnings as well as their ability to accommodate different ideological viewpoints.

The development of radical geography in the late 1960s onwards has had several outcomes, but one has been that many geographers now believe that space is neither a formal framework nor an explanatory variable but is something which has to be explained. The areal distribution of resources and unequal access is generated by social structures and the historic development of social relations of production. Moreover, it is the political economy of a nation and its insertion into the world capitalist economy which historically determines the pattern of both internal and external inequality.

The essays in Section One are primarily concerned with spatial analysis, but use it in rather different ways. The opening essay by

Songsore describes the use of multivariate analysis as a means of revealing the inequality in wealth between the north and south of Ghana. But in line with a more radical outlook he extends his spatial analysis by locating the north-south difference in Ghana within the context of colonial rule and the class dynamics it provoked. Thus space became not an explanatory variable but the resolution of social and economic relations. Ijere's essay on north-eastern Nigeria uses indices of social welfare, agricultural technology and extension services to illustrate different levels of development among a collection of administrative units. But as Ijere shows, the territorial principle of resource allocation by government is also shaped by these administrative units and produces its own inequalities. Henkel's essay directly addresses the issue of measuring inequalities. He provides a critique of several measures of spatial concentration and differentiation for the identification of people's access to resources and services. His essay also includes an application of one of them, the Gini coefficient, to the provision of medical services and schools in Zambia.

Falola's paper looks at the 19 states of Federal Nigeria and explores governments' attempts to provide an equitable distribution of health and educational services. Quite clearly a gap exists in the provision of these services between the north and south of the country and Falola concludes that the disparities are the result of ineffective policies. He argues that after 25 years of independence it is no longer sufficient to blame unequal access to basic resources and services on the colonial past; what is required is a more vigorous approach to these problems by government.

The essays in this section also look at spatial inequality at several different scales or levels; north-south, rural-urban and rural-rural. This can be seen as a welcome development in the debate about underdevelopment because in the social and political sciences there is a tendency to concentrate either on the micro-scale, that is the village or household, or the macro-scale, which only takes the nation-state as the unit of analysis. Small-scale household studies in recent years, along with farm systems analysis, have told us a great deal about how farmers and households work and survive (see Moock 1986), but there are dangers in extrapolating from these studies to make statements about wider areas and regions. The decline of regional analysis in geography (although now it seems to be making a comeback) and ethnography have contributed to the impoverishment of intermediate levels of analysis. Several essays in other sections of this volume also draw attention to the meso-level of analysis and not just through the use of administrative units within a particular region or country, but in terms of looking at constellations of villages, sub-regions of cities or groups of people. This kind of analysis is not a substitute for national studies or household surveys, but it does (and should) provide another kind of input into the development debate.

Inequality in rural and urban settings

While the essays in Section One are concerned with trying to identify and highlight where disparities in economic opportunities and social services occur, in Sections Two and Three the emphasis is on groups of people and classes, that is *who* gets what, where, with the emphasis on 'who'. Moreover attempts are made to explain why this is so. Explanations in all of these essays to a greater or lesser extent lie within particular ideological or conceptual frameworks. These frameworks range from the descriptive and structural-functionalist to the neo-Marxist, as well as the more populist approach to inequality and development. But almost all of the papers in Sections Two and Three display a strong sense of temporal and/or historical change: temporal in the sense of wanting to include time as a variable in their analyses, and historical in the sense of a concern with colonialism, its legacy, and the shifts and changes in the global political economy over the past 100 years.

The paper by Zinyama on Zimbabwe initially picks out the highly developed central corridor which was a product of the colonial period and domination by the white community. Along with Zambia and Kenya, Zimbabwe is perhaps a classic case of how European settlement and the control of commercial farming and industry produced levels of internal disparity in income which far exceed those found elsewhere in tropical Africa. The communal farming areas (formally the African Reserves) contain 60 per cent of the population who are primarily subsistence farmers living beyond the developed central corridor. This area has provided a challenge for the government, who face the political necessity of correcting the economic imbalance and of making the communal farming area something more than a labour reserve for the developed centre.

Kenya is another African country where a strong European presence led to the alienation of land. In Mackenzie and Taylor's paper they also point to the inequalities which were promoted by the colonial authorities, but unlike Zinyama they are less optimistic about attempts to improve the situation, and suggest that government policies have exacerbated rather than improved it. Mackenzie and Taylor discuss two important issues: the first is the role of women and changing inter-personal relationships in a situation where they have increasingly become heads of farming households and suppliers of farm inputs. The role of women in the African economy has provoked an ongoing debate, but apart from any moral issue about the way in which women are treated and the amount of work they do, it is important to understand their contribution to the total household economy and their relationships with men, particularly as this is crucial to the introduction of new technologies and crops.

This paper also raises the important issue of whether change can be effectively brought about through centralized programmes which rely on a 'trickle-down' effect. Mackenzie and Taylor reject this approach and believe that territorially based approaches are required where community control is a key element and where specific attention should be paid to gender relationships. The local community is in other words the scale or level wherein lies the knowledge and the understanding of local values, organization and environmental constraints which can bring about an effective change and improvement in personal and household incomes and welfare.

The papers on Kenya and Zimbabwe are a reminder of how different ideological stances taken by governments influence their development strategies and the way they unfold. In southern Africa there is the additional influence of the Republic of South Africa. The 'front-line' states are experiencing many difficulties as they try to reduce their economic dependence on the Republic while having to cope with the consequences and formulating policies to deal with them. For example, the decline in the numbers of migrant workers employed in South African mines has meant a reduction in employment opportunities for many households who have become dependent on this non-farm income. This is touched on in Arntzen and Silitshena's paper on Botswana, although their primary concern is access to land and farm incomes.

In Botswana there is an important distinction between arable lands and grazing lands and the income derived from cultivation, herding and non-farm work. Cattle ownership is skewed towards the prosperous, while poorer families are more reliant on arable farming and non-farm jobs. In an attempt to stimulate the economy, government schemes have been started to encourage commercial ranching and larger-scale arable farming through land leasing arrangements; in both cases they have favoured wealthier households and in some cases minority groups have been squeezed out of grazing areas. Furthermore the new Land Boards set up to allocate land and overcome the whims of traditional rulers who formerly controlled land seem to have advantaged an even smaller group of people.

This paper also looks at the complex problem of population pressure and land shortage. The rising human and animal population in Botswana is of some concern, especially when set against increased mechanization of arable farming and commercialization of herding, together with the falling number of non-farm jobs. Arntzen and Silitshena suggest that the shortage of arable land is only relative, while that for grazing is absolute. However, they make the important point that it is not simply access to land which matters, but the means to use it effectively by having enough labour, or draught animals and the fodder to maintain them. The increasingly differential access to land and resources in Botswana is apparently leading to an increase in the actual and potential 'land poor' and landless, especially in households headed by women, those without draught animals, and minority groups.

Baba's paper on irrigation schemes in northern Nigeria continues the theme of access to resources by rural people in the face of government intervention, as well as underlining the advantages of being able to monitor changes over time. The implementation of a series of irrigation schemes throughout northern Nigeria is in keeping with the desire of successive governments to redistribute accumulated wealth from oil revenues towards the less developed parts of the country. These objectives are being implemented in the north by the expansion and intensification of agriculture in selected river basins.

Baba's study started in 1970–1 and was repeated in 1979 in the Kano valley irrigation scheme, where he has studied the effects on farmers who have been brought within the scheme and who have had to adopt new cropping programmes designed by the managing authority. Two basic results emerge from the study: first, on the one hand there have been benefits in the irrigated areas measured through a substantial increase in the rate and volume of capital turnover (farm incomes, personal capital investment etc.) But it is also true that within the benefiting communities there have occurred increasing levels of inequality, and the conflict inherent in this situation is one which we return to at the end of this Introduction.

Finally in this section, Rangaswamy provides a traditional descriptive account of the differences in development between the tribal and non-tribal regions of Bharuch District in Gujarat, India.

The papers in Section Three transfer the issue of access to services by different groups of people to an urban setting. Tekie's paper on Manila describes the methods whereby the lowest-income earners (the bottom 40 per cent) acquire housing. Low-cost housing ranges from the most primitive squatter quarters to the purpose-built housing provided by government in its attempt to cure the housing problem.

The conclusion of Tekie's survey is in line with the work done by John Turner in Latin America, which suggests that government housing schemes and squatter resettlement are not always ideally suited to the people concerned; they are also inordinately expensive and a misuse of economic resources both within the urban and the national settings (Turner 1976; 1978). A better solution is to help people improve their existing housing by the provision of adequate services such as drainage, water supply and electricity, things which are conspicuously lacking even where government housing has been provided at considerable cost. This kind of pragmatic 'self-help' housing has attracted its critics; radical observers see it as petty-commodity housing, and yet another example of the marginalization of the poor in the interests of national bourgoisies, who are clients of the international capitalist system.

The linking of problems of internal inequality to the determinant power of international systems of production and exchange, is evident in the papers by Main and Cline-Cole. These papers are broadly structuralist in their approach to the causes of unequal access to resources and incomes; they suggest that the constraints on economic opportunities are neither fixed nor given, and certainly not a product of the distribution of natural resources. Main sees migrants to Kano as having their choices constrained by the lack of alternative jobs in rural areas, which reflect the development of the Nigerian oil economy from the mid-1970s onwards. Cline-Cole's study of domestic energy use in Kano and Freetown looks at fuel in terms of the dominant class interests, income profiles and whether the goals of energy use are expenditure minimization, or income generation. Cline-Cole sees the urban supply and use of domestic fuel as corresponding to spatial segments of the city which are dominated by particular class interests.

Both Cline-Cole's and Main's papers are concerned to point out that while external forces shape local inequalities none the less they take on particular configurations according to different geographic locations and the colonial and post-colonial experience of different groups of people. The structuralist approach to underdevelopment is much concerned with the linking or articulation of pre-capitalist and capitalist modes of production, wherein the preservation of the former in the interests of the latter ultimately creates underdevelopment. Because of their structural perspectives both these authors, together with Songsore (Section One), are keen to present space not as an independent variable, but as something which has to be explained, and a manifestation or resolution of the inequalities in local societies which are shaped by national and international economies.

Time, policy and development

The papers in Section Four extend the discussion of the role of the state to include policies which have been implemented nationally. The six papers consider diverse policy issues which include among other matters, income distribution in Sri Lanka, urbanization in Kenya, Tanzania and Uganda, and trade and ecology in Nigeria. The section begins with a paper by Samarasinghe on Sri Lanka.

Sri Lanka is a country where there are particular problems associated with a minority population, the Tamils and the dominant majority, the Sinhalese. But Samarasinghe's paper primarily touches on an issue which faces several Third World countries, that of the attraction of the free-market approach currently favoured by the IMF. This is in effect a return to the production thesis and contends that the reduction of state intervention in the economy allows higher growth and quicker returns nationally, although it may allow poor areas to become poorer. Alternative policies of equity and a wider distribution of investment and development produces slower growth in terms of national income and export earnings. In Sri Lanka from 1960–77 state control was evident in planned settlements in agriculture and the introduction of state industry in selected locations. After 1977 a more open economy was promoted, yet the political reality was such that the government is trying to make sure that although the better-off areas become richer, the poor areas are at least less poor.

Obudho's paper examines national policies towards urbanization and their relationship with the more general objectives of economic development. In Kenya, Tanzania and Uganda, historically levels of urbanization have been low, but currently they are experiencing high rates of urban growth, especially from rural to urban migration. Therefore national policies on urbanization are linked to wider issues of social and economic development and the containment of the already dominant capital cities of Nairobi, Kampala and Dar-es-Salaam. In addition to discussing urban housing policies charged with meeting the influx of population, Obudho compares the development policies of the three countries; Kenya has pursued a capitalist 'top-down' approach, while Tanzania has directed attention to agrarian reform and a 'bottom-up' strategy, while Uganda has followed a line somewhere in between the two. Since the 1980s Kenya has altered its stance to a modified 'bottom-up' approach and Obudho emphasizes that there is an increased concern in all three countries with the importance of medium-sized urban centres and their reinforcement with services and industries as a basis not only for checking urban migration, but as the means of achieving more balanced economic growth regionally.

The spreading of economic opportunity has also been a priority in Nigeria but this has been a particularly tricky issue in Africa's most populous country and one which embraces diverse interest groups associated with specific regions. This issue is taken up in the paper by Akintola-Arikawe which looks at two central industrial development banks, and evaluates their attempts to implement a 'convergence induction' policy in the regions of Nigeria. His conclusion is that as far as the industrial sector is concerned, divergence rather than convergence is the story of Nigeria since the 1970s. In Nigeria plans for a state-sponsored indigenous iron and steel industry date back to the early 1960s, when the high costs of imported construction materials became apparent. The promotion of the iron and steel industry has been bedevilled by the conflict between the economies of stole and attempts to locate the plants on an equitable basis *vis-à-vis* the different regional interests in Nigeria. The result is an imperfect, fragmented, over-priced industry with plant laterally integrated over vast distances. However there have been private initiatives in Nigeria in the field of light manufacturing, especially in the post-oil boom years. In the recent times of economic stringency, capital is now moving into agriculture and industry; principally because the easy options of large-scale trading using import licences, and contracting and building for an expanding public sector have now virtually disappeared.

While a number of essays in other sections discuss the progress of change, by comparing sets of data of different dates, or through fieldwork conducted over a number of years, Porter's essay is the only one which relies exclusively on archival data. This essay looks at Borno in the late-nineteenth and twentieth centuries, especially at trading networks within and beyond the 'core' of this ancient Sudanic state. These marketing systems are the means whereby Porter charts the changing social and economic structures of Borno. She points to the varying impact of colonial rule in northern Nigeria and how the north-east has become progressively peripheral and lacking in development, compared with the relatively thriving region of Hausaland to the west and south-west. The vigorous trading economy of Borno has gradually declined while that of Kano and its region have remained relatively vibrant during the past seventy years.

Mortimore and Binns' contribution, also located within Kano and ancient Borno, is the only one which directly addresses the issue of environment and inequality. Their essay combines two studies of how communities in different ways have been affected by disruption of their farming and pastoral ecologies and the consequences in terms of increasing inequality. The first uses information on drought-affected villages which Mortimore has assembled over the past 16 years: such a monitoring exercise must be virtually unique. The study looks at farming families in the semi-arid zone of Kano State and the adaptive response of poorer families to major agricultural drought. The thesis that indigenous structures were eroded during the colonial period leading to increased incapacity of farmers to cope with drought is examined by Mortimore and while he agrees that poor farmers have been disproportionately hit, evidence is produced to suggest that new methods and survival strategies have replaced former ones. The second study by Binns turns to the effects of state intervention through the Kano River irrigation project and how the alteration of the basin's hydrology has exacerbated unequal access to land and water by both farmers and pastoralists.

Whatever the long view of environmental disturbance may be, at the household level there remain the practicalities of survival. The business of short-run coping is one familiar to a majority of peasant and urban labouring households, and such occurrences chart their lifetimes. In some instances they resort to long-tried remedies or strategies, and often there are latent forces which determine their actions (see Bourdieu 1977). On the other hand the rural and urban poor continuously adapt and invent new methods of survival under adverse circumstances.

The issue of environmentalism is well known to geographers and also has a place in social sciences such as anthropology and economics. The distribution of natural resources was long held by geographers and economists to be an integral part of development and underdevelopment, and was also an important element in the theory of comparative advantage and inter-regional and international trade. In the 1960s and 1970s the static aspects of the theory of comparative advantage came under strong attack, especially the idea that natural resources were in some way fixed or given. Furthermore the Sahelian and other African droughts gave a strong impetus to radical anthropologists, geographers and historians to attack positivist positions on climatic change and other naturalistic reasons for disasters.

Yet while the radicals were right to denounce the dangers of environmental determinism, curiously enough they almost replaced it by another kind of dogmatic determinism. This determinism is well illustrated in the stagnationist view of underdevelopment and inequality espoused by the 'Dependency school'. Advocates of the dependency thesis maintain that peripheral economies are locked into the world's capitalist economy from which there is little escape. Indeed the continuance of capitalism in the metropolises hinges on the continuance of underdevelopment. This position has been attacked by numerous Marxists such as Brenner (1977) and Warren (1980), the former rejecting the pre-eminence given to exchange relations and the world trading systems in explanations of underdevelopment. In the accounts of the environment given by many neo-Marxists it appears it is not sufficient to contend (as many would) that the environmental circumstances are shaped by social and economic structures, but that they are necessarily fully determined and explained by them (Corbridge 1986). It follows that environmental disaster, and famine, are entirely the result of capitalist commodity relations.

While agreeing that climate and soils are mediated through social and political structures, environmental factors cannot be brushed aside as something capable of automatic solution given the correct political and institutional framework (Corbridge 1986). The environment and resource endowments are on the agenda of all states whatever their ideological commitments, although it might be conceded that some are able to cope with them better than others. While it may be undesirable to conduct analyses of development and inequality in a historical vacuum, equally they should not be conducted in an ecological one either.

Conclusion

With the ending of colonial rule there followed a period when people felt that governments had an almost unlimited capacity to promote economic and social welfare. There was a widespread feeling that privately generated change was too slow and ultimately inequitable. On the other hand it was believed that state-induced change would be faster and could be directed specifically towards selected objectives, locations and interest groups. This view was supported by economists and scientists who were cast in the role of experts who could map the routes politicians might take to achieve the transformation of their countries. In essence there was a convergence of political and scientific rationality, which in Rostow's phrase would lead to 'take-off into self-sustaining growth' (Rostow 1960). The conviction that rational scientifically based development would lead to increased welfare was shared by liberal and socialist régimes alike, although their political methods might differ. But time and time again the intended recipients of development inputs, such as fertilizers, credit, and machines, have not been the ones who have benefited, and one of the persistent themes in these essays is that intervention by the state has made things worse, not better.

If state intervention in general has increased inequalities rather than lessening them, why is this so, can it be remedied or is inequality inevitably part of the price to be paid for deep-rooted structural changes in society? These questions are easier to pose than answer. However, the list of reasons why development initiatives fail is a long one. Reasons for the inability of development programmes to promote widespread economic growth which reduces inequalities include administrative inefficiency, corruption, the implementation of inappropriate technologies and finally peasant ignorance and indifference. Attempts to remove corruption and administrative incompetence have been made through political putches and military coups, while proponents of the 'ignorant peasant' argument see the best hope to lie in programmes of education and better extension work.

In addition to these 'technical' reasons for the limited successes of development initiatives there are the 'structural' explanations for the continuance of poverty, inequality and underdevelopment. First, there are those who identify the persistence of the peasantry itself as the real stumbling block to agrarian change and progress – an 'uncaptured' peasantry who still retain some control over their means of production and who are not compliant with the objectives of either entrepreneurs or State managers (Hyden 1980). It was the continuance of peasant producers (albeit more passive ones than Hyden suggests) which led to the formulation of neo-Marxist explanations on underdevelopment and inequality in the 1960s. They pointed to the absence or limited extent of capitalist relations of production which according to orthodox Marxism would eventually lead to class conflict and the replacement of capitalism by socialism. The reasons for this blocking of the progression towards capitalism and socialism varied; on the one hand dependency theorists emphasized exchange relations and evisceration of local economies through the penetration of merchant capital and colonialism, while on the other those who emphasized production relations saw the inhibiting effects of the articulation of pre-capitalist and capitalist relations in Third World countries.

For most radicals the breaking of this deadlock is by a revolutionary means and withdrawal from the world capitalist system. But the problem for the Left is how this revolution is to be not only engineered, but maintained; how to raise the political consciousness of peasants and urban workers, and whether it can be done from the grass-roots upwards, or downwards via an intellectual vanguard. For Marxist-Leninists the answer lies in a rigorous centralized political system buttressed by an efficiently organized party. In other words it is in the party-state wherein lies the best hope of change and the move towards equitable distribution of resources and incomes.

When innovations in production and distribution have been initiated by both state capitalism and socialist régimes they have frequently met with passive or active resistance. It appears that peasants do not perceive that many large-scale development schemes lie within their immediate interest and there are those who argue that it is the state *per se* that is the enemy of peasant producers (Williams 1976). Taking the part of the peasants has been a feature of populist critiques of development, and a belief that the peasantry is robust, and capable of contributing significantly to the improvement of agricultural production, given the right conditions. Based on work in Sierra Leone, Richards (1983; 1985) believes that rural farming systems are both innovative and adaptive, and contain the capacity for what he describes as an indigenous agricultural revolution. This is not a view shared by Watts (1983a; 1983b) whose work in northern Nigeria indicates the difficulties experienced by farmers coping with the rigours of drought due to external constraints and the disruption of indigenous forms of production and distribution by the colonial and post-colonial state. Populist measures which invite farmers to set the agenda for change in association with development planners have many attractions, but as Watts (1983) observes, populism allows for competition but with none of the adverse effects. Furthermore, populist schema tend to ignore other classes, the state and industrialization. It should also be added that there are parts of Africa where rural households are heavily dependent on non-farm work which conditions their agricultural potential and status within the community.

While 'populist' and 'structuralist' paradigms may be the focus of much academic debate, in terms of actual policies being enacted in Africa there has been a shift towards the 'new economics' coming out of Europe and America. There has been a resurgence of arguments for the removal of state intervention, the encouragement of market forces and the expansion of agricultural exports by peasant farmers. It is argued that what farmers need are price incentives. Policies to achieve this kind of development are held to include targeting aid on areas with the greatest potential, encouraging larger farmers and a devaluation of the exchange rate to facilitate exports. These policies are contained within the World Bank's 'Accelerated Development in Sub-Saharan Africa – An Agenda for Development', published in 1981 and popularly referred to as the Berg Report as it was prepared under the supervision of Elliot Berg. The report shifts the development issue to domestic policy within Africa and argues that past trends in the terms of trade cannot explain the slow growth of African economies. The problem lies in the bias against agriculture, import substitution industries, over-valued exchange rates, urban wages and prices and over-expansion of a subsidized state sector.

The Berg Report has been influential in shaping World Bank policies and the conditions laid down by the IMF for negotiating loans and debt repayments while its impact has been felt in African countries in a variety of ways. Objections have been raised that it will intensify class divisions and create a class of *kulak* farmers while regional inequalities will also become greater. However, those in favour of freer markets believe that the development of rural and urban entrepreneurs will create sufficient forward and backward linkages with all sectors of the economy to promote a general rise in economic well-being. But as Loxley (1984) points out the successful implementation of the 'Agenda for Action' would entail far-reaching realignments of class interest and degrees of unacceptable (if not impossible) state coercion. The validity of this remark has been borne out by the political instability engendered by attempts to meet IMF conditionalities for example in Zambia, and during 1988 in Nigeria related to the increase in petroleum products. Whatever the merits of the World Bank and IMF packages may be they have to be set against the internal political problems of implementing them, when they involve increased landlessness, job losses and the reduction of already limited health and education services. Furthermore the Berg Report was premised on the belief that terms of trade were either neutral or positive, but the data it used do not capture the crisis of the world economy after 1978, which included world recession, high interest rates, spiralling debt and a collapse of the terms of trade for African countries (Loxley 1984).

A central feature of induced change (including colonial rule) is that it does not take place on a homogeneous plain inhabited by a uniform set of people. Development schemes frequently embrace different environments and people with different histories who are not easily disengaged from their perceptions of themselves, their pasts and their established relations of production. The essays in this volume suggest that there is a pressing need to acknowledge both the geographic and historic specificity of different countries and regions when either the nature or the effects of development are considered. Furthermore as Kitching (1980) has suggested there is a need to dismantle the 'grand theories' into lower level concepts which can be applied more widely. Rather than try to construct all-embracing modes of production which attempt to chart the shift from pre-capitalist to capitalist production, it might be more useful to look at the way in which the appropriation of surplus labour takes place, or the appropriation of nature, and how circulation (money and commodities) occurs. And for many observers the issue of gender, the division of labour and control of resources, is a crucial one. Inherent in most of the essays which follow is the idea of looking at development and inequality at intermediate levels such as regions, groups of villages, or subsets of the city.

In conclusion, the problem of inequality seems insoluble in as much as any fundamental change, induced or otherwise, is likely to cause disruption for some sectors of the population. Programmes of socialist reconstruction disturb the entrepreneurs and prosperous peasants, while the encouragement of capitalist relation of production and exchange bear heavily on those who are already disadvantaged. At the conclusion of the conference which produced these papers, there was a feeling that planners and academics should try to develop initiatives which would at least lessen the inequalities produced by change. This feeling might be described as a 'liberal-pragmatic' approach where the concern is not so much the creation of the right development projects, as the institution of policies to smooth the worst excesses and inequalities occasioned by interventionist strategies. This concern may be even more relevant given the effects of IMF prescriptions and programmes which have been adopted by some countries. However at the end of the day the policies, prescriptions and programmes we espouse are shaped by the way in which we recognize and analyse inequality. Rather like beauty, underdevelopment, inequality and their cure all lie within the eye of the beholder.

One thing does seem to be clear, and that is that policies and projects aimed at improving people's material conditions over a wide area are not going to succeed overnight. Many programmes of social and economic change are premised on a belief that they are going to provide a 'one-shot adjustment'. This may be the pious hope of politicians, and planners, and the legitimate claim of the hungry and dispossessed, but sustained improvement in people's well-being may be slow and erratic. It should also be remembered that efforts to engineer change, even when they fail, are part of the process of change, as they create resistance, adaptation and new sets of initiatives. Also, in the desire to analyse failures perhaps too little is made of the beneficial changes which have occurred in many underdeveloped countries. But to believe that a country, region or social group is forever locked into some peripheral or dependent status seems both unrealistic and unduly pessimistic.

References

Bourdieu, P. 1977. *Outline of a theory of practice* (Cambridge: Cambridge University Press)

Brenner, R. 1977. The origins of capitalist development. A critique of Neo-Smithian Marxism, *New Left Review*, vol. 104, pp. 25–92.

Bromley, R. and Geery, C. (eds). 1979. *Casual work and poverty in Third World cities* (Chichester: Wiley)

Clower, R.W. *et al.* 1966. *Growth without development: an economic survey of Liberia* (Evanston: N.W. Univ. Press)

Corbridge, S. 1986. *Capitalist world development* (New Jersey: Rowman and Littlefield)

Drakakis-Smith, D. and Williams, S.W. (eds). 1983. *Internal colonialism: essays around a theme*. Monograph No. 3 Development Areas Study Group, Institute of British Geography.

Eicher, C.K. and D.C. Baker. 1982. *Research on agricultural development in Sub-Saharan Africa: a critical survey*, MSU International Development Paper No. 1, Dept. of Agricultural Economics, Michigan State University, East Lansing.

Frank, A.G. 1967. *Capitalism and underdevelopment in Latin America* (London: Monthly Review Press)

Frank, A.G. 1978. *Dependent accumulation and underdevelopment* (London: Macmillan)

Friedmann, J. 1966. *Regional development policy: a case study of Venezuela* (Cambridge, Massachusetts: M.I.T. Press)

Gakou, M.L. 1987. *The crisis in African agriculture* (London: Zed books for U.N. University)

Hinderink, J. and Steckenberg, J.J. 1978. Spatial inequality in underdeveloped countries and the role of government policy. *T.E.G.S.* vol. 6 (1–2), pp. 5–16.

Hyden, G. 1980. *Beyond Ujamaa in Tanzania: underdevelopment and uncaptured peasantry* (London: Heinemann)

Kamarck, A. 1976. *The tropics and economic development: a provocative inquiry into the poverty of nations* (Baltimore: John Hopkins Press)

Kusnetz, S. 1955. Economic growth and income inequality. *American Economic Review*, vol. 45: pp. 1–28.

Kitching, G. 1980. *Class economic change in Kenya: the making of an African petite bourgoisie* (London: Yale University Press)

Lipton, M. 1977. *Why poor people stay poor: a study of urban bias in world development* (London: Temple Smith)

Loxley, J. 1984. 'The World Bank and the model of accumulation'. In J. Barker (ed.), *The politics of agriculture in tropical Africa* (Beverley Hills, USA: Sage)

Richards, P. 1983. The politics of African land use, *The African Studies Review*, vol. 26, no. 2, pp. 1–72.

Richards, P. 1985. *Indigenous agricultural revolution* (London: Hutchinson)

Rimmer, D. 1984. *The economics of West Africa* (London: Weidenfeld and Nicholson)

Rostow, W.W. 1960. *The stages of economic growth: a Non-Communist Manifesto* (Cambridge: Cambridge University Press)

Streeten, P. 1981. *First things first; meeting basic human needs in developing countries* (London: Oxford University Press)
Turner, J.F.C. 1976. *Housing by people* (London: Marion Boyes)
Turner, J.F.C. 1978. Housing in three dimensions. *World Development*, vol. 6 (9–10), pp. 1135–1145.
Wallerstein, I. 1974. *The Modern World System* (New York: Academic Press)
Wallerstein, I. 1979. *The capitalist world economy* (Cambridge: Cambridge University Press)
Warren, B. 1980. *Imperialism: pioneer of capitalism* (London: New Left Books)
Watts, M. 1983a. *Silent violence: food, famine and peasantry in northern Nigeria* (Berkeley: University of California Press)
Watts, M. 1983b. 'Good try, Mr Paul': populism and the politics of African land use, *The African Studies Review*, vol. 26, no. 2, pp. 73–83.
Williams, G. 1976. 'Taking the part of peasants: rural development in Nigeria and Tanzania'. In P.C.W. Gutkind and I. Wallerstein *The political economy of contemporary Africa* (Beverly Hills, California: Sage)

Section One: Measuring Spatial Inequalities

1
The spatial impress and dynamics of underdevelopment in Ghana

Jacob Songsore
Department of Geography, University of Ghana, Legon

Introduction

Literature in development studies evidences an increasing concern over ever-widening inequalities in the economic and social conditions of life between the advanced and underdeveloped countries of the world. Some have argued that there may be only one centre and one periphery (Frank 1967; Galtung 1971), as evidenced in the collective struggles between the 'North' and the 'South', in which the South is demanding global redistribution. Moving from a global to a continental scale, spatial variations in levels of economic development have been found. For example, in Europe they tend to be lowest in regions furthest removed from the main European centres of industrial activity, embracing England and the Rhine valley (Chorley and Haggett 1970, pp. 257–266). Similarly, in West Africa, the evidence suggests widening inequalities between a more developed south and an underdeveloped periphery in the north. At the next lower level of spatial resolution, regional inequalities in levels of development within countries have been extensively discussed.

In Ghana, a number of studies have emphasized the broad disparities between the North and the South in terms of levels of economic development and the general quality of life. These studies have all emphasized the relative backwardness of the North (Dickson 1968, 1974; Ewusi 1976; Forde 1968, Songsore 1983, see Figure 1). I have argued elsewhere that dependency and capitalist penetration, which under colonialism had shaped the internal production structure to fit the needs of the colonial metropolis, continue under neo-colonialism to distort the internal patterns of production, and the spatial organization of economic and social activity (Songsore 1979).

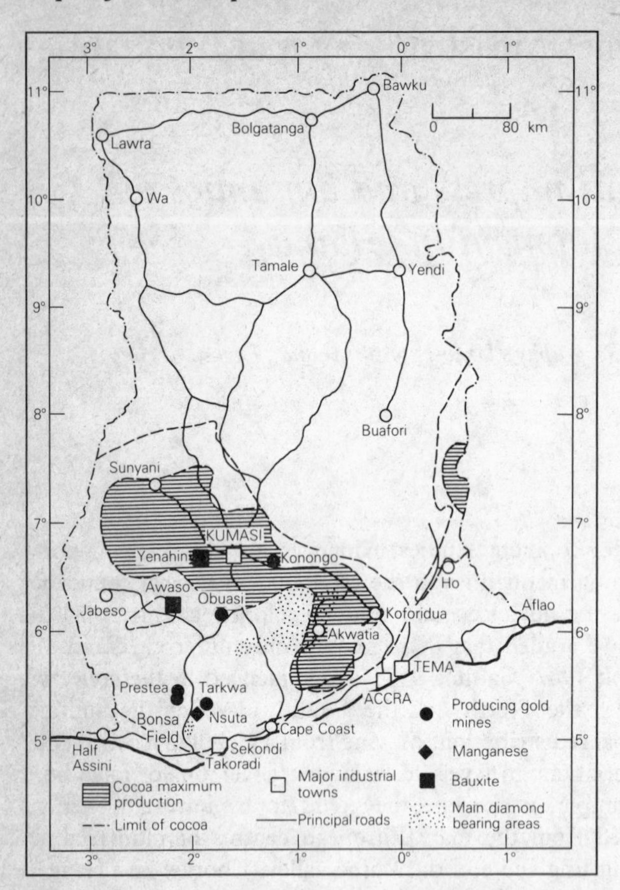

Fig. 1 The economic heartland of Ghana (adapted from K.B.Dickson and G. Benneh, *A new Geography of Ghana*.) pp. 71–92

Except in a few cases, spatial analysis has been undertaken in underdeveloped countries regardless of the past and present capitalist system. 'Yet this integration constitutes the very foundation of distinctions between underdeveloped countries and is at the root of the explanation of their internal spatial dynamics' (Coutsinas and Paix 1977, p. 97). As Mandel puts it, 'The unequal development between regions and nations is the very essence of capitalism, on the same level as the exploitation of labour by capital' (Mandel 1969, p. 43). There is also the need to recognize that spatial structures cannot be theorized without social structures, and *vice versa* (Gregory 1978, p. 121). It is important to emphasize this point, as some writers in the social sciences have taken for granted, or ignored, the crucial import of space in the understanding of social structures. 'Spatial reality is a dimension which is permanently engaged in its own readjustment under the influence of social and economic reality, but which at the same time exerts its own influence over that reality' (Santos 1977, p. 9).

The object of this present study is to provide an empirico-statistical test of the validity of the structured patterns of inequalities which were recognized in earlier studies. It will also investigate the inequalities that lie beyond the spatial units of administrative regions which in the past have been lumped together for the purpose of analysis. An attempt is made to advance beyond the spatial manifestations of inequality to an explanation of the pattern that emerges.

Methodology and data base

Some analysts of regional inequality in Ghana have tried to discuss regional disparities in development with the administrative regions as the basic units of aggregation (Ewusi 1976; Kudiabor 1974). The result of using such large units has been that the conclusions have been generalized. The choice of administrative regions as statistical units tends to hide the basic contradictions that exist between rural areas and urban centres. To avoid this pitfall, the present study aims at a lower level of spatial dis-aggregation – the administrative districts (see Figure 2). The administrative district is the smallest unit for recording statistical data. It is at this level that a more detailed picture of spatial variations in levels of economic health and social welfare within the country can be discovered. A broad range of socio-economic indices were collected from both census data and direct field survey, on a cross-sectional basis. These indices, when put together, were considered adequate surrogate measures of the level of economic health and social well-being in the early 1970s, as most of them were social welfare indicators. The indices employed in the analysis are listed in Appendix 1 on page 39.

The data were subjected to principal components analysis to isolate the key variables and remove the redundancy in the original data matrix (Gould 1970, p. 153). A final factor score matrix will help to determine the performance of the districts on the major factors isolated, and that provides a basis for comparing districts, according to levels of economic health, and delimiting homogeneous regions of underdevelopment. The data relate, of course, to a cross-section, but they display basic patterns of inequality which are not altered much by year-to-year fluctuations. They also reflect a structure brought about by processes operating over a long historical period. The data

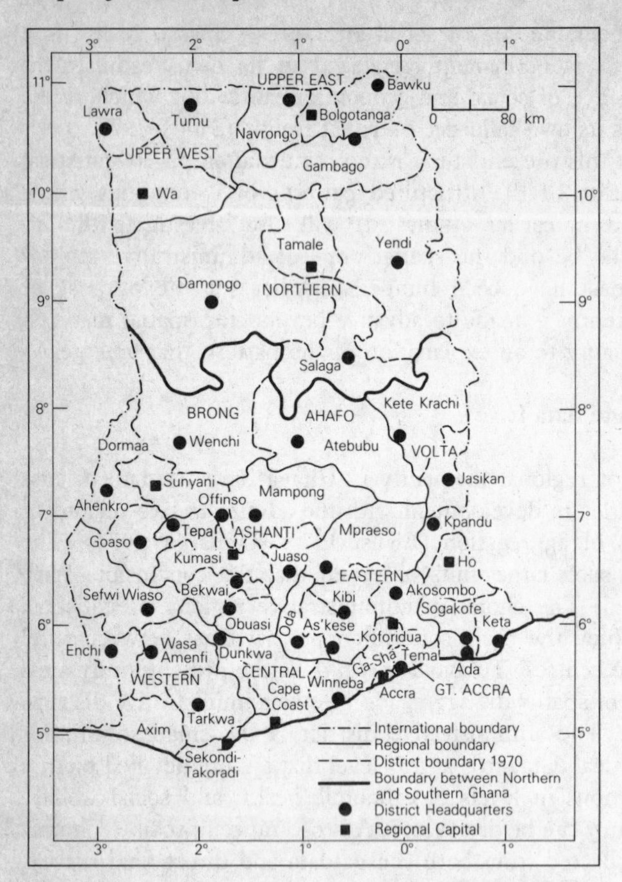

Fig. 2 Administrative regions and districts of Ghana

are based on both the Population Census of 1970 and other primary data collected in the early 1970s.

Four principal components were identified out of the original 22 variables (Appendix II). Only the first three, whose factor scores will be analysed, have been named. Component I has been identified as the general social welfare indicator, component II has been identified as the literacy factor, and component III which is a residual factor is difficult to interpret and is described as the ethnic mixture-electricity factor (Appendix III). Since all three principal components have been identified on the basis of high negative loadings, it follows that the best performing districts with regard to the three factors will be those with high negative factor scores. To all intents and purposes the first two factors are adequate to rank districts according to levels of access to social welfare services, and hence levels of welfare, as they account for over 73 per cent of the total variance.

Patterns of spatial inequalities in welfare

Figures 3 and 4 show the spatial patterns that emerge from mapping factors I and II and indicate the following contradictions in level of social well-being (Appendix III).

There is first and foremost the contradiction between the North and the South, the North having all the features of an underdeveloped region in relation to the South. At the next level of spatial resolution, one notices a contradiction between urban and rural. The patterns show a clear advantage for the urbanized regions at the level of living gap between urban and rural districts. Yet at the next lower scale there is a rural-rural contradiction between those rural areas more closely tied to commodity production for export and those more closely tied to subsistence production by peasants.

Finally, although this does not emerge from the spatial patterns presented, there are class contradictions in the urban areas between the military-bureaucratic bourgeoisie, together with the lower *petite-bourgeoisie*, and the workers and *lumpenproletariat*.

The military-bureaucratic bourgeoisie includes senior military and police personnel, senior civil servants, professionals and businessmen, whilst the lower *petite-bourgeoisie* includes teachers, nurses, senior clerks and some well-established petty traders, all with considerable relative wealth and status. State power in Ghana is exercised principally by the military-bureaucratic stratum. The *lumpenproletariat* includes the unemployed, and those in the petty-commodity sector living at the margins of urban society. A substantial group of wage earners comprises lower-level civil servants, clerks, other ranks in the military establishment, railwaymen, dockworkers and factory workers.

Factorial ecologies of urban spaces, if undertaken, would adequately reveal these contradictions. Similarly, in the rural areas there is a contradiction between the proto-feudal or chiefly elements, together with the *kulak* class, and the poor peasants and landless migrant labourers. These patterns will be discussed in greater detail for factors I and II respectively.

Figure 3, which discusses the regional patterns for factor I, illustrates the contradictions well, and this general social welfare indicator is by far the most important. There existed a sharp and marked inequality between Northern Ghana, comprising Northern and Upper Regions, and Southern Ghana which is the rest of the country. There

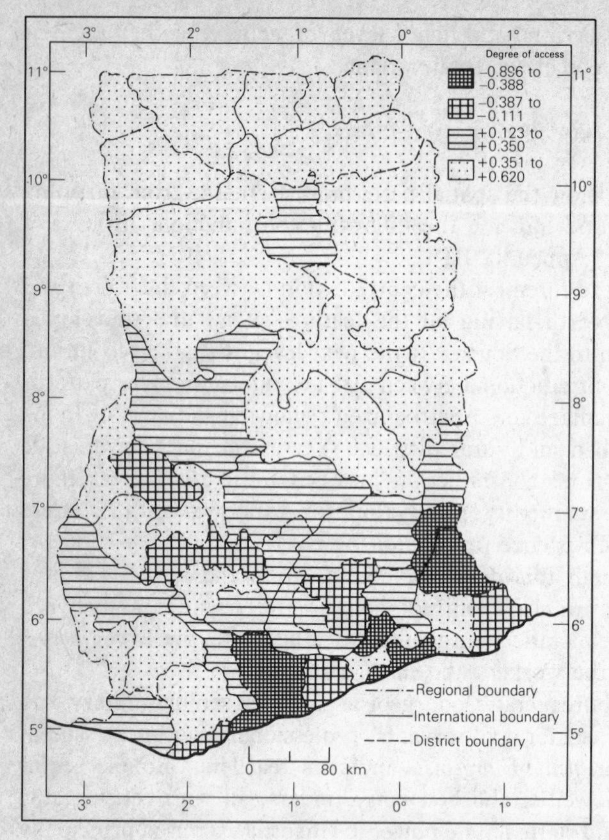

Fig. 3 Factor I: general social welfare

was not a single district in the North with a score in the second quartile and only one district – Tamale – within the third quartile. The remaining districts in Northern Ghana fell in the fourth (lowest). This is significant, as the distinction is not only geographical, but one which reflects a structural feature of Ghana. This has been the result of different policies pursued by the colonial state in the two main regions. The North was designated by the colonial political class as the labour reserve for the industry and agriculture of the South. The patterns had not changed, owing to the lack of any significant change in policy, and also because of the structural rigidities of colonial policy.

It is, however, naïve to treat either the North or the South as monoliths. One notices at the sub-regional levels an equally sharp contrast between rural and urban districts in terms of their performance on the welfare scale. In Northern Ghana, it was only Tamale District which attained the third quartile. This is because Tamale had emerged as the regional headquarters of the Northern Territories and had since become the most significant administrative, commercial and business centre in the area (Songsore 1977). The better performance of this district reflects the concentration of social services in Tamale town, which raised its score. And although the contradiction between town and country is blurred by the general underdevelopment of the region, the few urban centres in Northern Ghana outside Tamale also monopolize the few available social services in the region, as the policy has always been to locate social services in the administrative centres for the benefit of the bureaucratic élite (Songsore 1977, p. 116).

A similar pattern emerges when one examines the situation in Southern Ghana. The districts in the South with the best scores include Accra, Tema, Koforidua, Cape Coast and Kpandu. These include the most urbanized districts of Accra, Tema and Koforidua. Ho and Cape Coast are the regional capitals for the Volta and Central Regions, hence the location of numerous services in these towns, whilst Kpandu District lies in the most urbanized part of the Volta Region, which is also a cocoa producing district. These districts were followed in the next quartile by Kumasi, Sunyani, Sekondi-Takoradi, Kibi and Keta Districts. In this second group are included the capital districts of Sunyani for Brong-Ahafo, Kumasi for Ashanti, and Sekondi-Takoradi for Western Regions. The other three districts of Winneba, Kibi and Keta are highly urbanized and dominated by their district capitals. It is therefore clear that there was an urban bias in the provision of welfare services and this also reflects the unequal distribution of decision-making power between urban and rural interest groups.

It is the predominantly rural districts in Southern Ghana which fell into the lower quartiles. It is especially significant to note that Kumasi tended to have a primacy effect on all the other districts of Ashanti, but more especially the districts of Bekwai, Tepa and Ofinso, the close neighbours of Kumasi District, which are among the least developed districts in the country.

Outside Northern Ghana, Brong-Ahafo and Western Regions were the least developed administrative regions, with three districts each in the lower quartile. Both Western and Brong-Ahafo Regions are 'resource frontier' regions with much of the potential for cocoa, timber and mineral expansion. But being young regions with few significant urban centres, they are clearly under-represented in terms of welfare services.

Another striking feature of the pattern is that the Volta Region, contrary to popular opinion, lay in the constellation of better endowed regions consisting of Greater Accra, Central and Volta Regions. As many as three districts in the Region fall within the first two quartiles. There are a number of reasons for this. Ho District had a high score because it was the capital district for Volta Region. Kpandu District lies near the old cocoa producing district of Jasikan and is an important cocoa buying centre. For Keta District, the high score was partly the result of a high rate of out-migration, following the decline of its economic activity with the construction of the Volta Dam at Akosombo, and coastal erosion at Keta itself. Keta had been an important trading outpost from as far back as the mercantilist era, and also an old district administrative centre, with numerous services located there. Besides, for the Volta Region as a whole, political pressure exerted at the national level – in terms of threats of secession – had ensured the adequate provision of social services if not productive investments.

The poor performance of many of the rural districts in Southern Ghana partly derives from the fact that they are destination zones for most of the rural migrants from the economically distressed areas of Northern, Upper and Volta Regions. These migrant labourers help to depress the performance indices when they are standardized by the population base.[1]

At the next lower level one finds rural-rural inequalities, although they are not very clear. For example, the older cocoa growing rural regions perform much better than the non-cocoa growing rural districts of Southern Ghana, and even than the new 'resource frontier' area which is just being opened up to cash cropping. These are just as underdeveloped as Northern Ghana – for example, Dormaa-Ahenkro, Goaso and Tepa Districts. The rural-rural inequality is due to the greater bargaining power of old cocoa districts by virtue of their production of export crops. Like Northern Ghana, the non-export orientated rural regions of Southern Ghana are tucked in the backwoods of welfare.

Even in the most favoured urban regions with high per capita service ratios, it is a truism that physical availability of facilities does not necessarily guarantee access by all social classes. Although physical distance serves as a serious barrier to access in the rural regions, this disadvantage is not shared by all social classes. The degree of access of the peasantry and working classes to urban-based welfare services is not only much lower than that of the dominant classes, but also gets worse when a right-wing régime happens to be in power, as levies are imposed. The levies often take the form of increased fees for school children, high hospital fees and high transport fares. Retrenchment of labour often accompanies deflationary measures.

For example, although educational facilities are available in large towns, the working classes are still forced by economic pressures to keep their children out of school, or to be satisfied with the early completion of their school career. This ensures the reproduction of their kind. With reference to electricity and water supply, especially in urban areas, a socio-economic survey conducted in Accra-Tema metropolitan area reveals a number of important facts on the level of living gap. The working class neighbourhood of Nima was not supplied with electricity at all, although centrally located in Accra. Some working class districts were never supplied with water (e.g. Darkuman), or supplied with a few public stand-pipes. As a result most residents were buying water by the bucket from private stand-pipe operators. The average household spent as much as ₵40.00 per month on water. But most high-income and middle-income residential suburbs were provided with water supply in every household, and each family unit consumed three to five times more water than the average working class family. For all this, they paid an average of ₵2.00 per month per family (ATMA 1980). The same goes for health facilities, as the working classes are less able to pay for hospital services.

The same groups are often little involved in politics, as minimal effort is made at mass mobilization. They can afford to use the media less. They are, as a result, often ignorant of policy measures which directly affect their interest. Even when aware of such measures, they are unable to challenge the established order. This situation has been made worse by ethnic cleavages. A very similar pattern emerges for factor II, which is a literacy factor (Figure 4).

The general underdevelopment of Northern Ghana stands out in sharper relief in contrast to the more developed South. All the Northern districts are at the very bottom of the literacy scale whereas for the whole of Southern Ghana it is only five districts out of a total of 37 which fall in the lowest class. These include Kete-Krachi, Atebubu, Sunyani, Oda and Asamankese; Kete-Krachi was part of the Northern Territories and was discriminated against as regards educational services. The object of colonial policy was to keep the North backward so that cheap labour to the South could be guaranteed (Bening 1972). The anomaly is Sunyani District, which contains the capital of Brong-Ahafo Region, and performed well on factor I. This could, however, be explained by the fact that Sunyani was a rural centre before it became a regional capital. Brong-Ahafo was part of Ashanti, and like

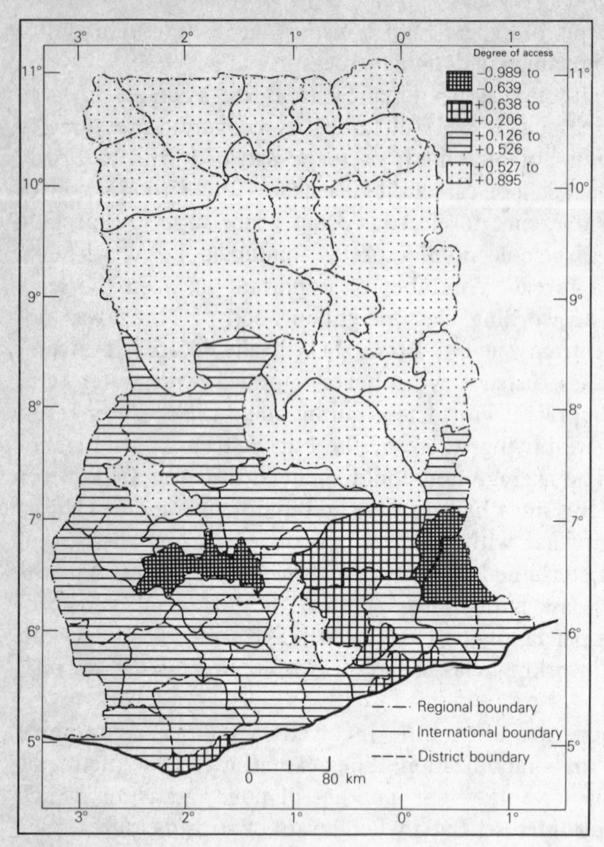

Fig. 4 Factor II: literacy

other areas outside Kumasi District did suffer from the primacy effect of Kumasi.

In the South, the contradiction between rural and urban districts is very stark. It is the more urbanized districts of Accra, Tema, Sekondi-Takoradi, Kumasi and Koforidua which are among the most developed as regards education, while both Kpandu and Ho Districts had a long history of missionary activity. This was enhanced in Kpandu District by the importance of cocoa purchasing. German colonialism in the Volta Region was characterized by more serious efforts to transfer German technology to the region, as the Germans meant to stay. Consequently, the German missionaries concentrated their educational activities in the technical sphere, that is in basic crafts and technology. Kibi and Mpraeso Districts have also good scores. Not as urbanized as the first five districts mentioned, they have nevertheless a cluster of medium-sized urban centres. They were among the earliest developed cocoa districts, with a long tradition of missionary and government educational activity.

The observed North-South and rural-urban contradictions, as with factor I, assume a class character as different social classes enjoy different levels of educational attainment, even within spatial domains, and access to educational services (or lack of it) has been one of the principal determinants of social mobility. Factor III emphasizes urban-rural polarity, especially with regard to electricity services. It is significant because of the relationship between electricity supply and the capacity for modern industrialization. The districts with high scores on this factor are the Southern regional capitals, and Tema District, which is part of the Accra-Tema metropolitan area. Kpando District is the only exception.

Having discussed the patterns of inequality, it is pertinent to attempt a general discussion of the underlying processes at work in the generation of these inequalities.

Interacting dynamics of class and spatial structures

It is clear that a proper understanding of the spatial and distributional imbalance between productive activities, and within the population as a whole, can only be achieved by an analysis of the dominant mode of production within the social formation.

Colonial dependency is at the root of the inequalities so evident in the Ghanaian space economy. Under the impact of colonialism the internal production structure had been divided into a dynamic modern export sector and a backward and underdeveloped subsistence sector which also served as a 'labour reserve' for the modern sector. This is at the root of the North-South contradiction, and also the other contradictions mentioned. In Northern Ghana, however, this process of underdevelopment pre-dated direct colonialism, and was in progress during the earlier era of European merchant activity on the coast. Prior to this, the north-western and north-eastern parts of Ghana had enjoyed considerable progress because of the 'middleman' role they played in the trade between the forest and the Sudan-Sahel zone further north. This encouraged the formation of states, and the development of a merchant class of Hausa and Dyula around the fifteenth century (Dickson 1968).

The decline of the North started when the trade which formerly passed northwards was reorientated south to the coast. This was followed in the eighteenth century by the emergence of Asante as a powerful state and its raids on the Gonja Empire which generated captives for the waiting slave ships, thereby enhancing the depopulation of the Middle Belt. This was followed by the export of labour from the North under the British administration. 'It was a consequence of the exploitative nature of the situation that the paramount powers whether before or after 1896 showed little inclination to foster the material advance of the north' (Ladouceur 1979). Northern underdevelopment stood in stark contrast to the relative development of the South.

The colonial state apparatus of governors, civil servants, soldiers and police facilitated the activities of expatriate merchant companies, mining and banking interests. Below this stratum of expatriate bourgeoisie and their agents, an intermediary stratum of *compradors*, professionals, and petty traders emerged. These were a crucial link, as their interests were to a large extent tied to the colonial economy. However, contradictions did occur between the colonial state and European capital, on the one hand, and the African bourgeoisie on the other hand, with regard to their share of the surpluses that were extracted from the peasant cocoa producers. On a number of occasions, the *comprador* bourgeoisie were able to mobilize the rural producers behind aims which would have principally benefited themselves. The cocoa hold-ups, during slumps in the trade, which were organized between 1900 and 1951 are the best examples of this conflict of interest (Grier 1979, pp. 145–234). Nevertheless these compradorial groups were incapable of independent existence outside their subordinate ties with imperialism. They have received new recruits with the achievement of flag independence, but their harmonious and yet ambivalent relations with imperialism continue unabated.

What has to be emphasized here is that these groups, like the expatriate bourgeoisie, were concentrated in the major urban centres of Accra, Sekondi-Takoradi and Kumasi, and at regional and district centres. Consequently, the distributional pattern of welfare services coincided with the locational pattern of these interests. The urban bias of these services reflects a specific class interest as services were established principally to serve these specific groups. The process of stratification in social space also became a process of stratification in geographical space. This explains, to a large extent, the rural-urban contradictions, and the class contradictions within the urban and rural spaces. 'It was division of class not work which separated the town from the country' (Blumenfeld 1972, p. 4).

Two societies were evolving in Ghana. According to one Member of Parliament, a wealthy urban society *feeds off the poor rural sector ..... These farmers feed the cities and pay for the mighty buildings in Accra, Kumasi and Takoradi. They pay for the big cars, trucks, trains, aeroplanes and the Akosombo dam and the pleasures and the very high standard of living which the cities enjoy. But Mr Speaker, sadly, these same farmers permanently suffer from disease, malnutrition, darkness, ignorance and from all the hardships of primitive people.*

(Grier 1979, p. 438)

Reinforcing the interests of class is the invisible hand of the market, for 'the modern city is a mode of social organization which furthers efficiency in economic activity' (Lampard 1964, p. 332). Urbanization economies or external economies were reaped by the fostering of a closer integration of interdependent functions, which the modern city brought about (Songsore 1977, pp. 123–4). Even where special services were designed for the needs of rural dwellers, these tended to benefit the wealthier sections of the rural community, and some urban interests as well. Examples include scholarships for cocoa producers' children, Agricultural Development Banks, Rural Banks, and Co-operative Credit Unions' financial credits to rural producers. These same interests have penetrated co-operative movements in the rural areas, and they have expropriated irrigated lands from the original owners, very often poor peasants.

The interesting aspect is that once class interests generate a distributional policy in space, these spatial structures, acting independently, reinforce class inequalities. Access to employment, education and welfare services has both a physical and social dimension. In the physical sense it relates to the distance to be covered by an individual in an attempt to secure employment or social service, and this may be an effective barrier, and a basis of social differentiation.

Socially, it relates to barriers of class, status or recognition which he may also have to overcome in the process. The factor of accessibility especially in its physical forms, means that individuals in certain localities or regions benefit less than others from the distribution of the product of social co-operation and development.

(Mabogunje 1980, p. 40.)

Spatial and class inequalities created to a large extent through colonialism have been exacerbated by the policies pursued by the intermediary strata, who captured state power at independence and used it to foster their class interest. This resulted in the phenomenal growth of the neo-colonial state apparatus. On the eve of independence, the inter-regional balance of class forces was such that a weak and inarticulate *petite-bourgeoisie* in the North could not have been expected to win any concessions, for the redress of imbalance at the national level, from the sophisticated and highly westernized *petite-bourgeoisie* from the Colony, Trans-Volta and Togoland, and the powerful cocoa interests of Ashanti. Nor could one expect hagglings in Parliament over the partition of government subsidies to be a sufficient force standing against the logic of capital accumulation which had created these inequalities in the first place (Mandel 1969, p. 45).

Although regional underdevelopment has long been a fact of life, its main victims – the mass of working people in the underdeveloped regions – are yet to become conscious of it. For example, never in the history of cocoa production have the most oppressed strata, namely the landless migrant producers from the underdeveloped North, and their class allies, the poor peasants from the South, been mobilized against the agro-commercial bourgeoisie, expatriate firms and the colonial or neo-colonial state. Ethnic consciousness prevented such an alliance.

The import substitution strategy of industrialization that was pursued after formal independence meant that the urban centres, which played a key role in the functional organization of the colonial economy, attracted all the industrial capital, giving rise to a further polarization of development. The 'big three', Accra-Tema, Sekondi-Takoradi and Kumasi, stood out as industrial centres, while the cocoa interests were subordinated to the state, trans-national capital and the nascent industrial bourgeoisie. As a result, members of the agro-commercial bourgeoisie were now relocating in the urban-industrial sector as *comparadors*, distributors or industrialists in their own right. Through allocative decisions of the state resources extracted through fiscal and macro-economic policies were concentrated in urban-centred investment in social overheads, and in manufacturing industry, to the neglect of the rural sector and interests. This sharpened the rural-urban contradictions, and by implication the North-South dualism, established during the colonial period (Ofori-Atta 1978). The North could only have benefited from a system-wide redistribution of resources in favour of rural areas and the peasantry.

It is important to emphasize that the portion of the surplus which was redistributed in favour of domestic urban interests was just a fraction of the total, as much was lost to imperialist monopolies through diverse mechanisms. These ranged from deterioration in the terms of trade and unequal exchange, to the withholding of reserves in the British Treasury. The key beneficiary has, therefore, always been monopoly capital in the metropolitan countries. In the urban areas, not all classes have benefited from the huge profits of multinational corporations and indigenously controlled investments.

What these patterns and explanation imply is that a regional planner interested in distributional justice must be committed to a fundamentally different kind of politics. One must watch the recent development of Workers' Defence Committees and Peoples' Defence Committees throughout the entire country, as they open up a prospect of increasing peasant and working class consciousness. It is only a worker-peasant alliance that can advance the struggles of these subordinate classes against the bourgeois state and the dominant class, thereby opening up the possibility of the transformation of the social relations of production and of the spatial organization of productive activities. Development geographers have the revolutionary role of 'helping to reveal the spatial malfunctionings and injustices, and contributing to the design of a spatial form of society in which people can be really free to fulfil themselves. This surely would be progress in geography' (Johnston 1979, p. 155).

Note

1 Population counts in Ghana are done by the *de facto* method which means that individuals are counted at locations where they spent the census night.

References

ATMA 1980. *Review of master plan for the ATMA water supply and sewerage project*, Accra-Tema Metropolitan Water Supply and Sewerage Project.

Bening, R.B. 1972. Development of education in Northern Ghana, *Ghana Social Science Journal* vol. 1/2, pp. 21–42.

Blumenfeld, H. 1972. *The modern metropolis: its origins, growth characteristics, and planning* (Cambridge, Massachusetts: MIT Press), p. 4.

Chorley, R.J. and Haggett, P. 1970. *Socio-economic models in Geography* (London: Methuen), pp. 257–266.

Coutsinas, G. and Paix, C. 1977. External trade and spatial organisation: a typology, *Antipode*, vol. 9/1, p. 97.

Dickson, K.B. 1968. Background to the problems of economic development in Northern Ghana, *Annals of the Association of American Geographers*, vol. 58/4, pp. 686–96.

Dickson, K.B. 1974. 'Generation and transmission of regional growth impulses: the case of Ghana'. In F. Helleiner and W. Stohr (eds), *Spatial aspects of the development process, Proceedings of the I.G.U. Commission on Regional Aspects of Development* (Canada), vol. 2, pp. 259–283.

Ewusi, K. 1976. Levels of regional development in Ghana, *Social Indicators Research*, vol. 3/1, pp. 75–100.

Forde E.R.A. 1968. *The population of Ghana: a study of the spatial relations of its socio-cultural and economic characteristics*, Northwestern University Studies in Geography No. 15.

Frank, A.G. 1967. *Capitalism and underdevelopment in Latin America* (London: Monthly Review Press)

Galtung, J. 1971. A structural theory of imperialism, *Journal of Peace Research*, vol. 12/2, pp. 81–117.

Gould, P.R. 1970. Tanzania 1920–63: the spatial impress of the modernization process, *World Politics*, vol. 22/2, pp. 149–170.

Gregory, D. 1978. *Ideology, science and human geography* (London: Hutchinson) p. 121.

Grier, B.C. 1979. *Cocoa, class formation and the state of Ghana* (Unpublished Ph.D Thesis, Yale University), pp. 145–234, 438.

Johnston, R.J. 1979. *Geography and geographers* (London: Edward Arnold), p. 155.

Kudiabor, C.D.K. 1974. 'Rural development, dispersal of industries and population redistribution' (Paper presented at the National Population Conference for Ghana, Accra)

Ladouceur, P.A. 1979. *Chiefs and politicians: the politics of regionalism in Northern Ghana*, (London: Longman) p. 35.

Lampard, E.E. 1964. 'The history of cities in the economically advanced areas'. In J. Friedmann and W. Alonso (eds), *Regional development and planning* (Cambridge, Massachusetts: M.I.T. Press), p. 332.

Mabogunje, A.L. 1980. *The development process: a spatial perspective* (London: Hutchinson), p. 40.

Mandel, E. 1969. Capitalism and regional disparities, *Socialisme*, no. 17 (Translated from French by Ted Richmond and Jim Peterson), pp. 42, 43, 45.

Ofori-Atta, J. 1978. Income redistribution in Ghana: a study of rural development strategies, *Ghana Social Science Journal*, vol. 5/1, pp. 1–25.
Santos, M. 1977. Society and space: social formations as theory and method, *Antipode*, vol 9/1, p. 9.
Songsore, Jacob. 1979. Structural crisis, dependent capitalist development and regional inequality in Ghana, *I.S.S. Occasional Papers*, no. 71, Institute of Social Studies, The Hague.
Songsore, Jacob. 1983. Intraregional and interregional labour migrations in historical perspective: the case of North-Western Ghana, *University of Port Harcourt, Faculty of Social Sciences, Occasional Papers Series*, no. 1.
Songsore, Jacob. 1977. Towards building a model of urban growth dynamics: the case of 'large' northern Ghanaian towns, *Universitas* (Legon) vol. 6/1, pp. 116, 123–4.

Appendix I: List of Indices of Social Welfare

X 1 = % of the total population born in other regions (1970 census)
X 2 = % of the total population born in West Africa (1970 census)
X 3 = % of the population born in other countries (1970 census)
X 4 = % of total population urban (1970 census)
X 5 = proportion of total population literate for 6–14 age group (1970 census)
X 6 = proportion of total population literate for 15–25 age group (1970 census)
X 7 = proportion of total population literate for 25+ age group (1970 census)
X 8 = % of public system secondary schools within the district (1974)
X 9 = proportion of total intake into public system secondary schools within the district (%) (1974)
X10 = % of registered importers within the district (1973)
X11 = % of registered industries in district (1973)
X12 = % of total number of localities within the district served with good drinking water (1970 census)
X13 = % of registered youth associations in district (1974)
X14 = % of Graphic Newspaper circulation consumed in district for 8 August 1974
X15 = % of localities within district with telephone facility (1974)
X16 = % of total units of national electricity consumption actually consumed within district (1972)
X17 = % of total number of branch establishments of commercial banks in Ghana located in district (1974)
X18 = % of total number of radio rediffusion stations located in district (1972)
X19 = % of total national radio box subscribers in district (1970)
X20 = proportion of localities in district with health establishments (hospitals, health centres, posts and maternity homes) (1971)
X21 = Ratio of population to hospital beds (1971)
X22 = % of total number of G.N.T.C. retail establishments in district (1975)

Appendix II: Contribution of principal components

Component	Eigenvalue	% Explained	Cumulative
1	12.879	58.54	58.54
2	3.202	14.56	73.10
3	1.440	6.54	79.64
4	1.159	5.27	84.91

Appendix III: Factor score matrix

District	Factor I	Factor II	Factor III
1 Axim	0.230	0.189	0.120
2 Sekondi-Takoradi	−0.111	−0.359	−0.337
3 Tarkwa	0.460	0.143	0.216
4 Wassa-Amenfi	0.477	0.159	0.125
5 Enchi	0.564	0.383	0.125
6 Sefwi-Wiawso	0.347	0.212	0.991
7 Cape-Coast	−0.602	0.149	−0.657
8 Winneba	−0.195	0.282	0.298
9 Dunkwa	0.326	0.150	0.906
10 Ga-Shai	0.476	0.218	0.934
11 Accra	−0.677	−0.304	−0.226
12 Tema	−0.898	−0.314	−0.558
13 Oda	0.194	0.623	0.656
14 Asamankese	0.162	0.574	0.644
15 Koforidua	−0.705	−0.206	−0.914
16 Akosombo	0.123	0.218	0.403
17 Ada	0.374	0.365	0.754
18 Kibi	−0.322	−0.258	0.446
19 Mpraeso	0.333	−0.297	0.688
20 Sogakope	0.479	0.226	0.158
21 Keta	−0.167	0.222	0.650
22 Ho	−0.495	−0.713	−0.219
23 Kpando	−0.550	−0.698	−0.198
24 Jasikan	0.211	0.309	0.874
25 Kete Krachi	0.541	0.590	0.140
26 Kumasi	−0.213	−0.989	−0.526
27 Bekwai	0.479	0.144	0.145
28 Obuasi	0.245	0.165	0.804
29 Juaso	0.204	0.286	0.794
30 Mampong	0.236	0.126	0.827
31 Offinso	0.408	0.218	0.132
32 Teppa	0.440	0.296	0.111
33 Goaso	0.407	0.310	0.772

Appendix III: Factor score matrix

District	Factor I	Factor II	Factor III
34 Sunyani	0.203	0.783	−0.333
35 Dormaa-Ahenkro	0.433	0.278	0.131
36 Wenchi	0.287	0.297	0.942
37 Atebubu	0.598	0.571	0.140
38 Damongo	0.514	0.763	0.165
39 Salaga	0.572	0.785	0.162
40 Yendi	0.527	0.895	0.167
41 Tamale	0.149	0.655	0.466
42 Gambaga	0.620	0.858	0.181
43 Wa	0.511	0.786	0.157
44 Lawra	0.447	0.637	0.174
45 Tumu	0.618	0.798	0.174
46 Navrongo	0.482	0.737	0.155
47 Bolgatanga	0.416	0.780	0.126
48 Bawku	0.520	0.853	0.168

2

Patterns of Rural Development in Borno State, Nigeria

J.A. Ijere
Department of Geography, University of Maiduguri, Nigeria

Introduction

Contemporary studies in development are often hampered by a lack of clarity on the exact meaning of the term 'development'. Conceptual shifts in its meaning, especially since the late 1960s, have produced several definitions.[1] Development is often equated with economic growth, level of technology, industrialization or modernization/westernization. Even though development may encompass all the above, these are products of a wider process of social change which may result in development or underdevelopment. There have to be positive and quantitative changes in the economic, socio-political and cultural lives of the people for development to take place. Development thus entails not only economic growth but also other conditions such as adequate food, employment, health, education, reduced inequality and self-reliance.[2] These attributes imply the satisfaction of human 'basic needs'.[3] The rural poverty pervasive in most less developed countries (LDCs) is due to poor performance in providing for these basic needs.

Since most LDCs are predominantly rural, rural development should be of paramount importance if real national development is to be achieved. Rural development is defined in terms of agricultural productivity, improved technology, rural welfare, rural security, rural employment, popular participation, equity in income distribution[4], and rural renaissance which induces positive changes in the lives of the rural people. Thus rural development is an holistic process in which transformations in the economic, social and political spheres are interwoven.[5]

The processes of rural development, occurring over time, are manifested in space as tangible and intangible spatial structures with distinctive observable patterns.[6] Patterns are of interest in rural development studies because they can be used to indentify problem areas, that is, areas of social deprivation. The dynamic nature of spatial patterns of development, which results from the on-going processes, brings to the forefront the question of the direction of change. Changes in patterns of development are inferred by measuring the various indicators of development.

Social scientists have used various statistics and data from various sources to analyse spatial and temporal patterns of development. Berry (1961) used factor analysis on 43 rank-ordered variables to analyse economic development in 95 countries in order to identify basic global patterns of economic development.[7] Weinand (1973) also used principal component analysis on ten variables to produce factor maps which depict spatial variations in economic development in Nigeria.[8] Less sophisticated statistics, such as rank correlations, descriptive statistics and proportions are also widely used in analysing relationships between development indicators and development outcomes.[9] Given the present meaning of development, the major obstacle in the measurement is the difficulty in quantifying its social and welfare aspects.[10] The indices used in any study and the correlations sought depend on the nature and availability of reliable data and also on the spatial units over which the data are collected.[11] The main problem in LDCs is that data on most variables used in measuring development are unavailable and, even if available, are unreliable.

The hypothesis in this paper is that there are problem areas (areas that are associated with low levels of rural development) in Borno State. The study, therefore, tries to identify and explain the patterns of rural development. The study area includes Maiduguri town because large areas of this administrative unit are rural both in structure and functions. However, the Chad Basin Development Projects in Kukawa, Monguno and Ngala Local Government Areas (LGA) are excluded because these projects are viewed as islands of development in a sea of underdevelopment. Their inclusion would have therefore led to distortion of the level of rural development in these local government areas.

Nature of data

An index of rural development, like development itself, is a multifaceted phenomenon and requires the measurement of several variables. Because of paucity of relevant data, only secondary data on five indicators made up of eleven socio-economic variables (Table 2.1)[12] for 1981, were used to derive patterns of rural development. However, some of these data have to be treated with caution. For example, it is an open secret that teachers sometimes inflate primary school enrolment to avoid the closure of their schools for lack of pupils. Secondly, the data on post-primary school enrolment tend to suggest that all students in post-primary institutions in an LGA are residents of that LGA. This is not true because government policy is to send some students to schools outside their LGAs to promote social integration in the state. However, the establishment of a post-primary institution brings satisfaction and self-esteem to the people and also positively influences secondary education where the school is located – hence the inclusion of this variable in this study. Thirdly, the reliability of the spatial patterns of development may be affected because the scores are standardized with the 1980/1 population estimates which are projections based on the controversial 1963 census in Nigeria. Fourthly, the length of roads and areas of the LGAs used in calculating the accessibility index were derived from measurements on a road map on a scale of 1:1,600,000.

Table 2.1 Variables used for measuring indices of rural development.

Index	Variable
Education	Primary schools
	Primary school enrolment
	Post-primary school enrolment
Health care facilities	Doctors
	Midwives
	Dispensaries
	Hospital beds
Agricultural technology	Farm tractors
	Other farm implements
Extension services	Extension workers
Accessibility	Length of roads

The spatial unit used in this study – the LGA – has been dictated by the fact that the data collected were based on the LGAs in Figure 5; hence all calculations presented in the analysis are based on these administrative units.

Derivation of rural development patterns

The location quotients

The position of each LGA on a rural development scale was determined

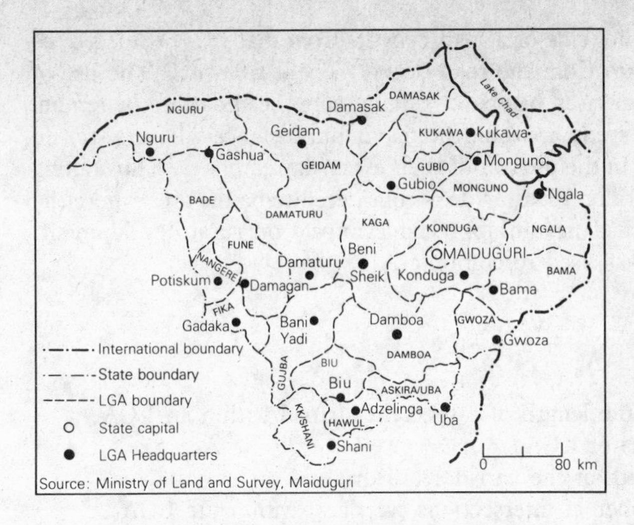

Fig. 5 Borno State – Local Government Areas

by computing the performance of the LGA on the five indices of rural development stated in Table 2.1. Location quotient analysis was used in computing the positions of the LGAs on the development scale on four of the five indices of rural development. The calculation of location quotient coefficients is based on the method used by Isard.[13] This is defined as:

$$\frac{S_i/S}{N_i/N}$$

where S_i is the size of the variable in LGA_i
S is the number of the same variable in all the LGAs
N_i is the population of LGA_i
N is the population of all the LGAs.

The location quotient (LQ) of each index of rural development was derived by calculating and then averaging the LQs for all the variables that make up that index. For example, the education index LQ for each LGA was obtained by summing the LQs for the number of primary schools and primary and post-primary school enrolments and dividing by three to get the mean LQ. An LQ which exceeds unity indicates that an LGA has more than its fair share of the development attribute measured, while an LQ less than unity indicates that the LGA is disadvantaged.

The accessibility index (AI) is based on distance from an all-weather (tarred) road. It was assumed that any point within 5 km (straight line distance) on either side of a road benefits from that road, while points farther than 5 km from the road do not benefit from it.[14] The use of 5 km as the limit was based on estimates by headmasters in remote villages (in the study area) on the maximum distance villagers trek to board vehicles, in the pursuit of their every-day activities. Thus, along any road, a corridor 10 km wide is considered to be the area where the presence of a road has an appreciable impact on rural development. This formula was used to compute AI:

$$AI = \frac{\Sigma dij \, . \, W - (W^2 \, . \, x)}{A_k}$$

where dij is the length of a segment of road within an LGA,
A_k is the area of LGA_k,
W is the width of the corridor (10 km) and
x is the number of intersections (vertices) within the LGA_k.[15]

An AI score indicates the proportion of the LGA that lies within 5 km from a road. An AI less than unity indicates that there are portions of the LGA that are inaccessible because they are beyond 5 km from any all-weather road, while an AI greater than unity indicates that no point within the LGA is beyond this limit.

The spatial patterns

The mean LQs of the LGAs on the four indices (education, health care, agricultural technology and agricultural extension) and the AI scores indicate how the LGAs performed on these indices of rural development. Table 2.2 lists each LGA's mean LQ and AI score. The mean scores for the LGAs are shown in a rank-ordered manner. Three methods of manipulating the mean scores were considered in generating composite patterns of rural development.

The first method was based on the mean score. The mean scores were arranged in descending order – the higher the score the better the performance on the development scale. Four categories (scales) of performance on the rural development scale, based on the clustering of scores, were derived (see Table 2.3). The distortion arising from this method is related to the weaknesses inherent in using an average to generalize for a population.

The second method ranked the LGAs by scores obtained on each index. Thus LGAs were ranked from 1 (the LGA with the best performance) to 23 (the LGA with the worst performance).[16] The ranks of each LGA were summed and the sum of ranks arranged in descending order (Table 2.3). The lower the sum of ranks the better

Table 2.2 Location quotient and accessibility scores on indices of development in 1980/1.

LGA	Education	Health	Accessi-bility	Agricultural Technology	Extension	Mean Score
Maiduguri	1.49	6.90	6.60	1.31	1.70	3.60
Gwoza	1.94	2.41	0.30	2.39	2.71	1.95
Biu	1.56	1.01	0.20	1.64	2.59	1.40
Askira/Uba	1.32	1.40	0.36	1.46	2.26	1.36
Bade	1.74	1.73	0.25	1.56	1.45	1.34
Fika	1.20	0.99	0.35	2.26	0.70	1.10
Gujba	1.22	0.36	0.11	1.67	1.97	1.06
Bama	1.24	1.01	0.17	1.27	1.40	1.01
KK/Shani	1.56	1.01	0.18	0.62	1.38	0.95
Hawul	1.56	1.01	0.32	0.59	1.19	0.93
Ngala	0.93	0.61	0.20	1.64	0.90	0.85
Nangere	1.20	0.99	0.75	0.31	0.70	0.79
Nguru	0.82	0.84	0.08	1.43	0.63	0.76
Damboa	1.31	0.18	0.08	1.22	0.92	0.74
Damaturu	0.78	0.27	0.27	1.00	0.80	0.62
Damasak	0.40	0.17	0.00	1.36	0.79	0.54
Fune	0.64	0.19	0.12	0.84	0.93	0.54
Monguno	0.78	0.18	0.26	0.89	0.49	0.52
Konduga	0.81	0.23	0.26	0.85	0.37	0.50
Kukawa	0.40	0.17	0.12	1.01	0.81	0.50
Geidam	0.57	0.58	0.05	0.63	0.48	0.46
Kaga	0.71	0.11	0.13	0.41	0.78	0.42
Gubio	0.40	0.17	0.06	0.53	0.33	0.29

Data sources: Borno State Ministries of: Education (1980/1); Health (1980/1); Agriculture and Natural Resources (1981); and Land and Survey (1981).

the performance on the development scale. Four categories of development were then derived from the sum of ranks based on the clustering of scores (Table 2.3). The limitation of this method is that the sum of ranks exaggerates the difference between the LGAs.

The third method was to rank the LGAs according to their performance on the summed ranks, and then arrange them in ascending order (Table 2.3). The LGAs were then divided into quartiles to produce patterns.[17] The limitation is that the division seems arbitrary since two LGAs with the same score may not necessarily be in the same category.

In observing the results so far obtained, it is apparent that the three methods are not independent of one another. There are only a few discrepancies in upward or downward movement between categories, indicating that the differential categorizations of rural development

Table 2.3 Different criteria for the ranking of level of development

Mean	Score	Sum of ranks		Ranked sum of ranks	
LGA	Score	LGA	Ranks	LGA	Final rank
Maiduguri	3.60	Gwoza	11.0	Gwoza	1
Gwoza	1.95	Maiduguri	23.0	Maiduguri	2
Biu	1.40	Askira/Uba	24.0	Askira/Uba	3
Askira/Uba	1.36	Bade	27.0	Bade	4
Bade	1.34	Biu	28.5	Biu	5
Fika	1.10	Fika	44.5	Fika	6.5
Gujba	1.06	Hawul	44.5	Hawul	6.5
Bama	1.01	Bama	47.5	Bama	8
KK/Shani	0.95	Gujba	49.0	Gujba	9
Hawul	0.93	KK/Shani	50.5	KK/Shani	10
Ngala	0.85	Ngala	53.0	Ngala	11
Nangere	0.79	Nangere	63.5	Nangere	12
Nguru	0.76	Damaturu	66.5	Damaturu	13
Damboa	0.74	Damboa	69.0	Damboa	14
Damaturu	0.62	Nguru	71.5	Nguru	15
Damasak	0.54	Konduga	77.5	Konduga	16
Fune	0.54	Monguno	78.5	Monguno	17
Monguno	0.52	Fune	79.5	Fune	18
Konduga	0.50	Kukawa	85.5	Kukawa	19
Kukawa	0.50	Damasak	90.0	Damasak	20
Geidam	0.46	Kaga	93.5	Kaga	21
Kaga	0.42	Geidam	94.0	Geidam	22
Gubio	0.29	Gubio	108.5	Gubio	23

Data Sources: same as in Table 2.2.

scales derived from these methods were quite similar. In this paper the first method was chosen for deriving the different patterns of rural development in Figures 6 and 7 because it relates more closely to the actual magnitude of distributions of socio-economic conditions in the state.

Further insights into the extent of spatial inequality in the distributions were derived graphically and mathematically using a programmed adaptation of the Lorenz curve and Gini, fair-share point and segregation indices.[18] For the indices, perfect equality of the measures of distribution is zero while a score of 100 indicates perfect inequality. Whilst these three indices are not perfectly correlated with each other, they can be useful for giving more insight into the magnitude of spatial, temporal and social inequalities in rural development.

An explanation of the patterns

Figure 6 summarizes rural development achievement in the LGAs based on each LGA's mean score. Many LGAs were disadvantaged. The most developed areas (first and second categories of LGAs, see Figure 6) stretch east and south from the north-western corner of the state to its eastern border in a crescent-shaped pattern. The less developed areas (third and fourth categories of LGAs) are in the northern and central parts of the state.

The distribution shows a regional pattern in levels of rural development. For example, three out of five LGAs in the first category are in the wetter southern and south-eastern periphery, while most of the LGAs in the fourth (last) category are in the drier north and north-east. The geographical pattern of the less developed LGAs (Figure 6) suggests that environmental factors contribute to the low level of development. With the 600 mm isohyet as the boundary between Sudan and Sahel zones[19], most of the LGAs in the first and second categories are in the Sudan zone while most of the LGAs in the third and fourth categories are in the Sahel zone. In these northern LGAs aridity is more severe, because the amount and duration of rainfall are more unpredictable. This factor tends to suggest that there is some relationship between ecological conditions and level of rural development in the state. However, the fact that one of the LGAs in the first category

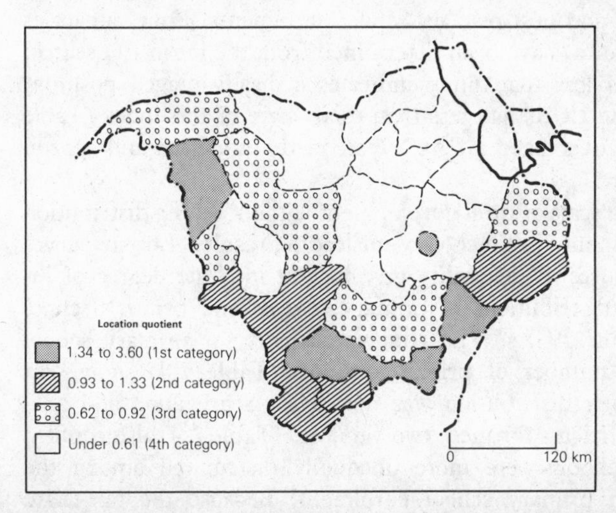

Fig. 6 Borno State – Categories of rural development in 1981

is also within the Sahel tends also to suggest that ecological conditions do not provide the only, and probably not even the principal, explanation for the present pattern of rural development in the state. Historical, economic, political and social factors are all important in the explanation of the patterns.

Understanding the composite pattern derived here requires knowledge of a particular historical process which led to the area's underdevelopment. Historically, the north-east region around Lake Chad (now relatively underdeveloped) was the ecumene of Bornu Empire in pre-colonial times.[20] The region performed an integrative role in trans-Saharan trade and *haj* movements to the Middle East and consequently the region prospered greatly.[21] Colonization led to the fall of Bornu Kingdom and the relocation of its capital from Kukawa to Maiduguri. The north-east region thus lost its integrative role in the development of the area. Maiduguri became the focus of trade, administration and transportation. The interplay of these factors set in motion a chain of social, political and economic processes which contributed more to the development of the southerly areas and the underdevelopment of the northerly and north-easterly areas. Details of these spatial inequalities in rural development are described and explained in the patterns that follow (see Figure 7).

Educational patterns

The educational patterns are based on the mean LQ performance of the LGAs (Table 2.2) on three variables: number of primary schools; primary school, and post-primary school enrolments. Four categories of LGAs (Figure 7a) have been determined from the mean LQ scores. Since a score of less than unity indicates a disadvantaged position, nearly half of the LGAs had less than their share of this index (Table 2.2). These disadvantaged LGAs are all in the northern and central parts of the state.

Measuring the scale of rural development without taking distribution into account can only produce very misleading results. Lorenz curves and other measures of inequality give insight into the degree of inequality in the distributions of primary schools and primary school enrolments in the LGAs. The Gini coefficients for primary school enrolment and number of primary schools (Table 2.4) show that inequality in their distribution was not great. Segregation and fair-share point coefficients for these two variables (Table 2.4) also confirm that primary schools were more unequally distributed among the population than primary school enrolment. Because the fair-share point index is a more sensitive measure of inequality, the fair-share

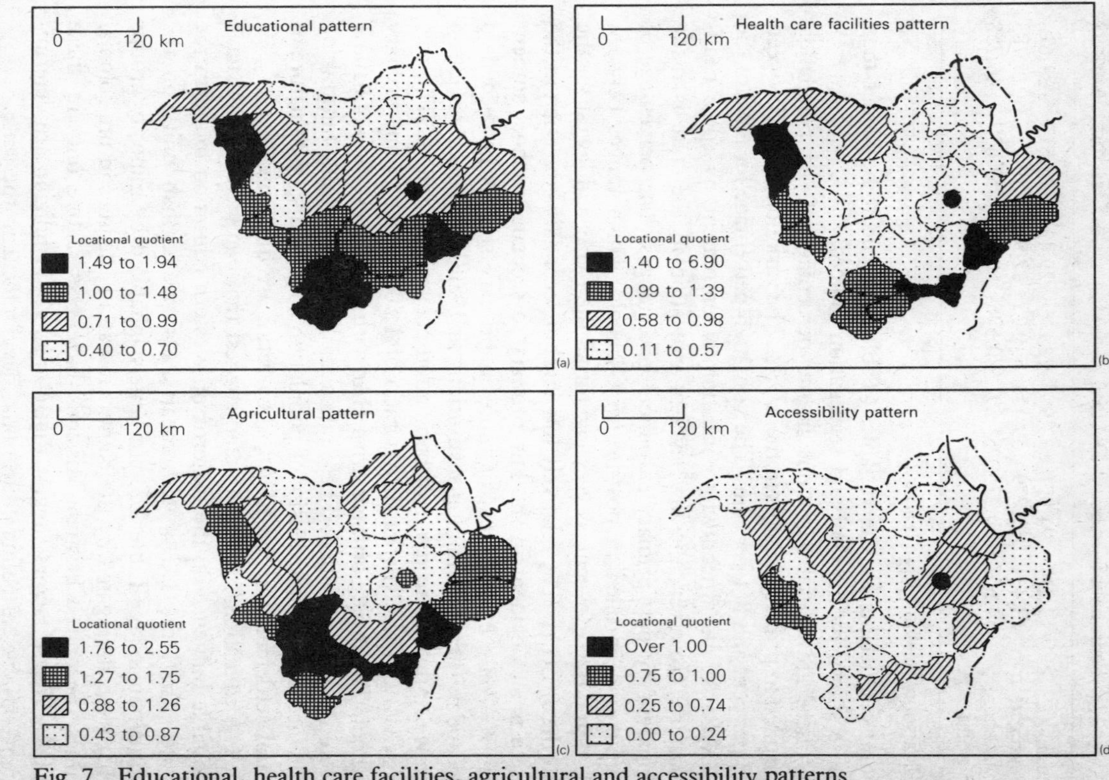

Fig. 7 Educational, health care facilities, agricultural and accessibility patterns

Table 2.4 Gini, segregation and fair-share point indices on the variables.

Index	Primary school enrolment	No. of primary schools	Doctors	Mid-wives	Dispen-saries	Tractors	Extension workers
Gini	19.217	24.971	77.949	72.099	29.434	26.517	28.620
Segregation	13.431	17.779	59.111	53.575	22.919	19.024	20.783
Fair-share point	54.607	70.175	67.391	80.576	60.667	57.635	46.758

Data sources: same as in Table 2.2.

point coefficients for the variables (Table 2.4) tend to be higher than those shown by the Gini and segregation indices.

There are spatial variations in the percentage of the population enrolled in primary schools in the LGAs. The variations range between 38 per cent and 8.4 per cent. The very high percentage for most of the LGAs may be attributed to inflation of enrolment by some headmasters. However, the low level of education in the state is made apparent by post-primary enrolment percentages. The percentage of population enrolled in post-primary schools, which ranges between 0.14 and 0.82 per cent, is very low for all the LGAs and lowest for the northern LGAs. The relatively low level of secondary education in the state is also evident in the low primary to secondary school student ratio – only 2.3 per cent of those in primary schools proceeded to secondary/ teacher-training institutions in 1980/1. The LGAs seem to be well provided in terms of population per primary school. The best served LGA was Gwoza with a ratio of 1,500 people to one primary school. The three north-eastern LGAs with the highest ratio of 6100:1 were the least provided. These ratios may seem reasonable but, taking into account the low density of population and the dispersed nature of rural settlements in the LGAs, such ratios are quite high.

The educational patterns noted suggest that two factors might have possible influence on the patterns of Western education found in the state. First, the LGAs with mean LQs greater than unity on the education index (Table 2.2) are largely inhabited by minority groups that were subjugated by the Kanuri in varying degrees in pre-colonial times. Second, Christian Missions have been active only in these LGAs. These factors suggest that ethnicity and religion are determinant variables affecting educational development in the state.

Health care pattern

This pattern is based on the mean LQ scores on doctors, midwives, dispensaries and hospital beds. Fifteen LGAs (65 per cent) were, in varying degrees, disadvantaged on this index. Furthermore, only metropolitan Maiduguri and Gwoza were not disadvantaged as regards the distribution of doctors. Other LGAs were, in varying degrees, disadvantaged also on the other variables that make up the health care index. Figure 7 shows some regional concentration. The LGAs with relatively high health care LQs, of one and above, are located in the north-western, southern and south-eastern periphery of the state, while the northern and central LGAs were in varying degrees disadvantaged.

The Gini coefficients for doctors and midwives (Table 2.4) show a very high degree of inequality in their distributions. The other two indices also confirm the high inequalities in the distribution of these two variables. The absence of any doctor in ten LGAs, with a combined population of 2.1 million and the non-availability of midwives in five LGAs, with a population of about 1.1 million, suggest that modern health care services were available only to a minority of the population in few locations. The Gini index of 29.434 for dispensaries shows that the distribution of dispensaries was more equal than that of doctors and midwives (Table 2.4). However, as the ratios of population per dispensary in the LGAs show (these range between one dispensary per 13,000 population and one per 71,800 population), dispensaries are still inadequate. This situation is exacerbated by the frequent lack of drugs in these dispensaries, thereby rendering them inoperative. Thus even this basic facility is poorly provided in the state.

Agricultural pattern

Table 2.2 shows the mean LQ scores for the two indices (agricultural technology and extension) of agricultural development. Like the other indices already considered, a number of the LGAs were disadvantaged. The Gini, segregation and fair-share point indices for the two variables (Table 2.4) show that the inequality in the distribution of these variables was not great. However, the ratios of tractors, which range from one tractor to 4,600 people and one tractor to 32,000 people, are not encouraging. The ratios of extension workers to population in the LGAs are worse for they range between 1:5800 and 1:42000. These ratios on the two indices suggest that traditional methods of agricultural production predominate, which may tend to lead to low output by farmers.

Figure 7c shows that the LGAs in the wetter areas of the Sudan Savanna were better served in the distribution of agricultural inputs. Since rainfall is the greatest impediment to agriculture in the state, it is possible that the ecological potentials of the wetter LGAs have strongly influenced the distribution of agricultural inputs.

Accessibility pattern

Roads are important infrastructures of development because they have direct effect on accessibility and indirect effect on agricultural productivity. Their adequacy is therefore imperative for rural welfare. Because there are few well-maintained roads, most LGAs are inaccessible. Over all, there were 2,188 km of all-weather roads[22] in the state by 1981. Since accessibility index (AI) of less than unity indicates that there are portions of the LGA which are inaccessible, many LGAs were, and are still, inaccessible.[23] Table 2.2 shows that the best served LGAs were metropolitan Maiduguri, where there is no point farther than 5 km from an all-weather road, and Nangere where 75 per cent of the LGA is accessible. Figure 7d shows that many LGAs scored less than 0.24, which means that over three-quarters of these LGAs were inaccessible all the year round by 1981. These figures point to the fact that many parts of the state were, and still are, inaccessible all the year round.

Other explanations of the patterns

The spatial variations in categories of rural development in Figures 6 and 7 may also be explained, at least in part, by examining the history of administrative structure in the state. The root of the present inequality can be traced to the colonial spatial organization of local administration in the area which led to the creation of five Native Authorities (NAs) and the designation of Maiduguri, Potiskum, Biu, Dikwa, and Gashua as NA headquarters (see Figure 8). Roads to

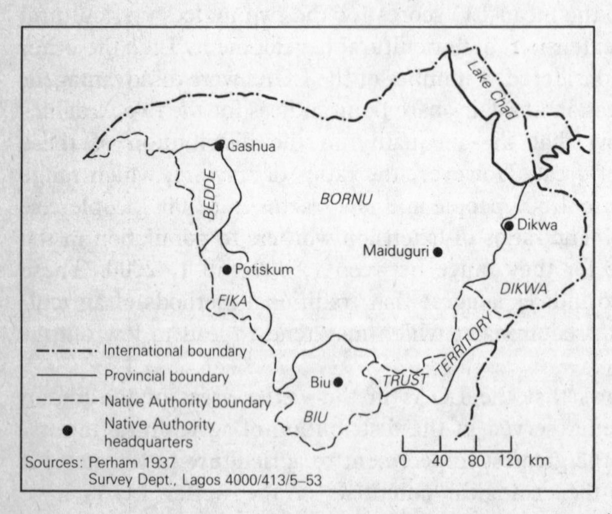

Fig. 8 Borno Province – Native Authorities

connect Maiduguri with these centres followed. It was also the policy of the colonial administration to site NA primary schools, post-primary schools, health facilities and other services in these headquarters.

Table 2.5 shows that the NA administration was in operation for seven decades. Bornu NA was the largest, with 64.4 per cent of the population and 65.9 per cent of the state's area.[24] All things being equal, the probability of development spreading from the headquarters of a small (in area) NA to all its corners is higher than is the case for a larger NA because of distance decay effect. Consequently Bornu NA (now comprising 12 LGAs) was at a greater disadvantage and therefore lagged behind. This partly explains why the bottom 11 LGAs on the rural development scale were in former Bornu NA. Conversely, Bade, in the same geographical area as these backward LGAs, which has been one administrative unit since colonical times, was among the top five on all the variables.

Table 2.5 Spatial structure of local governments 1902–81

1902–76	1976–80	1981	1984
	Maiduguri	Maiduguri	Return to structure of 1976–80
	Damboa	Damboa	
	Damaturu	Damaturu	
	Fune	Fune	
	Geidam	Geidam	
	Gujba	Gujba	
Bornu NA	Nguru	Nguru	
	Kaga	Kaga	
	Konduga	Konduga	
	Monguno	Monguno	
		Kukawa	
	Kukawa	Gubio	
		Damasak	
Dikwa NA	Ngala	Ngala	
	Bama	Bama	
		Biu	
Biu NA	Biu	Hawul	
		KK/Shani	
Fika NA	Fika	Fika	
		Nangere	
Bedde NA	Bade	Bade	
Part of Trust Territory/	Askira/Uba	Askira/Uba	
Sarduana Province	Gwoza	Gwoza	

Source: Perham (1937); and Ministry of Land and Survey (1981)

An important aspect in the spatial reorganization of local government in Borno State, between 1976 and 1980, was the designation of 23 centres as LGA headquarters. The headquarters, by virtue of their large numbers and more equitable spread (than the old NA headquarters), have greatly contributed to the reduction of the inequalities (since most allocations are based on administrative units) but they have not entirely alleviated either the residual inequalities that arose under the old spatial structure or brought about an entirely equitable distribution. Furthermore the non-centrality of many of the LGA headquarters (Figure 5) exacerbates the problems of accessibility and therefore contributes to the inequality within an LGA.

The territorial principle[25] which is still being used in the allocation of some resources also reinforces inequality in rural development. For example, a resource allocation formula which makes for the distribution of some grants and facilities, on an LGA basis, unwittingly promotes inequality because: (a) the principle does not take the area and population into account; and (b) such a policy is often not fully implemented, resulting in some units getting nothing in the long run. The first reason partly explains the good performance of the smaller LGAs like Gwoza, Bade and Askira/Uba, on some of the indices. This advantage was probably the main reason behind the widespread agitation for the creation of more LGAs during the Second Republic.

Limitations of the patterns

Rural development, being a multi-faceted phenomenon, includes economic, political and social variables. The indicators used in this study reflect mainly on the economic aspects, to the exclusion of the other aspects which can tell us more about the well-being of the population. Furthermore, the variables are mainly tangible inputs of the system instead of tangible and intangible outputs which tell us more about the well-being of people. Unfortunately evaluations of intangible conditions of well-being are hardly available in disaggregated forms.

Rural development calls for spatial as well as social equality. The patterns presented reflect on the latter and not the former. The location quotient and accessibility coefficients together with the Lorenz curve and the three indices depict equality of access. Thus the coefficients give the impression that the facilities/personnel are shared equally among the population in the LGAs. In reality this is not so. For example, access to health care depends not only on distance but also on other variables like income and social status. Therefore the analysis masks a lot of social inequalities within and between LGAs. Better insight would have been gained if patterns of social inequality, which emphasize the actual distribution of benefits among the population, are examined. Analysis of income distribution and social status will go a long way to eliminate this deficiency. Unfortunately, data on these variables are difficult to come by in developing countries.

A third limitation is that the spatial scale of observation (LGA) tends to be too large. The indentification of patterns of rural development, at this scale, masks the actual position in averages which are largely a reflection of conditions at the LGA headquarters where most of these facilities/personnel are located.

Finally, the result of the analysis gives the impression that the threshold of the facilities/services extends to all corners of the LGA. This is not true. The threshold of such facilities as hospitals cuts across LGA boundaries while some parts of the LGA are not reached. A better result would have been gained by examining and mapping the threshold of such facilities instead of using the coefficients to generalize for the whole LGA.

Conclusion

The unsophisticated statistical methods used in analysing patterns of rural development in Borno State in the period 1980/1 provide intuitive evidence that there are regional inequalities in rural development achievement as measured by the five indicators. The measures used have shown their capacity to identify areas of deprivation. With respect to the suitability of using these measures to show patterns of social inequalities in rural development, their limitation is admitted. A possible avenue for future investigation, to overcome this deficiency, might be the inclusion of data on income distribution and social status.

Finally, the rural development patterns that emerged are products of autonomous and policy-induced trends of spatial development. The reduction in spatial inequalities emanating from the spatial reorganization of local government in 1976 is acknowledged. However, the territorial principle of resource allocation, the great difference in the sizes of administrative units, the non-centrality of some LGA headquarters and the harsher environmental conditions in some areas will contribute to the persistence of regional inequalities in the state.

Notes

1 For a summary of these shifts see A.R. De Souza and P.W. Porter (1974), pp. 1–4.
2 This view of development was first given currency by Seers in his two articles (1977a and 1977b). The views expressed in these two articles still form the basis of the present meaning of development. Other concepts of development still have adherents in developing countries, among ordinary citizens, administrators and politicians responsible for development. This situation makes the realization of development more difficult.
3 There is no complete agreement on what constitutes 'basic needs' as these are culturally mediated. For these views see Seers (1977b) and Streeten (1977).
4 This view of rural development is based on the Asian experience: see Uphoff and Esman (1974). To a large extent this is also applicable to other less developed countries.
5 This holistic process should be viewed as a trinity. These spheres should be given equal attention if real development is to be achieved. In accepting this holistic concept, the complexity and interrelatedness of many variables which influence the quality of life in rural areas is recognized.
6 Spatial patterns can be expressed in terms of scale, distance, direction, mass, diffusion rate and nearest neighbour, and can be used to show real or perceived changes in the landscape: see Cohen and Rosenthal (1971).
7 The main limitation is that ranking distorts the magnitude of the difference between any two scales. However Berry in his study (1961) considered this to be insignificant since more faith is placed in the relative positions of the units than in the precise value of any index being measured.
8 The patterns derived in Weinand's (1973) study were highly generalized because the data were based on the provinces which roughly correspond to the present states.
9 Williamson's (1965) study makes use of coefficient of variation, squares of deviations and Spearman's rank correlation to derive patterns of regional inequality. Lipshitz (1981) used coefficient of variation to analyse regional inequalities in Israel. The coefficient of variation measures a single variable which is used as a proxy for measuring regional inequality. Board, *et al.* (1970) also used standard deviation measure to show patterns of economic welfare in South Africa. Z-score transformations were also widely used by Smith (1977).
10 The conceptual and practical problems of measuring some indicators of development and suggestions on how to reduce them are well treated in Seers (1972), Taylor (1972) and Drewnowski (1972).
11 For the purpose of generating more valid patterns of regional inequality smaller spatial units are advocated because the use of larger units leads to highly generalized patterns.
12 The main limitation of these variables is that they reflect more on inputs than outputs. Examples of output variables which reflect on various aspects of development abound in the literature. These include number of primary and post-primary school graduates, incidence of certain diseases, infant mortality, crime rate, floor space, unemployment rate, productivity in industry and agriculture, ethnic and religious fractionalization, participation,

etc. For more of these variables see Smith (1977; 1979) and Taylor (1972). A further limitation is that the variables reflect mainly on the economic aspect of development.

13 Location quotient measures socio-economic conditions based on per capita distribution. See Isard (1963), p. 124.

14 Accessibility, in this context, is used in a narrow sense to mean that overcoming distance is the only barrier to access to such facilities as hospitals, markets, farm service centres. In reality there are other barriers to access to these facilities such as income and social status. Therefore the accessibility index used in this study provides only a measure of people's ability to overcome distance in order to have access to a multiplicity of facilities within a given political unit. The 10 km wide corridor may seem arbitrary but this was the estimated threshold in the utilization of a road in the area. The width of the road can be adjusted to suit any local situation.

15 The formula was provided by Dr Assefa Mehretu. This formula takes care of double counting at an intersection, to be a distance of 5 km, where routes converge. However this is true only where four routes converge. For cases of more than four routes converging there will be some element of double counting. But since this was rarely the case in the study area this was used in the computation.

16 Ranking distorts the magnitude of differences between the scores by making the differences uniform. Despite this limitation it is widely used in the derivation of patterns. For example see Berry (1961); and Smith (1979), pp. 140–8.

17 For an example of this method of classification see Berry (1961).

18 Darden and Tabachneck's (1980) statistical programme computes and draws an adaptation of a Lorenz curve. The programme also calculates Gini, fair-share point and segregation indices to show the scale of inequality in distribution. The limitation of the Lorenz curve is that distributions with the same Gini value can have different Lorenz curves depending on whether distributions are concentrated at the upper or lower end of distribution (Smith 1979, p. 136).

19 In most climatic classifications rainfall in the Sudan zone varies between 600 and 1200 mm while in the Sahel it varies between 200 and 600 mm.

20 Bornu Empire at its zenith extended over hundreds of kilometres on all sides of Lake Chad. However the capital was all the time located near the western shores of Lake Chad around Kukawa. For details see Brenner (1973) and Hallam (1977).

21 The present north-eastern part of Borno State around Kukawa benefited economically, socially and culturally from trans-Saharan trade and *haj* movements in pre-colonial times. The location of Kukawa enabled the area round Lake Chad to play an integrative role and this led to the development of the north-east part of Borno State in pre-colonial times. See Cohen (1967) and Johnston and Muffett (1973).

22 Only tarred roads, which are usable all the year round by all ranges of vehicles, were considered as all-weather roads in this study.

23 Each AI was calculated using measured (on a map) lengths of all tarred roads within an LGA, the number of intersections (junctions) within that LGA and the 10 km width, which in this study is considered to be the threshold in people's day-to-day utilization of the road.

24 The area of the state is 116,080.8 sq km (Borno 1981). The area of each LGA was calculated using a planimeter. The sum of the areas of the LGAs calculated was less than the official figure by 3,512.8 sq km or 3 per cent. The population figures given are projections based on the controversial 1963 census.

25 This principle stipulates that resources are to be allocated on territorial basis irrespective of size. The territorial principle of resource allocation falls within the welfare distribution model. The disadvantage of using this formula for resource allocation is that the presence of pressure groups in some administrative units makes the authorities satisfy these units first and others later if funds are available. Rarely is this fully implemented. Therefore, in practice, the resources are allocated on the political placation model instead of the welfare distribution model spelled out in government policy objectives. The inequality observed in some infrastructural development in the state can be explained by reference to these two models. See Muir and Paddison (1981), p. 189, for more on these two models.

References

Berry, Brian J.L. 1961, 'Basic patterns of economic development'. In Ginsburg Norton (ed.), *Atlas of economic development* (University of Chicago; Department of Geography, Research Paper. no. 68); pp. 110–19.

Board, C.; Davis, R.J. and Fair, T.J.D. 1970. The structure of the South Africa space economy: an integrated approach, *Regional Studies* vol. 4, pp. 367–92.

Borno State, 1981a, *Local Government Areas* (Maiduguri, Ministry of Land and Survey)

– 1981b, 'Tractor equipment and their distribution in 1981' (Maiduguri: Ministry of Agriculture and Natural Resources)

– 1981c 'Extension personnel by LGAs – 1981' (Maiduguri: Ministry of Agriculture and Natural Resources)

– 1981d. 'Primary and secondary school enrolments by LGAs, 1980/1' (Maiduguri: Ministry of Education)

– 1981e, 'Number of primary schools by LGAs in 1980/1' (Maiduguri: Ministry of Education)

– 1981f, 'Health Establishments and Personnel by LGAs, 1980/1' (Maiduguri: Ministry of Health)

Brenner, Louis. 1973. *The Shehus of Bornu: a history of the El-Kanemi dynasty of Bornu* (Oxford: Claredon Press)

Cohen, Ronald. 1967. *The Kanuri of Bornu* (New York: Holt Rinehart and Winston)

Cohen, Saul B. and Rosenthal, Lewis D. 1971. A geographical model for political systems analysis. *Geographical Review* vol. 61, pp. 5–31.

Darden, J.I. and Tabachneck, A.S. 1980. Algorithm 8: graphic and mathematical descriptions of inequality, dissimilarity, segregation, or concentration, *Environment and Planning A* vol. 12, pp. 227–234.

De Souza, Anthony R. and Porter, Philip W. 1974. *The underdevelopment and modernization of the Third World*. Commission on College Geography Resource Paper No. 29 (Washington, D.C. Association of American Geographers)

Drewnowski, Jan. 1972. Social indicators and welfare measurement: remarks on methodology, *Journal of Development Studies* vol. 8 (3), pp. 77–90.

Hallam, W.K.R. 1977. *The Life of Rabin Fadl Allah* (Elms Court: Arthur H. Stockwell)

Isard, Walter. 1963. *Methods of regional analysis: an introduction to regional science* (Cambridge, Massachusetts: The M.I.T. Press), pp. 123–6.

Johnston, H.A.S. and Muffet, D.J.M. 1973. *Denham in Bornu* (Pittsburgh: Duquesne University Press)

Lipshitz, A.S.G. 1981. Regional inequalities in Israel, *Environment and Planning A* vol. 13, pp. 463–73.

Muir, Richard and Paddison, Roman. 1981. *Politics, geography and behaviour* (London: Methuen), pp. 183–9.

Perham, Margery. 1937. *Native administration in Nigeria* (Oxford: Oxford University Press)

Seers, Dudley, 1972. What are we trying to measure? *Journal of Development Studies* vol. 8, pp. 21–36.

– 1977a The meaning of development, *International Development Review* vol. 19 (2): pp. 2–7.
– 1977b The new meaning of development, *International Development Review* vol. 19 (3): pp. 2–7.
Smith, David M. 1977. *Human geography: a welfare approach* (New York: St. Martin's Press)
– 1979. *Where the grass is greener* (Baltimore: The Johns Hopkins University Press)
Streeten, Paul. 1977. The distinctive features of a basic needs approach to development, *International Development Review* vol. 19, pp. 8–16.
Taylor, Charles Lewis. 1972. Indicators of Political Development, *Journal of Development Studies* vol. 8 (3) pp. 103–9.
Uphoff, Norman T. and Esman, Miltion J. 1974. *Local organization for rural development: analysis of Asian experience* (Ithaca: Rural Development Committee, Cornell University)
Weinand, Herbert C. 1973. *Some spatial aspects of economic* development in Nigeria, *Journal of Developing Areas*, vol. 7, pp. 247–263.
Williamson, J.G. 1965. Regional inequality and the process of national development, *Economic Development and Cultural Change* vol. 13 part II.

Acknowledgement

I am grateful to Drs A. Mehretu, D.J. Campbell, J.T. Darden and M. Bratton all of Michigan State University, East Lansing, U.S.A. for their comments on an earlier draft.

3
Methods of measuring spatial inequality and their use: the example of Zambia

Reinhard Henkel
Department of Geography, University of Heidelberg, West Germany

Spatial differentiation or inequality is central to the study of human geography, yet surprisingly geographers have paid relatively little attention to developing measures of spatial inequality. Alternatively measures of concentration appear to be problematic for geographers and they are often handled incorrectly (Gaile 1983, p. 469).[1] For example, in an article on regional variations in China, Chu (1982) presents Lorenz curves which are 'kinked' and cross the equality diagonal, both impossibilities for correct Lorenz curves. These mistakes (which also resulted in the wrong calculation of concentration measures) were put right in a comment by Gaile (1983), but clearly there is need to have a closer look at these techniques. Even textbooks of welfare geography, whose major focus is the revelation and analysis of spatial inequality, show confusion in terminology, for example mixing the concentration index and Gini coefficient (Smith 1977; Coates *et al.* 1977).

There are three major questions which frequently appear in studies of spatial inequalities:

1 Are spatial inequalities within one region (or country) greater than within another?
2 Are spatial inequalities within a region for a certain variable greater than those of another indicator?
3 How does the extent of spatial inequality change over time? Is the distribution of a variable moving towards an equalization, or are the disparities growing?

All these questions can only be answered if one has a consistent method of measuring inequality. Therefore, in formal terms, we need to imagine the following situation: a non-negative variable is distributed over a region which consists of a complete system of **N** subregions.

We usually assume the variable relates to another variable of the subregions. In most cases this is the area of, or the population of the subregions, but sometimes it may be a certain part of the population.

Measures of inequality

A number of measures has been developed, mainly by economists, in order to measure inequality, usually income or social inequality (see also the survey by Gaile, 1977). Most of these can without much difficulty be applied spatially, that is, where the sub-units are subregions, rather than population groups or economic sectors. The three most important measures can be derived from different measures of relative dispersion (see Appendix p. 74). The easiest to handle (in mathematical terms) is the concentration index **C** (sometimes referred to as the Hoover, Kuznets or Schutz index). It is related to relative variability, which is itself based on the mean deviation of observations about the mean. Another is the Herfindahl-Hirschman index **H** which can be derived from the coefficient of variation, a measure of relative dispersion using the standard deviation. A dispersion measure, not very frequently used in statistics, is the sum of absolute differences between all observations. But it is used for a third very important measure of concentration, or of inequality, the Gini coefficient **G**, which is named after an Italian statistician. Both C and G are related to the Lorenz curve (for an example, see below, page 69) in that C is the maximum vertical distance between the equality diagonal and the Lorenz curve, whereas G is the ratio of the area between the diagonal and the curve (the 'concentration area') to the area of the triangle below the diagonal. Other measures have been proposed such as the Pareto index, or measures derived from the entropy concept (Gaile 1977) but they are either difficult to handle mathematically or not standardized. Indices C, H and G are or can be standardized, in that a value of zero denotes complete equality, and a value of 1.00 (or 100%) means complete concentration or inequality in the distribution of the variable. This is essential in order to work along the lines indicated by the questions raised above.

The relevance of a clear concept of inequality

The economist Kuznets (1955) stated that inequalities in *personal* income distribution necessarily increase in an early stage of the transformation process from an agrarian to an industrial and service society. These inequalities, however, stabilize and subsequently decrease with further development. Kuznets tried to prove this by analysing time series of the trends in several countries, using the concentration index C. Ten years later, Williamson (1965) published his well-known study investigating *spatial* income distribution. He arrived at analogous conclusions which have been termed the 'rule of the inverted U' (Figure 9).

Williamson applied the weighted coefficient of variation **V** as a measure of inequality. Many scholars working in the tradition of liberal theories of development concluded from these observations that increasing disparities in personal as well as in spatial income distribution must be regarded as inherent in the early stages of the development process. Whether a reversal occurs inherently in this process is a very important question for developing countries, because they need to know whether measures aimed at redressing spatial disparities have to be applied at an early stage, or whether there is no need to worry about this because 'it will take care of itself'. While the inverted **U** rule has been accepted as a more or less correct description of the past development of industrialized countries (see, for example, Lo and Salih 1981), its application to developing countries has been questioned. More recent data shows that there was no consistent relationship between per capita income and regional income disparity in a set of 14 developing countries (Figure 10), and also that regional disparities in developing nations are far wider than those in developed

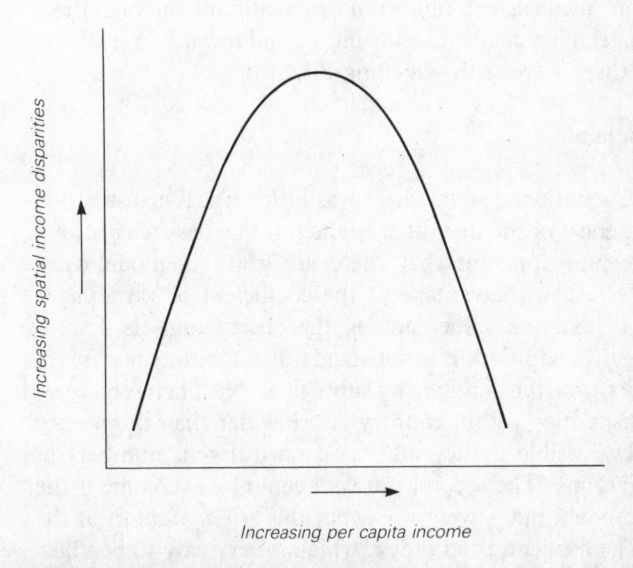

Fig. 9 The rule of the 'inverted U'

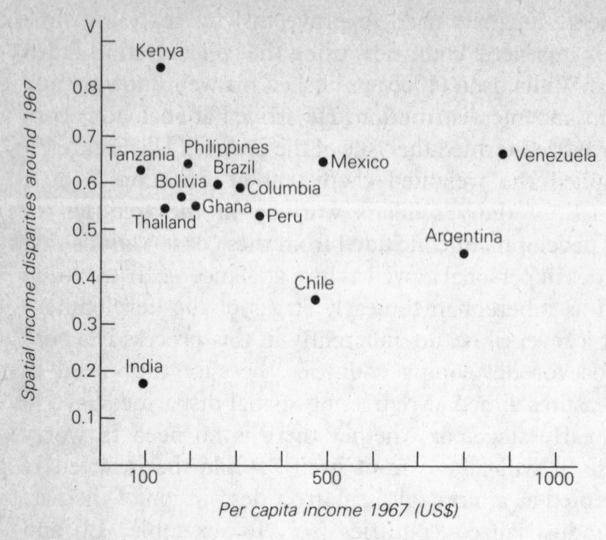

Fig. 10 Spatial inequality in 14 less developed countries

nations (Gilbert and Goodman 1976). The same authors also found that there was an inconsistent time trend in spatial inequality: there were as many developing countries showing a trend towards 'narrowing of the gaps' as there were with widening disparities.

Problems of application

In all the studies mentioned so far there was little critical investigation of the appropriateness of the measures applied. If one has a closer look at them, it becomes apparent that there are grave methodological deficiencies. A serious disadvantage of the coefficient of variation is that the effect of extreme values among the observations is disproportionately large. In addition, it is not standardized, but its maximum value is dependent on the number of subregions N. Therefore comparisons like 'disparities within country A are wider than in country B' are not really possible if they are based on different numbers of territorial subdivisions. The second problem could be overcome if the Hirschman-Herfindahl index were used, but this still suffers from the first problem. The concentration index, which is very easy to handle,[2] overcomes both problems, but there is another difficulty: an important aspect of any inequality measure is the effect of a transfer of (for example) from one subregion to another. If income is tran from a richer to a poorer subregion, the measure should tend tc equality. However the concentration index is not affected by income transfers on the same side of the mean.

The Gini coefficient and the closely related Lorenz curve are the most appropriate methods to measure and illustrate inequality. For the construction of the Lorenz curve, the cumulative percentage shares of the variable under investigation, and the population, for the spatial units are needed. These units have first to be ordered according to the ratio of advantage. To illustrate this Table 3.1 shows the distribution of doctors over the nine provinces of Zambia in 1978, and the population in these provinces.

Table 3.1 Distribution of doctors in Zambia (1978) and population, by provinces

Province	Share of doctors		Share of population		Ratio of advantage
	% x_i	cumulative per cent.	% p_i	cumulative per cent.	(doctors per 100,000 population)
Lusaka	38.8	38.8	11.5	11.5	39.8
Copperbelt	34.8	73.6	21.6	33.1	19.0
Central	6.5	80.1	9.0	42.1	8.5
Southern	5.9	86.0	12.1	54.2	5.7
Western	3.3	89.3	8.9	63.1	4.4
North-Western	1.7	91.0	5.4	68.5	3.8
Eastern	3.7	94.7	11.7	80.2	3.7
Northern	3.3	98.0	12.2	92.4	3.2
Luapula	1.9	99.9	7.4	99.8	3.0

For the Gini coefficient, few clear methods of calculation are available in the literature. However, that given in the Appendix is easy to use if the values needed for the construction of the Lorenz curve have already been computed.

For any data, G is always greater than or equal to C. And G still underestimates inequality, if the concentration area in the Lorenz diagram is accepted as an appropriate representation of the inequality (Figure 11). For strictly speaking, G does not measure the area between the diagonal and the Lorenz curve but the one between the diagonal and the Lorenz 'polygon' linking the points of the cumulative frequencies. This is because there is a limited number of spatial units.

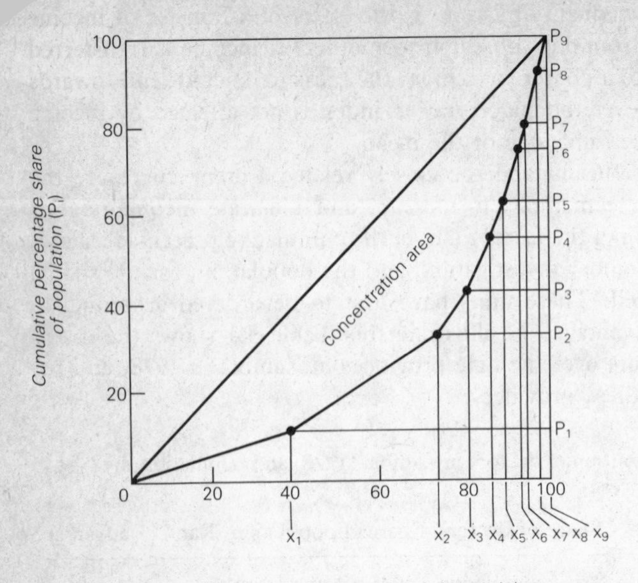

Fig. 11 Lorenz curve of the distribution of doctors over the nine provinces of Zambia

The greater the number of units, the more the polygon approaches the form of a 'real' curve. Even the Gini coefficient has its drawbacks; for example, different Lorenz curves can result in the same G values. In a discussion of different concentration measures, Smith (1977, p. 151ff) arrives at the conclusion that the measures related to the Lorenz curve are superior to others. Hence, the Gini coefficient is the most appropriate measure of inequality in most cases. Indices C and H are less useful, although their interpretation can sometimes lead to valuable insights.

All measures are dependent on the number of subregions. The greater the number, the greater we expect the inequality to be. Therefore it is essential that the level of spatial disaggregation is revealed. This is a formal weakness of Williamson's work: he compared levels of inequality in countries for which data on widely different disaggregative levels were used. In a study of the effect of scale on the concentration index (termed index of dissimilarity), Woods (1976, p. 173) arrives at the conclusion that the number of spatial sub-units not only influences the absolute value of the indices, but also their relative position. He continues by saying that these '... measures which although essentially simple to calculate and of widespread applicability can be extremely deceptive in their interpretation'. This warning is not confined to the concentration index but applies to the other measures too.

The example: Zambia

Zambia has been regarded a classic example of a less developed country with extremely wide spatial development disparities (Figure 12). Mining and industrial production, employment in the formal sector, and hence population are heavily concentrated along the 'line of rail', a small strip of land in the centre of the country. As a result of its mining industry, it is also one of the most highly urbanized countries in Africa. Partly because of this, personal income inequality is extreme in Zambia, with a Gini coefficient among the highest in the world, and inequality further widened after independence (ILO 1977, p. 292). Similar inequalities are found in the distribution of a whole range of services.

The provision of medical and educational services

Table 3.1 reveals that there are great inequalities in the distribution of doctors. The Gini coefficient is G = 48.5%, the concentration index

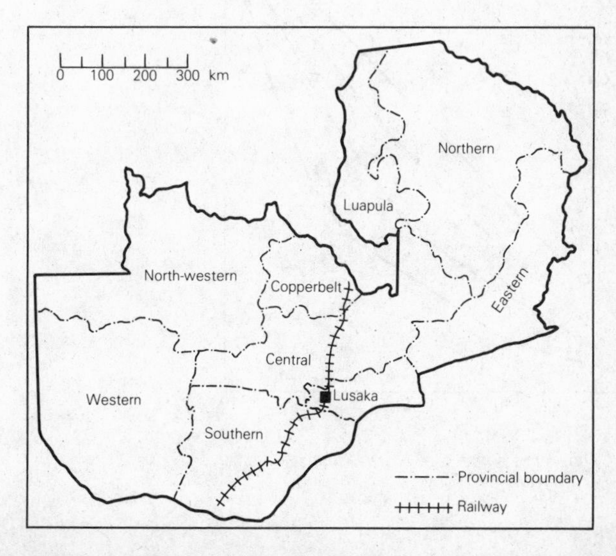

Fig. 12 The provinces of Zambia

is C = 40.4%. Highly qualified professionals such as doctors tend to be concentrated in the major urban nodes in most less developed countries[3], and not only there; for example, this is also the case in the Soviet Union (Smith 1979, p. 269–99), and China (Chu 1982; Gaile 1983). Another indicator of the availability of medical facilities, frequently employed and widely available is the number of hospital beds. These are much more equally distributed, as can clearly be seen in the Lorenz curve (Figure 13). Again for 1978 a Gini coefficient of G=12.7% was calculated, which indicates a slightly more equal distribution than in Kenya (G = 16.9% for eight provinces in 1978) and Tanzania (G = 15.6% for 17 regions in 1974, using data in Van den Berg 1979) and more equal than in Sierra Leone (C = 28.7 for 13 provinces in 1964, Coates *et al.* 1977, p. 39).

If one has a closer look at the bed distribution, it shows surprisingly that the rural areas are better served than the urban provinces. North-Western Province which is generally regarded the most remote and

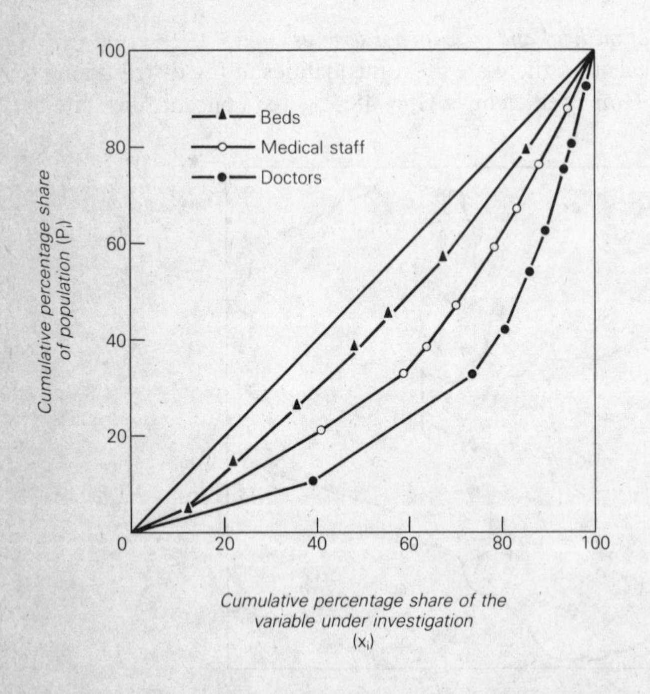

Fig. 13 Lorenz curves of three indicators of medical services in Zambia

underdeveloped part of the country, and Western Province, are the leading provinces, whereas the urban provinces of Lusaka, Central and Copperbelt are worst off (Figure 12). Two factors can be put forward as reasons. On the one hand, the missionary societies and the churches provided a significant share of the medical services, and concentrated their efforts in the rural areas (Henkel 1984); on the other hand, Zambia's national ideology of humanism puts emphasis on the availability of medical services for all citizens within an acceptable distance. Hospital beds have not always been as evenly distributed. At independence in 1964, the Gini coefficient was 20.2%, indicating greater inequality than in 1978. (As a methodological side-comment on the effect of scale, it should be mentioned that, with G = 22.8%, the Gini coefficient for hospital beds in the 52 districts in 1978 is considerably higher than that for the nine provinces.)

A government cannot ignore the locational preferences of doctors, and has to pay high salaries. The mere existence of hospital beds in a remote area does not by itself guarantee good health services. An alternative indicator of inequality is the number of all medical personnel – doctors, medical assistants and nurses. Particularly in the rural areas, it is the last two categories of staff who actually do the bulk of the work. The Lorenz curve for the distribution of all medical personnel lies between those of doctors and hospital beds, indicating a 'moderately unequal' situation. The Gini coefficient is G = 33.4%. When we compare the three measures G, C and H (Table 3.2), we note that G and C behave in a similar way. H is different, although it indicates the same direction. The achievement of more equality in the hospital bed distribution after independence is not as evident from H as from both other measures.

Table 3.2 Three measures of inequality compared

	Gini coefficient **G**	Concentration index **C**	Herfindahl-Hirschman index **H***
Doctors 1978	48.5%	40.4%	0.232
Medical personnel 1978	33.4%	25.3%	0.208
Hospital beds			
1978	12.7%	8.6%	0.126
1964	20.2%	15.5%	0.146

*H is standardized to range between 0 and 1
(data for 9 Zambian provinces)

In education, we can observe similar time trends in Zambia. Secondary school places were unevenly distributed at independence in 1964 (G = 37.5%),[4] but this imbalance was redressed significantly (G = 10.6% in 1980). Owing to the availability of data, we are able to trace development in primary education more closely (Table 3.3). Provision of primary school places was evenly distributed in spatial terms, because the missions, the major agents operating schools, were based in the rural areas. But in the course of the expansion of school facilities after independence (nationwide, 84% of children of primary school age were enrolled in 1980 compared with 32% in 1954), the government succeeded in reducing the imbalance to a level of G = 3.6% in 1970. This achievement compares favourably with Kenya, where we have Gini coefficients of 11.8% (1969) and 10.1% (1978).

In the seventies, inequality seems to have increased again, to a level of G = 8.6% (1980), this time at the expense of the urban areas. Owing to increased rural-urban migration of whole families, the Copperbelt and Lusaka are now the provinces worst-off, while the rural provinces do relatively well. In the present worsening financial situation, however, the Zambian government finds it extremely expensive to maintain this standard of provision of educational services. There were proposals to hand back a large number of primary schools to the churches from which they were nationalized in the years after independence, and recently there has been talk of reintroducing school fees.

Whereas there seems to have been some success in redressing regional imbalances in social services after independence, at least quantitatively, regional income differences are still high. Unfortunately, data to measure these are difficult to come by. Provincial data for 1969 indicates a Gini coefficient at that time of G = 49.0%[5]. Employment in the formal sector, reflecting job opportunities, may stand in its place. Here, a similarly high level of regional imbalance

Table 3.3 Gini coefficients G (in %) for primary school places in Zambia (8 provinces – Lusaka and Central combined)

Year	*G*
1954	12.1
1966	10.6
1970	3.6
1976	6.0
1980	8.6

exists. For 1977, G = 40.2%: far higher than that of the social services, except the distribution of doctors. But there had been a reduction from G = 51.0% (1966). In this respect, Zambia appears to have had slightly more success than Kenya, where regional imbalance in formal employment was reduced from G = 46.1% (1969) to 40.7% (1978). But the gaps are still intolerably wide.

Conclusion

Measurement of spatial inequality seems to be a complicated affair. And indeed there is great scope for errors, fallacies and misinterpretation. An attempt has been made to shed light on the usefulness and suitability of some measures. The Gini coefficient and the related Lorenz curve have been found to be the most appropriate techniques.

Using these, the development and status of spatial inequality in Zambia have been analysed. Whereas regional imbalances in social services are moderate, and have been successfully redressed after independence, differences in income and formal employment are still very high although they also seem to have diminished.

Notes

1 The widely-used techniques textbook by Toyne and Newby (1971, pp. 112–15) gives a wrong explanation of how a Lorenz curve (which is an important graphical representation of an inequality situation and which is closely related to some inequality measures) is constructed. The different spatial units are put into the diagram in an incorrect order and not according to the so-called 'ratio of advantage'.

2 If x_i is the percentage share of the variable under investigation in subregion i and p_i the percentage share of population in this subregion, then

$$C = \frac{1}{2} \sum_{i=1}^{N} |x_i - p_i|$$

with N = number of subregions.

3 In Zambia, 74% of the doctors are found in the two most highly urbanized provinces, Lusaka and Copperbelt, where only a third of the population is living. For Ghana, a similar level of inequality (C = 38.5 for 9 regions in 1969) is observed.

4 The calculation of measures of educational inequality is more tedious because one cannot (or should not) relate enrolment to the total population, but to the respective age cohorts, which may differ widely between provinces as a proportion of total population.

5 The corresponding coefficient of variation is V = 1.01, a value which is higher than any of those compiled by Gilbert and Goodman (1976) (Cf. Figure 10).

Appendix

Some measures of spatial inequality

1 (a) Coefficient of variation V

$$V = \frac{s}{\bar{x}} \text{ (s – standard deviation, } \bar{x} \text{ – mean)}$$

(b) Herfindahl-Hirschman index H

$$H = \sum_{i=1}^{N} \frac{a_i 2}{A} \quad (a_i \text{ – observation for ith subregion})$$

$$\left(N \text{ – number of subregions, } A = \sum_{i=1}^{N} {}_i\right)$$

$$= \frac{v^2 + 1}{N}$$

2 (a) Relative variability v

$$v = \frac{\bar{d}}{\bar{x}} \quad \left(d \text{ – mean deviation about the mean, } \bar{d} = \frac{1}{N} \sum_{i=1}^{N} |a_i - \bar{x}|\right)$$

(b) Concentration index C

$$C = \frac{v}{2}$$

3 (a) Sum of absolute differences between all observations

$$\triangle = \frac{1}{N^2} \sum_{j=1}^{N} \sum_{i=1}^{N} |a_i - a_j|$$

(b) Gini coefficient G

$$G = \frac{\triangle}{2\bar{x}} = 100 - \frac{1}{100}\left[X_iP_i + \sum_{i=2}^{N} X_i (P_i + P_{i-1})\right]$$

x_i and p_i- as explained in the text, p_i is the cumulative percentage of the share of the variable in question in subregion i).

References

Chu, D.K.Y. 1982. Some analyses of recent Chinese provincial data, *Professional Geographer*, vol. 34, pp. 431–7

Coates, B.E., Johnston, R.J. and Knox, P.L. 1977. *Geography and inequality* (Oxford: O.U.P.)

Gaile, G.L. 1977. Effiquity: a comparison of a measure of efficiency with an entropic measure of the equality of discrete spatial distributions, *Economic Geography*, vol. 53, pp. 265–82.

Gaile, G.L. 1983. Reanalyses of Chinese spatial inequality, *Professional Geographer*, vol. 35, pp. 467–9.

Gilbert, A.G. and Goodman, D.E. 1976. 'Regional income disparities and economic development: a critique'. In A.G. Gilbert (ed.) *Development planning and spatial structure* (London: Wiley), pp. 113–42.

Henkel, R. 1984. 'The distribution of the health care services in Zambia with special emphasis on the contribution of the churches' (Paper presented at the IGU Medical Geography Conference, Lusaka, April 1984).

International Labour Office (ILO). 1977. *Narrowing the gaps. Planning for basic needs and productive employment in Zambia* (Geneva: ILO)

Lo, F. & Salih, K. 1981. 'Growth poles, agropolitan development and polarization reversal: The debate and search for alternatives'. In W.B. Stöhr and D.R.F. Fraser (eds), *Development from above or below? The dialectics of regional planning in developing countries* (Chichester: Wiley), pp. 123–52.

Kuznets, S. 1955. Economic growth and income inequality, *American Economic Review*, vol. 45, pp. 1–28.

Smith, D.M. 1977. *Human geography. A welfare approach* (London: Edward Arnold)

Smith, D.M. 1979. *Where the grass is greener: living in an unequal world* (Harmondsworth: Penguin)

Toyne, P. and Newby, P.T. 1971. *Techniques in human geography* (London: Macmillan)

Van den Berg, L.M. 1979. On the measurement of regional inequality, *Journal of the Geographical Association of Tanzania*, vol. 18, pp. 87–99.

Williamson, J.G. 1965. Regional inequality and the process of national development: a description of the patterns, *Economic Development and Cultural Change*, vol. 13, pp. 3–45.

Woods, R. 1976. Aspects of the scale problem in the calculation of segregation indices: London and Birmingham, 1961 and 1971, *Tijdschrift voor Economische en Sociale Geografie*, vol. 67, pp. 169–74.

4
Spatial Inequalities in Nigeria's Social Services

J. Afolabi Falola
Department of Geography, Bayero University, Kano, Nigeria

Introduction

The phenomenon of inequality is widely recognized in Nigeria. It is epitomized in the use of such terms as 'advantaged' and 'disadvantaged' to describe the areas thought to be either comparatively well-off or lagging in particular attributes. Government awareness of inequalities is also evident from the policy objectives contained in the National Development Plans (NDP), especially since the Second Plan. In the second NDP (1970–4), for example, of the five principal national objectives outlined, three pointed to the need to ameliorate inequalities through appropriate policy measures, within the context of a general belief that:

> *a just and egalitarian society puts a premium on reducing inequalities in interpersonal incomes and promoting balanced development among the various communities in the different geographical areas of the country. It organises its economic institutions in such a way that there is no oppression based on class, social status, ethnic group or state. A distributive equity is, therefore, an important cornerstone in the set of national objectives for the government programme of reconstruction and social reform.*
>
> (*Second National Development Plan, 1970–4*)

A similar policy direction stipulated in the same document is 'the promotion of balanced development between one part of the country and another and especially between the urban and rural areas' (Federal Republic of Nigeria 1970, pp. 32, 34, 36).

In the third NDP, two specific objectives pointed to the issue of inequalities: (a) a more even distribution of incomes; and (b) balanced development to spread the benefits of economic growth so that the average Nigerian would experience a marked improvement in his living standard. It was further observed that in Nigeria, as in most other developing countries, development policy must be directed to three fundamental objectives among which was social equity (Federal Republic of Nigeria 1975, pp. 29–33). These objectives were carried forward into the period of the Fourth Plan in which it was stated that 'the overriding aim of our development efforts remains that of bringing about improvement in living conditions of our people.' To do this, there was a need for still 'more even distribution of income among individuals and socio-economic groups (and) balanced development – that is, the achievement of a balance in the development of the different sectors of the economy and the various geographical areas of the country' (Federal Ministry of National Planning 1981, p. 37).

Concern about inequalities in Nigeria has also been expressed by various social scientists. Mabogunje (1978a; 1980) for example, has pointed to the increasing inequality between major industrial metropolises and the other urban centres and, especially in welfare terms, between urban centres and rural areas. Similarly Udo (1975), Olatubosun (1975) and Teriba *et al.* (1975) have all vividly shown the disparities in opportunities and facilities between one rural area and another, and between the urban and rural areas of the country, using various economic and social indicators. But perhaps of particular interest is the work by Diejomaoh (1975) who has used a combination of socio-economic variables to describe the pattern of regional inequality in Nigeria, although because of data problems only education (school enrolment) and health (hospital bed facilities) were included as social variables.

Since the foregoing studies were undertaken not only has the country undergone further subdivision from twelve to nineteen states, in addition to a major local government reform, both of which have significant implications for regional planning and development (Adeniyi 1978) but, also, additional data on various aspects of the country's social conditions have become available through commissioned national surveys. These data, obtainable from the Federal Office of Statistics (FOS), are used in this study to measure spatial inequalities in various social services.

The paper is divided into five sections. The first section reviews some work on the measures of inequality; the second describes the components and variables of inequality used in this present study of Nigerian social services; the third presents the methodology; the fourth describes the pattern of distribution of inequalities and attempts an explanation for the observed distribution; and, finally, the fifth is the conclusion.

A review of measures of inequality

A number of indicators have been proposed for the measurement of inequality (See Coates *et al.* 1977; Smith 1977; and Morris 1979). Of particular relevance to the present analysis in Drewnowski's state of well-being (Smith 1977, pp. 35–6) which includes somatic status, educational status and social status; and the level-of-living index (including nutrition, clothing, shelter, health, education, leisure, security, social environment and physical environment). While the level-of-living index measures the flow of goods and services (inputs), the level-of-welfare, or state of well-being, measures the output of these activities (Morris 1979, p. 18). Furthermore, although the level-of-living list has been described as useful for the description of geographical variations (Smith 1977, p. 37), it is not an adequate measure of distributive performance because it is ethnocentric, being value-biased, in the context of the cultural structures within which people live (Morris 1979 p. 26).

In relation to health, for instance, it has been observed that a major decline in mortality in developing countries (and possibly in developed countries) came from general environmental improvements and from the extension of basic health facilities through the development of efficient administrative capacity rather than through the improvement of medical training and hospital facilities (Morris 1979, p. 26). The implication of this is that such indicators as hospital beds, physician per thousand population or expenditures on health services may be unsatisfactory measures of level of health in a poor country. But on the other hand, there is no denying the fact that elaborate medical facilities are indispensable in times of emergency as in cases of the outbreak of killer diseases such as cholera, meningitis and yellow fever. Furthermore, the importance of input variables such as basic social facilities (for example, health establishments, schools, etc.) is evident in the fact that their absence in the rural areas often accounts, in part, for the rural exodus in most developing countries. Also, the absence of social infrastructures often forms the basis of complaints which are put before government functionaries, especially in Nigeria.[1]

On the other hand, Morris (1979) has warned on the use of ethnocentric variables in identifying inequalities in a country such as Nigeria with a diverse cultural background and with varied exposures to external influences. For instance, it will be inadequate to use enrolment in the western-type educational institutions alone to gauge literacy, as such indicators often either do not provide information about results, or simply reflect the benefits that may be going primarily to élite groups. In contrast, a basic literacy indicator not only records gains going to the very poor but is also able to identify literacy gains made via informal mechanisms as well as those resulting from formal schooling (Morris p. 38). Nevertheless various levels of educational attainment are good measures of social mobility and, to a large extent, economic mobility, while basic literacy enhances 'social participation and control over one's environment' (Morris 1979).

The foregoing discussion points to the fact that the phenomena involved in the measurement of social inequality are complex: 'as such one cannot arrive at a true solution but can only choose among a set of alternatives, selecting in order to minimize inconvenience' (Morris, p. 13). And, in our own circumstances, where there is extreme paucity of data on social conditions, we can only select a very few variables. For instance, there are no comprehensive data on infant mortality, life expectancy and literacy on which Morris based his physical quality of life index (PQLI). We are thus left with no choice but to use both 'input' and 'output' measures. This approach is however still considered to be satisfactory for the present study because our aim is not to derive a composite index of well-being but, rather, to identify the different performance rates of the States of the Federation, and to understand the reasons which underlie the variations. To do this, four variables are used, namely: access to medical facilities; health and nutritional status; educational status; and basic literacy.

Description of components

Access to medical facilities

Four variables were used as indicators of access to medical facilities. They are: access to all types of health establishment; access to comprehensive health establishments; access to maternal health establishments; and hospital beds per capita. This disaggregation was important as health establishments vary by type and also in size and range of services offered to clients. Thus, all establishments were lumped together in the first variable to include teaching hospitals, general hospitals, specialist hospitals, clinics, dispensaries, etc. Their combined effect and spatial occurrence were judged to be important because of the relationship between them, since the large service centres usually serve as referral centres to the medium and small health centres. On the other hand, in order to reduce the undue influence of the small centres, a separate index of comprehensive health establishments was derived to include only the larger service centres. The supply of maternity hospitals and homes was considered in the third variable as they influence anti-natal and post-natal care and, therefore, the health of both the mother and the baby. Included in this variable were maternity hospitals and homes, and general and teaching hospitals. The latter two usually have maternity and child-welfare units. The last variable, hospital beds per capita, in addition to measuring accessibility, also points to the capacity and, sometimes, the quality of the available infrastructure.

Health and nutritional status

For this kind of analysis, health indicators should include life expectancy, infant mortality rates (IMR), crude death rate (CDR) and nutritional status. The data that exist on life expectancy, IMR and CDR are however only summaries of the national situation, thus precluding the derivation of any index to measure inequality through them. The nutritional status data exist as percentage of children aged 60 months or less who are below −2 standard deviation units of weight-for-height indicator (FOS 1985d).[2]

The health data used were of illness rates per thousand population based on the reported presence of any illness during 14 days prior to interview. These two variables were judged important because, as the saying goes, 'health is wealth', which reflects the close association between health status and the general socio-economic well-being of a population. Malnutrition does affect the physical and mental development of children and, thus, the human capital of the future, while the incidence of illness may result in loss of days from usual activities.

Educational status

Education is regarded as an engine of growth and plays a unique role in economic development and the social transformation process (Fourth NDP, p. 255). This is because it is the means by which skilled national manpower supply is derived. It also affects the pattern of employment, income, housing, food and nutrition, and, thus, the level of well-being. In the absence of statistics on the level of education and the stock of trained manpower, proxy indicators in the form of enrolments in primary and post-primary schools were used. The post-primary institutions included were secondary grammar and commercial schools, technical and vocational training schools, and teacher-training colleges. Post-secondary enrolments could not be incorporated into the analysis for lack of clearly disaggregated data.

Basic literacy

Basic literacy is defined as the ability of the population aged [illegible] and above to read and write a short composition in any language. This definition is particularly helpful as it takes care not only of those who attended the western-type formal education institution but also those literate in Quar'anic education and those who acquired their proficiency through adult education classes or some other informal means.

Methodology

Sources of data and scope of analysis

The analysis draws on a stock of secondary data including: 1981/2 education and health statistics (FOS 1985a); 1983/4 survey data on basic literacy and employment (FOS 1985b and 1985c); and the 1983/4 survey data on health and nutrition (FOS 1985d). The frame of analysis is the 19-state structure of Nigeria. Generally, a three-fold analysis was attempted: rural-rural, rural-urban and urban-urban, except in the cases of access to medical facilities and educational status, where data did not allow such disaggregation. Also, where possible, analysis covered observed inequalities between the sexes.

Analytical methods

Well-being and level-of-living are relative concepts. Since the essence of the analysis is to identify the different rates of performance of the states, the 'comparative approach' was adopted (Diejomaoh 1975, p. 237; and Coates *et al.* 1977, p. 17). In this context use was made of two variants of location quotients (cf. Isard 1960, pp. 124, 251–2) and the mean of the location quotients. The first variant of location quotient used was of the form:

$$LQ = \frac{x_i/x}{P_i/P} \quad \ldots\ldots \ (1)$$

Where x_i is number of attribute x for ith state

P_i is population or areal extent (km^2) of ith state, and

$$X = \sum_{i=1}^{N} x_i; \; P = \sum_{i=1}^{N} P_i$$

where N is number of states.

As facilities are provided on the basis of certain population thresholds, the adoption of the population-facility ratio is widely accepted and, thus, the use of population in the calculation of the quotients. But Mabogunje (1980, p. 40), discussing development as social justice, has pointed not only to the nature of goods provided by government but also to the question of the accessibility of these goods to different social classes. Accessibility is measured as physical or social: physical in terms of the distance to be covered to use it; and social in terms of a class barrier. In an aggregate analysis attempted here, it was not possible to analyse the latter for lack of suitable data. All the same, the former is equally important, as the factor of accessibility in its physical form means that individuals in certain localities benefit more or less than others. This consideration underlines the use of areal extent in deriving the **LQ** for health establishments (all types put together).

For variables such as basic literacy, and health and nutrition status, data already exist as percentages to total population of household. The variant of the location quotient used in these cases was therefore of the form:

$$LQ = \frac{SX}{NX} \quad \ldots (2)$$

where S_x is the state's % of attribute x
N_x is the national % of attribute x

In interpreting the results of the LQs derived using both equations 1 and 2, except in the case of health and nutritional status where the reverse holds, the value of LQ greater than unity indicates that a state is a 'good performer' and so 'better off'. On the other hand, a value of LQ less than unity shows that a state is a 'slow performer' or 'worse off.'

Limitations of data and analytical methods

The analysis of school enrolment should, ideally, be as a proportion of the total number of children of school age while the use of maternity hospitals and maternity homes should be as a proportion of the total female population of childbearing age. It was not possible to do either of these as the exact structure of the Nigerian population is not known, two censuses taken in 1963 and 1973 having failed to produce accurate figures. For this reason, total population, which is itself an estimate from the 1963 figures, was used with the assumption that the states have retained similar population structures. In addition, the school enrolment figures did not exclude drop-out rates which may arise from transfers, dismissals, deaths or other causes since, except for death, it was not possible to ascertain whether it was inter-state or intra-state transfer or whether the pupils dismissed were not reabsorbed even within the same state. The quality of pupils trained from schools was also disregarded as there were no data.

On the method of analysis, the derivation of the LQs and the mapping techniques treated the variables and components as if they were evenly distributed within each state. This definitely is not the case as the problem with some of the variables analysed was not only that of insufficiency but also of spatial concentration. Thus, although the methods showed inter-state disparity, intra-state variations by local government area, by settlement, etc., are completely hidden. Similarly, it is widely known that boundaries do not impose a complete barrier on interaction between states as facilities such as hospitals are used by people from outside the states in which they are located. The state however remains a convenient unit for our analysis because it is the basis for planning and implementing projects in the country.

Description and explanation of patterns

In order to grasp the description and explanation of the patterns that follow, a word about the political evolution of Nigeria will be in order. As a political entity, Nigeria dates only from 1900 at which date its northern and southern parts were governed as two distinct protectorates. In 1914, the two were amalgamated, and Lagos was chosen as the country's capital. Three regional political units were created in 1946 from the two protectorates: these were the Northern Region (representing the whole of the former Northern Protectorate) and Western and Eastern Regions, carved out of the previous Southern Protectorate. The Mid-West Region was further carved out of the Western Region in 1963. In 1967, the Northern Region was divided into six states, the Western Region into two, with a part joining the Lagos colony, while the Eastern Region was divided into three. The Mid-West Region remained as an entity. The 12-state structure of 1967 was reconstituted into 19 with a new Federal Capital Territory at Abuja (now under construction) in February, 1976 (Figure 14). This consists of ten states from the former Northern Region and nine states from the former southern regions (cf. Mabogunje 1978b).

Access to medical facilities

In 1982, there were 10,265 health establishments in Nigeria. This was composed of 704 general hospitals, 2,369 maternity hospitals and homes,

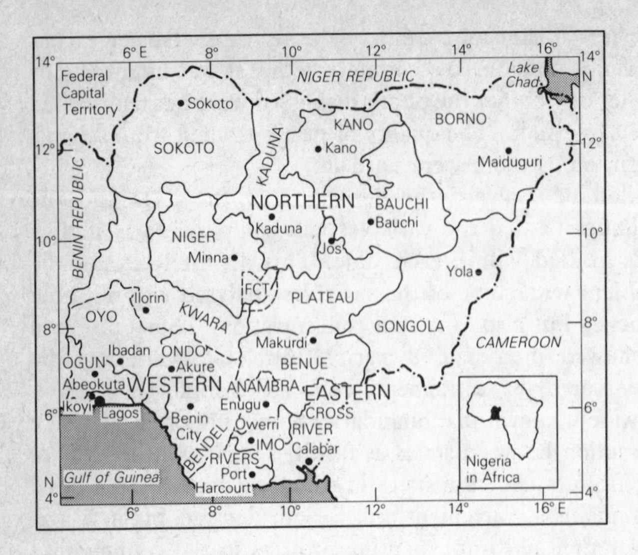

Fig. 14 Political map of Nigeria

33 infectious disease hospitals, 12 of each of teaching hospitals and psychiatric hospitals, and three orthopaedic hospitals. Private, missionary, community, industrial and joint hospitals, clinics and dispensaries formed 69.5%. At the same time there were 83,014 hospital beds, about 75 per cent of which were found in general hospitals (55.5 per cent) and maternity establishments (20.2 per cent). Also, there were 9,623 doctors, 425 dentists and 33,598 nurses. With an estimated national population of 89,100,000 in that year, this meant one doctor to 9,260, one dentist to 209,671 and one nurse to 2,652 people. At current estimates, life expectancy at birth in Nigeria is about 46 years. Infant mortality-rate estimates for the period 1975–9 were 63.8 per 1000 in the urban and 88.5 per 1000 in the rural areas. At the same period the child mortality rate was 116.4 per 1000 in the urban and 150.6 per 1000 in the rural areas (National Population Bureau 1984).

Figures 15a to 15d show that inequality was more marked in the distribution of all health establishments (15d) than it was in the cases of maternity homes and hospitals (15c), comprehensive health establishments (15a) and hospital beds (15b). This pattern is explained by the unequal participation, in each state, of the several organs that handle health-care delivery in the country. These included both government (for example, Federal, state, and local government, and the corporations) and non-government (for example, missionary, private, community industrial and joint) agencies. The extent of involvement of each of

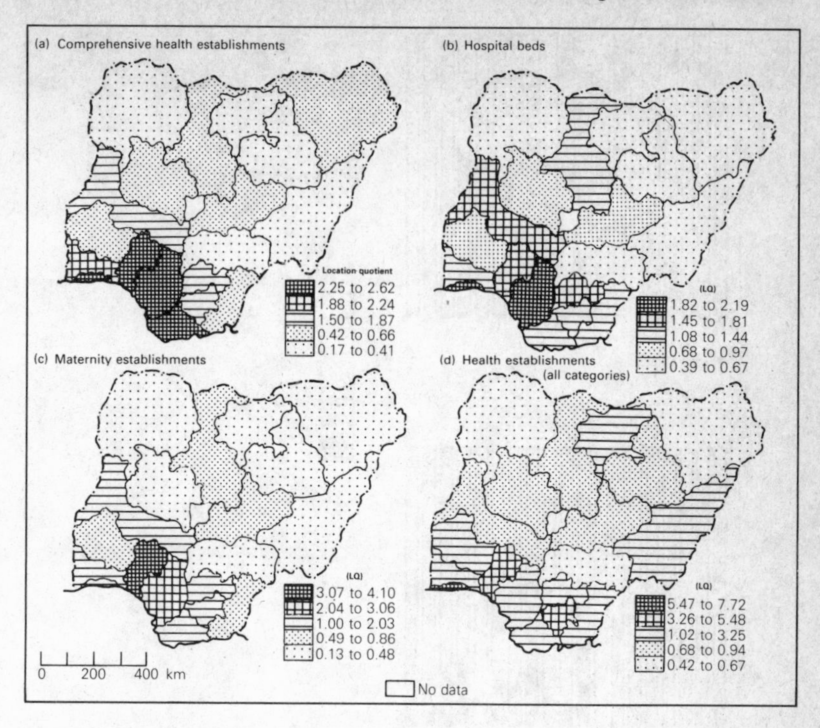

Fig. 15 Spatial patterns of access to medical facilities

these bodies in the provision of health facilities is shown in Figures 16a and 16b. From Figure 16a local government can be seen to have owned the highest percentage of establishments, on the average. This was because they provided lower-order centres like clinics and dispensaries, compared with federal and state governments which managed comprehensive health establishments such as general and teaching hospitals, which cannot be easily duplicated as they require a higher calibre of personnel and large capital outlay. This explains the lower disparity between states in the distribution of comprehensive health establishments, since state governments have broadly similar policies on health-facility locations.

The greater the mix of participating interest groups in the founding and running of health establishments, the higher the accessibility of the facilities. Thus, states such as Bauchi, Borno, Gongola, Kaduna, Niger, Plateau and Sokoto which depended almost exclusively on federal, state and local governments, had lower access than southern states such as Anambra, Imo, Oyo, Ondo, Ogun and Cross River

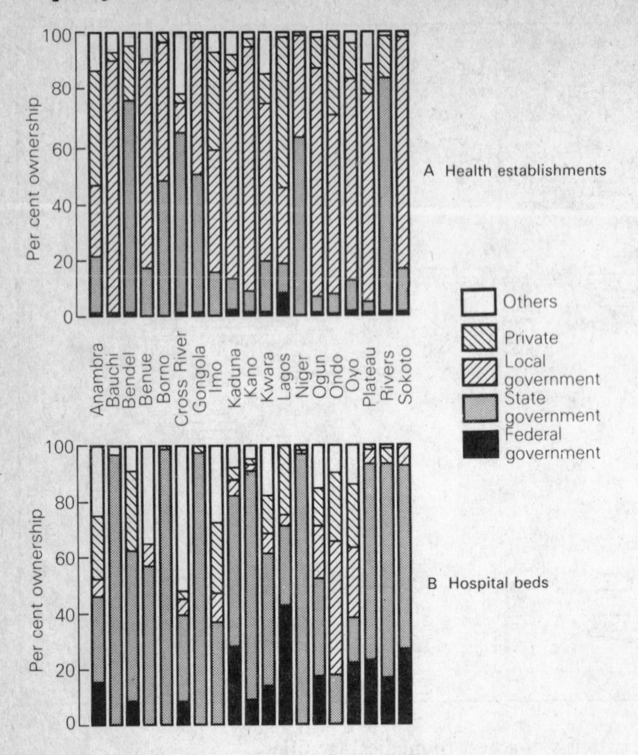

Fig. 16 Ownership of health establishments and hospital beds (1982)

which had greater community and missionary participation. Private influence was also dominant in the southern states and, to a lesser extent, in Kwara, Plateau and Kaduna States in the north. Private participation seemed to be related to urban (market) influence and probably to the presence of indigenous medical practitioners.

The quality of health establishments under each ownership category is shown in Figure 16b in relation to the proportion of hospital beds owned. The federal government, though having fewer establishments (largely teaching and specialists hospitals), owned a high proportion of the beds. The same is true of state as against local government.

As regards maternity hospitals and homes, the southern states also showed a greater degree of accessibility than the northern states. In most of the southern states, maternity establishments were built by local governments, communities and missions. Their use has also been facilitated by the population's higher literacy and educational status, consequent upon earlier exposures to Western influence. Today, some communities in the south-west of the country enforce the use of maternity homes by imposing fines on those who give birth at their homes.

Health and nutritional status

The pattern of health status showed greater inequality among states in urban than in rural areas (Figures 17a and 17b) although there was, on the average, a higher illness rate in rural than in urban areas (95 per 1000 against 75 per 1000). The southern states showed poorer health status than the northern states with the exception of Gongola rural areas, which had the highest rate of illness according to the survey data. The lower illness rates in the urban areas (when compared to rural areas) may be indicative of better living conditions among urban dwellers. But, strangely, urban areas showed slightly lower nutritional status than the rural areas (Figures 17c and 17d) as 20.9 per cent fell below −2 standard deviation units of weight-for-height indicator in the urban area as against 19.7 per cent in the rural. This situation might be related to the presence of a high proportion of urbanites who live just at, or below, subsistence level. Also, several urban poor have

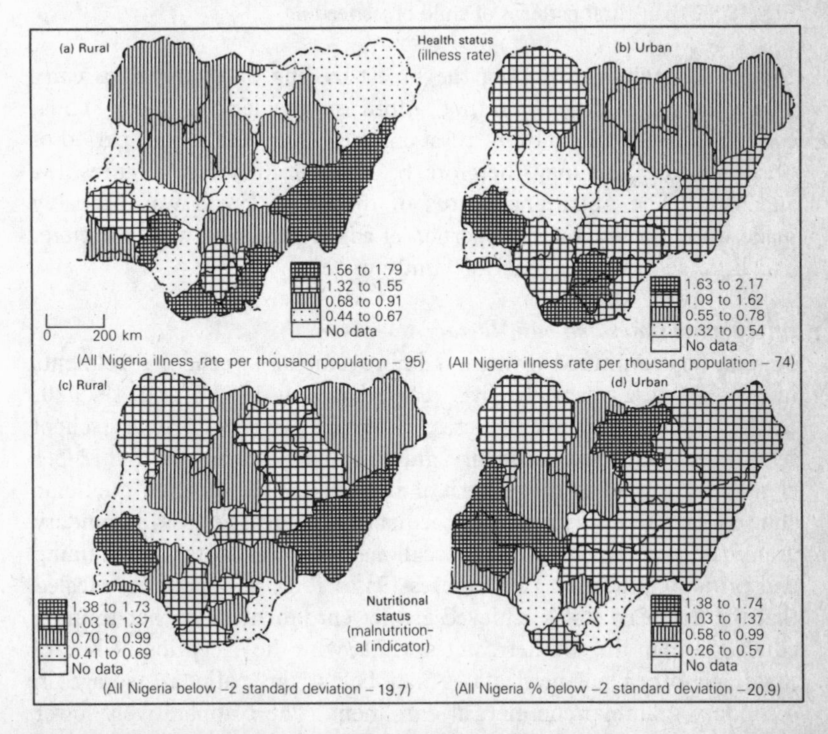

Fig. 17 Spatial patterns of health and nutritional status

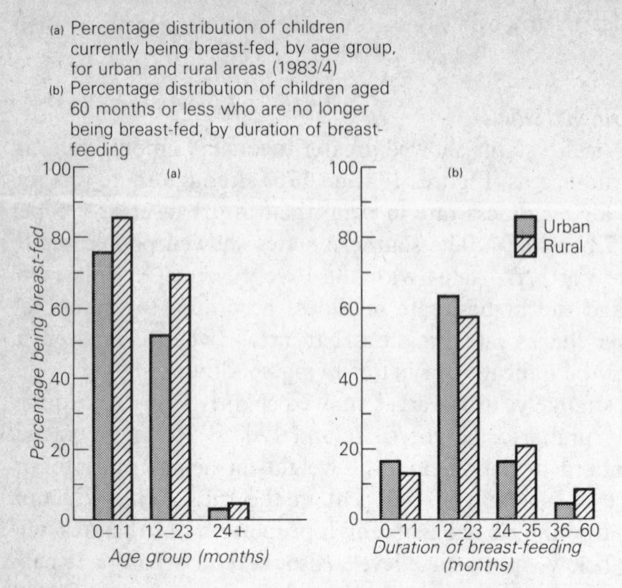

Fig. 18 Urban-rural patterns of child breastfeeding

copied the rich by stopping the breast-feeding of their babies early when, in fact, they could not afford supplementary food. Thus, compared to urban children, rural children enjoyed a longer period of breast-feeding and may therefore be more healthy (see Figures 18a and 18b). The nutritional status of the urban north was probably made worse by the lower proportion of adults employed who, therefore, had little access to income for family upkeep.

Educational status and basic literacy

Nigeria has continued to witness improvements in school enrolments in the last few years. In five years, between 1975/6 and 1979/80, teacher-training enrolment increased by 100 per cent, primary school by 114 per cent and secondary grammar and commercial by 12 per cent. With regard to the pattern of enrolments, the location quotients showed that the magnitude of inequalities decreased from secondary grammar/commercial through vocational/technical to teacher-training and primary education (see Figures 19a to 19d). The pattern revealed that the northern states achieved greater enrolment in teacher-training education than the southern states while, with the exception of Kwara State, all other northern states had below the national average in secondary grammar/commercial enrolment. The comparatively lower enrolment in teacher-training colleges in such southern states as Ogun,

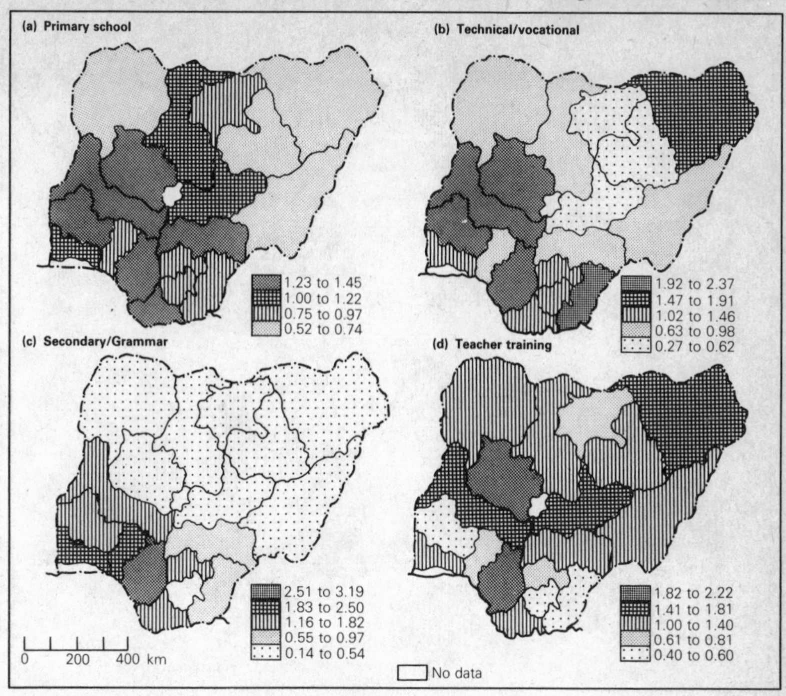

Fig. 19 Spatial patterns of educational status

Ondo and Oyo is, in fact, indicative of a move towards stability rather than backwardness. These are among the so-called educationally advantaged states, and actually had a higher proportion of qualified teachers and better teacher-pupil ratios than the north. Indeed, by 1984 the supply of teachers in the southern states was such that in Bendel, Lagos, Ogun, Ondo and Oyo States all unqualified teachers (Grade II failed and untrained teachers) had been relieved of their jobs. Furthermore, Ondo State restricted admission of pupils into only two teachers' colleges in the 1985/6 school year while other teacher-training colleges were converted to special secondary schools as qualified Grade II teachers had been over-produced in the state.

In general, there was inequality between the sexes in access to education, to the advantage of the male sex. Thus, on average in the urban areas 31.0 per cent of the male and 22.6 per cent of the female population of school age were in school, while for rural areas the corresponding figures were 22.6 per cent and 18.0 per cent. Furthermore, using basic literacy as surrogate for the stock of educated population, Figure 20a-d shows that there was greater inequality between male and female literacy in rural than urban areas. Indeed, in all the

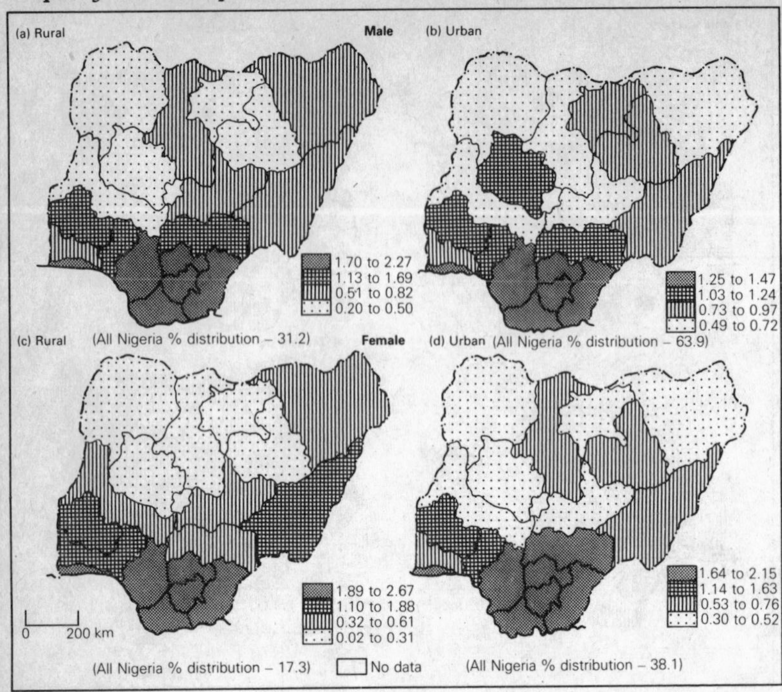

Fig. 20 Spatial patterns of basic literacy

states there was a clear disparity between male and female literacy rates, in favour of the former.

The northern states generally achieved the lowest literacy rate in spite of the inclusion of Quar'anic education in the analysis. The reason for this disparity is historical. According to Mabogunje, the beginning of this aspect of social disparity in Nigeria was the colonial period when in the southern half of the country more people were exposed to Western-type education, while in the northern half the predominant social and educational influence remained Islamic. He observed further that:

> *The background to this regional difference was the agreement entered into by the colonial administration at the time of the subjugation of the Fulani emirs of Northern Nigeria. This agreement was to the effect that Christian missionaries would not be encouraged to proselytise within the emirates. But it was these same missionary bodies which were, throughout the colonial period, in the vanguard of educational development in the country. Indeed, to be a Christian in those days was to become literate and to have the prospect of educating one's children. By refusing the missionaries easy access to the north, the*

colonial administration helped to create an imbalance in the proportion of educated people between the southern and the northern halves of the country.

(Mabogunje 1978a, pp. 17–18)

To validate Mabogunje's observations, the first school in the country was established by the Christian missionary in Badagry (Lagos State) in 1843 while the first known Muslim primary school established by colonial government was in Lagos in 1899. It was not until 1907 that two schools were established by a Christian missionary in Zaria (Kaduna State), and another primary school by government in Kano in 1909. On the contrary, in Yorubaland, during this period, Christian missionary schools were established in practically every town and village without restrictions. Indeed, as early as 1922, the competition already entered into by the Christian missions in the area of establishment of schools in the south was joined by Muslim missions. Private and, later, community efforts were also intensified in the south while practically all schools founded in the north were being financed from public funds (cf. Fafunwa 1980).

Shortly before independence, the Western Regional Government and the Lagos Federal Territory introduced free universal primary education in 1955 and 1957, respectively. Apart from the fact that the north could not join the race for financial reasons, it was noted that:

while some Northern political and religious leaders were keen to expose the child to the modern educational system most leaders in Northern Nigeria were reticent about the blessings of Western education as compared with the Islamic system.

(Fafunwa 1980, p. 174)

Conclusion

From the foregoing analysis and discussion, it seems clear that, except in the case of health and nutritional status, the southern states scored more highly in the distribution of social infrastructures and services than the northern states, and the urban than the rural areas. These results therefore generally confirm the notions of a 'north-south' duality (cf. Abumere 1978) and an urban-rural dichotomy in Nigeria's social transformation process. A basic challenge in the future development of the country is therefore the narrowing of the gap between the northern and southern states, and between urban and rural areas.

This problem of gap-narrowing is one that demands drastic reorientations of policy. For example, the north-south duality is commonly seen to be rooted in the events of the colonial past. It is however our view that after 25 years of independence there is hardly any excuse for the persistence of the gap, except on the ground of lack of a sound policy to create the right atmosphere for advancement in the backward areas. Indeed, certain government policies have only made the situation worse. For example, the takeover of Voluntary Agency Schools in many states of the Federation since 1970 has only increased the burden of government at a time of diminishing financial resources; hence a fall in educational standards. A reversal of that policy, and active encouragement of Voluntary Agency Schools, particularly in the northern states, will go a long way to help bridge the educational gap between the northern and southern states.

Similarly, although a policy of universal primary education has been pursued since the mid-1970s, it has not been effective in the bulk of the northern states where a large proportion of school-age children still remain unschooled and where withdrawal rates are high. Hence, nothing short of a policy of *compulsory* universal primary education and stricter prohibition of child withdrawal from school will be needed to mitigate the imbalance. Similar radical policies will be needed country-wide to correct the present imbalance between the sexes, and between urban and rural areas, in terms of access to basic social infrastructures and services. A possible direction for such policies, especially in the northern states, is the promotion of community, self-help projects, in order to break the traditional overdependence on government, and to put within easier reach of each community the essential infrastructures and services.

Notes

1 For example, speaking on behalf of the Ndoni Community of River State, Anothony Egobueze asked the governor '..... will the promise of former Governor ..... to declare open a health centre next month .... still be fulfilled?' To this the governor responded 'I don't see why I wouldn't be there to open it, if it is ready. So prepare for me. I would be in Ndoni in November to open it.' Speaking in the same vein on behalf of Ogba/Egbema district, J.O. Nwachukwu, a redcap chief said, 'Over the last three or four years, we have been listening to the slogan: "Health for all by the year 2000." We do not know how far this government is irrevocably committed towards achieving this objective. If the government is serious why is it that no positive steps have been taken to complete some of the health projects that are meant for the benefit of the man at the grassroots ......?', citing the non-completion of the nurses' quarters and a general hospital in his districts. (*The Guardian*, 7 October 1986, p. 11.)

2 The Federal Office of Statistics (FOS) which collected the data indicated its recognition of the fact that 'the age group less than five years (that is, 59

months or less) is commonly used to present data on children's nutritional status. In the pilot study, it was found that some children who were not quite 5 years old were reported as being of that age already. When no birth date was given, the age of such children was recorded as 60 months. It seemed prudent to ask about children listed as 60 months of age because of this tendency' (FOS 1985d, p. 27).

References

Abumere 1978. The regional distribution of income in Bendel State of Nigeria. *The Journal of Tropical Geography*, vol. 47 pp. 1–12.

Adeniyi, E.A. 1978. 'Regional Planning in Nigeria'. In J.S. Oguntoyinbo *et al.* (eds), *A Geography of Nigerian development*. Ibadan: Heinemann

Coates, B.E., Johnston, R.J. and Knox, P.L. 1977. *Geography and inequalities* (Oxford: Oxford University Press)

Diejomaoh, V.P. 1975. 'Regional Dimensions of Poverty in Nigeria'. In O. Teriba, A.O. Phillips and E.O. Akeredolu-Ale (eds) *Poverty in Nigeria* (Proceedings of the 1975 Annual Conference of the Nigerian Economic Society), pp. 237–55.

Fafunwa, A.B. 1980. *History of education in Nigeria* (London, George Allen & Unwin) 7th Impression.

Federal Republic of Nigeria 1970. *Second National Development Plan, 1970–74: Programme of Post-War Reconstruction and Development*. (Lagos: Federal Government Printer)

Federal Republic of Nigeria 1975. *Third National Development Plan, 1975–80* volume 1 (Lagos: Federal Government Printer)

Federal Ministry of National Planning. *Outline of the Fourth National Development Plan, 1981–85* (Lagos: Federal Government Printer: Ministry of National Planning).

Federal Ministry of National Planning 1981. *Fourth National Development Plan: 1981–85* vol. 1 (Lagos: Ministry of National Planning)

Federal Office of Statistics 1985a. *Annual Abstract of Statistics 1985 Edition*. (Lagos: F.O.S.)

F.O.S. 1985b. *National Integrated Survey of Households (NISH): Report of General Household Survey 1982–1983*. Survey Report No. G.H.S. Household survey unit (Lagos: F.O.S.)

F.O.S. 1985c. *Nigeria National Integrated Survey of Households (NISH): Report of General Household Survey April 1983 – March 1984*. Household Survey Unit (Lagos: F.O.S.)

F.O.S. 1985d. *The health of Nigerians 1983/84: Health and Nutrition Status Survey*, A module of the National Integrated Survey of Households (NISH) April 1983 – March, 1984 (Lagos: F.O.S.)

Isard, W. 1960. *Methods of regional analysis: an introduction to regional science*, (Massachusetts: M.I.T.) 9th Print, 1973.

Mabogunje, L. 1978a. 'Growth poles and growth centres in the regional development of Nigeria'. In Antoni Kuklinski (ed.) *Regional policies in Nigeria, India and Brazil*; U.N. Research Institute for Social Development vol. 9, Geneva. (The Hague: Mouton)

Mabogunje 1978b. 'Geographical perspectives on Nigerian development'. In J.S. Oguntoyinbo *et al.* (eds) *A geography of Nigerian development*. (Ibadan: Heinemann).

Mabogunje 1980. *The development process: a spatial perspective* (London: Hutchinson)

Morris, M.D. 1979. *Measuring the condition of the world's poor: the physical quality of life index* (Published for the Overseas Development Council. New York: Pergamon)

National Population Bureau 1984. *The Nigeria Fertility Survey*, vol. 1 (Lagos: Government Printer)

Olatubosun. 1975. *Nigeria's neglected rural majority* (Ibadan: University Press)

Smith, M.D. 1977. *Human geography: a welfare approach* (London: Edward Arnold)

Teriba, O, Philips, A.O. and Akeredolu-Ale, E.A. 1975. *Poverty in Nigeria*: Proceedings of the 1975 Annual Conference of the Nigerian Economic Society, (Ibadan: Ibadan University Press) (See following: V.P. Diejomaoh, 'Regional dimension of poverty in Nigeria', pp. 237–55; B.A. Etim and F.N. Erontimi 'Personal income distribution in Nigeria, 1969/70–1971/72', pp. 295–312; O. Fajana, 'The distribution of personal income in Nigeria' pp. 277–93; A. Ogunpola and A. Ojo, 'Housing as an indicator of urban poverty: the case of Metropolitan Lagos, pp. 111–22).

Udo R.K. 1975. *Migrant tenant farmers of Nigeria: a geographical study of rural migrations in Nigeria* (African University Press)

Section Two: Inequality in Rural Settings

5
Spatial Inequalities in Zimbabwe with Reference to the Communal Farming Areas

L.M. Zinyama
Department of Geography, University of Zimbabwe

Developing countries are generally characterized by wide regional disparities in levels of socio-economic development and standards of living. These inequalities are most apparent between the major urban centres and large-scale commercial agricultural areas on the one hand and extensive subsistence agricultural areas on the other. The former are generally better provided in both quantity and quality of services such as health, education, transport, housing, sanitation, as well as having higher per capita incomes. The backward rural areas, where the majority of the population live, are generally inadequately serviced with social and economic infrastructure, have low per capita incomes and low living standards. The absence of infrastructure and services may also retard the development of agriculture and other economic activities in rural areas. The low incomes and poor quality of rural life also provide the 'push factors' in the migration of people to the major urban centres, thereby creating numerous social and political problems for both source regions and recipient regions.

The administrative and demographic structure of communal areas

In Zimbabwe, there are presently three main systems of rural land use, namely (i) large-scale commercial farming which is dominated by white farmers; (ii) small-scale commercial farming on medium-sized farms by black farmers in areas formerly known as African Purchase Areas; and (iii) small-scale subsistence agriculture in the communally held land areas (formerly called African Reserves or Tribal Trust Lands). Following some reorganization of local government soon after independence in 1980, the 160 or so communal land areas, together with some of the small-scale commercial farming areas, were grouped into 55 administrative districts. Each district has a district council of elected representatives and a few ex-officio members (usually the local chiefs). The district council is assisted by a small number of civil servants appointed by central government, headed by a District Administrator who is the chief executive officer. District councils are responsible for a number of development functions within their areas, such as the construction and maintenance of roads, resource conservation, the establishment of rural service centres and, subject to the provisions of the relevant national legislation and the approval of the ministries concerned, the establishment and maintenance of health and educational services (Zimbabwe 1982a). They can raise revenues from various local sources such as taxes and licence fees, although at present most of their administrative and development costs are paid for from grants given by the government.

According to the 1982 census, the 55 districts had a total population of 4·27 million, or 56·6 per cent of the 7·54 million people in the country. The rate of growth in the whole country is approximately 3·3 per cent per year, with an estimated 30,000 to 35,000 new households being added to the rural population each year (Zimbabwe 1982b). In 1982, the population in the district council areas ranged from 9,823 in Nyaminyami in the Zambezi Valley to 228,467 in Cheziya Gokwe, also in the north (Figure 21). The district council areas range in size from 368 sq km for Harava south of Harare (the capital city) to 13,327 sq km for Cheziya Gokwe. The average population density is 25 persons per sq km, with densities for individual districts ranging from three per sq km in Nyaminyami to 77 per sq km in Harava.

Apart from the resident rural population, many urban dwellers still retain close ties with their communal land areas of origin, have some property there such as houses and livestock, and retain cultivation rights. Their families frequently spend the summer season working on their arable lands, and join their husbands in the towns during the dry months. Consequently, it can be said that the communal land areas support to varying degrees many more people than the permanently resident population, although remittances from the urban dwellers help to sustain the rural population.

Another feature of the district council areas is their fragmentation, a legacy of the past colonial government policy of apportioning land into small tribal reserves. Many of the districts, such as Gwanda, Bulilimamangwe, Matobo and Maungwe, consist of two or three tracts of land separated by areas of commercial farmland. This fragmentation creates problems in the administration and co-ordination of development within individual districts as well as between adjacent district council

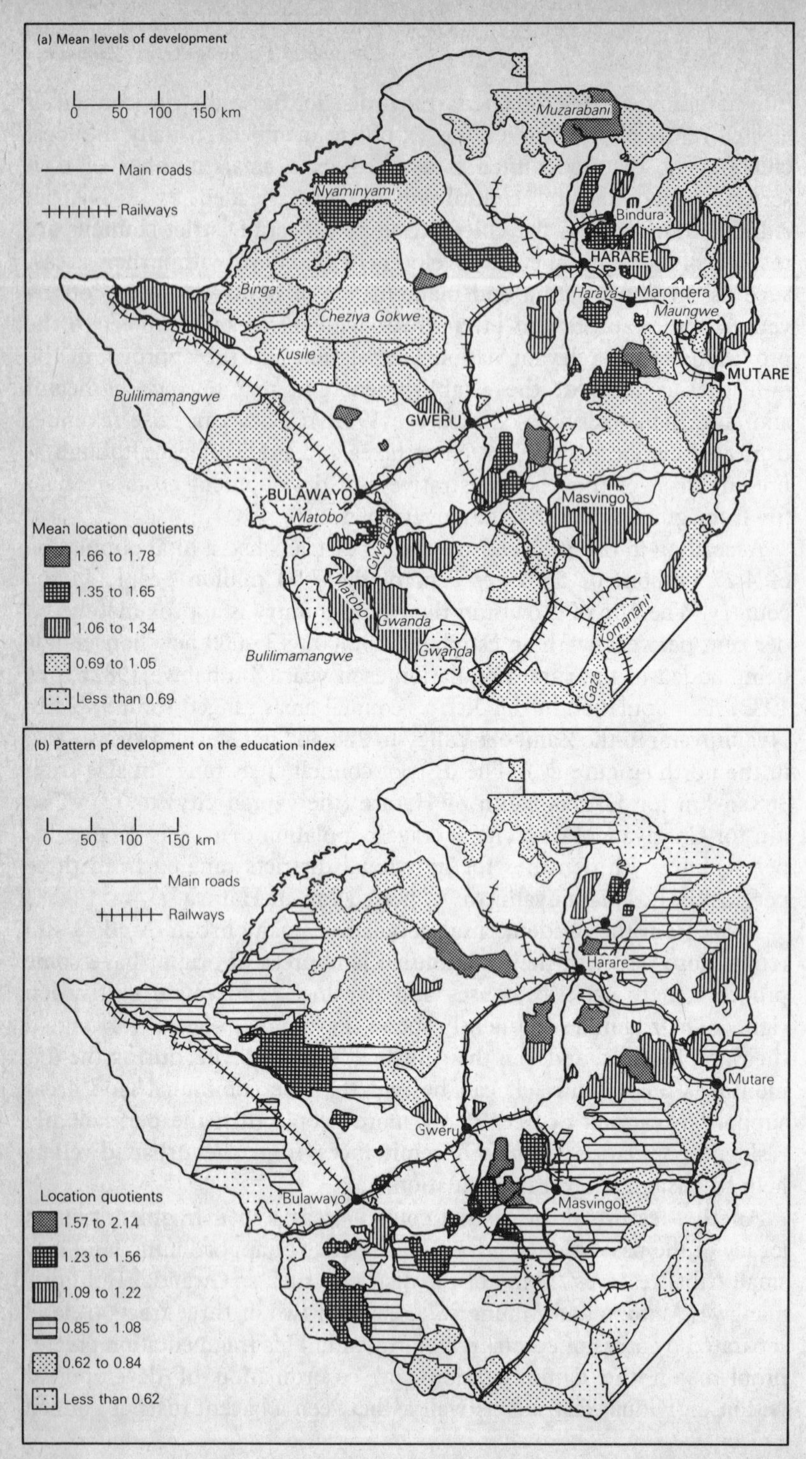

Fig. 21 Mean levels and pattern of development in district council areas, Zimbabwe, 1982

and rural council areas. (The latter are responsible for the administration of the commercial farming areas. At the time of writing, proposals are under consideration to amalgamate the two branches of local government in the rural areas, as well as the resettlement areas which are presently administered by the Ministry of Lands, Resettlement and Rural Development.)

Spatial inequalities and the role of government in Zimbabwe

The inequitable distribution of social and economic infrastructures and services that is characteristic of developing countries is true of Zimbabwe. Here, spatial disparities have been accentuated by 90 years of white minority colonial administration, from 1890 to the attainment of political independence in 1980. During this period, national resources and socio-economic development were unequally distributed among the two major racial groups, to the benefit of the white community in the urban areas and in the large-scale commercial farming sector. Yet the white population has never constituted more than five per cent of the total population. The provision of services such as schools and health facilities in the communal areas was largely left in the hands of benevolent missionary organizations and, from the 1960s, of inadequately funded local and provincial authorities. The division of land by race, which commenced with the establishment of the first reserves for blacks in 1894, and became legalized under the Land Apportionment Act of 1930 and subsequent legislation, restricted the black rural population to the drier, sandy and less fertile parts of the country.

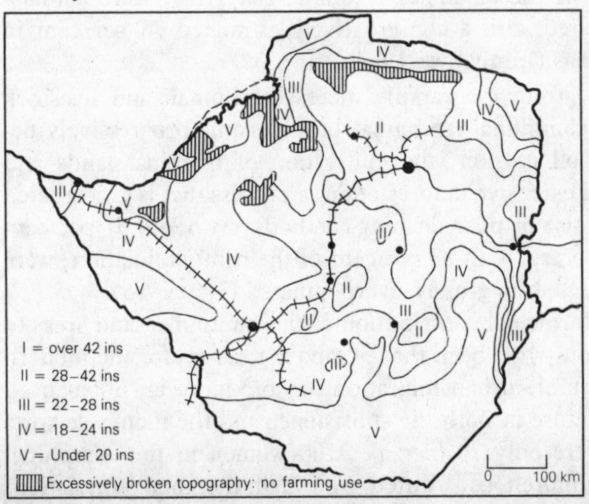

Fig. 22 The natural regions of Zimbabwe

Table 5.1. Distribution of land by category and Natural Region during the 1970s (in percentages)

Category	I	II	III	IV	V	Total
Communal land area	0.8	7.7	17.3	44.9	29.3	100
Commercial land	2.8	27.6	20.6	25.7	23.3	100
African Purchase land	0.5	17.8	37.9	36.9	6.9	100
Other land	2.3	0.5	12.2	51.3	33.7	100
Total–Zimbabwe	1.8	15.0	18.7	37.8	26.7	100

Source: Zimbabwe (1982b)

For farming purposes, the country is divided into five regions, mainly on the basis of rainfall (Figure 22); conditions become increasingly marginal for agriculture moving from Natural Region I to Natural Region V as rainfall decreases in amount and reliability. Land alienation was such that, in the 1970s, over 30 per cent of the white-owned commercial farmland fell within Natural Regions I and II, the zones most suited for agriculture (Table 5.1). On the other hand, only 8.5 per cent of the communal farming areas fell within the same ecological regions; instead, 74 per cent were situated in Natural Regions IV and V, areas that are subject to low and unreliable rainfall, periodic seasonal droughts, and are considered suitable only for extensive commercial livestock and game ranching. Even the small-scale commercial farming areas (former Purchase Areas), where aspiring black farmers could acquire medium-sized farms on freehold or leasehold tenure, were largely situated in marginal areas. Moreover, only 21 per cent of the potential arable land in the large-scale commercial areas, and 18 per cent in the small-scale commercial areas, were actually cultivated, compared with a conservatively estimated 73 per cent in the communal areas (Zimbabwe 1982b, p. 65).

Under pressure from the rapidly increasing human and livestock populations, the communal land areas have become progressively degraded through soil erosion, the cultivation of marginal lands and grazing areas, and extensive deforestation, a process that is exacerbated by the continued use of poor farming methods. By 1969, 57 per cent of the communal areas, with 83 per cent of the rural population, were already overpopulated or grossly overpopulated (Kay 1975).

Until now, the principal contribution of the communal land areas to the national economy had been that of labour reserves for the modern sector. Selective rural–urban migration has produced an unbalanced demographic structure in both the subsistence and the money sectors. In 1969, there were only 70 men per 100 women in the communal land areas and children constituted over half the total population.

Conversely, in the commercial farming areas and in the 12 main towns, the adult black population was predominantly male (175 men per 100 women) and children comprised less than two-fifths of the population (Kay 1972, p.17). Such demographic imbalances have significant social and economic consequences on the patterns of development and spatial inequalities in the country.

Until the attainment of independence, a variety of racially discriminatory policies – such as the denial of agricultural credit and marketing facilities, poor transport, remoteness and inaccessibility to major urban markets – coupled with adverse climatic and soil conditions, inhibited the development of communal land agriculture (Yudelman 1964; Gapare 1976; Ndlela 1981). For instance, some 59 per cent of the white-owned farmland was located within 32 km (20 miles) of a railway line and only six per cent was more than 80 km (50 miles) away. On the other hand, 40 per cent of the communal land areas and the African Purchase Areas were situated more than 80 km from the railway services and only a little more than five per cent fell within 16 km (10 miles) of the railway (Kay 1972, pp. 22–23). It should be noted that the railway lines generally run parallel to the network of main all-weather roads in Zimbabwe. A levy on agricultural commodities marketed by black farmers was introduced in 1949 to raise funds for primary development work in the communal and small-scale commercial farming areas. As a result of the levy, farmers in the two areas received between 60 and 80 per cent of the official guaranteed price received by white farmers. The levy, which remained in force until independence, was in effect a form of taxation on the more progressive, market-orientated farmers.

Since 1980, the government has, in pursuit of its stated policy of 'Growth with Equity', given priority to the development of these previously neglected areas in an effort to raise the quality of life of a majority of the population. This is being done, among other measures, by the improvement of the rural road network, the provision of agricultural credit, marketing facilities and extension services in order to raise agricultural productivity and incomes, the establishment of rural service centres, the development of health and educational services, and the resettlement of landless people from overpopulated communal lands on to underutilized former commercial farmland. In the provision of health services, the government objective is that every household should be within 10 km of a health facility. There has been a change in emphasis from a curative to a preventive health service, and towards this end, village health workers working at grassroots level are being given training in basic nutrition, hygiene and sanitation, and in the treatment of minor ailments. The village health workers, who are chosen by the communities from among themselves, are to become the vanguard in the struggle against disease in the rural areas. In 1976 there were 152 secondary schools (of which only 27 were government schools) for black children throughout the country, with a total enrolment of 40,686 pupils, including 13,519 in technical secondary schools. By 1983 the numbers had more than quintupled to 790 schools with 316,438 pupils of all races. This includes several hundred rural day secondary schools constructed by the district councils and the government, with the parents providing much of the labour, bricks and other locally available materials.

In order to make agricultural marketing facilities more accessible, receiving depots are being established in the communal areas, with the objective that producers should not have to transport their commodities more than 60 km to a marketing depot. Similarly, there has been a considerable redirection of agricultural credit granted to farmers by the parastatal Agricultural Finance Corporation from an estimated 4,500-strong commercial farming sector to the communal and resettlement farmers (Table 5.2). The Small Farm Credit Scheme was only established in April 1978; until then, only a small amount of money had been available for lending to small-scale commercial farmers alone from the government and from private sources (Hughes 1974; Ndlela 1981). The decrease in the number of loans to the commercial sector is attributable to the decrease in the number of white farmers as a result

Table 5.2 Loans granted by the Agricultural Finance Corporation to farmers by agricultural sector, 1978/9 to 1983/4. (Values in Z$ million)

	Small Farm Credit Scheme				Resettlement credit scheme		Large-scale commercial	
	Communal areas		Small-scale commercial					
Season	*No.*	*Value*	*No.*	*Value*	*No.*	*Value*	*No.*	*Value*
1978/9	0	0	1,290	1.07	0	0	2,675	67.89
1979/80	2,850	0.48	1,498	1.18	0	0	2,233	75.65
1980/1	18,000	7.90	3,333	(a)	0	0	2,500	86.91
1981/2	30,150	9.05	3,589	4.50	900	0.42	2,100	88.91
1982/3	38,912	13.24	2,929	4.41	4,173	1.55	1,746	88.71
1983/4	50,036	23.40	2,539	5.90	18,277	8.55	1,332	102.24

(a) included under Communal Areas

Source: AFC Annual reports

of emigration and, to a lesser extent, the acquisition of underutilized land by government for the resettlement programme; while the increase in value of loans is largely due to the rise in cost of farm inputs, particularly fertilizers, in recent years.

The response of the communal area farmers to the improved economic opportunities is shown in part by the increasing volume of agricultural sales during the last few years. This increase is particularly remarkable since it has occurred at the time of a very severe three-year drought, from 1981/2 to 1983/4. Until 1980/1, communal area and small-scale commercial farmers produced less than 10 per cent of the maize delivered to the Grain Marketing Board, the parastatal organization responsible for all the domestic and external commercial marketing of several 'controlled' agricultural commodities such as maize, groundnuts, sorghum, soya beans and wheat. Since 1980, following the removal of the institutional constraints which had previously inhibited commercial production, the two agricultural subsectors have increased their sales of maize to the Grain Marketing Board almost fourfold from less than 90,000 tonnes to over 340,000 tonnes during the first

Table 5.3 Maize deliveries to the Grain Marketing Board by agricultural sector, 1974/5 to 1984/5

	Large-scale commercial sector		Small-scale commercial communal sectors		Total delivered
*Intake year**	*tonnes*	%	*tonnes*	%	*tonnes*
1974/5	1,290,253	96.5	46,683	3.5	1,336,936
1975/6	957,588	95.1	49,358	4.9	1,006,946
1976/7	874,555	91.2	83,982	8.8	958,537
1977/8	856,799	91.1	84,265	8.9	941,064
1978/9	813,420	92.7	63,605	7.3	877,025
1979/80	473,736	92.5	38,184	7.5	511,920
1980/1	728,532	89.4	86,296	10.6	814,828
1981/2	1,650,574	82.0	363,269	18.0	2,013,843
1982/3	1,021,892	73.5	369,374	26.5	1,391,266
1983/4	464,337	75.3	152,414	24.7	656,751
1984/5**	547,863	61.7	340,427	38.3	888,290

* the GMB intake year, which runs from 1 April to the 31 March following, is the year following that of production, that is, the crop planted in November 1980 for the 1980/1 season was delivered during the 1981/2 intake year.
** figures for the first seven months to 31 October 1984 only.
Sources: GMB annual reports and GMB Producers Registry records.

seven months of the 1984/5 intake year (Table 5.3). A fortuitous coincidence of favourable weather conditions, the end of hostilities, the distribution of free seed and fertilizer packs as part of an internationally assisted post-war reconstruction programme, and a 41 per cent increase in the pre-planting price of top grade maize to Z$120 per tonne were responsible for the record harvest of 1980/1. Deliveries of seed cotton from the small-scale commercial and communal area farmers have also increased from 36,928 tonnes or 20 per cent of total output in 1980/1 to over 101,000 tonnes or 40 per cent during 1984/5. The transformation of agriculture in the communal farming areas is therefore taking place through both the commercialization of traditional food crops and the adoption of new industrial crops such as cotton and tobacco.

Rural–rural inequalities

The preceding paragraphs have examined the patterns of spatial inequalities between communal, predominantly subsistence agricultural areas on the one hand and modern urban-commercial agricultural areas on the other, and some of the efforts being made to improve the quality of life in the former. As the redirection of scarce national resources towards rural development gets under way, it is necessary to undertake baseline studies concerned with the identification and measurement of spatial inequalities that exist among them, and of the magnitude of inequity; national resources can then be more effectively allocated in line with the government objective of achieving an egalitarian society.

Data for assessing inter-rural inequalities were obtained from the Central Statistical Office's report *Social Conditions in District Council Areas 1982 (Preliminary Tables)*. The compilation of this report marks the first comprehensive effort to bring together data from various government ministries and departments on social and economic infrastructure and services, within the boundaries of the district council areas. The data were presented in tabular form by district council area and by province.

Methodology

For each district, data were obtained on 11 variables. These were then grouped into five development indices for each district (Table 5.4). For each variable except road density, the share of each district relative to all the 55 districts was computed using Isard's location quotient (**LQ**) (Isard 1960, p. 124).

$$LQ = \frac{S_i/S}{N_i/N}$$

where S_i is the number of the variable in district i;
S is the total number of the same variable in all the districts;
N_i is the population in district i;
N is the total population in all the districts.

Since the study is concerned with welfare conditions, and with per capita distributions of infrastructure and services for rural development, population size rather than areal extent of the districts was chosen as the most appropriate base.

Table 5.4 Variables used to measure levels of development in the district council areas

Development index	Variable
1 Education	Number of primary schools
	Number of secondary schools
2 Accessibility	Length of motorable roads (km)
	Number of bus permits
	Road density (metres per sq km)
3 Health	Number of approved clinics
	Number of hospital beds
	Number of nurses and medical assistants in hospitals
4 Commercial activity	Number of general dealer leases granted
	Number of grain mill leases granted
5 Extension	Number of agricultural extension workers

Given the level of provision throughout all the communal areas, a location quotient greater than one indicates that a district has more than its fair share of a facility or service. A location quotient of less than one suggests that the district has less than its fair share. The location quotient for each development index is the mean of the LQs for its constituent variables. Thus, for the health index for each district, three LQs were calculated for the numbers of approved clinics, hospital beds, and nurses and medical assistants in the district's hospital(s). The mean of the three LQs is the health index.

It was not possible to use the Isard formula for road density. Instead a value similar to a location quotient was obtained by computing the ratio of a district's road density above or below the average road density for all districts. Therefore, a district whose road density was the same as the average (129 m per sq km) would have a value of 1.00; a district with a density of 114 m per sq km would have a value of 0.88; while a density of 337 m per sq km would give a value of 2.61. These values were added to the location quotients for the length of motorable roads and the number of bus permits. The result was then divided by three to give the accessibility index for the district. The LQs on the five indices were then added together and their mean obtained. This mean value measures the overall level of development of infrastructure and services in the district, relative to all the other districts. The five indices and the overall mean for each of 55 districts are set out in the Appendix (page 110).

The variables chosen comprise a spectrum of services that have a direct effect on the quality of life of the rural population and on their level of agricultural production and incomes. They are almost all self-explanatory, except for those used to measure the level of development of commercial activities. Both general dealers and grain mill operators perform a crucial function in the rural areas. The former, who run small shops at service or business centres, make manufactured goods from the towns more widely available to the rural population. The diesel-operated grain mills grind maize and other small grains into mealie meal (or flour) which is then cooked into a thick porridge, the staple diet amongst the indigenous population. In the absence of commercially produced grain meal, the presence of these mills greatly reduces the drudgery of food preparation, particularly for rural women. However, it should be noted that the granting of a lease by a district council to run a business does not necessarily mean that these services were operational at the time the data were collected.

Although the use of the location quotient gives a measure of the development of certain services and infrastructure in a particular district, two limitations should be noted. First, equal weight is given to all the variables. No account is taken of differences in the quality of the facilities and the differential impact which quality may have on living standards and prospects for rural development. For instance, many of the rural schools that have been established during the last few years are still poorly equipped, are without properly trained and qualified staff and do not have enough textbooks. Likewise, the mission hospitals and clinics in the rural areas are generally understaffed, lack adequate funds and, especially since the introduction of a free health service for all low-income persons (that is, those earning less than Z$150 per month), are overcrowded. Second, the variables used here are biased towards development inputs provided by either central government or the district councils. A more realistic measure of disparities in development levels should give greater weight to the outputs of the development effort, such as agricultural production levels, school enrolment as a proportion of the total number of children of school age, infant mortality rates, literacy levels, etc. The choice of variables used in this study was determined by the availability of data covering all the districts.

Discussion

A variety of reasons, including political, historical, economic and geographical factors, and even the effect of missionary activities, explain the pattern of service development in the communal areas of Zimbabwe. The results (Figure 21 and Appendix) suggest that there are small but fairly significant differences in levels of development, particularly between the best and the least served amongst the district council areas. A factor of three or more separates the mean LQs of the three best districts from the three poorest-served districts, and a factor of two or more separates the best five from the ten least developed districts. The five districts with the highest mean LQs (greater than 1.66) generally have scores well above unity on at least four of the five indices (the common exception being the commercial activity index), and are particularly well served with health facilities. Their high LQs on the health index are due to the presence of mission hospitals in these districts, often to complement the government hospitals and council clinics. On the other hand, ten districts had no hospitals at all, although in some of them the residents would have access to hospitals in adjacent rural council or urban areas. The hospital services in the latter are frequently of a higher quality than those within the communal areas. This was certainly true for Harava District which is situated near the towns of Harare, Marondera and Chitungwiza, or Kubatana Bindura District near the town of Bindura.

It would be expected that higher mean LQs would be found in districts located adjacent to the major urban centres and the national development corridor as a result of the diffusion, through time, of development impulses outwards from the modern sector. Figure 21 suggests that such a pattern, although not very pronounced, does exist in Zimbabwe, as 12 of the 14 districts with a mean LQ of 1.35 or more are located adjacent to the national economic heartland that stretches from Mutare in the east through Harare to Bulawayo in the west. The two exceptions are Nyaminyami and Muzarabani in the north which, although located in peripheral areas, have high mean LQs of 1.38 and 1.70 respectively. In reality, Nyaminyami is one of the least developed districts in the country, most of the few services having been established only during the last few years. The low actual level of development is indicated by the fact that it ranks 48th on the education and health indices and 54th on the commercial activities index, with LQs of 0.69, 0.45 and 0.35 respectively. Road density at 74 m per sq km was 43 per cent below the average for all district council areas, and only two bus permits had been granted to operate in the area by 1982. The apparently high overall level of development suggested by its mean LQ is explained by the very high scores it obtained on only two variables, the length of motorable roads and the number of extension workers. The considerable length of motorable roads in Nyaminyami and the other districts on the country's borders is due to a programme of construction of security roads by the previous Rhodesian government to curtail cross-border infiltration from neighbouring independent countries by nationalist freedom fighters during the 1970s.

Apart from Nyaminyami and Muzarabani, districts in peripheral locations generally have low mean location quotients. Of the 17 districts on the country's borders, nine had mean LQs of less than unity, including the large but sparsely populated districts of Cheziya Gokwe, Binga and Kusile in the north-west. The nine are particularly ill-served with health and commercial services, with LQs of less than 0.50 on these indices. For instance, Gaza Komanani in the extreme south-east had LQs of 0.43 for commercial activities and 0.27 for health services, while Binga and Bulilimamangwe had 0.11 and 0.41 respectively for commercial services. The low population density and the dispersed settlement pattern in these peripheral districts raises the costs of providing services. A number of pilot schemes have already been launched to regroup some of these dispersed communities into larger village units to facilitate the provision of services. The low LQs obtained by these peripheral districts on commercial services provided by private entrepreneurs are due to the fact that potential investors find these areas unattractive. The development of commercial services is hampered by the problems of transporting goods from the urban centres over long distances with poor gravel roads, and by the low level of demand due to low incomes.

The effect of distance from the national development corridor is most noticeable with respect to the pattern of development of educational services (Figure 21b). Of the ten districts with the highest levels of development of educational services relative to their populations, five are located within close proximity of Harare, two are close to Bulawayo, the second largest city in the country, and the remaining three are situated close to the regional centre of Masvingo in the south. On the other hand, the ten poorest-served districts, with location quotients of less than 0.72 on the education index, are situated on the borders of the country. The effect of distance and geographical location on service availability in general assumes even greater significance, because not only do people in districts adjacent to the national economic heartland have more services per capita within their own district boundaries, but they also have greater access to better quality services within the modern sector.

Concluding remarks

Spatial inequalities in Zimbabwe have been examined from two perspectives. First they have been analysed in terms of the dichotomy between the subsistence and the modern economic sectors. Such an analytical approach is valuable in enhancing our understanding of the historical colonial origins, and the magnitude, of the disparities in levels of living between the different economic areas in the country. The post-colonial government has, since 1980, addressed itself to ameliorating the squalor and poverty of the communal farming areas, a task that is manifest in the considerable redirection of public resources of finance and manpower. Second, disparities between the district council areas have been examined using data on selected infrastructure and services available within the district boundaries. All the communal areas are still at low levels of development. Spatial inequalities between them are still fairly small, although there is evidence that the more remote and peripheral districts are relatively worse off in the per capita provision of services than those nearer to the national development corridor. As the country seeks to achieve its objectives of 'Growth with Equity' and the uplift of the quality of life in the communal farming areas, it is essential that the emerging pattern of inequalities is monitored and remedial policies adopted to avoid their intensification. The periodic examination of per capita distribution of services along the lines attempted in this baseline study can provide a valuable framework for development planning, and the allocation of scarce resources on the basis of spatial equity and social justice.

References

Central Statistical Office 1982. *Social conditions in District Council Areas 1982 (Preliminary Tables)*, Statistical Monographs No. SS 1/82. (Harare: CSO)

Gapare, R. 1976. Problems in crop production as seen by a Tribal Trust Land farmer, *The Rhodesia Science News*, vol. 10, no. 10, pp. 249–251.

Hughes, A.J.B. 1974. *Development in Rhodesian Tribal Areas* (Salisbury: Tribal Areas of Rhodesia Research Foundation)

Isard, W. 1960. *Methods of regional analysis: an introduction to regional science* (Cambridge, Massachusetts: M.I.T. Press)

Kay, G. 1972. *Distribution and density of African population in Rhodesia*, Miscellaneous Series No. 12. (University of Hull, Department of Geography)

Kay, G. 1975. Population pressures and development prospects in Rhodesia, *The Rhodesia Science News*, vol. 9, no. 1, pp. 7–13.

Ndlela, D.B. 1981. *Dualism in the Rhodesian colonial economy*, University Lund Economic Studies 22. (University of Lund, Department of Economics)

Yudelman, M. 1964. *Africans on the land* (Harvard University Press)

Zimbabwe 1982a. *District Council Handbook, Vol. 1: Administrative* (Harare)

Zimbabwe 1982b. *Transitional National Development Plan 1982/3– 1984/5* vol. 1. (Harare)

Appendix: Location quotients for five infrastructure and service development indices, 1982

District Council Area	Population density per km²	Education index	Accessibility index	Health index	Commercial activity index	Extension index	Overall mean
Hlangabeza	36	1.39	1.94	3.23	0.49	1.85	1.78
Sanyati	46	1.20	0.82	4.18	0.87	1.79	1.77
Wedza	40	1.76	1.51	2.24	1.81	1.41	1.75
Muzarabani	5	1.06	1.45	3.71	0.38	1.91	1.70
Takawira	40	1.56	1.46	2.58	1.14	1.54	1.66
Shurugwe	51	1.84	1.25	1.48	1.84	1.21	1.52
Goromonzi Kubatana	71	2.14	2.43	1.38	0.86	0.69	1.50
Rudhaka	59	2.05	1.67	0.83	1.56	1.24	1.47
Chikomba	49	1.14	1.30	1.07	1.58	2.07	1.43
Chiweshe	66	1.13	1.07	2.20	1.31	1.33	1.41
Chirorodziva	28	1.87	2.04	0.85*	1.27	0.87	1.38
Nyaminyami	3	0.69	2.14	0.45	0.35	3.29	1.38
Kubatana Bindura	50	0.98	3.03	0.46	1.07	1.26	1.36

District Council Area	Population density per km^2	Education index	Accessibility index	Health index	Commercial activity index	Extension index	Overall mean
Umzingwane	38	1.22	1.68	1.54	0.87	1.46	1.35
Mabvazuva	46	0.84	1.14	0.57	1.64	2.14	1.27
Zaka	50	0.92	1.06	2.29	1.01	1.04	1.26
Mhondoro	46	2.13	0.68	0.95	1.15	1.33	1.25
Ngezi	46	1.20	1.05	1.59	0.77	1.61	1.24
Manyame	59	1.21	1.10	0.66	0.83	2.31	1.22
Insiza	27	1.32	1.51	0.86	0.73	1.64	1.21
Murewa Kubstana	68	0.94	1.59	1.33	1.02	0.93	1.16
Harava	77	1.05	1.35	0.62	1.45	1.26	1.15
Hwange	10	1.03	1.50	1.03	0.61	1.59	1.15
Chaminuka	56	1.36	1.12	1.17	1.05	1.01	1.14
Chitepo	65	0.89	0.85	1.14	1.54	1.29	1.14
Zvishavane	36	1.29	1.94	0.79	0.86	0.84	1.14
Mutoko	33	0.98	1.01	1.63	1.01	1.01	1.13
Bikita People's	45	0.82	1.07	1.72	0.92	0.97	1.10
Nyanga	22	1.12	0.85	1.08	1.18	1.18	1.08
Gwanda	16	1.02	1.23	0.26	1.21	1.66	1.07
Masvingo	45	1.04	1.14	1.36	0.99	0.77	1.06
Matobo	21	1.33	1.38	0.77	0.71	1.09	1.06
Gazaland	42	0.51	0.87	0.92	1.17	1.44	0.98
Kusile	11	1.28	1.11	0.78	0.63	0.97	0.95
Pfura	22	0.44	0.96	1.54	0.97	0.86	0.95
UMP Zvataida	30	0.94	1.27	0.77	0.74	0.93	0.93
Tsholotsho	12	0.99	0.65	1.46	0.71	0.84	0.93
Beitbridge	8	0.70	1.69	0.25	0.48	1.45	0.91
Gaza Komanani	12	0.61	0.96	0.27	0.43	2.28	0.91
Guruve	13	0.80	0.53	1.00	1.31	0.92	0.91
Mutare	43	0.75	0.97	0.66	1.27	0.82	0.89
Nkayi	20	0.94	0.94	0.92	0.93	0.62	0.87
Cheziya Gokwe	17	0.77	0.83	0.50	1.23	0.95	0.86
Maungwe	49	1.18	1.03	0.64	1.15	0.27	0.85
Binga	6	0.91	1.34	1.39	0.11	0.45	0.84
Mberengwa	40	0.97	0.70	1.29	0.87	0.28	0.82
Gutu	40	1.08	0.71	0.87	1.01	0.36	0.81
Buhera	31	0.99	0.68	0.47	1.03	0.82	0.79
Mudzi	17	0.72	0.93	0.45	0.73	0.85	0.74
Nyaningwe	44	0.94	0.89	0.13	0.69	0.86	0.70
Mashambazhou	34	0.76	0.75	0.32	1.03	0.62	0.69
Hurungwe	20	0.66	0.81	0.47*	1.06	0.48	0.69
Bulilimamangwe	16	0.46	0.63	0.97	0.41	0.65	0.62
Rushinga	21	0.44	0.81	0.37	0.73	0.54	0.58
Batanai	36	0.56	0.85	0.29	0.42	0.59	0.54

* data on one hospital (number of beds and number of nurses) not included

6

Inequality in Murang'a District, Kenya: Local Organization for Change

Fiona Mackenzie and D.R.F. Taylor
Department of Geography, Carleton University, Ottawa, Canada

Introduction

The intention in this chapter is to discuss the relationship between inequalities in rural Kenya and government policies directed towards the rural sector. It will be argued that government policies, congruent with a highly centralized and functional model of development pursued during both the colonial era and the period of 'national developmentalism' (Sandbrook 1982) after independence, have exacerbated rather than reduced spatial and interpersonal inequalities. It is suggested that although the rural situation is a complex one and that solutions to rural inequalities cannot be framed in isolation from power relationships of the state, local initiatives, which have arisen as a direct response to contradictions in the rural areas, indicate the practicability of an alternative paradigm of development.

The argument will be illustrated using empirical evidence from Murang'a District, Central Province (Figure 23). However, in order to set the scene for this, we will first briefly outline the dimensions of inequality in Kenya as a whole. It will be evident that although Central Province is among the more resource-rich areas of Kenya, macro-economic and social indicators mask severe inequalities. Analysis will then centre on a discussion of the impact of specific agricultural policies in Murang'a District, and the nature of local responses to these. Drawing on this, the final section considers the theoretical, practical and policy implications of local, small-scale solutions to the development problematic. To a very real extent, the conceptualization of 'development from within' which is indicated here is concerned with *struggle* rather than *strategy*, *politics* rather than *policies* (Weaver 1984, p. 138) at the local territorial level.

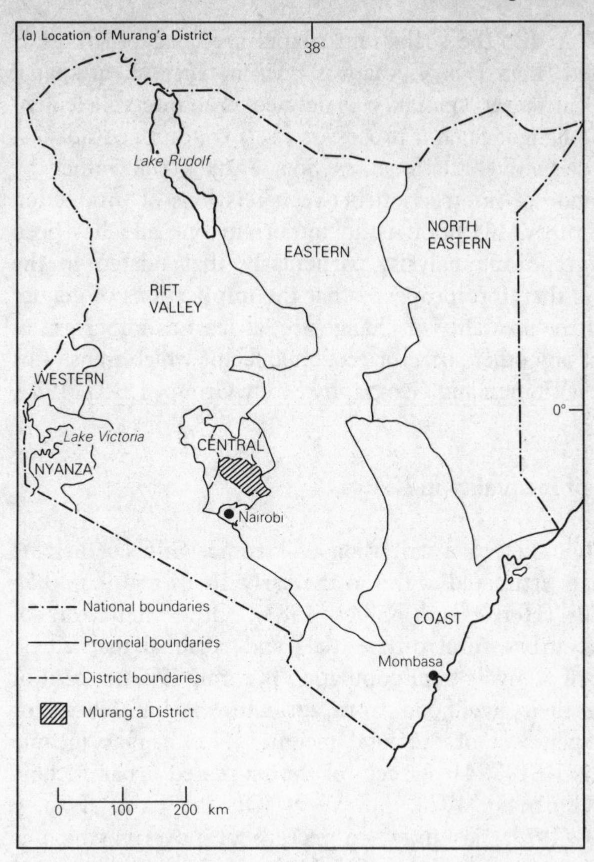

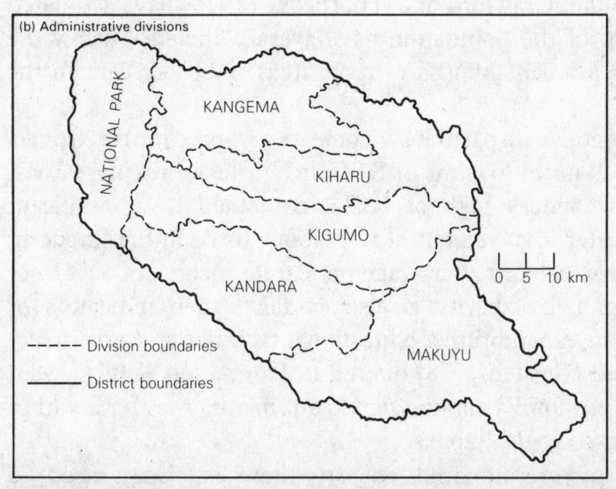

Fig. 23 Murang'a District, Kenya – location and administrative divisions

It will be evident that the social and spatial are conceptualized as dialectically related (Soja 1980). Analysis does not centre on spatial inequality *per se*, but rather 'spatiality' is defined as an integral element of any process of change. Such a process is itself conditioned not just by changes in productive relations, as Soja argues, but rather by changes in the mode of intersection between relations of production and of reproduction.[1] This point is an important one and has been neglected in geographical analysis, particularly that related to the Third World. It is therefore proposed that the implications of gender in any analysis of the spatiality of change are 'at least as important as the implications of any other social or economic factor which transforms society and space' (Women and Geography Study Group, I.B.G. 1984, p. 21).

The dimensions of inequality in Kenya

Kenya has a highly skewed distribution of income. Gini coefficients have been variously estimated at 0.6 in the early 1970s and 0.5–0.55 in the mid–1970s (House and Killick 1983). Other indicators of inequality include urban-rural differentials and regional disparities. Over 88 per cent of Kenya's total population is rural, 79.6 per cent of the total earning their livelihood from agriculture. Yet this sector receives only 47 per cent of the total income. The average income from agriculture is K£188, 41 per cent of the estimated urban income (Crawford and Thorbecke 1978, pp. v–9). On the basis of these figures, the ILO (1979) has drawn a picture of poverty which is primarily a rural one. Crawford and Thorbecke (1978) have estimated that 44.8 per cent of the population have average incomes below the poverty line, five per cent living in urban areas, 39.8 per cent in the rural sector.

In terms of regional disparities, income per capita ranges from a high of K£338 in Nairobi to a low of K£16 in Western Province. Coast Province has a secondary high of K£76, explained to a significant degree by the greater involvement of the labour force in the 'modern' sector. Central Province has an average per capita income of K£42 per annum. This regional disparity is also evident when indicators of health facilities and expenditures, educational facilities and infrastructure are considered (Bigsten 1978, quoted in House and Killick 1983, p. 36). The rural economy contains significant inequalities both within and between agro-ecological zones.

In defining a picture of rural poverty there is also a need to differentiate households according to the sex of the household head.

Available data concerns only the smallholder population. Even here it is difficult to present an accurate view as definitions of household head have changed. The Integrated Rural Survey of 1981 gives the definition as 'the senior member of the household resident in the household compound or though residing elsewhere returns at frequent intervals' (p. 23). On this basis, approximately one quarter of smallholder households in Kenya are headed by women, an indication that some rural households are unable to generate enough income from the land and therefore migration, generally of males, occurs. Barnes (1983) indicated substantial differences between households headed by married men and those headed by women, and within the latter households headed by unmarried women, generally widows, are the most disadvantaged. Households headed by women tend to be located in the areas of lower agricultural potential, although they may also be found on very small farms in high-potential areas. Their holdings tend to be below the average size and their access to labour is less than that of male-headed households. In addition, they have less access to non-farm income, a significant determinant of rural poverty. Unmarried women household heads are in a particularly difficult position here, only seven per cent receiving K£15 or more per month from non-farm income. This compares with 22 per cent for married women, and 26 per cent for married men household heads. In households headed by married women, remittances from absent spouses sometimes assist the household economy. In general, male-headed households have a total cash income 19 per cent greater than female-headed households. Households headed by women, and especially those headed by unmarried women, depend more on their holding for a living than those headed by males (Barnes 1983).

A fairly comprehensive picture of inequalities within Murang'a District may be drawn from a variety of sources. It should be noted that this district is an area of relatively high agricultural potential compared to Kenya as a whole, 80 per cent of its area of 2,476 sq km being considered suitable for agriculture, and 65 per cent classified as lying in agro-ecological zones of high and medium potential. Here 96 per cent of the households derive their livelihoods from agriculture, and for the most part operate small farms, which occupy 64 per cent of the land, according to the Draft District Development Plan (DDDP) of 1979 (pp. 4–7). Of the five Divisions within the District, only in Makuyu are large farms the norm. The sizes of holdings vary, but 80 per cent of those in the smallholder sector are under two ha, 46.5 per cent being under one ha (Statistical Abstract 1970, p. 81). The distribution of the population (648,333) reflects the agricultural potential:

densities ranging from over 600 sq km in Kamahuha Location in Middle Murang'a to 75 sq km in Mitumbiro Location in the lower zone (Census of 1979, quoted in Jaetzold and Schmidt 1983, p. 581).

Despite its agricultural resources, the Murang'a District Development Plan (MDDP) of 1984–8 (p. 12) estimates that 30 per cent of the households in Kandara, Kigumo, Kiharu and Kangema Divisions lie below the poverty line. The comparable figure for the fifth Division, Makuyu, is 70 per cent. The poverty line is presently estimated to lie at K£477 for a family of 4.5 adult equivalents, one quarter of this amount being required to meet the family's food budget. Current data on the numbers of smallholders, who form the largest category of poor, are not given. Estimates in the DDDP (p. 5) suggest that 53,000 smallholders in the marginal areas, particularly of Makuyu Division (where lack of rainfall and its unreliability are critical), and a further 27,800 with less than one ha in areas of high and medium potential in Kangema, Kiharu and Kandara, are close to or below the poverty line. It is estimated in the MDDP that two additional categories of poor existed in 1984: 30,000 squatters and 22,000 landless; and the DDDP estimated 65,300 adult dependents in 1979 (p. 5). The numbers of all categories of poor are increasing owing to the continuing subdivision of holdings, the decreased opportunities for resettlement, and a perception of the limited benefits of outmigration, whether to urban or rural areas. Outmigration and resettlement provided viable alternatives for many in the 1960s and early 1970s.

Among other estimates of poverty an analysis of the pattern of moderate protein energy malnutrition shows that it affects 39 per cent of children aged between one and four years in Central Province. Again, the situation is most severe in Makuyu Division and among landless (DDDP 1979, p. 78).

The disproportionate representation of the poor in Makuyu Division is not only the result of its location in the area of least agro-ecological potential. The DDDP for Murang'a which dealt extensively with access to basic needs and the distribution of poverty, noted that there are wealthy farmers in marginal areas: generally those who own large coffee and pineapple estates with irrigation facilities. Irrigation water however, is not generally available for the smallholder who grows food crops. The DDDP (p. 77) indicates that there has been little emphasis on identifying suitable cash crops (sunflower, cotton) for the drier areas until very recently. In addition, little research had focused on food crops which are drought-resistant.

A significant part of the unequal distribution of poverty in Murang'a results from the fact that attention in terms of development has been directed to those areas where high capital returns may be expected, hence infrastructure has been located in areas producing export crops such as tea and coffee. These areas not only have a higher proportion of bitumenized and all-weather (murram) roads, but are better served by education and health facilities. A further difficulty farmers face in the marginal areas is the lack of access to credit. Whereas smallholders in high- and medium-potential areas have title deeds to their land, those in Makuyu, although they own the land, do not yet have a title deed, either because the land was subdivided from large estates, or because they form part of a settlement scheme. The DDDP considers the lack of collateral in the form of a title deed as a significant constraint for loans to local farming.

Precise data on inequalities between households headed by men and women is not available at the district level. In Central Province as a whole, 23 per cent of the households are headed by women. In 1971/2 Kimani and Taylor (1973) found that 29.4 per cent of a sample of over 5,000 farms were run by women. Unofficial estimates from Murang'a in 1984 suggest an even higher percentage of female household heads particularly in Kandara Division, where the proportion may rise to 60·3 per cent. Such estimates are supported by the age-sex ratios for the district, which indicate female majorities for the age groups 20–65, the result of high rates of male out-migration for all divisions except for Makuyu (MDDP, pp. 8–11).

In the rural areas a major source of inequality on both a regional and interpersonal level is unequal access to land. The issue of land and land tenure is a complex one which will be more fully discussed in the next section. In Murang'a there is a strong correlation between the amount of land owned and income levels.

In 1962, Taylor (1966) carried out a random sample survey of 250 farms from all over the District. The largest holding was just under 40 ha and the smallest 0·12 ha. The average holding was 2·02 ha, and 19.8 per cent of the holdings were under 1·2 ha. Land Consolidation records for the whole District in 1962 were available for 75 sublocations. The sublocations are the smallest administrative units. The average size of the 4,254 holdings recorded was 2·06 ha, 44·8 per cent under 1·2 ha. Considerable spatial disparity existed between different ecological zones of the District and also within each of those zones. The smallest average holding size for a sublocation was 0·8 ha, the largest 6·3 ha. The next largest unit is the location, which may consist of up to 15 sublocations. Table 6.1 shows figures for location 2 in the Tea-Pyrethrum Zone and Location 10 in the Coffee Zone. Disparities in

Table 6.1 Landholdings in two locations. Murang'a District, 1962

Location	Sub-location	Total number of holdings	Holdings over 3 acres (1.2 ha)	Holdings under 3 acres (1.2 ha)	Average holding size (ha)
Location 2					
(Tea, pyrethrum)	a)	718	620	98	3.09
	b)	161	150	11	6.26
	c)	718	620	98	2.61
	d)	227	202	25	4.18
	e)	286	270	16	4.72
	f)	943	632	311	1.96
Total		3053	2494 (81.69%)	559 (18.31%)	3.80
Location 10					
(Coffee)	a)	726	134	592	0.83
	b)	366	114	252	1.95
	c)	831	403	428	1.33
	d)	824	542	282	1.66
	e)	326	72	254	0.91
	f)	522	223	299	2.48
Total		3595	1488 (41.39%)	2107 (58.61%)	1.45

(Source: Taylor, 1966)

the size of landholdings between these two ecological zones, and within each zone, are striking.

In 1972, Kimani and Taylor (1973) sampled over 5,000 farms in the District. The average size was 2.02 ha, but there was considerable variation, 3.7 per cent of the farms being under 0.4 ha and 1.2 per cent over 20 ha. By 1979, the number of smallholdings in the District had reached 131,264, largely as a result of the subdivision of existing holdings (although 1,837 holdings were added as a result of incorporating a new Division into the District). Table 6.2 shows the range in size by Division, and again considerable variation is apparent. The definition of a smallholding is 0.5–20 ha, and it is likely that the situation is even more extreme than the table shows. Holdings of less than 0.5 ha would either not be recorded, or recorded as 0.5, whereas those over 20 ha would be recorded as 20.

These figures show both the increase of population pressure on the land and the inequities in landholding size over time. It is perhaps

Table 6.2 Landholding size by Division, Murang'a District, 1979

Division	Number of smallholdings	Size range (ha)
Makuyu	1,837	2.0– 4.0
Kandara	30,306	1.3– 2.3
Kangema	34,566	0.5– 3.0
Kiharu	51,342	0.8–20.0
Kugumo	13,213	1.5– 6.5
District total	131,264	0.5–20.0

Source: Murang'a District Development Plan 1984 (p. 53)

worth noting that registered land owners made up no more than 20 per cent of the total population of the District in 1984.

The distribution of poverty in Kenya is far from static. The evidence suggests that regardless of the scale at which this is considered, or the spatial unit used for comparison, both spatial and interpersonal inequalities in Kenya are increasing both in relative and absolute terms.

National agricultural policy: elements of inequality

It is not possible to discuss fully the wide range of agricultural policies applied to Murang'a District during and after the colonial period. We have chosen to select those policies which pertain specifically to land tenure and export crop production, in order to provide an historical perspective in which the local response to change may be placed. These policies are of central importance in the local economy. Land remains the main means of production for the majority of households, and the need for cash to meet basic needs is 'the dominant economic force operating at the household level today' (Barnes 1983, p. 48); a significant source of cash in Murang'a is the sale of export crops.

The beginnings of a colonial agricultural policy in Kenya may be traced to the alienation of several million hectares of land from 1887 onwards. The division of territory into scheduled areas reserved for European agriculture and Non-Scheduled areas for Africans was superimposed on pre-existing socio-economic and cultural organization. It laid the basis not only for a highly skewed distribution of land between large and small farming systems (Okoth-Ogendo 1981), but also for a two-pronged agricultural policy.[4] One branch of this was directed to the European sector and comprised policies to facilitate the development of a viable base for a colonial economy: employment rules which allowed the procurement of African labour on terms favourable to Europeans; the provision of transport and other infrastructure; preferential or exclusive access to markets; and research, extension and credit facilities directed to their needs (Heyer 1981).

Policy directed to the million smallholders in the Non-Scheduled Areas can only be understood in relation to this other policy: it was designed to facilitate the expansion of European agriculture. To the extent that this did not compete with markets or the provision of an exported labour supply, some intensification of agricultural production was advocated. Thus food crops such as maize and cassava were advanced at the expense of millet and sorghum as they required less land and labour per unit of production (Fisher 1952). To a limited extent, low value cash crops such as wattle and cotton were introduced, the latter often with no regard to the labour constraints faced by women, which resulted in its failure (Pala 1980). Growing coffee, tea or pyrethrum for the export market and maize and dairy produce for the urban or inter-regional market was prohibited during this period.

The impact of these policies on a growing population confined to a curtailed land base, together with the imposition of hut and poll taxes, meant that the export of labour became essential for survival. Kitching (1980, p. 250) has estimated that this affected 41.7 per cent of the adult males aged 15–45 years in Fort Hall (now Murang'a) District in 1928. As wages were hardly sufficient to meet the workers' subsistence needs, the reserve functioned, through the production of food crops by women, as the area of reproduction of the labour force. With the spatial division of labour that this entailed, the women became increasingly responsible for agricultural production, yet the men's integration into the cash economy meant the beginning of their involvement in that sector which provided the basis for increasingly assymetrical gender relations.

Opposition to the government in the early 1950s culminated in the violence of the Emergency. Recognizing that agricultural policies were no longer tenable, two new policies were introduced which reversed, in part, previous policy, and these have continued to form the basis of post-independence strategy:

1 Intensification of African agriculture on the basis of land tenure reform and production for the urban and export market, proposed by the Swynnerton Plan in 1954.
2 A limited African resettlement of Scheduled Areas was recommended by the Royal Commission Report of 1955, primarily in order to safeguard European farming interests (Okoth-Ogendo 1981).

Our comments will be confined to the first set of policies.

The Swynnerton Plan attempted to impose a pattern of integrated rural development, to create a politically stable, land-owning peasant class more interested in economic gain than in further radicalization of the tense political situation. In the Reserves the three-part strategy involved: the adjudication of land ownership; consolidation where necessary; and the registration of individual title to the land. Although these measures were frequently referred to as land reform, they involved no move towards more equitable access to the land (Leys 1975; Lamb 1974). In fact, land consolidation tended to freeze existing land distribution, including inherent inequalities, at a particular point in time. These policies represent the beginning of a commitment, since continually endorsed, to the individualization of land tenure as a basis for increased agricultural productivity. Benefits expected to ensue from these measures included the following: legal title would increase security and therefore lead to long-term investment and provide collateral for credit; time and money spent by the farmer walking between the land parcels would be reduced; it would be easier both to protect crops and provide extension advice; more intensive land use would result in greater employment (Heyer 1981).

Although it is still argued that greater agricultural productivity results from these measures (see House and Killick 1983, for a summary), others contend that the production increases of the 'fifties and 'sixties were due rather to the rapid adoption of coffee, tea and dairy enterprises, once restrictions were relaxed (Heyer 1976; Smith 1976). Scepticism of the reforms may be voiced on several points. Firstly, Haugerud's (1983) analysis in Embu lends support to the view that kin relations continue to exist in contradiction to the formal system of individual land tenure. The District Land Registry thus may bear limited relationship to the actual division and use of land. Moreover, the *de facto* subdivision of land on inheritance, notwithstanding *de jure* ownership, has led to conflict; only the possessor of the title has the right of sale or access to credit. Second, evidence indicates that with a change to an individualized system of land tenure, women's access to land becomes less secure. Research by Barnes (1983) and Pala (1980) gives evidence of the implications of women's subordinate position in access to land, and their insecurity because of this. This situation is examined below. Third, questions have been raised about the institutionalization of a landless class as a result of this policy. Swynnerton saw this as 'a normal step in the evolution of a country' (quoted in Leys 1975, p. 52) and argued the majority of such workers would then be employed on the larger holdings. Evidence from Embu, while substantiating the view that inequality in holding size (and thus landlessness) is increasing, suggests that much of the land accumulated (principally by those with access to non-farm income) is not farmed immediately. Rather, it is held for speculation or future inheritance. Increased employment has therefore not been the result of an increasingly skewed land distribution pattern (Haugerud 1983; more generally, House and Killick 1983).

The second major component of the Swynnerton Plan for small farm areas was the promotion of cash crops. Coffee, previously grown almost exclusively on European holdings, was restricted initially to a small élite of 'progressive farmers' and a tightly controlled co-operative marketing system was established. Expansion was immediate and rapid. Tea, pyrethrum and dairying were also introduced as cash earners (Heyer 1981). As a result of these changes, and related investment in infrastructure, processing and marketing, the marketed output from small farms increased to 51.7 per cent of the total marketed output at the national level in 1982 (Economic Survey 1983).

In the post-independence period, the increasing integration of the economy into capitalist relations of production both nationally and internationally (Buch-Hansen and Kieler 1983) has resulted in a continued emphasis on high value export crops. With the exception of the development of hybrid and composite maize varieties and more recent emphasis on other food crops, services (research, extension and credit) and inputs have supported this strategy. The impact has been uneven both regionally (Central Province having benefited the most) and in terms of stratification of the population (House and Killick 1983).

The introduction of export crops resulted in a further widening of the split between the subsistence and monetized sectors of the economy, radically affecting gender-productive relations (Smock 1977). In general, colonial ideology, as expressed through agricultural policy, served to reinforce patriarchal elements in society and with male control of cash crops such as coffee, gender relations became increasingly hierarchical. Blumberg (1978) has explained this in terms of one gender's participation in significant or strategic productive labour, resulting in both increased remuneration and prestige. In contrast, women's contribution to agriculture lay chiefly in the subsistence, or domestic, sector.

With increasing male out-migration from many areas, there is now a less precise division of labour by sex in agriculture, but although women have taken over responsibility in many areas for export crop production, seldom do they control the proceeds of this labour (Stamp 1975/6).

Local response to national policy: Murang'a District

From their earliest contact with external influences the Gikuyu people have responded to change in an innovative way in order to survive (Marris and Somerset 1971). This section will concentrate on the impact on, and the responses of, women to national government policies which we contend are as much part of the problem as the solution to the development issues.

Issues of land

Prior to the individualization of land tenure, the *githaka* system of land tenure prevailed in the area occupied by the Gikuyu. Essentially this meant that the *mbari*, the kin corporation (Sacks 1982), as defined by lineage relations tracing descent patrilineally from a common ancestor, was the land-owning unit (Sorrenson 1967). Under this system, farmland was allocated to a woman by her husband and was inherited by her sons. Although women did not, in general, inherit land, they did have automatic usufruct rights to land on marriage (Stamp 1975/6).

In addition, women not infrequently retained use-rights to land as 'sisters' in their natal kin corporations after marriage.[5] This may have involved the *mugunda wa muiritu*, a small piece of land given them at the age of 14 or 15 by their father for cultivation (Fisher 1952), or a piece of land closer to their residence as a wife (MDCH).[6] Such rights were retained for varying lengths of time, almost always reverting to brothers as they needed it. Whether women could accede to such rights as 'sisters' clearly depended both on distance from the place of birth and on mobility. In certain other cases women had more control over the allocation of land, for example, as a female husband (Leakey 1977, p. 800: MDCH), although such land was still inherited patrilineally, or less frequently where a woman decided not to marry but bore children. In such a situation her sons inherited through her (Leakey 1977, p. 536).

While ethnographic literature presents a static view of the relationship of a kin corporation to land, this relationship was very far from static, as shown by evidence from the Maxwell Commission's report on *Native Land Tenure in Kikuyu Province* (1929), and the Report of the Kenya Land Commission of 1934. Individualization of landholding, and the buying and selling of land (although not irredeemably unlike Kiambu District to the south), had begun at this time. The specific effect on gender relations to land is not mentioned in these reports.

The individual rights to land provided under the Swynnerton Plan were, however, qualitatively different. Registration of individual title meant that the power of individual men to allocate land was equated with the 'registrable interest', and thus, with very few exceptions, men became the owners of the land. To a very real degree this resulted in increasing insecurity for women, as Smock notes: 'In a situation in which the clan cannot effectively impose sanctions, the clan also cannot protect women's prerogative' (1977, p. 48).

Nevertheless, as Haugerud (1983, p. 76) has argued for Embu, kin relations are far from being 'eclipsed' by statutory law. She states: 'In the intersection of the new *de jure* system with *de facto* continuation of pre-reform practices, pre-existing rights become less secure, and new sources of domestic conflict fester'. Land registration was carried out much earlier in Murang'a than Embu, but evidence exists of an area of fluidity in kin versus statutory legal claims to land. A case presently awaiting a hearing before the High Court in Nairobi may illustrate the nature of the conflict. A widow from Kandara Division, with title deed to the land originally her husband's, is claiming the right to pass the land on to her two daughters in the face of clan opposition acting on behalf of her husband's brother. In pre-registration times this land would have passed to her brother-in-law's sons (MDCH).

Recognition of the insecurity women face in rural areas, whether based on insecure access to land or to cash, is evident at different socio-economic levels in the district. Since independence in 1963, an average of 11.7 per cent of land purchases have been made by women

Table 6.3 Land sales, Murang'a District, by gender

Year[a]	Total sales	Sales to women %	Sales to men %
1984*	923	11.7	88.3
1979**	1,413	12.5	87.3
1974	1,928	12.2	87.8
1969	923	13.0	87.0
1964	374	6.7	93.3
1963	165	13.9	86.1
1962	78	1.3	98.7
1961	6	0	100.0
1960	66	1.5	98.5
1959	67	9.0	91.0
1958	6	0	100.0

* 1984 Sales up to and including 8 December.
** 1979 Data from 7 to 31 December were missing.
[a] After 1984, data are given for every fifth year because the large increase in land sales made annual estimates difficult.
Source: Murang'a District Land Registry, Presentation Books

(Table 6.3). This figure represents the surmounting of incredible difficulties on the part of these women. Not only do women have far less ready access to cash with which to purchase land, but there is frequently pressure on women who wish to purchase land to register it in their husband's name (MDCH).

It will be evident from Table 6.3 that sales for 1984 were significantly lower than for 1979, the direct result of a measure introduced by the Land Boards in Murang'a in 1982/3. All land cases, including those requesting permission for sale, must be heard initially by the Land Board at the Location level (Chief's Camp). Since 1982/3, in response to the evident insecurity of women whose means of livelihood could be sold by a husband facing financial strain, it has been mandatory for the spouse of the land owner (and if adult, a child) to appear before the Board to indicate both their awareness of the proposed sale and agreement with it. As a result of this measure, land sales throughout the district have decreased.[7]

Export crops and access to cash

Within Gikuyu society, men's and women's tasks were sharply differentiated. Women, in addition to their exclusive responsibility for household maintenance and other reproductive tasks, were responsible for the planting, weeding and harvesting of food crops. Men's tasks centred on clearing the land, tending perennial (tree) crops, and livestock (Fisher 1952). In general women exercised control over the allocation of labour in their *myumba* (the land allocated to them) and controlled the products of their labour, although it is likely that women's autonomy here was sometimes an area of dispute (Kitching 1980, pp. 120–30). Men's greater access to cash in the colonial economy, outmigration, and their later control of export crops such as tea and coffee resulted in their greater control of earnings, and the prestige associated with this. Women's responsibility for food crop production continued to be vital, but as priority was accorded to export crops and more land was turned over for export crop production, women produced food crops on reduced land. In turn this meant less surplus for sale in local markets, and reduced access to cash. Kitching (1980) extrapolating from Fisher's (1952) data on Murang'a, argues that with greater commoditization of the economy, it is likely that dispute increased over women's control of the disposal of the products of their labour. There is need here, however, to differentiate between households, and Kershaw's (1975/6) evidence from Kiambu suggests a high degree of variation in decision-making power of the sexes with the socio-economic stratum of the household.

Table 6.4 Njora Coffee Growers' Co–operative Society

Year	Cumulative total membership	New members M	F	Female as % of new members	Subsequent change of shareholder M to F	F to M
1951	3	3	0	0	0	0
1952	3	0	0	0	0	0
1953	10	6	1	14.3	1	0
1954	19	8	1	11.1	0	0
1955	63	42	1	2.3	2	0
1956	70	7	0	0	1	0
1957	82	10	1	9.1	1	0
1958–60	218	135	1	0.7	4	0
1961	299	76	5	6.2	1	0
1962	409	108	2	1.8	2	0
1963	469	58	2	3.3	2	0
1964	802	323	10	3.0	8	0
1965	1,256	440	14	3.1	15	0
1966	1,290	33	1	2.9	0	0
1967–9	1,483	187	6	3.1	5	0
1970	1,596	106	7	6.2	0	0
1971	1,656	47	13	21.7	2	0
1972	1,671	14	1	6.7	1	0
1973	1,936	250	15	5.7	2	1
1974	2,560	595	49	7.9	5	0
1975	2,875	285	30	9.5	1	1
1976	3,549	601	73	10.8	4	0
1977	3,952	458	45	11.2	2	0
1978	4,224	242	32	11.8	3	0
1979	4,572	286	62	17.8	2	0
1980	4,999	367	60	14.1	3	0
1981	5,165	143	23	13.9	1	0
1982	5,260	84	11	11.6	0	0
1983	5,481	200	21	9.5	0	0
1984	5,663	149	33	18.1	0	0

(1 Nov.) Female members as percentage of total members (1984) 10.4

Male to male transactions are not included
Source: Njora Coffee Society Registers[8]

The precise impact of the introduction of export crops on gender relations, and the response to this, varied according to the crop, labour requirements, marketing and other organizational factors. The case of coffee only will be considered here, focusing on the marketing arrangements of that crop. Since its introduction to the District in the 1950s, the processing and marketing of coffee has been organized co-operatively. At present, Murang'a Union, uniting 26 coffee societies, has a total membership of 61,000 (MDDP 1984–8, p. 39). As Table 6.4 however indicates for one coffee society, membership is overwhelmingly male. Females make up only 10.4 per cent of the total. In general, the land owner is registered as the co-operative shareholder. This has two sets of implications for the majority of women farmers.

First, given the blurring of customary patterns of the division of labour with high rates of male out-migration, many women are now responsible for labouring for export crop as well as food crop production. Payment however, has (at least until very recently) been made exclusively to the shareholder in the society. As in Kiambu (Stamp 1975/6) evidence from Murang'a indicates widespread dissatisfaction on the part of women who worked to produce the coffee but depended on the will of their husbands for remuneration. Women responded with varying degrees of withdrawal of labour from coffee production, or at least not according coffee production the highest priority, resulting in poorer quality produce (MDCS). Problems associated with migrant men having access to their accounts, and the difficulties of families depending on this source of cash, led to a recent drive for joint accounts by the four Savings and Credit Sections of the Union.

Table 6.5 Maragua Savings and Credit Section, Murang'a Farmers' District Co-operative Union Ltd. (November 1984)

Society	Total accounts	Single men's accounts %	Single women's accounts %	Joint accounts %
Mugiori	3,757	52.5	14	33.5
Thanga-ini	3,827	16.9	4.9	79.2
Njora	5,003	71.0	11.9	17.1
Irati	3,345	31.1	13.5	55.4
Nginda	1,151	67.5	13.6	18.9
Kiangoma	2,006	59.4	10.5	30.1
Total	19,089	48.1	11.1	40.8

Table 6.5 shows the situation in six societies belonging to one of these sections of the Union. The wide differences in the percentages of joint accounts is explained by the Assistant Manager of the Maragua Savings Section as resulting from the degree of out-migration. Thus, Thanga-ini and Irati, with higher male out-migration, have a larger percentage of joint accounts. While this trend does not in itself

guarantee women's control over the proceeds of their labour, it may be seen as a step in that direction.

The second set of implications arising from the very limited degree of female membership concerns their difficulties in gaining access to credit. Co-operatives have become the major vehicle for credit provision in the smallholder areas in Kenya: 86 per cent in 1980/1 and 72 per cent in 1981/2, of new agricultural credit issued to small farmers was channelled through these institutions (calculated from Economic Survey 1983, p. 116). Credit extended through the Co-operative Production Credit Scheme (CPCS), Smallholder Production Services Credit Programme (SPSCP), Integrated Agricultural Development Programme (IADP), National Poultry Development Programme (NPDP), Smallholder Coffee Improvement Programme (SCIP) and the new Seasonal Credit Scheme (NSCS) *inter alia* has all taken this route. Rarely can smallholders gain access to credit through the Agricultural Finance Corporation (AFC) on account of the small size of loans generally requested, and here land is demanded as collateral, again putting women at a disadvantage.

The role of credit as a vehicle for agricultural developments has been questioned, for example, by Von Pischke (1976) and Gerhart (1974). Both have pointed to the lack of correlation between credit and the adoption or diffusion of coffee, tea or hybrid maize. Even the World Bank (1983) has indicated a recent change in policy in Kenya, favouring financing agricultural innovation through higher prices for agricultural products rather than through credit. Yet the demand for credit remains, and a workshop on the *Women's Programme in Agricultural Credit and Banking* (Nairobi, 1983) discussed the problems of women in obtaining loans, in terms of issues of efficiency (productivity) and of equity.

The failure of the IADP in Murang'a District (Kandara Division) has been attributed in large measure to problems associated with the provision of credit.[9] The Programme itself aimed to increase the level of living of smallholders by focusing on food crop production for the national market. It intended to remove constraints by strengthening existing credit, training and marketing institutions (such as co-operatives) and by providing a technological package (IADP Management Handbook, 1979). Unfortunately, the data on the Programme was not disaggregated by gender, but, given the very high degree of male outmigration from Kandara, and women's responsibility for food crop production, it is likely that women's inability to obtain credit through co-operatives was at least partly responsible for the Programme's lack of success (Mackenzie 1986).

Local organization

Within Murang'a, men and women have long organized collectively to meet their needs. This generally took the form of *ngwatio* (an arrangement whereby two or more people agreed to help each other, on a rotating basis, for example with agricultural work), or *gutumana wira*, (labour organized on a much larger scale for a specific task). This was not immediately reciprocal (Fisher 1952).

As Thomas (1982) has indicated, however, there is a qualitative and quantitative difference between such work organization and the women's groups in Kenya which have evolved since the early 'seventies. The latter may be understood rather in the context of a direct response to women's increasing insecurity and workload resulting from structural socio-economic change.

In Murang'a District at present a total of 30,350 women belong to 540 registered women's groups (MDDP, 1984/8). Table 6.6 gives the distribution by division, with some exceptions. Approximately 19 per cent of adult women (aged 20–60 years) are members of such groups. Preliminary analysis of data from 1977[10] lists 303 groups, indicating a substantial increase in the intervening years.

The vast majority of groups identified in 1977 gave their date of formation in the early 1970s, the catalyst frequently being a directive issued through the Community Development Officers or Chiefs. It was suggested that women organize to meet needs which were expressed in terms of their heavy workload (with increasing numbers of children attending primary school in the post-independence period), and their lack of cash. The majority of groups formed at this time, *mabati* groups (whose purpose was to purchase metal roofing for members), acted in essence as a revolving loan and savings association. Members

Table 6.6 Murang'a District: Registered Women's Groups (1984)

Division	No. of groups	Total membership
Kandara*	154	7,362
Kigumo**	60	1,975
Kiharu	149	6,813
Kangema***	65	3,437
Makuyu	83	3,153
Total	511	22 740

* for Muruka Location, only income-generating projects included
** CDA Kigumo gave figure of 121 groups. Maragua Ridge excluded
*** Reports missing for three locations

of this type of group pay monthly contributions (generally K.shs. 2–25), the amount varying according to the wealth of the group. Then each month, depending on the amount of contribution and the size of the group (generally 20–100 members), the total is allocated to one or more members. In some cases the decision as to what to do with the money is left to the recipient; in other cases the group decides. The 1977 data indicates that the majority of groups at this time were of this type: 163 were involved in roofing houses, 146 in the purchase of water tanks; 189 in buying household equipment; and 78 in purchasing grade cattle. They also often had a secondary function, one of social security: assisting members to pay school and hospital fees, or to meet wedding and burial expenses. In addition, 197 organized for a social activity such as dancing.

The data for 1984 (Table 6.7) illustrate the great increase in numbers of groups whose primary purpose is income generation. This substantial change in overall direction is illustrated both among new groups which had formed in the 1980s, and in the evolution of earlier groups to this type of function. These groups tend to have a membership of 20–30. Activities, as indicated in Table 6.7, range from specifically agricultural activities such as rearing livestock or keeping poultry, to buying a plot (generally with the intention of building a shop), buying land or land shares, running a hotel or store and buying and operating a maize mill. While the agricultural activities represent a departure from the past, in that the women involved have exclusive control over any proceeds from the activity, an objective such as the purchase and operation of a maize mill, or buying land, is a far more radical departure. The two mills bought and operated by women's groups in Kandara Division provide a service to women in their communities, and are indicative of a move by women to gain access to, and control over, technology from which they were previously excluded. The purchase of land is similarly a move of significance in gaining access as owners to the means of production.

Further analysis of the 1977 and 1984 data will indicate more clearly the characteristics of the groups and the spatial and ecological distribution of income-generating *vis-á-vis* savings and loans groups. A study by Thomas (1982), which included two Locations (Weithaga and Mbiri) in Murang'a appears to indicate that income-generating groups tend to be located in the areas of greater agricultural potential. It is here (e.g. Weithaga) that more income-earning opportunities exist (for example through working on coffee shambas), access to cash is therefore easier and women can find the means to fund, initially, an income-generating activity. Thomas (1982, p. 14) distinguishes be-

Table 6.7 Women's Group activities (1984)

Activity	Kandara	Kigumo	Kiharu	Kangema	Makuyu	Total
Not income-generating:						
mabati	31	1	39	4	11	86
home improvement	1	0	7	38	19	65
water tanks	1	0	0	18	0	19
contributions	37	24	34	6	20	121
buying ploughs/tools	0	0	0	0	2	2
dancing	0	0	0	0	1	1
Income-generating:						
rearing livestock	20	18	28	0	11	77
bees	2	1	3	0	6	12
tree nursery	1	0	0	0	0	1
poultry	8	1	0	0	7	16
cultivating	19	1	3	6	2	31
buying land	1	0	0	0	1	2
handcraft*	8	11	32	10	9	70
firewood/charcoal for sale	11	5	5	0	1	22
trading	4	0	0	0	0	4
buying plot	3	1	2	3	0	9
building shop	4	2	1	0	1	8
house rental	0	3	0	0	0	3
maize mill	2	0	0	0	0	2
selling paraffin	0	2	0	0	1	3
block making	2	0	0	0	0	2
running hotel	1	0	0	0	0	1
store	3	0	0	0	0	3
land shares	0	0	0	0	1	1
buying house	0	0	9	6	0	15
banking to start business	0	0	0	0	1	1

Some groups list more than one activity
* includes: sewing, knitting, baskets, pots, silkscreen

tween such groups which were born 'less out of economic hardship than out of economic opportunity' from those in Mbiri where access to cash is far more difficult. Confirmation of this analysis is needed from a larger sample.

The question has been raised, with reference to the Women's Programme of the Special Rural Development Programme of the early 'seventies (see Pala *et al.* 1975) as to whether there is a disproportionate representation of the rural élite in women's groups. Thomas (1982) suggests that in the resource-poor locations such as Mbiri there is high representation of women in the lowest income group. Where the location of a group is in a higher potential agricultural zone, membership appears to be drawn from all socio-economic strata. Often such groups will facilitate the payment of contributions of poorer members by accepting work in lieu of cash.[11] It is also evident from Thomas' analysis that the average literacy rate for members of groups is below the average for adult women in each location. In Mbiri 20 per cent of the members are literate, compared to a figure of 50 per cent for adult women in the location as a whole. The comparable figures for Weithaga are 40 per cent and 77 per cent respectively. There also appears to be a direct relationship, for reasons identified earlier, between a high percentage of female household heads and membership in women's groups. 34 per cent of the adult women in Mbiri, from which there is high male out-migration, belong to groups. (No comparable figure is given for Weithaga, but Thomas indicates that the percentage of membership is much lower in this area of low out-migration.) Very few members of any group had employment off the shamba which indicates that members were not drawn from the élite.

With the change in direction to income generation, the lack of working capital has become a major issue for women's groups. Some funds are available through the Women's Bureau in the Ministry of Housing and Social Services, although these are extremely limited, and through the Rural Development Fund (RDF). The latter was established in 1975 by the Kenyan government and the aid agencies DANIDA, NORAD and SIDA as an instrument to promote local participation in development activities. It is administered at the district level through the District Development Committee. A very few women's groups have benefited from funds from this source, but the vast majority are unable to obtain loans or gain access to credit. This is now identified as a major constraint by the Community Development Officer in Kandara, for example. Additional problems concern marketing: this is a particular problem associated with handcraft production, but supportive infrastructure is needed for other activities also.

In general, women's groups receive at least verbal support from the central government (although they are frequently warned not to become political), and often more tangible support locally from chiefs granting land for use or permits for shops. To a very real degree this support is the result of community activities carried out by the groups: the building of nursery schools, dispensaries or cattle dips. The Women's Bureau has a specific mandate of responsibility for women's groups but its position within the Department of Community Development, itself located under the Ministry of Housing and Social Services, gives it no structural or budgetary leverage.

Theoretical and policy implications

Sandbrook (1986, p. 319) has argued that most African states have not been equal to the developmental task they face and that the state is 'part of the problem of economic stagnation in much of sub-Saharan Africa'. He sees the emergence of personal rule as a major reason for this, and such rule as destructive in terms of economic development. His argument is that 'the political requirements of régime and personal survival take precedence over and can contradict the economic policies and practices needed to promote sustained economic expansion' (p. 321). Although Sandbrook's explanations of the failure of African states to meet the challenge of development may be debatable, the fact that they have been unable to do so is difficult to dispute (see Mars and White 1986).

The authors of this paper would argue that both in theoretical and policy terms a more 'self-reliant and communitarian' approach is not only possible but necessary in Africa today. This strategy has been designated 'development from within' and the nature and theoretical underpinnings of the approach have been more fully developed elsewhere (Stohr and Taylor 1981, Mackenzie and Taylor 1985, Taylor 1985).

The major criticisms of this approach have been that it is impracticable and too idealistic and that there is no empirical evidence that it will work. In reply two main points can be made. Existing approaches to development in Africa have led to increasing inequality and economic stagnation even in those nations, like Kenya, which are sometimes used as examples of economic success. The empirical evidence in this paper supports that contention. Inequality has not decreased over time and development has not diffused from the 'core' region of Central Kenya to the 'peripheral' regions as predicted by economic and geographical theorists. When growth and equality is examined within that case region itself they are seen to be highly skewed with the macro-indicators masking serious problems. The detailed empirical evidence from Murang'a District shows that such inequalities have increased over time (Taylor 1966; Kimani & Taylor 1973; Mackenzie 1978, Mackenzie and Taylor 1985) and additional evidence has been presented here. Women have been particularly adversely affected. Such policies were initiated in Kenya in the 1950s under a colonial government and continued by independent governments up until the present, and over a period of 30 years little positive change has taken place. Evidence from other sub-Saharan countries, with the debatable exception of Côte d'Ivoire, is similar and in many, such as Chad, Nigeria, Sudan, Zaire and Uganda, even more striking. Existing policies have had a fair trial and have failed to bring about the results expected of them. New responses are urgently required and as existing approaches have helped lead to a crisis situation, 'development from within' cannot make things any worse and is likely to lead to improvement, especially in meeting basic needs.

This failure is due to a complex set of both internal and external factors including the economic shocks of sharp increases in the price of oil, global recession and drought in the late 1970s and early 1980s which played havoc with the ability of even the stronger governments, of which Kenya is certainly one, to meet development challenges effectively.

The overall result has been a downward spiral of economic development which has brought most of sub-Saharan Africa into a state of crisis. In both absolute and relative terms, poverty and inequality are increasing and in some countries, the crisis has reached such proportions that thousands of people are dying. Sandbrook poses the question which many others have posed – 'How can this downward spiral be checked and reversed?' Somewhat reluctantly he arrives at the conclusion:

> *It is just possible that, for the people of countries caught in a devastating downward spiral, their best hope lies in building upon the very survival mechanisms that the current crisis has called forth. For countries in which state capacity remains more or less intact, a range of widely debated policy reforms are still a practical option. But elsewhere the outlook is grimmer. People fall back on local self-reliance as a prime means of survival in the context of economic deterioration and a corrupt and incapacitated state. Local communities in Zaire, Chad, Ghana, Uganda, Equatorial Guinea, and the Sudan, for example, cannot expect to build a better life through assistance from central authorities and planning agencies. They must, to a considerable extent, fend for themselves. This usually entails efforts to improve their informal economies so that many of their basic needs can be satisfied locally or through trade with nearby communities.*
>
> *This recourse to self-reliance is certainly a creative adaptation to a difficult situation. Many communities have, by withdrawing from the formal economy and the state, lessened the decline of their living standards. In so doing, perhaps the people have unwittingly demonstrated the practicability of a utopian strand in development theory.*

> *This regards small-scale community solutions as preferable under any circumstances. According to this 'development as liberation' school, grassroots self-reliance can prove liberating in two senses. Not only can it free communities from the rigours of material deprivation, it can also permit villagers, by defining their own needs, designing and implementing their own projects, to educate themselves in organisational dynamics and self-government. In time, this local capacity for organisation and confidence may increase popular pressure for change at the territorial level. Or so goes the theory.*
>
> *Is it wholly unrealistic to hope that out of systemic crisis and popular disillusion and withdrawal, can emerge the self-reliant and communitarian basis for the construction of more organic and satisfactory economic and political structures? Or are statist, top-down forms of capitalism and socialism the only practicable frameworks for economic development today?*
>
> *(Sandbrook 1986, pp. 330–1)*

This paper has presented evidence that women are organizing themselves to increase their income-generating activities. They struggle to implement a strategy for self-help to counteract the negative impacts on their quality of life brought about in part by inappropriate and ineffective government policy. 'Development from within' strategies have emerged in Murang'a District and are growing. Women are amongst the poorest of the rural poor and many are uneducated and illiterate, yet an alternative response is emerging. This experience is not unique, and further detailed investigation of the informal rural economy in Kenya and elsewhere is likely to reveal other innovative responses. In Murang'a there have also been innovative responses by men's groups, by individuals, by kin groups, and by individual households, although these have not as yet been the subject of detailed empirical investigation.

It is not suggested that 'development from within' is the only strategy, or that small-scale community solutions are preferable under any circumstances, but at this point in time and space in Africa there is need of a new balance of power between central state and local communities. This is unlikely to be achieved without struggle because it involves change in the balance of real political power with a devolution of many of the powers of the state to the local level. Perhaps a 'neopatrimonial' state structure as described by Sandbrook (1986), with the roots of personal power lying in the informal economy, will be more conducive to the development of new relationships emerging in response to African reality from the bottom up, than the statist models of capitalism and socialism devised from ideologies developed outside the continent. Out of the current crisis a new approach to development may emerge which is more suited to Africa.

Notes

1 Considerable confusion exists in the literature with respect to defining 'reproduction'. It is useful to draw attention to the distinctions made by F. Edholm, O. Harris and K. Young (1977). Three dimensions of reproduction are separated:
   a) Social reproduction, referring to those conditions necessary for the continuation of a social system. This concerns the transmission of resources generationally.
   b) Reproduction of the labour force: this includes the daily maintenance of workers and the future labour force.
   c) Human or biological reproduction: this involves childbearing and is the only aspect of reproduction necessarily female. Conceptually it may form part of (b), yet may be differentiated from it.

2 The Integrated Rural Surveys I to IV (IRS) are sample surveys carried out in the smallholder areas of Kenya by the Central Bureau of Statistics. Data is published only at the provincial level. It includes detailed socio-economic information on households which may be disaggregated according to the sex and marital status of the household head.

3 Estimated by the Community Development Officer, Kandara Division, December 1984.

4 By 1963, over 8 million ha, comprising 75 per cent of Kenya's high potential land, was in European hands as large-scale farms (Okoth-Ogendo 1981).

5 Sacks (1982, p.6–7) defines a 'sister' as 'one who is an owner, a decision-maker among others of the kin corporation'. She has autonomy as an adult, this position resulting from her membership from birth in the kin group.

6 MDCH – Murang'a District case history, denotes information given as part of the collection of oral agricultural history from farmers in the latter part of 1984.

7 According to the Chief, Muthithi Location, December 1984.

8 Figures for total membership in coffee societies are not aggregated by sex. It was necessary to examine the Society Registers themselves to accumulate the numbers which appear on this table.

9 Data collected during an evaluation of IADP Phase I in Kandara Division in May 1980 showed that 36 of the 45 farmers interviewed had decided not to continue with the IADP for reasons associated with the provision of loans.

10 Data from a joint survey of women's groups carried out by the Central Bureau of Statistics and the Women's Bureau of the Ministry of Housing and Social Services (1977).

11 Information from the Chairperson, Thuita Women's Group.

References

Barnes, C. 1983. Differentiation by sex among small-scale farming households in Kenya, *Rural Africana*, Winter/Spring, pp. 41–63.

Bigsten, A. 1978. *Regional inequality and development: a case study of Kenya* (University of Gothenburg)

Blumberg, R. 1978. *Stratification: socio-economic and sexual inequality* (Dubuque, Iowa: Brown Co.)

Buch-Hansen, M. and Kieler, J. 1983. The development of capitalism and the transformation of the peasantry in Kenya, *Rural Africana*. Winter/Spring, pp. 13–40.

Crawford, E. and Thorbecke, E. 1978. *Employment, income distribution and basic needs in Kenya* (Report of an ILO Consulting Mission, Cornell University)

Edholm, F., Harris, O. and Young, K. 1977. Conceptualising women, *Critique of Anthropology*, vol. 8/10.

Fisher, J.M. 1952. *Reports on the Kikuyu, Fort Hall District*, Miscellaneous Correspondence DC/HF 31 (Kenya National Archives)

Gerhart, J. 1974. 'The diffusion of hybrid maize in Western Kenya' (Unpublished Ph.D dissertation, Princeton University)

Haugerud, A. 1983. The consequences of land tenure reform among smallholders in the Kenya Highlands, *Rural Africana*, Winter/Spring, pp. 65–89.

Heyer, J. 1981. 'Agricultural development policy in Kenya from the colonial period to 1975'. In J. Heyer, P. Roberts and G. Williams (eds), *Rural development in tropical Africa* (London: Macmillan)

Heyer, J. 1976. 'The marketing system'. In J. Heyer, J.K. Maitha and W.M. Genga (eds), *Agricultural development in Kenya: an economic assessment* (Nairobi: Oxford University Press)

House, W.J. and Killick, T. 1983. 'Social justice and development in Kenya's rural economy'. In D. Ghai and S. Radwan (eds), *Agrarian policies and rural poverty in Africa* (Geneva: International Labour Organization)

IBG 1984. *Geography and gender: an introduction to feminist geography* (London: Women and Geography Study Group of the Institute of British Geographers, Hutchinson in association with the Explorations in Feminism Collective)

ILO 1979. D. Ghai, M. Godfrey and F. Lisk, *Planning for basic needs in Kenya* (Geneva: International Labour Organization)

Jaetzold, R. and Schmidt, H. 1983. *Farm management handbook of Kenya: natural conditions and farm management information*, vol. 2. (Kenya Ministry of Agriculture with German Agency for Technical Cooperation)

Kenya 1970. *Statistical Abstracts* (Nairobi: Government printer)

Kenya 1983. *Economic Survey* (Nairobi: Government printer)

Kitching, G. 1980. *Class and economic change in Kenya* (New Haven: Yale University Press)

Lamb, G. 1974. *Peasant politics* (Lewes, Sussex: Friedmann Publishing)

Leakey, L.S.B. 1977. *The Southern Kikuyu before 1903, Vol. 1* (London: Academic Press)

Leys, C. 1975. *Underdevelopment in Kenya* (Berkeley: University Press)

Mackenzie, F. 1978. 'A consideration of the potential role of the marketplace as a centre for the diffusion of innovations; exploration of an idea related to

Murang'a District, Kenya' (Unpublished M.A. Thesis, Carleton University)
Mackenzie, F. 1986. 'Land and labour: women and men in agricultural change. Murang'a District, Kenya, 1880–1984' (Ph.D dissertation, University of Ottowa)
Mackenzie, F. and Taylor, D.R.F. 1985. Scale and the question of rural development in Africa, *African Urban Quarterly*, vol. 1, no. 1.
Marris, P. and Somerset, A. 1971. *African businessmen* (London: Routledge)
Mars, T. and White, G. (eds) 1986. 'Developmental states and African agriculture', *IDS bulletin*, vol. 17/1.
Okoth-Ogendo, H.W.O. 1981. 'Land ownership and distribution in Kenya's large farm areas'. In T. Killick (ed.) *Papers on the Kenyan economy* (London: Heinemann)
Pala, A.O. 1980. 'Daughters of the lakes and rivers: colonisation and the land rights of Luo women'. In M. Etienne and E. Leacock (eds), *Women and colonization* (New York: Praeger)
Pala, A.O., Reynolds, J.E. Wallis, M.A.H. and Browne, D.L. 1975: 'The Women's Group Programme in the SRDP', *Occasional Paper, no. 13*, Institute of Development Studies, University of Nairobi.
Sacks, K., 1982. *Sisters and wives: the past and future of sexual equality. (Chicago: University of Illinois Press)*
Sandbrook, R. 1982. *The politics of basic needs* (Toronto: University of Toronto Press)
Sandbrook, R. 1986. The state and economic stagnation in tropical Africa, *World Development*, vol. 14/3, pp. 319–32.
Soja, E.W. 1980. The socio-spatial dialectic, *Annals of the Association of American Geographers*, vol. 70, pp. 207–25.
Smith, L.D. 1976. 'An overview of agricultural development policy'. In J. Heyer, J.K. Maitha and W.M. Senga (eds), *Agricultural Development in Kenya: an economic assessment* (Nairobi: Oxford University Press)
Smock, A. 1977. 'Women's education and roles in Kenya', *Working Paper no. 316* (Institute of Development Studies, University of Nairobi)
Sorrenson, M.P.K. 1967. *Land reform in Kikuyu country* (Nairobi: Oxford University Press)
Stamp, P. 1975/6, Perception of change and economic strategy among Kikuyu women of Mitero, Kenya, *Rural Africana* vol. 29, pp. 19–44.
Stohr, W and Taylor, D.R.F. 1981. *Development from above or below; the dialectics of regional planning in developing countries* (Chichester: Wiley)
Taylor, D.R.F. 1966. '*Fort Hall District, Kenya: a geographical consideration of the problems and potential of a developing area*' (Unpublished Ph.D. Thesis, University of Edinburgh)
Taylor, D.R.F. 1985. 'Rural development space in Africa'. In D.B. Knight (ed.), *Coherence in diversity: geographical essays in honour of G.C. Merrill (Ottawa:* Carleton University Press)
Thomas, B.P. 1982. 'Cash, credit, co-operation and community: responses of women's groups to socio-economic change in rural Kenya', *Paper presented at the Harvard/MIT Women in Development Group's Second Annual Workshop on Women, Work and Public Policy.*
Von Pischke, J.D. 1976.'A critical survey of approaches to the role of credit in smallholder development', *Discussion Paper, no. 233*, Institute of Development Studies, University of Nairobi.

Weaver, C. 1984. *Regional development and the local community: planning politics and social context* (Chichester: Wiley)
World Bank, 1983. *Kenya, growth and structural change; An IBRD Country Study* (Washington, D.C.)

Acknowledgement
The comments of Richard Sandbrook on a draft of this paper are gratefully acknowledged.

7

The Problems of Rural Inequality on the Kano River Project, Nigeria

J.M. Baba
Department of Geography, Federal University of Technology, Minna (formerly Ahmadu Bello University, Zaria)

The nature and scope of the problem

The 1970s saw the development of two strategies as the principal routes towards achieving not only better conditions of living in rural Nigeria, but also higher regional equity in the allocation of public investments. The first of these strategies was large-scale irrigation, which gained a clear focus in various states in the Sudan Savanna belt during the Second Development Plan, 1970–4 (Baba 1984). By the Third Development Plan period (1975–80) river basin development had become accepted by the federal government as a medium of regional planning and resource allocation, as well as for achieving development at the grassroots of Nigerian society. Thus by Decree No. 25 of 1976, the country was divided into 11 River Basin Authorities, each charged with the responsibility of generating and managing development projects in its area of jurisdiction.

The second strategy started in 1974 as World Bank integrated rural development projects at two locations: Funtua (in Kaduna State) and Gusau (in Sokoto State), later renamed Agricultural Development Projects (ADPs). This strategy is based on the premise that qualitative changes can be achieved in the rural sector by: (a) increasing agricultural productivity; (b) more equitable income distribution; (c) provision of social, economic and physical infrastructures; and (d) a high level of local participation. Initial positive results in the first years of the ADPs soon led to the replication of the strategy in various locations, including Gombe (1975), Ayangba (1977), Lafiya (1977), Bida (1979), and Ilorin (1980). Indeed, by 1980 the strategy had become adopted, in principle, for application over the entire country. It was partly in pursuit of this goal that a rural development policy was reaffirmed in the Fourth Plan (1981–5) with a view to:

promoting a more rapid development of the rural areas through sustained effort to raise agricultural productivity and provide basic human needs such as hygienic water supply, health facilities, access roads, electricity, etc. ... This strategy will also help to provide a basis for more geographical spread of physical development throughout the country, and help to counterbalance the strong trend towards rural–urban migration.

(*Nigeria 1981, p. 29*)

Various evaluations of both the irrigation projects and ADPs have already been undertaken, with particular emphasis on the social and economic impact of the projects (Baba 1975; 1981; 1983; 1984; Wallace 1979; 1980; 1981; D'Silva and Raza 1980; Mabogunje and Gana 1981). While these studies have yielded valuable information on policy and the social and economic trends in the project areas, not much attention has been focused on the issue of equality. Yet, the question 'What is happening to inequality' is now accepted as critical in the conceptualization and evaluation of development (Seers 1977).

Inequality in this context may be examined at two levels. There is, first, the regional levels within which may be outlined the differences between regions in terms of the spatial pattern of investments or resource allocation and then, second, the community or locality level at which may be seen the different degrees of access which individuals or groups have to benefits and services. Both levels of analysis are important to a full understanding of the impact of a development project. Our focus in this paper is on the latter dimension, not because it is necessarily the more important, but because it is the more easily neglected, as well as the more difficult to measure. The importance of the community level of analysis may also be seen in the fact that the regional allocations of resources actually become functional and acquire relevance to human needs at the level of the community. Hence, this is the level at which the impact of national resource allocation policies may be most meaningfully assessed.

Alhough the indicators of inequality span a wide range of social and economic variables (Coates *et al.* 1977; Smith 1979) we are restricting our analysis to two parameters: (a) land distribution: and (b) income distribution. Although this has arisen from the constraint of available data, it does not impose any serious limitations on the value of the study. Land is central to all rural resources and is the primary means to rural wealth. Its importance as an index of inequality specifically in Hausa rural communities has clearly come out in Hill's detailed studies of the Batagarawa community of the Katsina area and the Dorayi community of the Kano region (Hill 1972; 1977). The improvement of incomes, through improved productivity, is an important goal of the development process. The assumption is that through improved productivity and income an individual or community will become equipped with the means of satisfying basic needs and wants, and thus improving welfare.

Finally, the analysis emphasizes change over time rather than over space. The local scale of the study makes this inevitable. But Smith (pp. 18–19) has rightly stressed the danger of overemphasizing the importance of the spatial dimension in the measurement of inequality, which relates to the broader structure of society, and can therefore be best understood within an interdisciplinary context.

Methodology

Our main data sources are two sets of questionnaires applied at two stages of the Kano River Project (Phase I). The first stage was shortly before the take-off of the Project (in 1971) when the traditional rural economy was still largely intact. The second stage was eight years later (in 1979) when a substantial proportion of the planned change had been executed, and the traditional economy had substantially given way to a modern agricultural economy based on large-scale irrigation. Among other features, the questionnaires at both stages included items on a wide range of economic and social circumstances surrounding the individual respondent, including estimates of holding sizes, incomes, farm inputs and other forms of capital investment.

The sample respondents in the first phase of study comprised 115 farmers located in four village areas of Kura District. These were Kadawa, Kura, Karfi and Dan Hassan. The sample for the second phase, on the other hand, comprised 179 farmers who had already been drawn into modern irrigation in southern Kura District, but particularly in Kadawa and Chiromawa village areas (see Figure 24).

Although it would have been preferable to retain the same sample population for the two stages of the study, this was not practically possible. Eight years is too long a time to keep a sample population of over one hundred respondents intact. In spite of this limitation, however, it is believed that the sample for each stage presented a fair picture of the prevailing socio-economic conditions at the time of study. Comparison of the data for the two stages should therefore give us some idea of what had been happening to the parameters of development during the period.

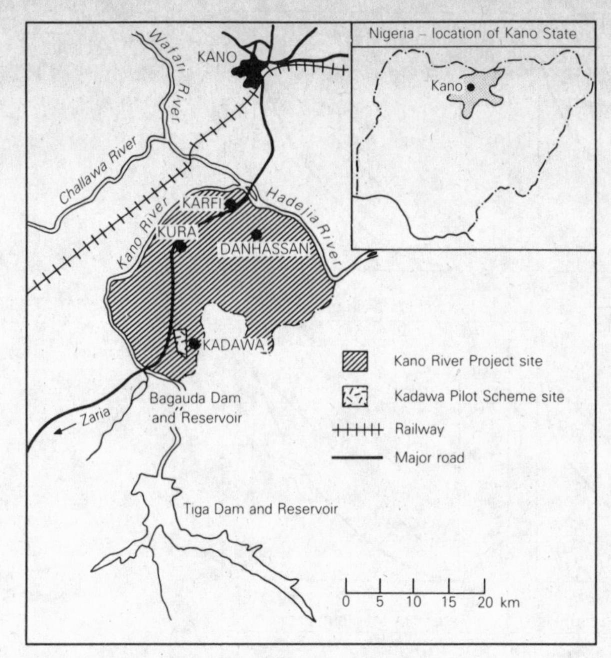

Fig. 24 The Kano River Project, Nigeria

A simple, but logical and informative, method of data analysis has been adopted. It involves the calculation not only of the central tendencies in the distribution of the two parameters chosen (that is, land and incomes), but also of concentration coefficients, using both tabulated percentile coefficients of advantage and Gini coefficients on Lorenz curves. The combination of these statistical measures has produced results which help us to answer the question, at least in part, as to what is happening to inequality within this project area.

Trends in land distribution

Land is the core of rural wealth, because it is the primary factor of production. Attempts to redistribute wealth in rural communities of the world have consequently concentrated on land reforms (de Wilde 1967: Walinsky 1977). But even in development projects where land redistribution has not been an issue, the processes of change have often involved covert alterations in land tenure institutions, as communities react to the opportunities implicit in the projects. Thus, although the policy in the Kano River Irrigation Project has been to reallocate to farmers an equivalent of the land which they held

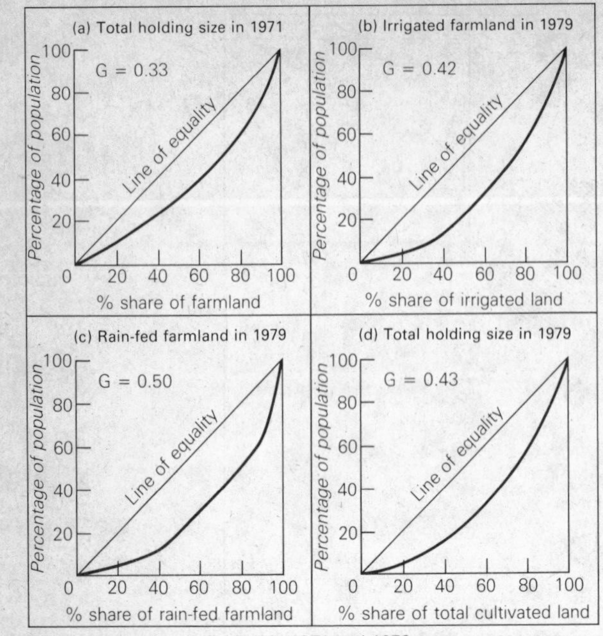

Fig. 25 Lorenz curves showing patterns of land distribution in 1971 and 1979

before irrigation development, the possibilities of new social processes, capable of distorting the traditional pattern of land distribution, are high.

Table 7.1 and Figure 25 summarize the changes in the distribution pattern of land between the base year, 1971, and 1979. The categorization of land into 'irrigated land', 'rain-fed cultivated land', and 'total holding' is important. Irrigated and rain-fed cultivation represent not only different categories of land use, but also different levels of economic opportunities and input requirements, even where physically the land involved is essentially the same. The typical holding now contains both irrigated land and rain-fed land.

Attention may be paid particularly to what is happening at the upper and lower levels of the community, as a way of establishing whether the rich are getting richer and the poor poorer in the distribution of land. The question is whether the concentration of land at the top is on a downward trend, to the advantage of the lower levels. In Table 7.1 it can be seen that in 1971 the top 10 per cent held 19.6 per cent of the land having a coefficient of advantage of 2. The bottom 10 per cent on the other hand, held only 2.4 per cent of the land.

Table 7.1 Patterns of land distribution, 1971 and 1979

% of population (1)	Share of total holding, 1971 (2)		Share of irrigated land, 1979 (3)		Share of rain-fed land, 1979 (4)		Share of total holdings, 1979 (5)		Coefficients of Advantage* in respect of:			
	Ha	*% Total*	*Ha*	*% Total*	*Ha*	*% Total*	*Ha*	*% Total*	*(2)*	*(3)*	*(4)*	*(5)*
Upper 10	49.2	19.6	115.4	34.4	168.4	35.7	251.8	33.2	2.0	3.4	3.6	3.3
Upper 20	91.8	36.5	159.1	47.4	234.8	49.7	366.8	48.4	1.8	2.4	2.5	2.4
Upper 30	124.0	49.4	194.3	57.9	284.6	60.3	445.7	58.8	1.7	1.9	2.0	2.0
Upper 40	156.4	62.3	223.5	66.6	325.1	68.9	515.4	68.0	1.6	1.7	1.7	1.7
Upper 50	181.1	72.1	251.0	74.8	387.0	82.0	572.9	75.6	1.4	1.5	1.6	1.5
Upper 60	202.7	80.7	274.5	81.8	416.6	88.3	622.7	82.2	1.4	1.4	1.5	1.4
Upper 70	220.3	87.7	295.1	87.9	437.2	92.6	666.0	87.9	1.3	1.3	1.3	1.3
Upper 80	235.5	93.8	312.6	93.1	454.3	96.2	704.9	93.1	1.2	1.2	1.2	1.2
Upper 90	245.2	97.6	326.3	97.2	467.2	99.0	735.6	97.1	1.1	1.1	1.1	1.1
Upper 100	251.2	100.0	335.6	100.0	472.1	100.0	757.5	100.0	1.0	1.0	1.0	1.0

* Coefficient of Advantage is obtained by dividing corresponding % values under (2) – (5) by values under (1).

Source: Author's fieldwork, 1971 and 1979.

Nearly half of the land (49.4 per cent) was concentrated in the hands of the top 30 per cent of the sample population, while the bottom 30 per cent held only 12.3 per cent. These figures suggest a land distribution pattern that was inequitable prior to the development project, even if the degree of inequality may not be comparable to what is known elsewhere in the world. Figure 25 shows that the distribution pattern had a Gini coefficient of 0.33 on the Lorenz Curve.

Table 7.1 shows a significant change in the distribution of land during the period under study, with a tendency towards higher inequality. For example, in 1979 the top ten per cent held 34.4 per cent of the irrigated land (with a Coefficient of Advantage of 3.4) while the bottom ten per cent held 2.8 per cent. Also, nearly half of the land (47.4 per cent) was held by the top 20 per cent, while the bottom 30 per cent held only 12.1 per cent (Column 3).

Very similar results have been obtained for rain-fed cultivated land. Whereas 35.7 per cent was held by the top ten per cent (Coefficient of Advantage = 3.6) only one per cent of the land was held by the bottom ten per cent. Also, whereas about 50 per cent of the land was held by the top 20 per cent, only 7.4 per cent of the land was held by the bottom 30 per cent of the farmers (Column 4). As would be expected, the picture is the same when the total holding (that is irrigated plus rain-fed cultivated land) is considered. A movement of the average size of holding from 2.2 ha in 1971 to 4.73 ha in 1979 can be seen primarily as the effect of multi-cropping, implicit in irrigation development (Column 5).

The foregoing results clearly show worsening inequality in the distribution of land in the first eight years of the Kano River Irrigation Project. Figure 25 gives a graphical representation of this trend. Thus, whereas the distribution of land in 1971 had a Gini coefficient of 0.33, this value had gone up to 0.42 for irrigated land, 0.50 for rain-fed land and 0.43 for total holding size, in 1979. The results are symptomatic of the emergence of new social and economic forces within this area with the coming of large-scale irrigation. This is not surprising: irrigation generally represents the extension of production possibilities and, hence, a means towards the maximization of profits in a quasi-capitalist environment. The means of production has thus become the object of speculation, giving rise to different forms of transaction and a new distribution pattern – a process in which the wealthier members of the community are at an advantage.

Table 7.2 reveals the relative importance of various forms of land right in 1971 and 1979. Although the table shows a preponderance of inheritance in both years, the percentage of the land held under this

Table 7.2 Relative importance of different categories of land rights, 1971 and 1979

Category of right	Occurrence (by per cent of land involved)	
	1971	*1979*
Inheritance (*gado*)	67.9	62.0
Purchase (*saye*)	26.7	20.0
Lease/Loan (*aro*)	5.0	16.8
Pledge (*jingina*)	0.4	1.2
Total	100.0	100.0

Source: Fieldwork, 1971 and 1979

right had declined slightly in 1979. Whereas purchased land had declined, leased or loaned land had substantially increased. This situation at first looks surprising. Purchase which gives permanent usufructuary rights should normally be preferred to lease or loan which gives only temporary rights of use. Indeed, the bulk of those respondents who had acquired land between 1971 and 1979 would have preferred acquisition by purchase. However, the new expectations raised by irrigation had led to a general reluctance among the farmers to dispose permanently of land during these transitional years. Hence, although there was a high degree of land mobility, this was along the lines of leasing, loans and pledging.

An item in the questionnaire for the second phase of study sought further details on the issue of land transactions. This was a question directed to find out the proportion of the respondents who had disposed of any land within the period of study, in addition to such other details as the types of land involved, the nature of the transactions and the reasons for the disposal. Some of the respondents had disposed of land within the period. A total of 37 persons and 61.9 ha were involved, of which 43.5 ha (70.3 per cent) were rain-fed upland while 18.4 ha (19.7 per cent) were irrigated. Table 7.3 summarizes the main modes of transaction, while Table 7.4 summarizes the main reasons for the transactions. The single most important mode was lease or loan, followed by sale and pledging.

The most important reason adduced was the need to raise money for emergencies, followed by labour shortage. The first suggests that land is increasingly becoming a medium of capital flow within the community, as well as the basis for new social relations between the various strata. As mentioned earlier, the wealthier members of the community are generally at the receiving end of land transactions.

Table 7.3 Modes of land disposal (n = 37)

Category of transaction	Incidence	
	No. of hectares	*Percent of total*
By sale (*sayarwa*)	24.9	40.2
By lease/loan (*aro*)	33.0	53.3
By pledge (*jingina*)	3.2	5.2
By gift (*kyauta*)	0.8	1.3
Total	61.9	100.0

Source: Fieldwork, 1979

Table 7.4 Reasons for disposing of land (n = 37)

Reason	Incidence	
	No. of respondents	*Percentage of total*
1 To raise money for other emergencies	14	37.8
2 Land held is in excess of available labour	12	32.4
3 To raise money for farm inputs	2	5.4
4 Others	9	24.3
Total	37	99.9

Source: Fieldwork, 1979

They are able to raise capital, not only to meet the high input demands of irrigation agriculture, but also to expand their holdings through purchases, leases and pledges. But observations in the field also showed that a proportion of those who had made acquisitions of land had come from urban Kano, including employees of the project management, suggesting a new and important dimension in the rural-urban relationships. The critical question arising from this is: will such projects ultimately become a stage for rural-urban competition, and a means towards greater rural-urban inequality?

The answers to these questions, as well as the ultimate outcome of the processes which have been outlined above can now only be speculated. These speculations are reserved for the concluding section.

Trends in income distribution

Incomes are normally difficult to measure in rural social surveys, partly because enquiries about them easily generate suspicion. There is also a lack of comprehensive information on the sources of cash flow. Next is the problem of memory lapse (in the absence of records) even when the respondent is willing to provide information. Yet incomes provide an important quantitative parameter by which the production goals of development projects may be measured, and also by which trends in inequality may be monitored.

In spite of the difficulties of obtaining data, therefore, efforts were made to gather information on incomes. In 1971 emphasis was put on the cash derived from the sale of farm products during the preceding season (the 1970/1 growing season). In 1979, however, emphasis was put on the savings which were made on individual holdings during the previous year (i.e. 1978). While the former stands for gross farm income, the latter stands for net farm income. Neither, however, stands for total income as the non-farm sources have not been considered. But in spite of the limitations, the available information gives indications of trends not only in terms of the changing level of incomes but also in its distribution among the population.

Table 7.5 (column 2) shows the farm cash income distribution shortly before the onset of the development programme. The mean farm cash income of N75.00 pointed to the general poverty in the area. But there was also an initial state of inequality. Whereas 36.9 per cent of the income was concentrated in the hands of ten per cent

Table 7.5 Distribution of farm cash incomes and farm savings, 1971 and 1978

% of Population (1)	Share of farm cash income. 1971 (2)		Share of farm cash savings. 1978 (3)		Coefficients of Advantage* (4)	
	Amount	*% of total*	*Amount*	*% of total*	*(1) & (2)*	*(1) & (3)*
Upper 10	3,180	36.9	22,310	45.3	3.7	4.5
Upper 20	4,984	57.8	30,010	61.0	2.9	3.1
Upper 30	6,020	69.8	35,335	71.8	2.3	2.4
Upper 40	6,812	79.0	39,400	80.0	2.0	2.0
Upper 50	7,350	85.2	42,605	86.5	1.7	1.7
Upper 60	7,844	90.9	45,300	92.0	1.5	1.5
Upper 70	8,174	94.8	47,170	95.8	1.4	1.4
Upper 80	8,434	97.8	48,538	98.6	1.2	1.2
Upper 90	8,592	99.6	49,227	100.0	1.1	1.1
Upper 100	8,626	100.0	49,227	100.0	1.0	1.0

* Coefficient of Advantage is obtained by dividing corresponding % values under (2) and (3) by values under (1).
Source: Author's fieldwork, 1971 and 1979.

of the population (Coefficient of advantage = 3.7) only 0.4 per cent of the income was shared by the bottom ten per cent. Further, about 70 per cent of the income was shared by the top 30 per cent of the population, while only 5.2 per cent was held by the bottom 30 per cent. The grossness of this initial inequality is shown graphically in Figure 26(a). The Lorenz curve shows a distribution pattern with a Gini coefficient of 0.58, which by any standard can be rated high. The question arises therefore, as to the extent to which the Project has been a means towards more equitable income distribution.

Table 7.5 (column 3) gives the distribution of net farm cash incomes (savings) in 1978. The mean income had risen by at least 338 per cent from the 1971 level[1], owing to the new high output levels associated with irrigation development. An implication of this is a substantially improved purchasing power and strong potentials for the improvement of personal welfare. But, on the other hand, the problem of inequality was far from redressed. Rather it has been aggravated. Thus the top ten per cent of the sample controlled 45·3 per cent of the net farm savings, while the bottom ten per cent recorded no savings at all. While the top 30 per cent controlled 71·8 per cent of the savings (coefficient of advantage = 2·4), the bottom 30 per cent shared only 4·2 per cent. In Figure 26 (b), the Gini coefficient can be seen to have risen to 0·62. This trend is not surprising. It is a logical outcome of the growing inequality of land distribution and other factors of production. It suggests that a significant positive correlation may be expected between size of holding and farm cash incomes.

The problem of income inequality is complex, being an outcome of the mutual interaction of various factors of production, including labour. A development project which entrenches inequality in the initial distribution of any factor is therefore likely to intensify the

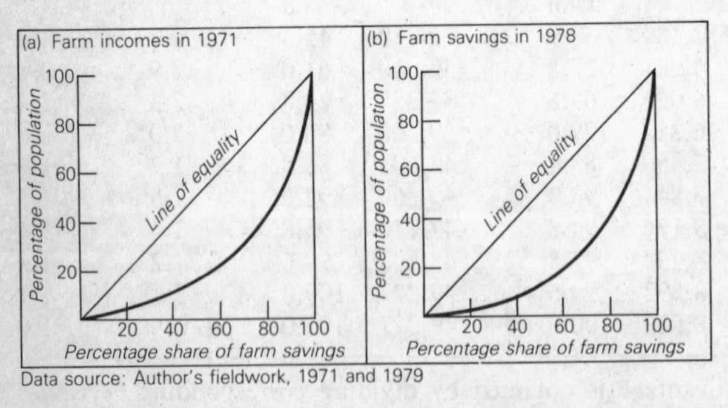

Fig. 26 Lorenz curves showing the distribution of farm incomes (1971) and farm savings (1979)

problem in respect not only of that factor but of related factors as well. The prevailing policy in the Project under study entrenches the initial inequality in land distribution and access to capital. The latter dimension derives from the lack of viable modern credit institutions which would give effective access to capital for all farmers and, hence, curb the tendency to increase the gap between the rich and the poor.

Wider implications

The relevance of this analysis goes beyond the experience of one project. The results are a reflecton of the situation not only in similar irrigation projects but also in the country's Agricultural Development Projects. In the former, the experience in the Bakolori Project, in Sokoto State, is fairly well documented. In an evaluation of the impact of this project, Etuk and Abalu (1982) have reported the under-utilization of land and, hence, the shortfall of actual yields below potential yields for most crops. This they have attributed to several factors, including the practice whereby poor farmers either rent out their land to richer farmers or leave it under fallow.

In the same vein, Igbozurike and Diatchavbe (1982) have examined the social cost of the same project and have noted the fact that 'most of the land is now in the hands of land speculators, teachers and civil servants and not necessarily in the hands of either the original owners or tenant farmers' (p. 349). According to them, the small and poor farmers 'lost ownership through cajoled sale, renting and letting out of their farms'. This corroborates Wallace's (1980, p. 68) earlier observation that at Bakolori 'small farmers are already selling land cheaply to schoolteachers, businessmen in Gusau, Sokoto and Gombe – maybe because they have gone so deeply into debt.'

The picture in the Agricultural Development Projects is not necessarily different. Indeed, policy has been designed deliberately to favour the 'big farmer' who enjoys easier access to such inputs as loans, fertilizers and extension services (Wallace 1980; D'Silva and Raza 1980; Mabogunje and Gana 1981) and thus fuelling the propensity for the rich to get richer and the poor, poorer. It is now also common knowledge that more and more of the 'big farmers' are located in the urban centres.

Thus, from these examples, it is clear that the experience of the Kano River Project (Phase I), is not unique. Several issues can therefore be raised from the trends which we have established in our analysis, and which are relevant to the major rural development strategies in Nigeria. Four of these issues are considered to be of primary importance. They are posed as questions: (a) Development for whom? (b) Development by whom? (c) What technological choice? and (d) What direction of policy?

Development for whom?

This question naturally arises from the results of our analysis. Among other features, the development process is normally concerned with the elimination of poverty and the mitigation of inequality in society (Seers 1977; Stohr and Taylor 1981). This implies a concern not only for the rural sector, but also for the poorer members of the rural community.

With growing inequality in the access to land and income in the Kano River Project area, and in related projects in the country, there is evidence to suggest the growing marginalization of the poorer segment of the rural community. Although this has been a strong tendency in such an apparently successful project as the Gezira of the Sudan Republic (Barnett 1981), it is nevertheless a negation of the basic principles of the development process. What is needed is redirection of policy in a way that focuses on the poorer segments of society in the provision of access to productive resources.

In the same vein, these projects are designed to benefit primarily the rural population, and to act as a means towards reducing existing rural-urban inequality. With the ample evidence of encroachment on rural land by urban residents, a major objective of the development process also becomes endangered. The greater this urban encroachment, the greater will be the tendency towards rural marginalization. The rural-urban dimension of the problem is therefore yet another area needing policy redirection.

Development by whom?

Current rural development theory holds that adequate local participation in decision-making is a means towards achieving the objectives of the development process (Lele 1975). This notion is an important aspect of the concept of 'development from below' which 'considers development to be based primarily on maximum mobilization of each area's natural, human, and institutional resources with the primary objective being the satisfaction of the basic needs of the inhabitants of that area' (Stohr and Taylor 1981, p. 1).

Although our data does not cover the institutional arrangements of project management, it is now common knowledge that the local farmers have hitherto had little say in the process of decision-making. The concentration of power in the hands of urban-based bureaucrats and the alienation of the rural population from the processes of decision-making can be seen as strong factors facilitating the unequal opportunities of access to productive resources. The arrest of growing inequality thus becomes also an issue of creating appropriate institutional structures for more active participation by the local population in the processes of decision-making.

What technological choice?

It has been suggested elsewhere (Igbozurike and Diatchavbe 1982) that large-scale irrigation and imported technologies are naturally unsuited to Nigeria's rural social milieu, and therefore have the potential to disorganize society and negate the goals of development. This argument may be further stretched to state that growing inequality is a manifestation of societal disorganization and a negation of the goals of development.

Should the argument be valid, the problem of inequality in project areas becomes inevitable and, perhaps, irredeemable as long as the technological choice is upheld. While the disruptive influences of alien technologies may not be denied, however, it is also true that modifications in the cultural milieu as well as in the technology itself are possible. With such appropriate modifications, not only can an alien technology be accommodated but full advantage can also be taken of the benefits proceeding from it.

It can therefore be safely concluded that inequality persists primarily because of the failure to adapt the chosen technologies to the cultural milieu or to achieve appropriate modifications of the latter, or, indeed, both. This, once again, takes us to the realm of policy.

What direction of policy?

From the foregoing discussion the central importance of policy stands out. Policy is the key by which the course and mode of change may be determined. The issue of persistent inequality in these development projects must therefore be seen primarily as a problem of policy failure, or of lack of appropriate policies. In the context of this study, the key issue is the need for effective policy towards achieving not only an increase in rural wealth, through improved production, but also a narrower gap between the rich and the poor. But to ensure improved production goes beyond the provision of irrigation and other physical infrastructures, it demands effective access to the means of production. Policies on land distribution are therefore of paramount importance.

Specific issues arising from the present trends of the distribution and mobility of land include: (a) how effective access may be guaranteed to the poor farmer; and (b) how the rural population may be shielded against urban encroachers and speculators.

The first issue goes beyond sheer physical access. Indeed, more important than this is access to the resources which would make the land productive. The absence of these resources (particularly capital) accounts for the increasing rate of land leases both among the farmers themselves and between them, on the one hand, and urban encroachers, on the other. The issue of effective access to land thus becomes one of creating appropriate institutions which would facilitate the flow of capital and financial resources to all strata of society. Appropriate institutional provisions would also facilitate participation of farmers in the processes of decision-making. Strong farmer cooperatives would be both appropriate and effective.

As for the second issue, while enterprising urban residents should be encouraged to participate in agricultural production, that process must not be permitted to marginalize the rural population. Appropriate policies in both the rural and urban sectors can help to prevent rural marginalization. At the rural front, the registration of land ownership as well as the documentation for all transactions may inhibit urban encroachment. There may also be room for expropriation and redistribution of land where farmers demonstrate their inability to cope with the amount of land they hold.

Finally, there is the possibility of creating more non-farm employment opportunities in both urban and rural centres, to act as absorbers of the rural labour which may become displaced from land for whatever reason. The diversification of products and increased output within these project areas particularly establish strong possibilities for agro-allied industries in the rural areas.

With policies such as these, rural development through either large-scale irrigation projects or agricultural development projects would focus on the elimination of poverty and the mitigation of inequality.

Conclusion

This study has shown some evidence of worsening inequality in the Kano River Project (Phase I) area, using data on the distribution of land and farm cash incomes. Although the Project has brought more wealth into the area (with increased farm incomes between 1971 and 1979) the worsening distribution of both land and incomes negates an important objective of the development process – the objective of mitigating inequality. The results have been shown to point to the need for policy redirection in ways that would ensure not only increasing rural wealth through improved production, but also, the narrowing of the gap between the rich and poor, on the one hand, and the rural and urban sectors, on the other.

Finally, this study, in spite of its shortcomings, is of methodological and utilitarian importance. It points not only to the need to monitor the impact of rural development projects on inequality, but also presents a procedure by which the evaluation may be made. Of central importance is the gathering of data on parameters of societal welfare in project areas, at regular intervals, with a view to monitoring change. But for future research there will be a need to develop a more comprehensive set of parameters than we have been constrained to use in this study. Reviews of policies should also normally be made where inequality persists and, even more so, where it is on the increase.

Note

1 From ₦75.00 in 1971 (mean cash income) to ₦328.20 in 1978 (mean cash savings). Although this direct comparison may be questioned on methodological grounds, the increase in mean disposable incomes must have been greater.

References

Baba, J. M. 1975. 'Induced agricultural change in a densely populated district: a study of the existing agricultural system in Kura District and the projected impact of the Kano River Irrigation Project, Kano State, Nigeria' (Unpublished Ph.D. Thesis, Ahmadu Bello University, Zaria)

Baba, J.M. 1981. Large-scale irrigation development in Nigeria: the constraint of labour, *The Nigerian Journal of Agricultural Extension*, vol. 1, no. 1, pp. 44–57.

Baba, J.M. 1983. Rationalising rural settlements for large-scale irrigation development: the case of the Kano River Project Phase I, Kano State, Nigeria, *Aman: (Journal of Society, Culture and Environment)* (Centre for Social, Cultural and Environmental Research, University of Benin), vol. III, no. 1.

Baba, J.M. 1984. Developing rural Nigeria through capital-intensive irrigation projects: a critique, *Journal of Issues in Development* (Centre for Social and Economic Research, Ahmadu Bello University) vol. 1, no. 1. (June), pp. 1–17.

Barnett, T. 1981. 'Evaluating the Gezira Scheme: Black Box or Pandora's Box'. In J. Heyer *et al.* (eds) *Rural development in Tropical Africa* (London: Macmillan, pp. 306–24)

Coates, B.E., Johnston, R.J. and Knox, P.L. 1977. *Geography and inequality*, (Oxford: Oxford University Press)

D'Silva, B.C. and Raza, M.R. 1980. Integrated rural development in Nigeria: the Funtua Project, *Food Policy*, vol. 5, no. 4, pp. 282–97.

Etuk, E.G. and Abalu, G.O.I. 1982. 'River basin development in Northern Nigeria: a case study of the Bakolori Project', *Fourth Afro-Asian Regional Conference of International Commission on Irrigation and Drainage* (Lagos), vol. II, pp. 335–46.

Nigeria 1981. *Guidelines for the Fourth National Development Plan 1981–5* (Lagos)

Hill, P. 1972. *Rural Hausa: a village and a setting* (Cambridge: Cambridge University Press)

Hill, P. 1977. *Population, prosperity and poverty: rural Kano 1900 and 1960* (Cambridge: Cambridge University Press)

Igbozurike, M. and Diatchavbe O. 1982. 'The social cost of irrigation: the case of Bakolori', *Fourth Afro-Asian Regional Conference of International Commission on Irrigation and Drainage* (Lagos), vol. II, pp. 347–52.

Lele, U. 1975. *The design of rural development: lessons from Africa*, (Baltimore: World Bank/The John Hopkins University Press)

Mabogunje, A.L. and Gana, J.A. 1981. 'Rural development in Nigeria: case study of the Funtua integrated rural development project, Kaduna State, Nigeria', *UNCRD Project 509/80* (Nagoya, Japan: The United Nations Centre for Regional Development)

Seers, D. 1977. The meaning of development, *International Development Review*, no. 3, p. 3.

Smith, D.M. 1979. *Where the grass is greener: living in an unequal world*, (Harmondsworth: Pelican Books)

Stohr, W.B. and D.R.F. Taylor (eds) 1981. 'Introduction', *Development from above or below? The dialectics of regional planning in developing countries* (Chichester John Wiley)

Walinsky, L.J. 1977. *Agrarian reform as unfinished business: the selected papers of Wolf Ladejinsky*, (Oxford: Oxford University Press)

Wallace, T. 1979. 'Rural development through irrigation: studies in a town on the Kano River Project', *Research Report no. 3*, (Centre for Social and Economic Research, Ahmadu Bello University, Zaria)

Wallace, T. 1980. Agriculture projects and land in Northern Nigeria, *Review of African Political Economy* vol. 17, pp. 59–70.

Wallace, T. 1981. 'The Kano River Project, Nigeria: the impact of an irrigation scheme on productivity and welfare' In J. Heyer, P. Roberts and G. Williams (eds) *Rural development in Tropical Africa* (London: Macmillan, pp. 281–305)

Wilde, de J.C. 1967. *Experiences with agricultural development in Tropical Africa*, vol. II (The case studies) (Baltimore: John Hopkins/IBRD)

8

Access to Land and Farm Income in Botswana

J.W. Arntzen
Institute for Environmental Studies, Free University, Amsterdam
and R.M.K. Silitshena
Department of Environmental Science, University of Botswana

Introduction

This case study deals with Botswana which is a large country with a small population (Figure 27). The case study shows how inequalities in access to land and farm income can be generated and perpetrated by a number of factors, some of which have their roots in the past. It also shows, among other things, how these inequalities can be exacerbated by government policies.

The paper is divided into six parts. The first part is the background, which seeks to provide the context in which the inequalities in access to land and farm income exist. Topics treated in this section are population and its structure, the physical environment, the agricultural systems, the structure of the economy, socio-economic groups, settlement and land use in rural areas, and institutional arrangements. The second part defines access to land in the context of Botswana; it treats determinants to access to land and looks in detail at both arable and livestock farming in this respect. The third part looks at access to farm income. The fourth section reviews five of the crucial government policies in this area. The fifth section deals with impending land shortage; in particular it looks at the causes and effects. The last part is the conclusion.

In this paper we address ourselves to the situation in communal lands, which account for 71 per cent of all land. Two other forms of land tenure are state land, accounting for 23 per cent of the land, most of it comprising national parks and game reserves, and freehold, which accounts for the remaining six per cent of the land and is found in areas that were formerly reserved for European occupation (Figure 28). Freehold land has been omitted from the discussion. However,

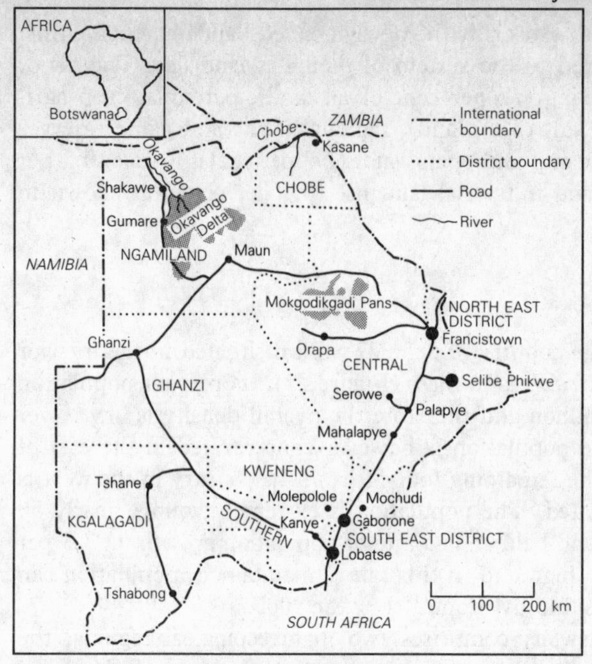

Fig. 27 Botswana: position, districts and major settlements

Fig. 28 Botswana: land use circa 1985

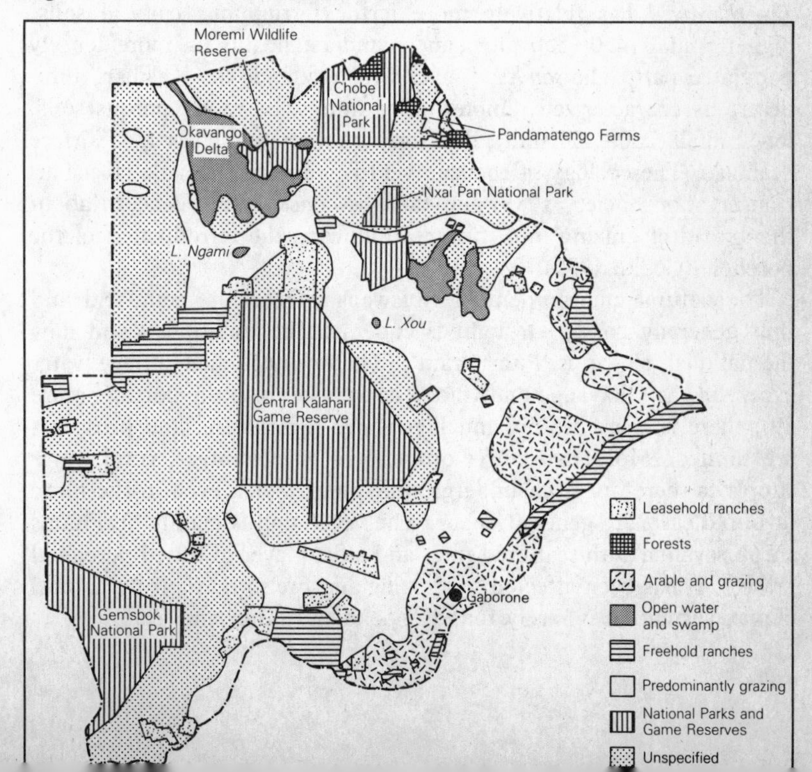

access to state land, especially the newly created Pandamatenga farms, is included. Aligned to the system of tenure is land use. The major land uses are grazing (77 per cent of all land), perennial crop agriculture (two per cent of all land), national parks and game reserves (17.5 per cent), swamp and open water (2.7 per cent), forests (0.5 per cent) and urban and industrial land use (0.1 per cent), as shown in Figure 28.

A background

Botswana is a large country of 585,227 sq km situated in the interior of the southern African land mass (Figure 27). Its present population is just over one million and therefore the overall density is low. Over 80 per cent of the population is however concentrated in the east of the country and the remaining four-fifths of the country in the west is very thinly populated. The population is extremely young, nearly 50 per cent aged 14 and below. The rate of population growth, at 3.3 per cent per annum is high and, if this rate is maintained, population can be expected to double by around the year 2000.

Physically, Botswana comprises two main ecological regions, the *hardveld* in the eastern part of the country and the *sandveld* in the west; the latter covers about four-fifths of the country (Figure 29). The *hardveld* has relatively more fertile ferruginous tropical soils, higher rainfall (450–550 mm), and is understandably the more densely populated part. The *sandveld*, over which extends the Kalahari semi-desert, is characterized, among other things, by sandy porous soils, low rainfall (250–450 mm), high evaporation rates and lack of surface drainage. The ecology of the sandveld is considered fragile (Kalahari Conservation Society 1983) and there is consequently concern about the spread of grazing into this area following the introduction of the borehole (Cooke 1985).

The natural environment of Botswana is therefore semi-arid and thus generally harsh. Drought is endemic: the traditional, and now the national, slogan is 'Pula' ('rain'). There is not much surface water except in the Okavango and Chobe river systems in the north (Figure 29); there is therefore not much irrigated agriculture, and prospects are limited. More than three-quarters of the country's rural water supply is therefore from underground water. Soils, even in the more favoured east, are generally poor. The vegetation is mainly deciduous shrub savanna with scattered trees and a field layer of tufted perennial grasses. It has been affected by grazing and fire so that a truly natural climax vegetation is rarely found (Cooke and Silitshena 1986).

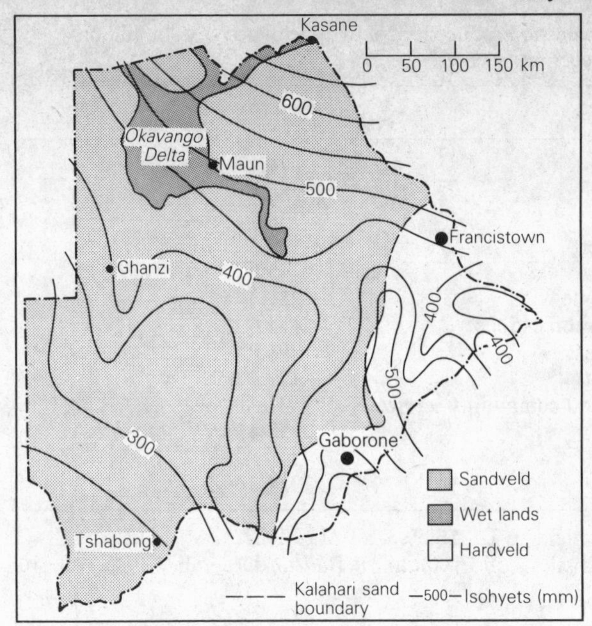

Fig. 29 Botswana: ecological regions and rainfall

Climate is, however, the major determining factor of economic activities. It is generally unfavourable; being characterized, among other things, by high daytime temperatures (mean maxima in summer 30–35°C and in winter 20–25°C) which cause high rates of evaporation and transpiration; and a highly seasonal, variable and unreliable rainfall. The rainfall varies from 650 mm in the north to 250 mm in the south and 500 mm in the east. The country is consequently drought-prone. Given this climatic background, agriculture, especially crop farming, is a very risky business. Prolonged droughts however, do also affect livestock farming. Dry land arable agriculture is potentially economic in only five per cent of the country and is generally not the most attractive proposition.

Table 8.1 shows the gross domestic product (GDP) in 1982/3. The dominance of the mining sector, contributed mainly by the three diamond mines, is obvious. The manufacturing sector is small. Although the mining sector accounts for nearly 80 per cent of exports it employs only six per cent of the 117,100 employed in the formal sector (1985 figures). The remaining estimated 400,000 active labour force have to derive their living from traditional agriculture.

Traditional agriculture is composed of livestock (mainly cattle) farming and subsistence crop farming. In 1984 there were an estimated

Table 8.1 Gross Domestic Product 1982/3 by type of activity (in million Pula* at current prices)

Activity	GDP
Agriculture	74.1
Mining and quarrying	286.4
Manufacturing	78.7
Electricity and water	29.7
Construction	45.0
Wholesale, retail trade	225.3
Transport and communications	30.6
Financial institutions	98.0
General government	171.4
Household, social and community services	37.5
Dummy sector	–52.4
Total	1024.3

* One Pula is equivalent to US $0.59 as of May 1987.
Source: Central Statistics Office; *Statistical Bulletin* December 1985, vol. 10 no. 4, p. 5.

2.4 million cattle, the ownership of which was concentrated in a few hands. An agricultural survey in 1983 revealed that 50 per cent of rural households owned 14 per cent of the cattle and the average herd size was about 12. At least 30 per cent of rural households owned no cattle. The top four per cent of the households owned more than 30 per cent of the total national herd (Ministry of Agriculture 1983). Traditional farmers keep cattle for a number of reasons such as draught power, cash and prestige. Their strategy is to accumulate as large a number as possible to minimize losses during the time of drought. The rangelands in communal areas are consequently severely overgrazed.

The major crops grown are sorghum, maize, millet and beans. Agriculture is of the extensive type and there is little use of manure or fertilizer, which accounts for low productivity (about 270 kg per hectare). The other major contributor to this situation is the hostile environment, although unremunerative prices have also been mentioned as a factor (Republic of Botswana 1976). The government is currently concentrating a considerable amount of financial and manpower resources towards arable agriculture in order to create employment and increase incomes in this sector and to achieve national self-sufficiency in cereals (see later in this chapter).

Although there are many ethnic groups found in Botswana, the most dominant is the Tswana group. The Tswana have traditionally been characterized by, among other things, a centralized political system, a stratified society and a preference for nucleated settlements. The chief of the main Tswana group and his relatives formed the top layer of society at the bottom of which were subject tribes, which included Basarwa 'Bushmen' (Schapera 1953). The latter tribes were incorporated into Tswana States in the last century; a process that invariably led to the loss of their land rights. Members of these tribes were treated as serfs by the dominant Tswana. Some of the attitudes towards formerly subject tribes unfortunately still persist.

Land use comprised nucleated settlements called villages or agro-towns, cultivated areas or *lands* and grazing areas known as *cattleposts* (Figure 30). Villages, some of which had populations exceeding 20,000, were centres of the Tswana economy. In the past the locations of these villages used to change frequently as the soil and firewood around became exhausted (Silitshena 1983). Since the early part of this century they have tended to occupy permanent sites because, among other things, of provision of modern facilities such as schools and clinics, use of permanent materials such as brick and corrugated iron in

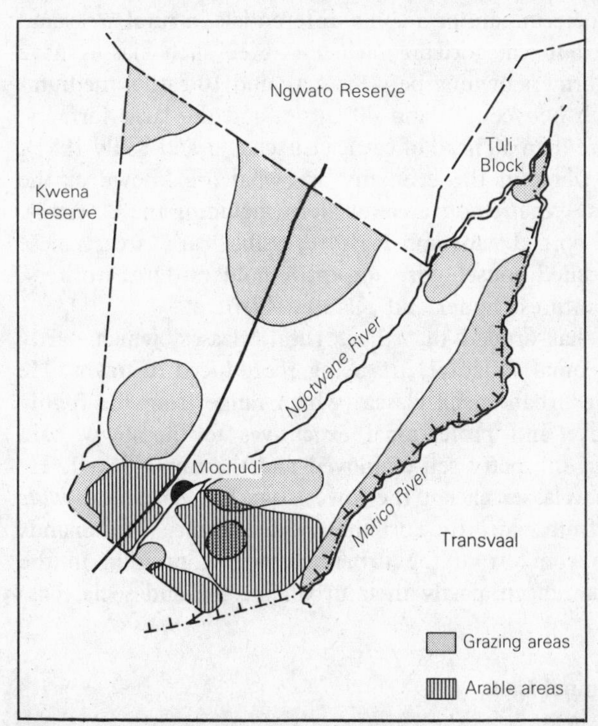

Fig. 30 Sketch map of the Kgatla Reserve

constructing houses and dependence upon assured water supply from boreholes.

Lands were normally found just outside the village boundary. One consequence of the permanence of village sites, in a situation of extensive agriculture, has been an increase in distances between villages and *lands* as the fields near the village became exhausted (Silitshena 1983, p. 86). This increase in distance brought about a system of seasonal movements between villages and *lands*. During the agricultural season people lived in their temporary huts near their fields, moving back to their village homes after harvesting.

The third element in land use was grazing, which normally took place in the distant grazing stations called *cattleposts*. *Cattleposts* were selected on the basis of availability of grass and water. In modern times the use of boreholes to water livestock has made the selection of *cattleposts* more flexible.

Modern rural Botswana is also stratified according to income derived mainly from cattle. The main market for Botswana beef is the EEC and the farmers receive a good price for their cattle. Cattle ownership is thus the main determinant of income differentials in rural areas and is frequently used in categorizing farmers; three such classes have been identified: farmers owning between zero and 10 cattle, medium-sized farmers with between 10 and 40 cattle, and the large farmers, those owning more than 40 head of cattle (Litschauer and Kelly 1981). Those that fare worst in the economy are what are known as the vulnerable groups – the remote area dwellers (including the Basarwa), who live in the more distant and least accessible rural areas; these include female-headed households, non-cattle holders, farm workers, herdboys and destitutes (Egner and Klausen 1980).

Cooper (1982) has argued that these rural 'classes' which partly reflect the pre-colonial situation, are being reproduced in towns. He has identified five urban social classes which range from the highly paid administrative and professional executives to the lowly paid domestic workers, the petty self-employed and the unemployed. He found that all the classes except the lowest one had *lands* and *cattle posts* in the areas from which they originally came. Hence the demands on the land also come from the urbanites, whose position in the agricultural sector reflects partly their urban income and social position.

Access to Communal Land

As already explained we are dealing mostly with communal areas which support around 80 per cent of the population and their activities. The introduction of the Tribal Grazing Land Policy has led to a significant reduction of land under communal terms through the establishment of leasehold ranches on tribal land. This policy and its effects are discussed below.

As Botswana is a large country with a small and scattered population, access to communal land in the strict sense of the word is generally no problem, unlike small countries such as Lesotho or countries where communal areas form a relatively small portion of the total available land. *Every Motswana is in principle able to gain access to land for crop and livestock production.* This generalization, however, deserves qualification.

Table 8.2: Development of human and livestock population

	Human population	Cattle	Smallstock
1964	515,833	1,347,000	
1971	596,944	2,092,000	1,391,000
1981	941,027	2,967,000	761,000

Sources: Human Population: Population Census 1964, 1971, 1981.
Livestock: Agricultural Statistics

Firstly, increased land pressure is now occurring because of increased human population and livestock numbers: both have approximately doubled since independence in 1966 (Table 8.2). Such pressure has already caused widespread land degradation and has started a vicious circle of degradation – lower productivity – extra land needs. Other signs of land shortage observed in the country are:

1 Smaller average herd size and arable allocation in small districts. For example, the land board in South-East District allocates fields of 2·5 hectares compared with 16 hectares in the larger districts (Gulbrandsen 1984). The average herd size of cattle was 15 in 1985 compared with 39 for the entire country (Ministry of Agriculture 1986).
2 Increasing land conflicts. For example, arable encroachment into grazing land is a major concern in Barolong (Gulbrandsen 1984).
3 Increased exclusive use of boreholes by their owners such as in Kgatleng (Peters 1981).

Apart from the increase in human and livestock population, land pressure may regionally and locally be aggravated by mechanization which allows the cultivation of larger areas as in Barolong; and by the reduction in the number of Botswana workers in South African mines, whose numbers have been reduced from a peak of 60,000 in the mid-1970s to about 20,000 at present.

There are various factors that have brought this situation about. Gulbrandsen (1984) rightly points out that land pressure is partly artificial. Old land use claims are usually still respected even though cultivable land may have been out of arable use for a considerable period of time. The land boards have to face (and often acknowledge) claims to allocations that are supposed to have been made prior to their establishment. In addition, they have not yet used their power to set boundaries for the various land use activities and to reallocate arable land which has not been used for at least five years. Unlimited access to land in future will be impossible and is, undoubtedly, undesirable. This calls for effective land use planning in order to minimize conflicts between human activities such as crop damage inflicted by cattle, and to select the 'best' form of land use in view of local ecological conditions and socio-economic needs (see for example Communal Area Research Group, 1984).

Secondly, access to land requires the availability of adequate resources to put the land to productive use. At least one-third of the rural population does not hold cattle and a lower percentage has no arable land; the latter may be due to lack of need to cultivate as a result of better income opportunities elsewhere, or lack of basic means to work the land (Gulbrandsen 1984; Arntzen 1984). The National Migration Survey found that 20 per cent of rural dwellings had no fields while households with working members were less likely to have no cattle but have arable land: 28 per cent versus 40 per cent (Kerven 1982). In other words, the availability of better employment opportunities elsewhere affects participation in crop production. Cattle form an important interaction between livestock and crop production in this respect. Animal draught power is an important means (and constraint) for cultivation. As we have pointed out before, the possibility of using scarce labour for both livestock and crop production, is an important impetus for mixed farming by resource-poor farmers. Another important factor is that where there is land pressure and associated land degradation, additional resources are required to reach the same level of production. Extra efforts are needed, for example, to supply cattle with grass, fodder and water; at the same time, exclusive use of such resources by owners is becoming more common. Formal or informal socio-cultural systems to pool such resources have weakened at the expense of the resource-poor households (Peters 1981). Resource availability, in summary, does not only determine the level of land-based activities but also, (and more importantly, in future) actual participation in or dropping out of such activities.

Beyond the *cattlepost* zone was the hunting zone. Within the hunting zone also lived subject tribes. Land here and its occupants were parcelled out to Tswana royals and favoured commoners. 'The low status groups were required to provide tribute in the form of meat, skins and other goods to the Tswana. In addition, they worked as guides for hunting parties and as servants in the camps of hunting parties' (Hitchcock and Holm 1985, p. 8). These groups, particularly the Basarwa who compose about 3.6 per cent of Botswana's population (Hitchcock and Holm 1985), are the most disadvantaged with limited access to land. They and their children could be 'owned' and passed down by generations of Tswana families (Hitchcock and Holm 1985). With the creation of commercial farms in Ghanzi (see Figure 27) and the spread of *cattleposts* to this area, the denial of Basarwa land rights was almost complete. Those who continued to live in these areas provided cheap labour to European or Tswana farmers.

Land use in Botswana right up to the colonial period was characterized by this division into almost exclusive but interlinked zones. Cattle, except the draught oxen, were not allowed in the *lands* areas during the agricultural season. No ploughing was allowed at *cattleposts* and every man had to have a permanent home in the village (Schapera 1943). This system of land use was organized by the traditional institutions – the chief and his various subordinates – which applied the rules rigidly (Schapera 1943).

Since independence in 1966 the functions of land allocation and management have been transferred to newly created statutory institutions called land boards. Land boards, which started operating in 1970, are composed of representatives of government, district councils and traditional institutions. In the absence of cadastral maps, land boards have, of necessity, to rely on the local headmen when they allocate the land. There have been complaints against land boards which include poor record-keeping, and poor knowledge of the relevant laws and procedures (Noppen 1982).

The new institutions do not appear to be as effective as the chiefs they have replaced in separating arable from grazing. Other social and economic changes have contributed to this situation. Firstly, the shortage of young male labour resulting from schooling and employment in urban areas have made it necessary for the households with few cattle, which cannot afford to pay a herder at the *cattlepost*, to keep their livestock in the *lands* (Kooijman 1978). Secondly, however, the *lands* in some cases are so distant that it is uneconomic or virtually impossible to operate from the village (Silitshena 1983). Thirdly, the government is now providing schools and health services in the *lands* and *cattleposts* and thus further reducing the pull of villages (Silitshena 1983). As a result the neat separation of land use is no more, as land use is increasingly mixed (see Figure 31).

Thirdly, large regional differences in access to land exist. For example, shortage of land has been a serious problem in small districts such as South East and North East Districts since the 1940s (Schapera 1943) and attempts to acquire additional freehold land have offered only slight relief. Land has been a serious constraint for the growing human population in these districts ever since the 1940s and densities and stocking rates are consequently high (Table 8.3). Such regional differences have continued after independence because land allocation remained the primary concern of individual districts (although as already noted, the institutional structure changed in the early 1970s).

Fourthly, physical conditions generally favour land-extensive practices. For example, the potential carrying capacity of the grazing areas varies between 12 and 20 hectares per livestock unit and livestock requires even larger areas during drought, and under degraded grazing conditions. Most land boards allocate fields of 16 hectares in order to satisfy household needs (only achieved by 10–15 per cent of the rural population: FAO 1974). Again, land pressure conflicts with land-intensive practices. Pressure is leading to the utilization of less productive areas but it also calls for more land-intensive practices especially

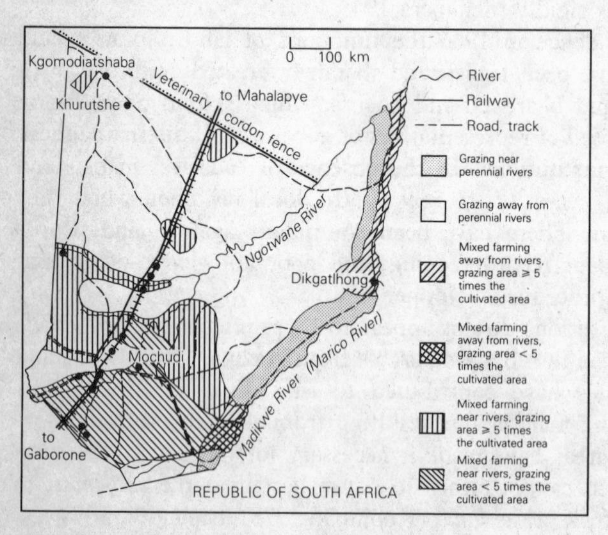

Fig. 31 Land use zones of the Kgatleng District

Table 8.3 Regional Differences in land pressure

Size	Districts	Area (sq km)	Stocking rate 1984 ha/LSU*	Rural population density 1981 per sq km	Percentage cultivated area (mid 1970s)
1 Small	South-East	1,492	4.0	16.9	15.5
	North-East	5,300	5.2	7.0	11.0
	Kgatleng	7,650	8.3	5.8	6.9
2 Large	Central	147,730	18.8	2.2	2.2
3 Botswana		585,227**	28.5	1.4	1.4

* Livestock Unit = LSU
Cattle = 0.7 LSU
Goats/Sheep = 0.1 LSU
Donkey = 0.4 LSU
Horses = 0.6 LSU
** Total surface including water, freehold areas etc.

Sources: DHV Consulting Engineers (1980) *Countrywide Animal and Range Assessment Project*, Gaborone, Ministry of Commerce and Industry.
Population Census (1981) Gaborone, Central Statistics Office.
Agricultural Statistics (1984) Gaborone, Ministry of Agriculture.

as the diversification of the economy does not offer adequate relief to unemployment. An example of the first adaptation is found in the expansion of livestock into western sandveld areas with a lower carrying capacity and a more fragile environment (Cooke 1985). Increased land-intensive practices, on the other hand, increase farmers' risks and are difficult to accept for the majority of farmers with limited resources. The two dominant forms of rural land use, that is livestock holding and crop farming, are discussed below in more detail.

Livestock holding

As shown before, livestock distribution is highly skewed but at the same time it is the most rewarding rural income opportunity, particularly for better-off farmers (see, for example, Kerven 1982, and Republic of Botswana 1976). In order to appreciate the relationship between land and livestock it is necessary to deal briefly with some management practices.

Access to water is the key issue with respect to livestock holding. This seems to contradict the fact that, as a result of widespread land degradation, lack of grazing and not lack of water is nowadays widely considered to be the main problem for livestock holders. However, it is explained by the fact that access to water provides *de facto* access to surrounding grazing areas. Although farmers use a variety of seasonal and permanent water sources during the year, access to ground water is decisive for the use of grazing during the crucial dry season period.

A number of threshold levels of herd size, each with their own socio-economic and spatial characteristics, can be identified (Carl Bro Int. 1982). Herds of less than 40 head are mostly kept in mixed farming areas. This enables owners to attend to both livestock and crop production but exposes cattle to generally poorer grazing conditions and the owner to risks of crop damage and subsequent compensation claims. The Livestock Management Survey found that stocking rates in mixed farming areas are double those in grazing areas: 7.5 hectares and 13.9 hectares per livestock unit in 1983 respectively. Crop damage by cattle is a common problem faced by most crop growing farmers. The livestock holder is usually requested to compensate the crop farmer for the estimated loss caused by livestock damage.

Herds of over 40 head are mostly kept at separate *cattleposts*. Farmers with more than 100 head of cattle are more likely to have their own water sources, mostly boreholes at these *cattleposts*. In Kgatleng District most permanent water sources in grazing areas are run by syndicates. Syndicates have on average 14 members with an average herd size of 88 as compared with 27.5 for the whole district (Peters 1981). Peters describes this phenomenon as privatization of communal grazing areas. In Kgatleng District, 20 per cent of large cattle holders have control over of 64 per cent of the grazing areas (Arntzen 1985). In view of the crucial role of boreholes in livestock holding and grazing management, it is surprising that knowledge about spatial distribution and ownership of boreholes is incomplete. Consequently, it is not exactly known how full grazing areas are nor whether there are any opportunities left to drill additional boreholes. Obviously, this puts the present borehole owners at an advantage but raises also the question as to what will happen with the majority of farmers who do not have direct access to ground water.

Crop production

Farmers' strategies and resources determine to a large extent the relationship between land and crop production. As with livestock holding, the yields are distributed in a skewed manner, though to a lesser extent. As crop production is not the most attractive proposition in the country, most farmers prefer to allocate their scarce means to other activities first, such as wage employment and livestock holding. As a result, most crop producers adopt a low-input and risk-aversive strategy. Alverson (1984) shows improved arable management practices do not fit into this strategy at present. Households plough on average around 4–5 hectares in a reasonable rainfall year and productivity as already noted is low.

The availability of arable land is not yet a constraint generally felt by farmers. This is a result of two factors, viz:

1 the Land Board has not yet zoned grazing and arable land as requested in the Tribal Land Act; and
2 individual land rights such as arable ones appear to receive implicit priority over communal grazing rights.

Consequently, arable encroachment into grazing occurs constantly, probably to be stopped only when grazing areas near boreholes are reached. Due to the slow arable development in the past, encroachment has so far been mostly limited. For example, in Kgatleng District, such encroachment involved less than 3 per cent of the grazing areas in the period 1963–82 (Arntzen 1985). As noted before, arable encroachment is reported to be most serious in Barolong with its large tracts of arable land.

Most fields are only partly cleared of vegetation, indicating that lack of means such as draught power, funds and labour are more important constraints than land. The Arable Land Survey and other research in Kgatleng show that on average only 60 per cent of each arable field is cleared (Odell 1980; Arntzen 1984). However, it is increasingly difficult to find fields in the proximity of villages. Fields at larger distances from villages are less attractive for resource-poor farmers without transport and unable to hire transport. Hiring charges can amount to ten per cent of the harvest. In addition it is becoming more difficult to gain access to different types of soil, either in one field or through the acquisition of a second field. Access to different types of soil is a traditional tool to reduce risks involved in cultivation. Sandy, loamy and clay soil are differently suited for the erratic rainfall patterns in the country. If farmers have fields at different locations they also reduce the risk of being struck by local rainfall failure.

Continued arable expansion is likely to result in the cultivation of less productive areas in the long run. However, there is no evidence as yet that new arable areas are less fertile. Countrywide, only 1–2 per cent is annually cultivated at present whereas up to 5 per cent of the country is assumed to be suited for crop production. Actual arable land use is highly related to livestock holding, that is, as a means of production, draught power as well as source of cash). Table 8.4 reveals that both the cultivated area and yields are much higher for large cattle holders.

Table 8.4 Cultivated area and yields according to herd size (%)

Herd-size	1980/1			1983/4		
	(1)	(2)	(3)	(1)	(2)	(3)
0	31.6	19.8	14.0	28.7	16.7	14.3
1–10	15.8	12.6	8.5	21.2	15.5	9.5
11–20	17.3	17.5	13.5	14.9	17.1	10.8
21–40	18.1	19.8	19.9	17.0	24.5	17.3
41+	17.1	30.3	44.1	18.2	26.2	48.3

(1) % holders (2) % cultivated area (3) % production.
Source: Ministry of Agriculture (1984)

Access to farm income

Although comprehensive rural income data are old (1974), they are likely to be still relevant. Table 8.5 summarizes to what extent various activities such as crop and livestock production contribute to the income of ten income groups. Economic developments in the country since 1974 have probably even sharpened the income differences and the dependence of socio-economic groups on particular sources of income. Salaries are likely to play a more prominent role now for the better-off households. Crop production provided in 1974 at most 10 per cent of the household income. Livestock was the major source of

Table 8.5 Income profiles for the rural population (1974/5)

Percentile Income Groupings	Crops	Animals	Wages	Manufacturing	Trading	Services	Hunting	Gathering	Housing	Transfers	Other	Total
Poorest 10%	9	14	9	10	–	2	9	22	11	19	−5	100
10%–30%	10	13	17	6	1	3	1	16	10	19	4	100
30%–50%	10	19	21	5	2	2	1	12	9	14	5	100
50%–70%	11	31	17	6	1	2	1	7	6	11	7	100
70%–90%	8	39	20	4	1	1	3	5	5	8	6	100
Richest 10%	5	40	38	1	1	2	4	3	2	5	−1	100
Total	9	27	20	5	1	2	3	10	7	13	4	

Source: C. Colclough and P. Fallon (1983) 'Rural poverty in Botswana: dimensions, causes and constraints'. In D. Ghai and S. Radwan (eds.) *Agrarian Policies and Rural Poverty in Africa* (Geneva: ILO)

income for the better-off households (up to 40 per cent of the income) whereas remittances and gathering were prime income sources for the poorest households. Income levels were generally higher in the large villages.

As results from the recent nationwide Rural Income and Expenditure Survey are not yet available (the results will probably be published late 1987), the best up-to-date source is the annual Farm Management Survey conducted by the Ministry of Agriculture. The sample is countrywide but biased in favour of cattle holders. In 1984, 86 per cent of the sample farmers held cattle as compared with national figures of 71 per cent; the average herd size was 40 in both cases. Most households derive income from a mixture of farm and off-farm activities. The latter become obviously more important during droughts and are of greater value for the smaller farmers. According to the Farm Management Survey, 32 per cent of the income of the sample farmers came from off-farm activities during year 1984, double the percentage of 1981 before the onset of the drought (Table 8.6). Wages constituted in 1984 68 per cent of the non-agricultural income whereas beer brewing contributed 15 per cent and remittances 10.5 per cent (Ministry of Agriculture 1984).

Table 8.6 Proportion of farm and non-farm income by farmer group (1984)%

Farmer group	Criterion 1*		Criterion 2**	
	Farm	Non−Farm %	Farm	Non−farm %
Top one-third (1984)	80	20	68	34
Middle one-third (1984)	82	18	82	18
Bottom one-third (1984)	43	57	7	44
All farmers 1984	68	32	68	32
All farmers 1981	84	16	84	16

* Farmers are ranked according to the gross-margin 1 hectare.
** Farmers are ranked according to production level 1 hectare.

Source: Ministry of Agriculture, 1984.

The lowest third of the farmers rely for over half of their income on non-agricultural activities such as beer brewing (females) and wage labour (males). During the period 1978–84, the annual contribution of crop production to total average farm income fluctuated between negative and 25 per cent with a median of 12.4 per cent (Ministry of Agriculture 1984). More importantly, arable income is far less stable than that of livestock (Table 8.7), and livestock is to some extent being used to stabilize average non-farm income. In view of the survey's bias, we can assume that small farmers depend more heavily on crop production alone, and hence are forced to compensate income losses from drought through off-farm activities.

Table 8.7 Average farm income 1978–84

Absolute (in Pula)	1978–84	1978	1979	1980	1981	1982	1983	1984
Crops	(S = 65.84) 59.36	42	11	143	139	7	−19	93
Livestock	(S = 359.97) 662.70	298	345	419	773	1,229	1,033	541
Total agriculture	(S = 340.15) 722.90	340	356	562	912	1,236	1,013	637
Percentages								
Crops	8.2	12.4	3.1	25.4	15.2	0.6	0.0	14.6
Livestock	91.8	87.6	96.9	74.6	84.8	99.4	100	85.4
Total agriculture	100	100	100	100	100	100	100	100

Source: Ministry of Agriculture, 1984.

The Farm Management Survey (1984) shows a positive relationship between agricultural involvement and farm income for 1984, but in 1981 the picture is less clear. Farm income appears conversely related to the number of livestock but in 1981 the average area ploughed for the better-off farmers was less than average; in 1984, they ploughed more than average. This pattern probably reflects the marginal position of arable production from the income point of view. Larger farmers may have the means to plough more but do not always consider it desirable to do so whereas the poorer households have usually no choice but to attempt to plough.

Impact of some government policies

Below we consider some of the policies that have been enacted primarily to increase agricultural production, but also to reduce range degradation and their impact or implication on access to land and farm income. We discuss each policy in turn.

Spacing of waterpoints
Throughout the history of livestock development, water development has played a central role, though the emphasis has changed. Initially,

extensive grazing areas were not accessible for livestock because of the absence of ground water resources (wells or boreholes). Water was seen as the major constraint for livestock development (e.g. Pim 1937; Schapera 1943; Roe, 1980). During this period various borehole drilling programmes were undertaken by the Protectorate Administration and tribes (e.g. Bakgatla). Such programmes were advocated for two reasons:

1 to support further growth of the livestock sector by opening up new grazing areas.
2 to alleviate local overgrazing by a better spatial distribution of livestock.

One of the effects was that boreholes quickly took over the role of wells. Whereas in 1927 Central District relied almost entirely on 227 wells (compared with only one borehole), boreholes have now become widespread and most important (Roe 1980). The need to regulate both the distance between waterpoints and the number of livestock permitted at each waterpoint was already recognized in the 1930s and 1940s. Under the assumption of an average of 500 Livestock Units per waterpoint, traditional authorities used a rule of thumb to keep at least 8 km distance between waterpoints. However, despite the recognition of the need for a rule for maximum numbers of livestock per waterpoint, such a rule has never been implemented (for example, in Kgatleng; see Peters 1983).

This is likely to have contributed to the situation today where grazing and no longer water is seen as the major constraint for livestock development. However, opportunities to open new grazing areas can no longer be easily found. This has brought to an end the situation during the period 1946–74 where the growth of livestock numbers was satisfied by an adequate (but no more than that) increase in the number of boreholes (Sandford 1983). Particularly in smaller districts, borehole spots can no longer be found despite the fact that the 8 km rule has been restricted to boreholes only (it is not exactly known when this change occurred). This pressure on water resources has had two effects:

1 an appeal to reduce the required distance between boreholes. In spite of some ministerial action to this effect, the 8 km rule appears in practice to be still applicable.
2 a trend towards more exclusive use of the boreholes by their owners (Peters 1983). Farmers who purchased water from borehole owners are increasingly turned away and therefore have to keep their livestock in mixed farming areas.

In the absence of stock limitation per borehole, the outcome of this process has been stocking rates well in excess of the estimated carrying capacity. Such overstocking has set into motion the gradual process of land degradation through bush encroachment, erosion and finally local desertification.

National Policy on Tribal Grazing Land

To deal with the problems of overgrazing and its effects on incomes, especially of small farmers in eastern Botswana, the government announced a National Policy on Tribal Grazing Land (TGLP) in 1975. Its aims were given as:

1 to stop overgrazing and degradation of the range through grazing control and better range management;
2 to promote greater equality of incomes in rural areas; and
3 to allow growth and commercialization of the livestock industry on a sustained basis (Republic of Botswana 1975).

These aims were to be achieved by zoning the country into three categories: commercial, communal and reserved land.

In the commercial areas, which are now located in the *sandveld*, six 400 hectare ranches were to be created and leased on 50-year heritable leases to large cattle owners or syndicates (a minimum of 400 cattle being the requirement). The ranches were to be fenced and the farmers were expected to adopt improved livestock and range management practices. In exchange for exclusive use of land, farmers in commercial areas were originally expected to pay economic rents, which would be used to improve conditions in the overgrazed communal areas. At the same time it was assumed that exclusive use of land would give farmers sufficient incentive to care for the land.

In the communal grazing areas, most of which would continue to be located in the *hardveld*, an improved grazing system, including stock limitations, would be introduced, although land would still be held communally. It was hoped that the removal of the larger herds to the ranches would create more grazing space and this would lead to the improvement of the quality of livestock (and consequently of incomes) of small farmers.

Reserved areas were to be set aside for future use: 'They are safeguards for the poorer members of the population . . . Those who have only a few cattle at present' or none at all (Republic of Botswana 1975, p. 7).

Implementation started in 1978 and was concerned exclusively with the demarcation of commercial farms (see Figure 28), which according to the white paper should have been done last 'after taking into account communal, reserved and national needs' (Republic of Botswana

1975, p. 11). The TGLP ranches account for 10 per cent of all land and the present situation with regard to TGLP is indicated in Table 8.8.

Table 8.8 Progress on creation of ranches as of 3 April 1986

No. demarcated	393	Leases signed	187
No. advertised	257	Ranches already with some development	149
No. dezoned	95		
No. allocated	242	Ranches reserved for associations/ syndicates etc.	16

Source: Ministry of Agriculture.

Among the major problems that have been experienced during implementation has been the discovery that there are already many claims to the land that was supposed to be empty by those with *cattle-posts* and boreholes, the small cattle owners depending on boreholes of others, people without cattle and Basarwa hunter-gatherers (Hitchcock 1982: p. 13–14). Ninety-five farms have subsequently been dezoned and returned to communal land. Priority in ranch allocations has consequently been given to those large cattle owners with boreholes in the area. Some of the boreholes were drilled in anticipation of the policy and at a time when there was a freeze on borehole drilling. One report noted:

> *The reason for this seems to be that cattle owners are becoming aware that good grazing with reasonable prospects for sucessful drilling is getting scarce. They want to establish their own cattle posts, boreholes and grazing rights in the remaining areas of good potential so that, if they are finally compelled to take out TGLP leases on the land, they will enjoy free and unrestricted use of the grazing in the area.*
>
> *(Carl Bro Int. Vol. II, 1982: 1.08)*

The second group to benefit from ranch allocations has been the professionals and traders looking for a place to put their money (Bekure and Dyson-Hudson 1982). Consequently the policy has not resulted in the reduction of overgrazing in the communal areas; the reverse in fact appears to be happening. The farmers who own small herds are being forced to move back into communal lands (Machacha 1986). But the large cattle farmers have not renounced their claims to communal lands (Carl Bro Int. Vol. I 1982: 2.07). Instead they return their herds to communal lands after overgrazing their ranches (Machacha 1986; Rep. of Botswana 1983: IX). Most ranches are overstocked. The good husbandry requirements are not being enforced. Rents have been fixed at a sub-economic figure of 4 Thebe per hectare or P256 for a ranch per annum.[1]

The policy is therefore seen as a trick worked by the rich cattle owners, some of them senior civil servants and politicians, to enrich themselves; the conservation and social equity aspects seen as a coating to sell the policy to the donors (Parson 1981). Bekure and Dyson-Hudson have concluded:

> *It has no ability to halt or reduce damage to range resources – if anything, the reverse. It has no ability to avoid, let alone encounter, such negative effects as widening the income gap between rich and poor, permanently concentrating the country's land resources in the hands of a tiny percentage of its occupants and depressing the already limited subsistence capacities of its poor citizens.*
>
> *(Bekure and Dyson-Hudson 1982: p. 2)*

Only a small number of farms have been reserved for syndicates of small herd owners (Table 8.8) and no land has been preserved for future use.

Fears that the policy might lead to landlessness were confirmed when reports of evictions of people from certain *cattleposts* that were expected to be in the commercial zone were received. This was done by large cattle farmers in order to avoid counter claims and to eliminate the costs of compensation in the event of the area being designated commercial (Carl Bro. International Vol. I, 1982: 2.08). The hunter-gatherers and other poor groups that are displaced are being accommodated in special areas within the farms called Communal Service Centres. The Communal Service Centres vary in size but average about 18,500 hectares and are all considered too small to support the Basarwa foraging economy (Hitchcock and Holm 1985). Furthermore they lack alternative forms of employment and social services. The social consequences of the policy will be felt for a long time to come.

Large-Scale Arable Programme – Pandamatenga farms

Parallel to TGLP is another scheme whose aim is to boost cereal (sorghum) production so as to achieve national self-sufficiency. Fifty farms averaging 500 hectares were demarcated in 1985 and 1986 in the better-watered Pandamatenga area and have been leased to big farmers (Figure 28). Some of these farmers have been assisted with huge loans and grants (to finance capital and labour costs) from the National

Development Bank[2]. The minimum capital costs are half a million Pula, with the farmer expected to contribute at least 25 per cent.[3] The beneficiaries include large commercial farmers already in possession of large chunks of land elsewhere in the country and senior serving or retired civil servants. Like TGLP this policy is seen as benefiting the rich and widening the gap in incomes.

Arable Lands Development Programme (ALDEP)

The main policy aimed at helping the small farmers is the Arable Lands Development Programme (ALDEP). The target group of ALDEP is the 60–70,000 poor households, with less than 40 cattle, half of whom do not have draught power. Among this group are the female-headed households that lack labour and capital as well. The goals of ALDEP are:

1 to increase production of food crops to achieve national self-sufficiency and even to export agricultural surpluses;
2 to improve incomes of small farmers; and
3 to create employment (estimated number was 10–12,000 jobs) and thus reduce rural-urban migration.

The aim of ALDEP is to remove the major constraints faced by small farmers by assisting them to acquire draught power, implements, fencing materials and to develop water resources on their lands. The assistance is in the form of a grant and generally covers 85 per cent of the total cost. Most popular packages are fencing and implements. The total project cost is US $29.4 million. Expenditure up to December 1986 totalled P10.4 million (ALDEP 1986).

The policy was launched in 1980 at the start of what has turned out to be the worst and most prolonged drought for many years, and therefore its full potential impact may not have been felt. However, the Progress Report for the period July – December 1986 notes:

> *some findings from the 1986 annual survey indicates that participating farmers have performed better than non-participating by planting and harvesting larger areas per farm, obtaining higher per farm production and by achieving a higher ratio of farms harvested to planted.*
> *(ALDEP, 1986)*

An evaluation survey carried out in 1982 showed that ALDEP was not reaching the poorest farmers. Only 10 per cent of farmers assisted had 10 or less cattle and less than 10 per cent (this figure had increased to 30 per cent in 1985/6) of farm households were female-headed (ALDEP 1983). However, 25 per cent of the assisted households belonged to the category with over 40 cattle, while the average herd size for a participating household is 35.6 cattle. However, in terms of hectarage, the average participating household falls within the ALDEP limits – being 8 hectares. In general it does appear that ALDEP is not touching large numbers of poor farmers who depend upon extra-farming activities and remittances for their income. The gap in income between the rich and poor farmers can be expected to widen rather than increase. Indeed there have already been claims that the main beneficiaries from ALDEP are in fact the better-off farmers (Opschoor 1983).

Accelerated Rainfed Arable Programme (ARAP)

The last major agricultural policy is the Accelerated Rainfed Arable Programme (ARAP) which was launched in 1985. Its target was the middle-level farmers not covered by any of the existing schemes but in its implementation it appears to be somewhat undiscriminating. The programme is to last five years and estimated to cost P29,890,000 (Ministry of Agriculture 1985).

There are six packages in the programme, and when the policy was conceived eligible farmers were to qualify only once for any of them, but this has since been relaxed. The first package is assistance towards destumping fields – up to a maximum of ten hectares per farming household at a rate of P50 per hectare. The second package is assistance towards the cost of draught hire, which includes ploughing (P50 per hectare), row planting (P10 per hectare) and weeding (P5 per hectare). The input procurement package includes provision of improved seed (8 kg per hectare up to maximum of 10 hectares) and a free distribution of 600 kg of fertilizer to cover three hectares. The fencing package is meant to enable the farmer to cover the costs of fencing up to six hectares of his field. Under the water development package farmers are provided with funds to meet the costs of equipping their boreholes and of reticulating water at their *lands* areas. The last package is the crop protection programme under which the Ministry of Agriculture has established the Crop Protection Unit whose main function is to deal with emergency outbreaks of *quelea* birds, pests of all kinds, and weed or bush encroachment.

The demand for ARAP funds, which are seen as a bonanza from the Government by some farmers, has been overwhelming. By March 1986 over P9 million had already been spent and, with some claims still in the pipeline, that figure was likely to be exceeded (ARAP 1986). Allocations for planting and draught power were severely overspent. Demands on extension staff time were heavy and in some cases farmers' committees had to be engaged in measuring fields (ARAP 1986). This latter practice resulted in overpayments and had to be discontinued. Indeed a few cases of corruption involving extension staff – authorizing payment for the ploughed fields they have not even seen – have been exposed. The scheme has generated demand for arable land with a number of people living in towns rushing back to claim their land rights.

Impending land shortage and its effects

Even if a decline in population growth were to occur, pressure on land in the near future is likely to increase significantly. The degree of success with regard to diversification of the economy may play an important role in reducing such pressure, but there are many constraints (for example participation in the Southern African Customs Union,[4] the proximity to more industrialized Zimbabwe and South Africa, and the small and scattered domestic markets) which are likely to limit this possibility. Even the low population growth scenario in the National Development Plan, 1985–91 would result in a doubling of the population by 2001. Also, cattle numbers grew by an average of 3.6 per cent per annum between 1971 and 1981. If growth of the national herd recurs after the drought, even an annual growth of only 2 per cent would imply a national herd of 3.9 million by the year 2000. Although the expansion of arable land is not clear and may be relatively low as in the past, this expansion will add to the overall land pressure.

At this point, it is necessary to dwell in some detail on the concept of land pressure and land shortage. At present there is no consensus as to whether land shortage already exists or not (see for example Marquardt 1982; Gulbrandsen 1984; Arntzen 1985). If one takes access to arable land as the criterion for land shortage, it does not exist (Marquardt 1982). If one takes a broader view, relative land shortage does exist, as people cannot easily acquire arable land as and where they wish, and this affects the resource-poor farmers chiefly. For example, it was found in Kgatleng that poor farmers continued to work old fields near Mochudi as they could not afford to open a field away from the village (at least 20 km distance). Gulbrandsen (1984) introduced the concept of 'artificial land shortage', which refers to a situation whereby land out of use may be inaccessible to people needing land because the previous users still have a claim on it. This concept explains land shortage around villages where land appears to be available but cannot be allocated because of old users' rights. In some instances this can involve a large portion of available land. Relative and artificial land shortage are expressions of increasing land pressure and are signs of impending absolute land shortage, when land is simply short in absolute terms for the requirements. Finally, it is essential to realize that land shortage is time- and situation-specific. Land shortage relates to the specific practices at one particular moment. The introduction of more land-intensive practices, for example, could reduce land shortage in future. This is also related to the institutional factor. The headmen still have considerable influence on land allocation through the requirement that they issue a note of 'no objection' before a formal application to the land board can be made. This offers headmen the opportunity to claim areas for members of their ward and to confirm any claims that may be alleged to have been made before land boards came into existence. The effect is that large areas of land may be out of the control of the land board. The extent to which this occurs, however, is not known. Successful introduction of intensive practices as well as development of the non-agricultural sector appear to be the main challenges to avert rural land shortage and its undesirable effects.

In summary, we would describe the present situation in the country as one where grazing land is short in absolute terms and there is a relative shortage, partly artificial, of arable land. This co-existence of two different levels of land shortage is possible because no clear zoning of land for various purposes is yet enforced. This situation requires due consideration to be given to the factor of land as a possible constraint in rural development planning. The need to do so has been illustrated by Opschoor and Maribe (1982) who argued that the objectives of the Arable Land Development Programme could not be achieved in small districts such as Kgatleng because of shortage of land. The rural population is generally quite aware of impending land shortage. For example, Gulbrandsen noticed in 1984 that 'the view that land is about to become acutely short was strongly pronounced by virtually all families I interviewed . . . quite different from what I had recorded during previous fieldwork in the Ngwaketse (1979)' (Gulbrandsen 1984: p. 3).

Land pressure and emerging land shortage have a number of potential economic, social and environmental effects which are directly in conflict with the four overall development objectives set by the government (economic growth, social justice, substained development and economic independence). Moreover, these effects are closely linked; in other words, environmental effects have economic and social consequences and vice versa.

The major social effect is further polarization of the population (Peters 1983; Lawry 1983). There is a tendency to acquire more exclusive rights or to utilize existing rights more exclusively. An instance of the former can be found in the acquisition of leasehold land under the TGLP. The latter is exemplified by reported problems of non-borehole owners in purchasing water and by the emergence of calls from borehole owners to fence off surrounding grazing land. Increased production costs and lower returns, as a result of land pressure and associated degradation, affect the poorer part of the population most seriously and may push an increasing number of people out of livestock holding and even cultivation.

Major environmental effects are many and include the already occurring over-exploitation of natural resources. Over-exploitation affects productivity and may, where it reaches a serious level, be only reversible at considerable cost to society or land user/owners. Land shortage also leads to a situation where activities which are dominating (from a societal/institutional point of view) encroach into less suitable areas. In the past, Botswana has experienced two main forms of spontaneous encroachment without due consideration for land suitability;

1 arable encroachment into grazing areas and
2 livestock encroachment into wildlife areas.

This calls for land use planning which takes into account the local natural resources base as well as the needs of local people.

Economic effects include lower production levels because of the use of less suitable land such as overgrazed ranges and overworked arable land. Secondly, a conflict between grazing and arable results in the destruction of crops by livestock. Another economic effect concerns higher production costs for farmers as a result of less suited degraded land, higher transport costs (related to relative land shortage) and higher production costs associated with more land-intensive management practices. Other effects include the rise of share-cropping between the small farmers, who are not able to use all their land, and the commercial farmers in need of large chunks of land to cultivate. There is also an incipient commercialization of arable land which reflects relative shortage of land.

Conclusions

Access to land *per se* is not yet a widespread problem in Botswana. Every Motswana is in principle able to acquire land for cultivation or livestock grazing. However, *real* access to land depends largely upon possession of resources to work the land. The poor non-livestock holders such as female-headed households may thus be prevented from the use of land.

Although there is not yet a serious scarcity of land, there are signs of impending land shortage resulting from a combination of factors. These factors are rapid population growth, slow growth of non-agricultural employment exacerbated by curtailment of mine recruitment to the South African mines, the land-extensive nature of agricultural activities, the low incomes of the majority of farmers, and some commercialization of arable agriculture in localized areas. The relative and artificial land shortage that already exists reflects the weakness of modern institutions in regulating land use in the rural areas. This weakness is not only because of their lack of power and experience but also because they are controlled by the big farmers. It is ironic, therefore, that the institutions which were set up to curtail the whims and corruption of chiefs in the allocation of land should operate in the interests of even fewer people than was the case before.

There is a widespread awareness of impending shortage of land which is driving people into actions that are aggravating the situation – clinging to old fallows that should be returned to the general pool of land, excluding other land users, hoarding land for their children, and, in exceptional circumstances, even buying land. The shortage of grazing land is now absolute and there is increasing encroachment on game reserves.

The groups with limited access to land and who face the immediate prospect of landlessness as land becomes scarce include:

1 the poor households without draught power;
2 unmarried women, whose rights to land are traditionally not clearly defined but whose numbers are on the increase and many of whom have their own households; and
3 members of the formerly subject tribes living at the *cattleposts* and whose access to land depends upon the master-servant relationship.

The shortage of land is much more intense in small districts.

Data on rural incomes are scarce but indications are that remittances and gathering are the main sources of income for the poor whereas livestock holding provides the bulk of income for the better-off and is a major determinant of income from agriculture. Crop production is a limited source of income, except for a small percentage of households, and this income is in any case highly variable. This reflects in part the arid nature of the country. One consequence of this is heavy reliance on non-agricultural activities, which increases tremendously during the times of drought.

The government has introduced policies to deal with some of the problems noted above. These policies appear to be benefiting better-off farmers and thus contributing to the widening rather than the narrowing of the income gap between rich and poor. Secondly, they appear to be increasing the demand for land and some of them are even advocating the privatization of common land without sufficient compensation to the society that has to forgo its rights to such land.

It seems therefore that government intervention should focus on two areas of concern – social justice and the ability to sustain growth. Other areas for government action include the strengthening of institutions, particularly the land boards, assistance to poor farmers regarding arable production, diversification of the rural economy and the rehabilitation of the degraded lands. It can only be hoped that current initiatives, particularly the National Food Strategy and National Conservation Strategy, will address effectively some of these problems.

Notes

1 Thebe is a unit of the Pula, Botswana's currency.
2 Amounting to about P7 million by June 1987 for 13 operations owning 23 farms between them (Source: NDB).
3 Source: NDB.
4 Botswana is a member of the Southern African Customs Union which comprises South Africa, Lesotho, Swaziland and Botswana.

References

ALDEP 1983. 1982 ALDEP: *Baseline data and evaluation* (Gaborone: Ministry of Agriculture)

ALDEP 1986. *ALDEP Progress Report July to December 1986* (Gaborone: Ministry of Agriculture)

Alverson, H. 1984. The wisdom of tradition in the development of Dryland Farming: Botswana, *Human Organisation*, vol. 43, Part 1, pp. 1–18.

ARAP 1986. *ARAP – Annual Report June, 1986* (Gaborone, Ministry of Agriculture)

Arntzen, J.W. 1984, *Agricultural resource utilisation in Mmathubudukwane*, NIR Research Notes No. 15 (Gaborone: University of Botswana)

Arntzen, J.W. 1984. *Determinants of field location in Kgatleng District*, NIR Research Notes No. 16 (Gaborone: University of Botswana)

Arntzen, J.W. 1985. *Land use agricultural development in Eastern Botswana: the case of Kgatleng District*, NIR Working Papers No. 50 (Gaborone: University of Botswana)

Bekure, S.N. and Dyson-Hudson N. 1982. *The operation and viability of the second Livestock Development Project: selected issues* (Gaborone: Ministry of Agriculture)

Carl Brothers International 1982. *An evaluation of livestock management and production in Botswana (Vols. I-III)* (Gaborone, Ministry of Agriculture)

Communal Area Research Group (CARG), 1984. *Report on land use planning in Botswana* (Gaborone: NIR University of Botswana [Mimeo])

Cooke, H.J. 1985. The Kalahari today – a case of conflict over resource use, *The Geographical Journal*, vol. 151, Part 1 pp. 75–85.

Cooke, H.J. and Silitshena, R.M.K. 1986. 'Botswana – an environment profile' (Unpublished report prepared for United Nations Environment Programme, Nairobi)

Cooper, D. 1982. 'An overview of Botswana urban class struggle and its articulation with the rural structure: insights from Selebi-Phikwe'. In Renee Hitchcock and M. Smith (eds) *Settlement in Botswana* (Marshalltown: Heinemann)

Egner, E.B. and Klausen, A.L. 1980. *Poverty in Botswana*, NIR Working Paper No. 29 (Gaborone: University of Botswana)

FAO and Republic of Botswana 1974. *A survey of constraints on agricultural development in the Republic of Botswana* (Gaborone: Government Printer)

Fortmann, L. *et al.* 1983. *A study of local institutions and resource management in the North East District* (CFA Gaborone: Applied Research Unit, Ministry of Local Government and Lands)

Gulbrandsen, 1984. *Access to agricultural land and communal management in Eastern Botswana* (Gaborone: Applied Research Unit, Ministry of Local Government and Lands)

Hitchcock, R.K. 1982. 'Tradition, Social Justice and Land Reform in Central Botswana'. In Richard P. Werbner (ed.) *Land reform in the making: tradition, public policy and ideology in Botswana* (London: Rex Collings)

Hitchcock, R.K. and Holm, J.D. 1985. Political development among the Basarwa of Botswana, *Cultural Survival Quarterly* vol. 9 (3) pp. 7–11.

Kalahari Conservation Society 1983. *Proceedings of a symposium 'Which way Botswana's wildlife'* (Gaborone: Kalahari Conservation Society)

Kerven, C. 1982. 'Effects of migration on agricultural production'. In Central Statistics Office (ed.) *Migration in Botswana: patterns, causes and consequences*, vol. 3 (Gaborone: Central Statistics Office), pp. 526–625.

Kooijman, K. 1978. *Social and economic change in a Tswana village* (Leiden: African Studies Centre)

Lawry, S. 1983. *Land tenure policy and smallholder livestock development in Botswana*, Research Paper No. 78 (Madison: Land Tenure Centre)

Litschauer, J.G. and Kelly, W.F. 1981. *Traditional versus commercial agriculture in Botswana* (Gaborone: Ministry of Agriculture)

Machacha, B. 1986. 'Botswana's land tenure: Institutional reform and policy formulation'. In J.W. Arntzen *et al.* (eds) *Land policy and agriculture in Eastern and Southern Africa* (Tokyo: The United Nations University)

Marquardt, M. 1982. *Access to land in Communal Areas* (Gaborone, Ministry of Local Government and Lands)

Ministry of Agriculture 1983. *Botswana Agricultural Statistics 1983* (Gaborone: Ministry of Agriculture)

Ministry of Agriculture 1984. *Farm Management Survey 1984* (Gaborone: Ministry of Agriculture)

Ministry of Agriculture 1985. *ARAP – Accelerated Rainfed Arable Programme: Address to Parliament by Minister of Agriculture, September 1985* (Gaborone: Ministry of Agriculture)

Noppen, D. 1982. *Consultation and non-commitment: planning with people in Botswana* (Leiden: African Studies Centre)

Odell, M.A. 1980. *Planning for agriculture: a report on the Arable Land Survey* (Gaborone: IDM/Ministry of Agriculture)

Opschoor, J.V. 1981. *Environmental resources utilization in Eastern Communal Botswana*, NIR Working Paper No. 38 (Gaborone, University of Botswana)

Opshcoor, J. 1983. 'Crops, class and climate: environmental and economic constraints and potentials of crop production in Botswana'. In M.A. Oommen *et al.* (eds) *Botswana's economy since independence* (New Delhi: Tata McGraw-Hill)

Opschoor, J. and Maribe, M. 1982. *Land availability and arable land development in Southern Kgatleng*, NIR Research Notes No. 3 (Gaborone: University of Botswana)

Parson, J.D. 1981. Cattle, class and the state in rural Botswana, *Journal of Southern African Studies* vol. 7 (2) pp. 236–55.

Peters, P.A. 1983. 'Cattlemen, borehole syndicates and privatization in Kgatleng District in Botswana' (Ph.D. Thesis, Boston University)

Pim, A.W. 1937. *Financial and economic position of the Bechuanaland Protectorate* (London: HMSO)

Republic of Botswana 1975. *National policy on Tribal Grazing Land* (Gaborone: Government Printer)

Republic of Botswana 1976. *The rural income distribution survey in Botswana 1974/5* (Gaborone: Government Printer)

Republic of Botswana 1983. *Report of the Presidential Commission on Land Tenure* (Gaborone: Government Printer)

Roe, E 1980. Development of livestock, agriculture and water supplies in Botswana before Independence, Cornell University Occasional Papers No. 10.
Sandford, S. 1983. *Management of pastoral development in the Third World* (London: ODA/Wiley)
Schapera, I. 1943. *Native land tenure in the Bechuanaland Protectorate* (Cape Town: The Lovedale Press)
Schapera, I. 1953. *The Tswana* (London: International African Institute)
Silitshena, R.M.K. 1983. *Intra-rural migration and settlement changes in Botswana* (Leiden: African Studies centre)
Williamson, R.G. 1973. *Poverty and progress* (London: Methuen)

Acknowledgements

We are grateful to Mr G. Koorutwe for drawing the maps and to Mrs F. Nunoo for typing the manuscript.

9
Regional Inequalities in Bharuch District in Gujarat

Rangaswamy Vimala
Department of Geography, M.S. University of Baroda, Baroda, India.

In this study, an attempt is made to evaluate the disparities in levels of development between the tribal and non-tribal regions of Bharuch District, using the data available from government sources. Varied geographical factors, social traditions, economic conditions and isolation have been responsible for creating these disparities.

Bharuch District forms a part of Gujarat (Figure 32) in Western India. There are three main regions of the District, namely the coastal belt, the alluvial plains in the centre and the hilly area of the east. Much of the eastern area forms part of the tribal region of Gujarat which extends from the semi-arid region in the north, through drought-prone areas to the comparatively wet areas of Surat, Valsad and Dangs (Figure 32).

Fig. 32 The Tribal Region in Gujarat

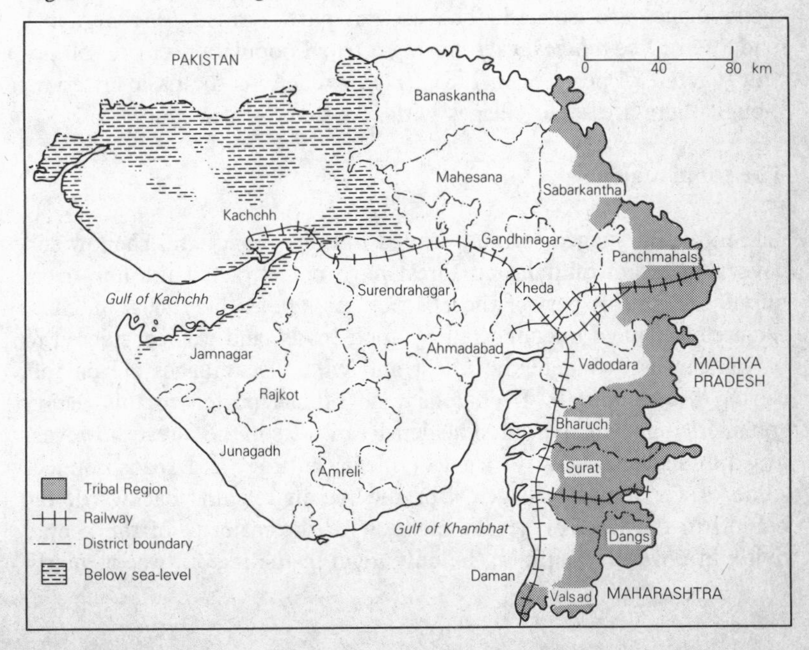

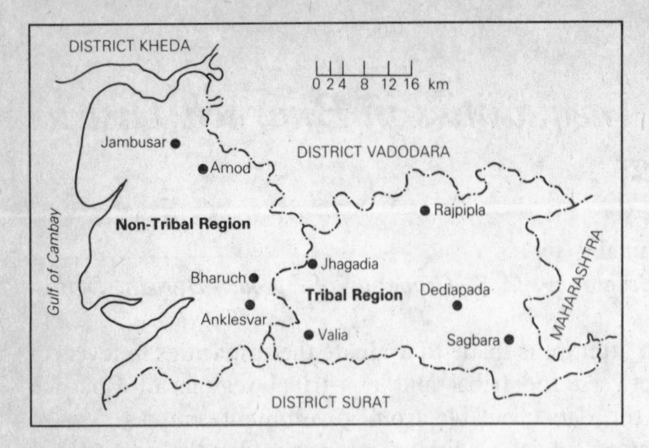

Fig. 33 Bharuch District Gujarat

Apart from the striking physical contrast between the western and the eastern parts, the District displays a marked contrast in its population and also in levels of development. For the purpose of the present study, the division is made on the basis of a *taluka* (an administrative division) having more than 50 per cent of its population of tribal origin (persons of scheduled tribes).[1] The western part, termed here *non-tribal region* consists of six *talukas* where the overall tribal population is 23 per cent (1981). This does not mean that there are no villages where the tribal population is not over 50 per cent, but such villages are isolated. The eastern part, termed *tribal region* is made up of five *talukas*, each having a tribal population of over 50 per cent (overall 74 per cent in 1981). Homogeneity is the basic criterion, though there are some villages with less than 50 per cent.

The tribal region

The hilly and rugged terrain, eroded hilltops, rocky and shallow soil cover, uncertain rainfall and forest have not attracted the non-tribal population to this part of the District. As late as the 1960s, much of the area remained unconnected by good roads, and was considered to be dangerous owing to the forest and wild life. Villages are cut off during heavy rainfall. Even today, an official posted to this region considers it a trying period. The density of trees in the forest, however, has diminished, owing to legal or illegal cutting, and roads connect some of the distant villages. But the region remains backward, far behind in the level of development, with the majority of the people living in poverty. Rajpipla, the only town in the region, was formerly the capital of the state. The region contains 70 per cent of the total population of the District.

The non-tribal region

Situated on the western traffic corridor connecting the cities of Bombay and Delhi, the region is a great contrast to the east. It has fertile alluvial soil and moderate rainfall. Accessibility by road, rail and also to some extent by water, is good. There are five towns: Bharuch, Ankleshwar, Jambusar, Amod and Hansot. Bharuch, although it has lost its ancient importance as a port, continues to be an important industrial centre and commercial depot for cotton, coconut and fresh-water fish. Industrialization is taking place, with the setting up of the Gujarat Narmada Fertilizer Corporation and the industrial estate. Other small-scale industries carried on in the traditional way are carpentry, *bidi* making (indigenous cigarettes), shoe making, bamboo working, tanning, smithing, coir industry and oil seed crushing. Bharuch is a distribution centre for coconuts imported from Kerala by the sea route.

Ankleshwar is an important cotton trading centre and a junction on the main line of the Western Railway. It has become a trans-shipment centre for the railway, with the result that there has been an increase in trading activity. Its growth has been rapid after the establishment of the Oil and Natural Gas Commission and an industrial estate. Jambusar and Amod are centres for cotton ginning and pressing. Industrialization has created job opportunities, but urbanization has not been rapid, and the region continues even today to be predominantly agricultural. Between 1971 and 1981, the urban population increased by 27 per cent and the rural by 32 per cent. Bharuch increased by 22 and Ankleshwar by 67 per cent, Jambusar by 17 per cent, Amod by 15 and Hansot by only one per cent. This region contains 30 per cent of the tribal population of the District.

The contrast between the tribal and non-tribal regions will now be explored using data on land use, population and occupational structure.

Land use

The tribal region is wetter (1,158 mm in 52 rainy days) than the non-ribal region (838 mm in 38 days; see Figure 34(a)).[2] The tribal region covers an area of 5,120km ^{2} and includes 806 villages. Table 9.1 shows that 27 per cent of the region was covered by forests in 1971, (see

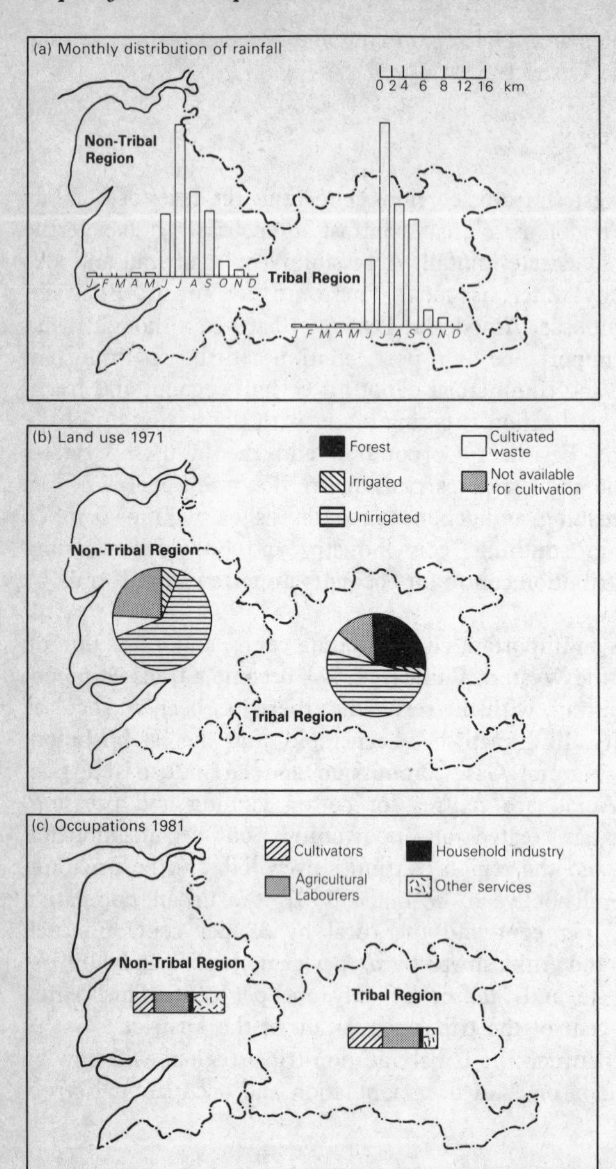

Fig. 34 Rainfall, land use and occupational structure in Bharuch District

Figure 34(b)). Forest resources, especially teak trees and bamboo, have been depleted in much of the area. Thick jungle untouched by man can be seen only in the north. Timber and bamboo are sent to the depots and to Rajpipla. Charcoal and other minor forest produce, such as leaves for *bidi*-making, bark, gum, and roots for medicines, are collected by the Forest Department and the Forest Development Corporation. An effort is being made to utilize the resources prudently and extend them by reafforestation, wherever the forest area has been laid bare. By contrast, the forest area in the non-tribal region is negligible.

Table 9.1 Land use (per cent)

Region	Forest	Irrigated	Unirrigated	Cultivable waste	Not available for cultivation	Total
Tribal	26–91	1.91	51.09	6.49	13.60	100
Non Tribal	0.16	6.09	63.58	6.30	23.87	100

Source: Census of India, District Handbook: Bharuch, 1971

Of the cultivated land, which formed 53 per cent of the total area of the tribal region, only two per cent is irrigated. This shows that most cultivation relies on rainfall, which is uncertain and at times comes in heavy downpours. The thin soil cover and the absence of irrigation facilities permit the farmer to grow only coarse varieties of cereals and inferior millets. Rice is an important crop in the hilly and forest areas of Valia, Dediapada and Sagbara *talukas*. The farmer in the tribal region makes very little effort to increase the productivity of the land. His methods of cultivation are traditional and his agricultural implements are simple. The area under food crops is 45 per cent and under non-food crops 37 per cent. In the black soil tracts groundnuts and cotton are also grown, and castor in the *talukas* of Sagbara and Dediapada.

In the non-tribal region, land under cultivation forms 70 per cent of the total area, of which six per cent is irrigated. Wells are the chief source of irrigation water. Wheat is important in the *talukas* of Vagra and Jambusar. Rice and *jowar* (a variety of millet) are also grown. Non-food crops occupy 63 per cent of the total cropped area. From time immemorial, cotton has been an important cash crop, especially in Bharuch, Jambusar and Vagra *talukas*. The other non-food crops worth mentioning are oilseeds: groundnuts in Ankleshwar, sesamum in Jambusar and castor in Jambusar and Vagra. Among the non-food crops, cotton and fodder crops occupied most of the irrigated area.

In the hilly tracts of the tribal region, sizeable areas lie as cultivable waste land, which includes open pasture land and groves. The livestock of the tribal farmers are driven to these pastures which are covered with bushes and grass, naturally grown. In the non-tribal region, a similar amount of cultivable waste is found.

Land classified as not available for cultivation was 14 per cent of the tribal region. Much of this land lies unused because of thin soil cover, or it is dissected by gullies or infertile. In the non-tribal region, more land (24 per cent) is not available for cultivation. This is on account of roads, buildings and building sites, which occupy up to 36 per cent of Jambusar and Vagra *talukas*. The tract called Bara, along the sea-shore, is subjected to tidal effects all the year round. There is a scarcity of potable water. Percolation wells in this area are mostly brackish, and hence a large percentage of the area is not available for cultivation.

The size of holdings in the regions varies according to the condition of the soil, the crop pattern, the financial condition of the farmer and the extent of absentee landlordism. Table 9.2 shows that holdings of 0–2 ha and 2–10 ha are equally distributed in the tribal region. In the forest areas the holdings are bigger, owing to the unproductive nature of the area. Elsewhere, holdings are small, owing to scarcity of fertile land and also to subdivision among family members. Many holdings are scattered over the village, the *taluka* and other *talukas*. In some villages, where progressive non-tribal farmers live, intensive use of the holding is made by employing better methods of cultivation with modern agricultural implements, fertilizers and manure, and high quality seeds, whereas the tribal farmer carries on agriculture with traditional ways and simple agricultural tools. With the new policy of distributing land to the landless tribals, there is a fear among the progressive farmers that they will have to part with some of their fertile and well-cared for farmlands. The tribal farmer, who is not wealthy, will not be able to give the same attention, and in course of time this will reduce the economic value of the land. The tribal farmers rarely have a surplus of production from their farms.

In the non-tribal region, the percentage of holdings of 0–2 ha is larger than that of 2–10 ha (Table 9.2). A large number of these small holdings lie in the alluvial plains, where a smaller area comprises an economic unit. The high percentage of land under non-food crops, especially cotton, the small size of holdings, and the rich soil show the intensive nature of cultivation in this region. Cultivation is done with the help of tractors, and electric pumps are used for the supply of water.

Table 9.2 Landholdings (per cent)

Region	0–2 ha	2–10 ha	Over 10 ha	Total
Tribal	46	48	6	100
Non–tribal	53	40	7	100

Source: District Statistical Tables, 1977–8. District Panchayat Office, Bharuch

Livestock and poultry form important resources of the tribal region. Bullocks are used in farm work and their large numbers indicate their importance also in rural transportation. Cows and she-buffaloes are mainly kept for milk. Livestock owned by the tribal people are weak and unhealthy as they are not stall-fed, but are allowed to graze in the open pasture land. The yield of milk is also low. Keeping of poultry is an important cottage industry in rural areas. Fowls and eggs are sent to the towns of Rajpipla, Ankleshwar and Bharuch. In the non-tribal region bullocks belong to a superior variety. She-buffaloes are growing in popularity because of their milk yield and the incentive offered by the Dairy Plant at Bharuch.

Population

In the tribal region the density of population is only 143 per sq km The density of the rural area is only 136 per sq km. The tribals were originally a wandering people in the jungle areas. It is only in the last 25 years that they have taken to a sedentary way of life. Of the villages 65 remain uninhabited, and are located either in the dense jungle or on rugged terrain. In contrast to the sparse population of the rural areas, the town, Rajpipla (6495 per sq km), linked by a narrow gauge railway line, is a planned town with good roads, water supply, electric supply, parks and gardens, schools, hospitals and other amenities. With two important river projects in the vicinity, the population grew by 13 per cent during the period 1971–1981 to 29,226. The lopsided development of the urban and the rural areas can be attributed to the fact that the tribal population was kept in isolation from the rest of the district until recently.

On the other hand, the population in the non-tribal region is relatively homogeneous. The overall density is 190 per sq km, 140 in rural areas and 2,075 in urban areas. This region has had connections with the outside world for a very long time. The population consists of people from different parts of India, belonging to different cultures, and the tribal percentage is small.

Occupational structure

Table 9.3 shows some socio-economic attributes of the population considered by region (tribal or non-tribal) and divided between rural and urban areas. The categories 'main' and 'marginal' workers were introduced in the census of 1981 to distinguish those in work for more or less than six months in the year. A great proportion of 'main workers' was found in the non-tribal region (54 per cent) and of 'marginal workers' in the tribal region (62 per cent). This is because tribal workers migrate seasonally to urban areas, in the agricultural off-season, in search of temporary jobs.

Table 9.3 Socio-economic characteristics of the population, 1981 (per cent)

Region	Scheduled tribes	Literates	Main workers	Marginal workers	Overall
Tribal:					
Rural	77	34	41	7	95
Urban	18	66	27	0	5
Total					100
Non tribal:					
Rural	27	48	37	4	72
Urban	13	60	31	1	28
					100

Source: Census of India, 1981; series 5 Gujarat Part 11B; general population tables; Primary Census Abstract, Ahmedabad

Agriculture is the main occupation in the District and a very large majority of the population is engaged in it (Figure 34). Cultivators may be classified into different strata according to the size of the holdings they cultivate and the income they derive from the cultivation. Table 9.2 clearly reveals that a majority of cultivators hold less than 10 ha of land. A large percentage of people work as agricultural labourers, including peasants who possess 0–2 ha. Such people make their living by hiring out their labour in return for wages, paid generally not in cash but in kind. Some may be technically described as landholders because they own land, but the extent of the land they own may be so small, and the income they derive from it so meagre, that for all practical purposes they are landless. Except in irrigated tracts, the agricultural labourer seems to get much less than is necessary to keep him in a state of physical efficiency throughout the year.

This is due not to low wages, because the concentrated demand for labour ensures a fair rate, but to the lack of regular employment throughout the year. Field investigations also reveal that the tribal people do not remain at the service of rich farmers for long in spite of food, clothing and shelter offered to them.

Classification of the occupational structure (Table 9.4 and Figure 34) shows that the percentage of people involved in secondary activities in the tribal region is very small. Therefore secondary activities do not form a source of income for this region, contributing to the low level of development. People employed in the tertiary sector also form a small percentage of the working population in the tribal region. Much of the trade and commerce, and other tertiary activities, are concentrated in the single town of this region. The development of Rajpipla in this sector has been rather rapid in the last decade because of the construction of two major river projects nearby on the Rivers Narmada and Karjan. Selamba, near Sagbara, is the only settlement where a weekly market is held, and the chief articles sold are clothes, vegetables, groceries, spices and other articles of daily use. Some of the sellers are themselves producers of the goods and others are dealers' agents from the neighbouring villages. The buyers are the people of the market-place and the villages round about and the transactions are usually done on a cash basis. Most of the settlements are ill-equipped with services of all kinds, which may be attributed to the smallness of the villages and their inaccessibility.

Table 9.4 Occupational structure of workers, 1971 (per cent)

	Primary sector	Secondary sector	Tertiary sector
District total	*81*	*7*	*12*
Rural	90	4	6
Urban	20	26	54
Tribal region	*89*	*4*	*7*
Rural	92	3	5
Urban	17	22	61
Non-tribal region	*74*	*10*	*16*
Rural	88	5	7
Urban	21	26	53

Source: Census of India, District Handbook: Bharuch, 1971

The non-tribal region also shows a high percentage of workers engaged in primary activities; but there has been a rapid increase in secondary activities after 1965, especially in the decade 1971–81. The urban areas show a considerable proportion of workers employed in tertiary activities. Bharuch and Ankleshwar, located on the important traffic route, have developed trade and commerce and other services.

The scheduled tribes provide most of the labour force in the tribal region: 83 per cent of the cultivators, 91 per cent of agricultural labourers, 49 per cent of workers in household industry and 40 per cent of other workers. By contrast, in the non-tribal region their contribution is predominantly as agricultural labourers: 62 per cent, compared with 5–16 per cent of the other three categories. Even in urban areas they work as agricultural labourers. This is related to the low level of economic development in the tribal region.

Conclusion

Table 9.5 shows that the tribal region is much behind its neighbouring non-tribal region in almost all aspects relevant to economic development. Even in villages having schools, they may not be utilized as they should be. Roads are repaired year after year in the hilly tracts, owing to very heavy rainfall. Many villages remain virtually cut off for three months in the rainy season. The percentage of literacy is low, and this adds to the ignorance of the tribal people. The pace of development is also influenced by other factors: the growth of transport facilities, freedom from all forms of exploitation, willingness of the people to accept change and participate in the efforts of various agencies to raise their levels of living.

The object should be to make full use of the land and human resources of the region by giving all possible help and incentives. Regional disparity is bound to exist, but full use of the available resources would improve the productivity and living conditions of the poor people.

> *Wealth of an area is the product of (a) the material resources of man's environment, (b) the biological resources of social personnel and (c) the social resources for mobilizing the common will to make the fullest use of the first two.*
>
> *(R.P. Misra 1969, p. 20)*

It may not be possible for the people of such different regions to attain the same level of income, but more effort could be made to attain the basic essentials of life. There is a marked difference in the economic prosperity which exists between the tribal and the non-tribal regions. It is important that economic factors which influence the growth potential should be given primary consideration in the development of

Table 9.5 Comparison of the tribal and non-tribal regions of Bharuch District.

Details	Tribal region No.	Tribal region per cent	Non-tribal region No.	Non-tribal region per cent
Number of *talukas*	5		6	
Number of villages	807		403	
Towns	1		6	
Total population	548,732	42	747,719	58
Area (sq km)*	5,120		3,926	
Density (per sq km)	143		190	
Total urban population	29,226	12	212,283	88
Total rural population	519,506	49	535,436	51
Density (per sq km)	136		140	
Scheduled tribes		70		30
Literates		33		67
Workers		46		54
Area under food crops (ha)	93,024	45	113,083	55
Area under non-food crops (ha)	90,886	37	151,630	63
Per cent of cultivated area, under irrigation		7		11
Number of tractors	67		279	
Number of oil engine pumps	2,858		1,383	
Number of electric pumps	498		2,080	
Livestock	214,280	66	108,464	34
Poultry	163,491	72	64,183	28
Per cent of villages having:				
metalled roads		27		42
unmetalled roads		76		80
primary schools		70		96
higher secondary schools		4		12
other educational institutions		9		10
dispensaries		4		14
power supply		10		33
water taps		7		44
wells		77		97
Post Offices		20		55
telephones		1		3
bus facilities for the whole year		21		34
bus facilities during fair season		22		47
no bus facilities		58		19

* The area used for reporting land use is less than the total for the District (3,832 sq km for Tribal and 3,929 sq km for Non-Tribal Regions)

Source: (i) Census of India 1971, Series 5 Gujarat District; Census Handbook Broach District;
(ii) Census of India 1981 Series 5 Gujarat Part II B General Population Tables – Primary Census abstract Ahmedabad;
(iii) Broach District statistical tables 1977–78. District Panchayat Office, Broach.

the region, such as: power, transport, and irrigation facilities. It is not the prosperity of the agency that should matter, but the effective implementation of schemes to improve the economic standard of backward people, and thus achieve the goal which is set for the rest of the country.

Notes

1 Scheduled tribes are aboriginal populations who are granted safeguards under the Indian constitution, including the reservation of seats in assemblies, councils and Parliament.
2 Averages for 17 years (tribal region) and 50 years (non-tribal region) to 1970; a rainy day is defined as a day with at least 2·5 mm of rain.

References

Misra, R.P. (ed.) 1969. *Regional planning: concepts, techniques, policies and case studies* (University of Mysore)

Section Three: Inequality in Urban Settings

10
Low-income housing in Metropolitan Manila, the Philippines

M. Tekie
Division of Human Settlements Development, Asian Institute of Technology, Bangkok

Introduction

About 25 per cent of the urban population in the Third World live in slums and uncontrolled settlements, and one of the major problems facing low-income groups is adequate housing. There is great concern not only because of the large numbers who are poorly housed, but also because the situation is deteriorating rapidly.

This paper focuses on Metropolitan Manila, the primate city of the Philippines, where the average population density is 11,240 persons per square kilometre. Being a primate city, Metro-Manila is the centre of industrial, social, political and administrative activity and consequently it employs 40 per cent of the country's non-agricultural labour force and pays more than one-half of the labour force engaged in manufacturing (Laquian 1966). Of an estimated labour force of 1.20 million, about 1.07 million (88 per cent) are in employment, 26 per cent of whom are in the service sector. In sharp contrast to the wealth, commerce and vitality of Metro-Manila, 20 per cent of the population live in slums and squatter settlements, one-third of which are in the central or core city. Urban renewal and housing, therefore, are two of the more pressing concerns of the metropolis.

The housing problems of Metropolitan Manila have been in existence for the last three decades, but they have never been more pressing than in the past 15 years. The basic reasons for this are a rapidly growing population and the economic primacy of the city. Annual population increase rose to a staggering 4.9 per cent in 1970 and of this figure 2.4 per cent was attributed to migration (IBRD 1975; Nierras 1979). Population increase was only slowed down to 2.6 per cent in 1975 when the government, through its various agencies, instituted measures to curb population, yet Metro-Manila is still expected to contain 12,590,136 people in the year 2000 (NCSO 1975).

This rapid increase in Metro-Manila's population has created several problems. For one, the metropolis does not have enough housing to accommodate immigrants, who usually cannot afford to pay even highly subsidized rents. As a result, squatter colonies have cropped up all over the urban area. Public and private land, vacant plots, parks and areas along river banks have been invaded, and vacant plots can become occupied overnight with makeshift houses. In Metro-Manila, numerous approaches have been tried in different situations to solve the low-income housing problem. All these approaches have their merits, and weaknesses, but the question that should concern planners is how well housing in any sector fulfils its desired function and contributes to the general socio-economic development of a country.

Purpose of the study and methodology

The search for solutions to the low-income housing problem has been a global phenomenon over the past years and while a multitude of methods have been tried, we still find people in dire need of adequate shelter. Since the 1960s there has been increasing emphasis on self-help housing, a theme which has been developed notably by John Turner (Turner 1976). Turner has argued for 'do-it-yourself' housing complemented by dweller control, with government guaranteeing access to resources and amenities. It is argued that formal housing – either government or private sector, does not fulfill the immediate and pressing needs of low-income groups without shelter. Furthermore, official intervention through slum clearance may aggravate the situation, while minimum standards enforced for new housing may be economically unviable. Turner's advocacy of self-help housing has not been without its critics (see for example Burgess, 1978), but it will be apparent from the following study of Manila that in this writer's opinion, there is much to commend it.

This paper is based on research aimed at uncovering the structure of low-income housing in Metropolitan Manila and how people obtain their housing. Seven low-cost housing sub-systems have been identified (Figure 35). Each sub-system will be explored concentrating on its strengths and weaknesses, government involvement, the extent of amenities available, and people's priorities for the improvement of existing amenities and services. In conclusion, some consideration is given to how best government can help to improve the housing situation.

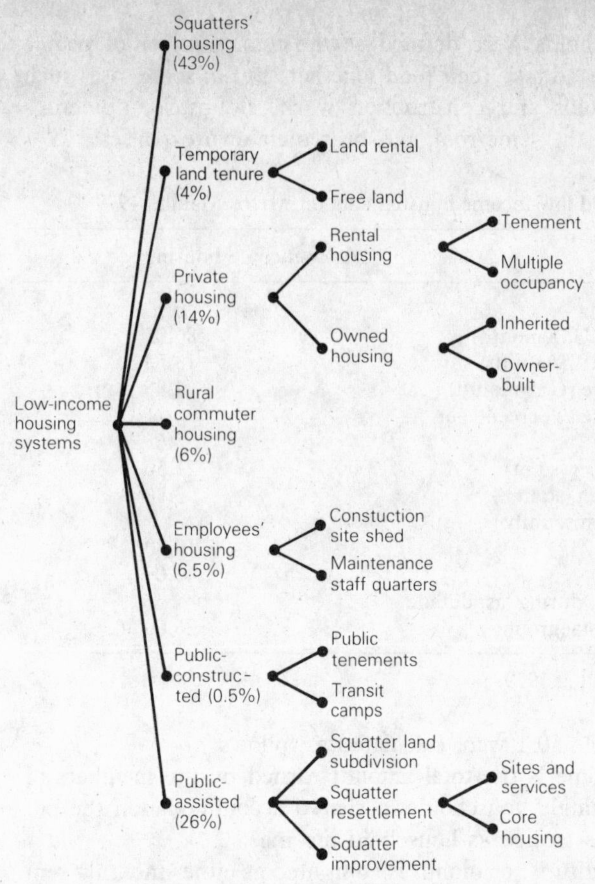

Fig. 35 Low-income housing systems in Metro-Manila

Using the 1975 income distribution data for Metro-Manila, together with adjustments based on wage indicators and variations for 1979, the upper limit of low-income earnings as applied in this research is 10,110.75 pesos (US$ 1,263.84) per annum or 842.57 pesos (US$ 105.32) per month. Some 2,820,967 people are in this category out of a total urban population of 7,052,477) or 462,452 families with an average household size of 6.1 persons. Low-income settlements were identified with the aid of aerial photographs, maps and field survey and a one-page structured questionnaire was administered to 2,000 households scattered over the low-income areas. Selection of households was done with a random-start procedure and systematically every fifth household in the community was interviewed. Those whose income was beyond the upper limit of the low-income boundary were discarded. Households were defined as the total number of people who live together and take their food together. But in some cases such as single households and construction workers' hostels, numerous people live under the same roof, but bear their own expenses.

Table 10.1 Averaged low-income housing data for Metro-Manila, 1979

Item	Low-income housing
Household size	6.1
Household income (US$/month)	86.05
Per capita income (US$/month)	13.53
Housing expenditure (US$/month)	4.86
Housing expenditure as percentage of income	5.65
Floor area of dwelling (sq m)	21.50
Floor area per person (sq m)	3.40
Length of stay in community	
Average (years)	10.80
Maximum (years)	40.0
Recent migrants i.e. during last decade as a percentage of total group	26.00

Source: Survey results, 1979

The items in Table 10.1 were calculated as follows:

1 Household income is the total amount earned by the members of the house. In single households in shared accommodation the per capita income is treated as household income.

2 Housing expenditure per month is computed as either monthly rent or one per cent of the present cost of the house (a rule of thumb) for owner-occupiers. In the case of single households who sat together, where all members equally share the rent of the room they live in, per capita housing expenditure was computed to get the aggregated average at sub-system and system level.

3 Floor area: only the area of the main house was counted because in many cases low-income people share some common spaces with others.

4 Those who came to the city during the last ten years were considered as recent migrants and the value was considered as a ratio of the whole.

Systems of low-income housing provision

While low-income groups are found all over the city, their settlements are usually concentrated either in the central urban area or in the periphery, on swampy areas and on land which is unusable for other development purposes. Also these locations tend to be crowded and unhealthy as well as in areas which are not easily reached by public transport. Low-income housing provision takes a variety of forms which may be either organized or spontaneous. Seven forms have been identified in this study which are termed sub-systems; they are: squatter, temporary land tenure, private housing, rural commuter housing, employees' housing, public constructed housing, and public assisted housing (Figure 35). These sub-systems can exist in any part of the city, but they differ from each other according to institutional arrangements, social interaction, economic conditions and residents' preferences. Each sub-system may contain several types of housing.

Amenities and essential services, such as toilets, baths, water supply, sewage and garbage disposal are mostly absent or found to be in a poor state. The most common problem in low-income settlements is the availability of water supply and in a majority of cases, a common water outlet services several hundred households. Drainage problems are not only widespread in these settlements, but throughout Metro-Manila. Opinions of respondents with regard to services and amenities and priorities for its improvement reflect the pathetic state of these essential facilities and services. It clearly reflects the substandard housing and health hazards of low-income communities.

Squatter housing

In 1979 squatters in Metro-Manila numbered approximately 190,000 families who were scattered throughout the main urbanized area (Figure 36). Squatters comprise the largest element of the low-income housing system (43 per cent), the majority occupying makeshift houses or 'barong-barongs' which are easy to build, and quickly constructed. The value of these houses ranges from a few hundred pesos to a little over a thousand pesos. A majority of squatter households have no toilet facilities although a small part of the house is reserved as a bathing place, but most people do not have an individual water supply. Footpaths in squatter settlements range in width from 0.5 to 1.0 metres and are mostly made of gravel. Drainage is one of the main problems in squatter areas.

In pure squatter settlements people erect houses on land which does not belong to them without the consent of the landowner. Squatter colonies usually crop up on vacant land which usually belongs to the government and houses are made of waste materials. In Metro-Manila, squatter colonies can appear overnight, and because there are so many

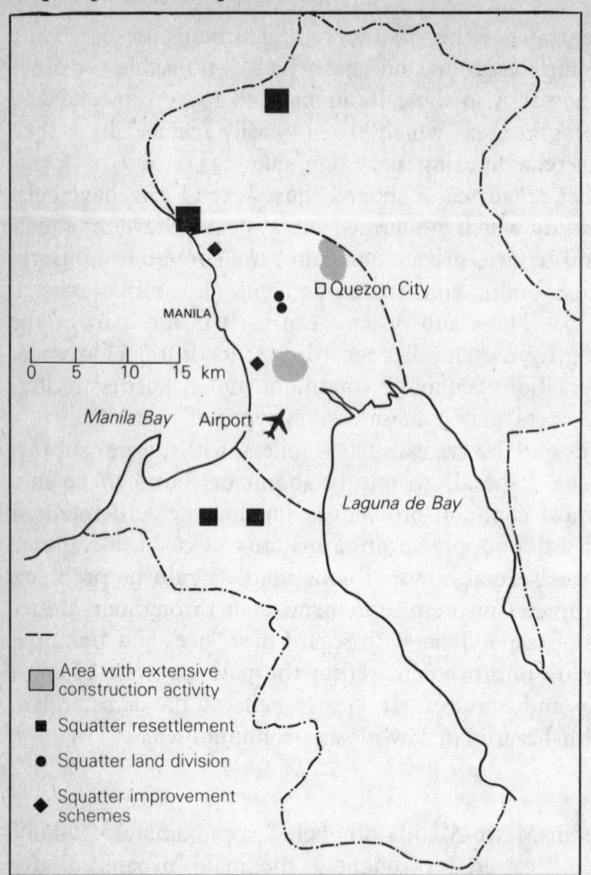

Fig. 36 Distribution of low-income housing in Metro-Manila (a)

of them sprawling all over the city, outright eviction is not possible. About 22.5 per cent of the squatter households are recent migrants (recent being defined as in the last ten years). This figure would run as high as 70 per cent if migrants were defined as those who came during the last two decades. Generally people in the squatter settlements are from rural areas, who come to the city in search of better opportunities, although statistics on income and housing indicate their relatively poor situation. In this type of settlement, people form informal associations through which they try to secure tenure of the land they occupy. Rural traits are found to be very strong in squatter settlements, as migrants carry with them their original cultures, yet although individual families exhibit close ties, the diverse mixture of cultures ensures that social conflict is common in squatter areas.

Materials used to construct houses are mainly wood, old galvanized iron, sheets and boards. Most dwelling units are one storey high and many people share one toilet while drinking water is collected from stand-pipes and tube wells installed for public use. These settlements are dirty, crowded, unhealthy and an affront to human dignity. But in spite of the pathetic condition of their environment, people are apparently happy and do not like to leave their communities. They are however dissatisfied with their present state, especially with the water supply, drainage and roads which are either absent or in poor condition. The government has initiated several schemes to improve squatter settlements and foremost among those which have been implemented are the squatter improvement schemes and the resettlement projects, which are discussed later.

Temporary land tenure housing

In this sub-system, people acquire a measure of security through temporary land tenure either by paying rent, or by an employer providing free land. Under both arrangements, land is provided by a third party and the house is constructed by the user. The settlement pattern in this sub-system is quite similar to that of squatters, but the major difference is the legality of land occupation and security of tenure. This sub-system is mostly found in the form of small communities, although a few independent and isolated structures can be found in some areas of the city. People who obtain housing of this type are again basically recent migrants. However, many old city residents who cannot afford to own a piece of land are also found in this sub-system. Houses are scattered throughout all residential areas but particularly in the periphery. Government involvement in this settlement type is limited to the formulation of land laws which prevent the imposition of exorbitant land rentals.

Under land rental arrangements people build their own houses on land obtained from a private owner at a fixed rent for a particular period of time. Houses, often two storeys high, are usually built by the people themselves with the assistance of a few skilled workers. They are of the semi-permanent type, slightly larger than the average 'barong-barong' and built of old wood and galvanized sheets. Generally, the houses have their own toilets and bath facilities and an individual water and electrical supply. Drainage is the chief problem and most of these houses are located where there is no direct access to public roads and transport.

When land is provided by employers for their employees, the latter pay no rental and the right to occupy the dwelling they construct is conterminous with employment. Since the arrangement is often precarious, houses are of the temporary type. People usually do not invest much in structure and houses are classified under the 'barong-barong' category. In fact, in terms of floor area, dwellings have a smaller floor area than those of squatters. This settlement type is frequently found near big business establishments. The average household size is only 3.8 which reflects employer preferences for employees with small families, and among the different sub-systems households belonging to this classification earn the least. Yet people expressed some satisfaction with the security offered and because these houses are only found near work sites, households often enjoy good facilities such as roads and transportation. In addition, they also have free services and facilities such as water supply, electricity and garbage collection. Improvements of the said services and facilities however are deemed essential by the settlers.

Private housing

Private housing is the third largest sub-system in Metro-Manila, housing 14 per cent of low-income households. This sub-system, which is comprised of older houses, occurs almost everywhere in the city and works without any assistance from the government or other institutions. There are two types of private housing; rental housing and owned housing.

Under private rental agreements individual households acquire houses from landlords at a monthly rent or on a lease for a mutually agreed period. These houses are either built specifically for renting or were formally used by their owners, and tenants have no direct involvement with the design and construction of the dwelling units. Rental housing can be subdivided into tenement and multiple-occupancy housing; government involvement mostly affects the rental of the latter and includes rent control laws.

There is in fact only one tenement project undertaken by the private sector for low-income groups, which is the Sambahayan Condominium Project in Mandaluyoung. This tenement project is a complex of several buildings clustered together with all the necessary facilities. Tenement houses are concrete multi-storey structures divided into apartment units for occupancy by low-income families. Each unit is provided with toilet and bath and a household occupant pays a monthly rent which is credited as monthly instalments against the purchase of the unit. Ownership of everything outside the apartment is socialized. It differs from the tenement houses of the government (see later) by the fact that people not only rent the units, but ultimately will own them. Government tenements are fully owned by the state and tenants are only expected to pay rent. Another difference is that units in the Sambahayan Project are bigger in floor area (34 sq m). Each tenement unit is valued at an average of US$ 2,062 which is paid on an instalment basis.

One special feature of this type is that it is not only the housing conditions of the residents that are better but also their personal involvement. Within the tenement complex a residents' association has been formed, which regularly meets to discuss common problems and to try to formulate solutions or precautionary measures. Management of the complex is also vested in the residents themselves, which is unique to this type of housing system. Because of restrictions imposed on applicants regarding household size, the average is relatively low, 5.8, and floor area per person is the highest among the whole low-income housing. The expenditure on housing with respect to income is 29.7 per cent, representing the highest figure within the entire system. People seem to be satisfied with all facilities, but they indicated that if improvements are to be introduced, highest priority should be given to water supply and access to public services. This housing type was conceived by several business leaders of the country as a contribution by the private sector to the low-income housing problem. At first, the Sambahayan Project was intended only for the very low-income group, but in the later stages of development, the rules were changed to include the middle-income earners. Today, a majority of the residents of Sambahayan Condominium are from the middle-income earning group.

Multiple occupancy of large old houses formerly belonging to high-income earning families, is another type of rental housing which can usually be found in older sections of the metropolis. Because these are old houses, the high-income occupants have moved out and sold these houses or have subdivided them into several units for rental. Owing to the relatively low rent of the individual units and the bad shape of the buildings, they are occupied by the very lowest income groups. Occupants in this housing category have the highest average household size (6.83), with a low floor area per person (2.9 sq m). Housing expenditure is 7.9 per cent of household income, which is almost twice the average for all sub-systems. People housed in multi-occupancy dwellings are dissatisfied with water supply, space, neighbourliness, and the physical condition of dwelling units, roads and walkways. Indicated priorities for improvement are water supply, followed by lanes, paths, roads and landfill. Forty per cent of the people who live in this type of housing are recent migrants to the city.

No government involvement has been recorded in assisting occupants of this housing category.

Within the private housing sub-system owned housing is the most important, comprising 11 per cent of the entire low-income housing. Both house and land are owned by the occupant, and housing may either be old and of the permanent type, or relatively new but constructed of second-hand materials. Low-income owned housing can be found in older sections of the metropolitan area, and at the periphery, and generally the value of houses and expenditure on housing is well above average. There are two types of housing under this category: inherited houses and owner-built houses. The value of inherited houses is higher than that of owner-built houses although the former are generally much older in appearance. There are no recent migrants in this housing category and their occupants have been permanent residents for the last decade.

Inherited housing is found scattered throughout the metropolitan area and dwellings, usually two-storey buildings, are provided with all facilities and services. They are commonly situated where transportation is easily accessible and roads and walkways are good enough. Inherited housing has one of the highest average floor areas (34.6 sq m) in the whole system, and although family composition is relatively high too (6.5), the average floor area per person is high (5.30 sq m). The average value of houses is US$ 1,239 which is more than other dwelling types. However maintenance is costly, amounting to 18.3 per cent of household income; this is due to the state of these older houses.

Owner-built housing is in the private sector commonly found in the peripheral parts of the metropolitan area (Figure 37). It accommodates people who own land through inheritance or purchase, but with very meagre resources to build better houses. Houses are built by the owners themselves and construction is done in phases. This is basically how it differs from inherited houses, where present occupants make no direct contribution to the construction. Occupants build their houses with their own capital and resources, using family labour and, in some instances, aided by a few skilled workers.

Owner-built houses are semi-permanent in nature and have floors which are elevated and made of concrete or wood; walls are built of wood and in a few cases hollow blocks. Independent toilets and small bathing spaces are available to occupants, but services, such as underground drainage, electricity, sewage and garbage disposal are not available. Water supply is obtained from pumps or wells and in some cases from roadside stand pipes. A majority of the residents, however,

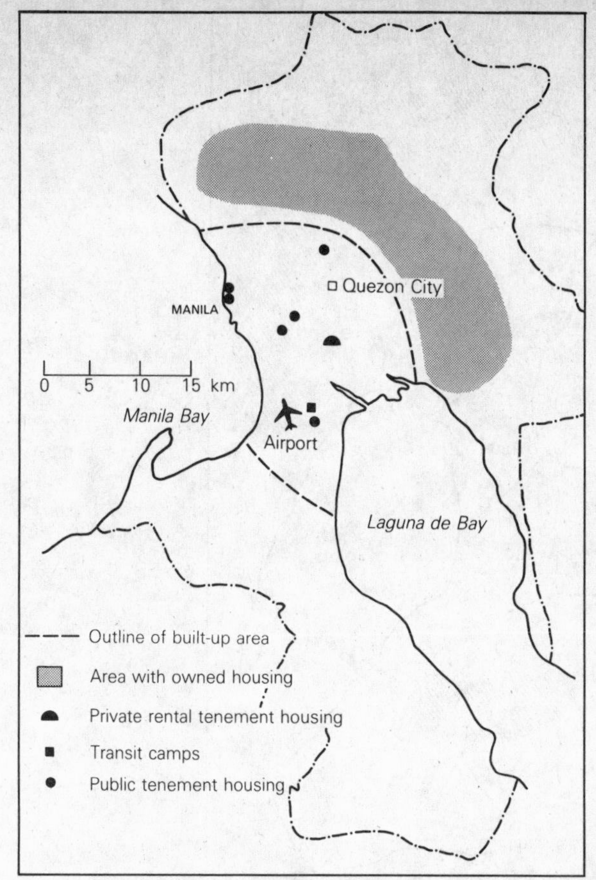

Fig. 37 Distribution of low-income housing in Metro-Manila (b)

have mains-electricity. As houses are usually located far from major streets, the condition of walkways leading to the houses is very poor.

Household size is comparatively small and has a high average floor area per person, and housing expenditure as a percentage of income is relatively higher than other types because of the price increases in construction materials in the local market. The inhabitants' first priority for improvement is the supply of water to their houses. This type of housing is receiving very little attention, if any, from the government.

Rural commuters housing sub-system

People in this type reside in the rural periphery of Metro-Manila, but commute into the centre for work (Figure 38). Both houses and lots

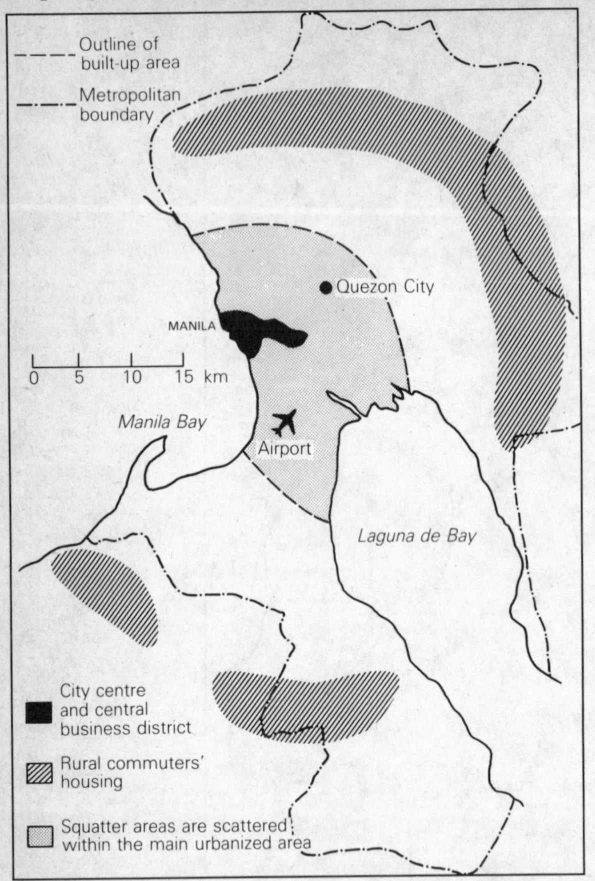

Fig. 38 Distribution of low-income housing in Metro-Manila (c)

are usually owned by the occupants, and the construction of semi-permanent houses is undertaken by the owners themselves with the assistance of a few skilled workers. Because of limited financial resources, house building proceeds in stages, although the cost of houses is much cheaper than those situated in the city. Concrete, wood and galvanized sheeting are commonly used for building and most of these houses have toilets and bath facilities, but water supply is the main problem. People who obtain housing of this type are better-off compared to the squatters in urban centres, which is evident from their relative household incomes (US$ 94.35) and the floor areas per person (4.84 sq m). There is no direct evidence of government offering assistance to this sub-system, and if there have been any efforts, it is in the form of transportation subsidies because of their location, together with the provision of roads, water supply and electricity.

Employee housing

Another housing type where the private sector is involved is the employee housing sub-system, and though not well recognized, it houses 6.5 percent of the total low-income population. Houses and lots or quarters are often constructed and provided by employers for their employees. Like the land rental system the arrangement is conterminous with the employee's work contract. This low-income group is found in those parts of the metropolitan area where construction activities and business establishments are concentrated, and where high- and middle-income earners reside. There are two types of employee housing, construction site dormitories and domestic staff quarters. These two types vary greatly in terms of the accommodation they offer. Construction site dormitories are more or less temporary, while domestic staff quarters are part of permanent structures. Household sizes and living units are very small in this sub-system, having an average floor area of 11.1 sq m, with limited floor area per person.

Construction site dormitories are temporary in nature, built by construction companies on the site to accommodate workers. These dormitories are sometimes built by the workers themselves out of materials provided by employers, or they are sometimes made of preformed lumber or waste materials. The size of these sheds varies depending upon the size of construction site, but usually they are laid out in lines. A majority, if not all, construction site dormitories have common toilets and baths. The electricity supply is good as it is used in construction activities, and the dormitories generally have an adequate water supply. Because all materials used in the construction of the shed are provided by the employers, housing expenditure for the occupant is zero. Satisfaction levels and improvement priorities were not answered by respondents, since the length of stay is temporary, ranging from a few to several months.

Domestic staff housing is either temporary, permanent or simply rooms which are part of the big houses occupied by their employers. This group comprises domestic servants, maintenance staff of government agencies, private companies, private organizations and individual high-income families. This housing type exists because of employers' need to be in close proximity to their staff round the clock. In most instances, domestic servants live in the same building occupied by employers while maintenance staff like drivers, cleaners, gardeners and security guards are housed in separate quarters within the compound of the employers' residence. Sometimes no quarters are provided for security guards but they can sleep anywhere inside the building.

Employees housed in this type generally enjoy the modern amenities and services which are available to high-income people. Those with separate quarters are provided with a toilet and bath. The roads that lead to their quarters or offices are well developed and all utilities are available. The estimated proportion of total households covered by this category is 2.70 per cent of the low-income population and these households enjoy a comparatively high per capita income (US$52.70), as only one person constitutes a household. Security guards and domestic servants are mostly single, and the families of those who are married in most instances live separately, usually in the provinces. Laws affecting occupants of this housing type relate to a minimum wage and in the case of security guards, qualities and qualifications are specifically stated.

Publicly constructed housing

This housing sub-system is one of the two sub-systems receiving direct government assistance. Dwelling units, mostly in the form of concrete tenements or transit camps, are available for rent or provided free and constructed as part of government schemes to house low-income people. However, the contribution of this sub-system towards the provision of low-income housing is minimal, providing for only 0.5 per cent of the total low-income population.

Public tenements comprise seven-storey concrete structures, divided into 24 sq m apartments at highly subsidized rents. There are 8 tenement blocks situated in Taguig, Metro-Manila with a maximum capacity each of 645 families. Each tenement block is virtually a self-contained community and all facilities are provided including recreation grounds, stores and elementary schools. However, sewage disposal and garbage collection is inadequate. The high average household size of 7.1 is coupled to a relatively high household income (US$99.80), although housing expenditure, which is 2.28 per cent of household income, is minimal as rentals are highly subsidized. Though these tenement houses were intended purely for the low-income group, we find that many of their tenants belong to the middle-income group. Only 10 per cent of the people in public tenements are recent migrants.

The other type of public housing is the transit camp. Transit camps are sites provided by the government to locate displaced low-income families, particularly squatters who are awaiting permanent relocation or resettlement. Basically, there are two kinds of transit camp; for the first kind the government provides land and a few facilities, such as water and communal toilets and baths. People are left to construct houses in the size and form preferred. There is only one camp of this kind in Metro-Manila – the Makati Health Center Relocation Area, which houses residents evicted from several sites in Makati. The second kind of transit camp comprises semi-permanent rows of houses constructed by the government for occupation by squatter families, particularly those coming from Tondo. This transit camp, which is a self-contained community in itself, is known as Tuluyan Project. Rows are divided into apartment units which are independently provided with essential facilities, and are occupied free. The floor area per person is 2.4 sq m, one of the lowest in the entire low-income system.

Public-assistance housing

Public-assistance housing is the second largest sub-system, housing 26 per cent of the entire low-income group. Three schemes were adopted to provide housing assistance: squatter resettlement (the most important), squatter subdivision and squatter improvement. The general difference between this sub-system and squatter housing is mainly in terms of facilities and condition of houses. A majority of the houses have their own toilet and bath while hardly any squatter settlements have the same facilities. The average value of houses is US$396, which is higher than those in squatter settlements, while expenditure on housing constitutes 7.20 per cent of household income. Of the families settled under this housing delivery category 22 per cent are recent migrants.

The most extensive government involvement in low-income housing is in resettlement projects. There are three in Metro-Manila which are situated in Carmona, Dasmarinas and Sapang Paley, accommodating a total of 60,000 by families (Figure 36). These areas are on government-owned or acquired lands, on the periphery of the metropolitan areas, which were developed with roads and essential facilities for the purpose of resettling squatter families from city centres. Parcels of 48 sq m lots were given out to squatters on very easy terms, households occupying a parcel of land and having 10 years in which to pay for it by instalments.

Government efforts are concentrated on this type of housing provision, the unique feature of which is the freedom to design and construct houses according to occupants' needs and tastes. The feeling of achievement and the value settlers attach to their houses are considered important aspects of this scheme. The household size of 6.3 is higher than the average for the whole system with a corresponding small floor area per person (3.60 sq m) and low per capita income

(US$11.29). Housing expenditure as a percentage of income is comparatively high (8.00 per cent) but houses are usually permanent and built in phases to suit the occupiers from all situations.

At the early stages of this venture, people were doubtful about the likely success of this scheme. Being located at the edge of the city with few job opportunities, a number of relocated settlers have returned to their old squatter locations in the metropolitan centre. However government authorities have recognized this problem and have therefore extended incentive programmes to encourage industrialists to locate their establishments in the vicinity of these sites and services. The government view this particular housing scheme as a major solution to the low-income housing problem, and intends to expand existing sites. Estimated government expenditure runs to many hundred million pesos, yet water supply, drainage, garbage collection and roads are all unsatisfactory and need improvement.

In addition to providing sites and services for resettled squatters another scheme provides 'core housing', which is relatively new. Government constructs 'cores' which consist of concrete floor slabs and compartments for toilet and bath, then sells to low-income families on very easy terms. These core houses are built in the resettlement projects. A householder granted permission to occupy the core of 24.5 sq m builds his house in phases and design is left to the occupant. Average housing expenditure as a percentage of income (8.8 per cent) is approximately the same as those located in sites and services projects. This figure is quite reasonable, but occupants are dissatisfied with the existing drainage, sewage and garbage collection systems and ranked these amenities as priorities for improvement. Again the chief setback of this scheme is the location, far from the workplaces of occupants. The same strategy as for sites and services projects was adopted by the government to circumvent this limitation.

Although the resettlement schemes are the major form of government intervention, squatter subdivision and squatter improvement make a minor contribution. While only 1.11 per cent of the entire low-income housing provision is covered by squatter land subdivision it is the most welcomed government intervention in housing. The land is usually in the form of privately owned plots within the urbanized built-up areas which have been idle and occupied by squatters. The sizes of these plots range from a few hundred square metres to several hectares. These lands were subdivided into smaller parcels and sold to their occupants at very reasonable prices within their purchasing capacity.

The only difference between this housing type and squatter settlements is that residents possess land tenure, and the fear of eviction is absent. But the general environmental condition is no better than that of squatter settlements. Houses may be permanent though most are still the same small 'barong-barong' type, spaced close together. In fact the average floor area per person is only 3.0 sq m, far lower than that of squatter houses. Toilet and bath facilities are not integral parts of the house, water is obtained from a communal source, and the surroundings are generally dirty. Not surprisingly, people are very dissatisfied with water supply, drainage, sewage and garbage collection systems and these amenities are their priorities if improvements are to be introduced.

'Squatter improvement' is the name given to settlements where the government has cleaned up the general environment of squatter and slum colonies. Roads and walkways have been widened, electricity lines provided, water supply, drainage, sewage and garbage collection facilities improved. Improved squatter areas are much better than pure squatter settlements, as houses are painted and enlarged, while the materials used in the construction of houses are no longer waste or second-hand materials. The average household size of 5.9 suggests that as one climbs the economic ladder, family size decreases. Complementary to this is the relatively high average income (US$97.25). Improved conditions are also reflected in the increased average housing expenditure from 4.4 per cent in the pure squatter type to 7.9 per cent in this category. One advantage of this scheme is its proximity to urban centres and places of work. Furthermore, the presence of a multitude of stores selling consumer goods is also an advantage compared with the resettlement areas.

Government housing policy

The failure to match housing standards with people's ability to pay is one of the serious factors which contributes to the aggravation of the low-income housing problem. Very high building standards are enforced beyond the capability of the majority of the population, which consists of low-income and lower middle-income groups.

The findings of a World Bank study conducted in 1975 pointed out three important aspects that undoubtedly demonstrate how building standards could affect the housing market.

1 If the extent of subsidy of total costs is not allowed to exceed 20 per cent and if the percentage of the family's income devoted to housing is not allowed to exceed 20 per cent, the average family cannot afford to purchase more than 15 sq m of living space.

2 If the subsidy is kept to 20 per cent and a minimum of 40 sq m is to be purchased, 38 per cent of the average family's income will be required.
3 If a minimum of 40 sq m is to be purchased and no more than 20 per cent of family income spent, 32 per cent of the total cost will have to be subsidized.

In the urban areas of the Philippines, the National Housing Authority pegged the minimum lot area at 180 sq m, and the minimum floor area at 46 sq m (NHA 1976). It recommended that the outside walls of houses should be made of 6 in. concrete hollow blocks and roof framing systems should be strong enough to be able to withstand zonal winds. If these standards were adhered to, then thousands of households would be unable to obtain shelter. A 180 sq m lot with a 46 sq m house would cost at least p.34,870 or $4,358.75. Assuming no subsidy and an interest rate at six per cent on a 25-year loan of p.34,870, monthly amortization would run to about p.227.31 or US$28.41. This amount is beyond the capacity of 40 per cent of the population of Metro-Manila, who only spend an average of p.38.88 or US$4.86 monthly for housing expenditure. If we accept that people's monthly savings plus their actual housing expenditure is fully spent on housing then the required monthly subsidy amounts to 75 per cent of the cost of the house and lot or p.167.63 (US$20.94) per house (average figures from survey results).

The role of government in low-income housing provision

Only two housing delivery sub-systems, covering 26 per cent of the total low-income population, receive direct government assistance out of the seven sub-systems discussed. These are the publicly constructed housing and public-assistance sub-systems where assistance is usually in the form of a subsidy. If we take 20 per cent of the household's income as normally allocated on housing expenditure, each transit camp family would then spend p.104.88 or US$13.11 per month on the average, but the survey shows that only p.2.64 or US$0.33 per month is being spent on housing. This would mean that the government is shouldering the balance of p.102.24 or US$12.78 per month per household. Taking the total number of households under this category, the aggregate government subsidy is p.47,352.00 (US$5,919.00) monthly or p.568,224.00 (US$71,028.00) per year. Adapting the same calculation for public tenement housing, we would arrive at a figure representing the subsidized amount equivalent to p.141.44 or US$17.68 per month per household. The total government subsidy then on public tenement housing amounts to p.261,638.56 (US$32,704.82) per month or p.3,139,662.70 (US$392,457.80) per year.

Public housing assistance is extended by the government through squatter-resettlement, squatter-improvement and squatter-land subdivision. Average household expenditure of families staying only in sites and services projects is approximately p.45.52 or US$5.69 per month. but if the normal 20 per cent of income is allocated for housing expenditure, each household would be actually devoting p.113.76 or US$14.22 per month and the difference between this figure and actual cash outlay is p.68.24 or US$8.53. This p.68.24 or US$8.53 balance then comes in the form of government subsidy. Since there are approximately 28,302 families residing in sites and services projects, the estimated government subsidy, covering cost of land, development cost and administrative expenses is in the region of p.1,931,328 (US$241,416) per month or p.23,175,936 (US$2,896,992) per year.

Core housing receives a bigger subsidy from the government because in addition to the sites and services development cost, construction of cores are undertaken. Estimated monthly government subsidy per household runs to about p.75.36 or US$9.42. Covering approximately 1,202.38 families, annual outlay is p.1,087,336 (US$135,917) or p.90,608 (US$11.326) each month.

Families residing in the squatter-improvement type of housing spend on the average p.61.44 or US$7.68 monthly on housing or about 7.90 per cent of their monthly income. If instead of the normal 20 per cent allocation for housing, we assume only 10 per cent of the income is spent because of slightly poorer conditions in this scheme, each family should be setting aside p.77.84 or US$9.73 per month, on the average, for housing expenditure. Since less is actually disbursed, the government covers the balance of p.16.40 (US$2.05) per month per household. The total subsidy in the tune p.1,462,240 (US$182,780) per month or p.17,546,912 (US$2,193,364) annually, covering 89,161 families. The squatter land subdivision scheme, which houses 5,133 households, receives p.610,648 (US$76,331) monthly or p.7,327,800 (US$915,975) annually in the form of housing subsidy.

In total, the estimated government cash outlay runs about p.52.8 million or US$6.6 million annually to subsidize the housing of 27.27 per cent of the low-income population. The squatters' housing subsystems, which covers the largest population – 43 per cent of the entire low-income population does not receive direct government subsidy. But the main objective of assisting the public-construction housing and public-assistance housing sub-systems is to accommodate people from the squatters' housing sub-system and upgrade their existing conditions. Temporary land tenure housing, rural commuters' housing, private housing and employee housing sub-systems, together forming 29.7 per cent of Metro-Manila's low-income population, do not receive any direct government subsidy.

The study has covered a total number of 2,000 households in Metro-Manila area. Data reveal that 80 per cent of the low-income people live in ordinary houses built mostly of wood; an average floor area available per person in these groups is found to be 3.4 sq m. Data on public utilities and services reflect the poor condition of low-income communities. It has been found that more than 70 per cent of the low-income people do not have any bathing facilities and 75 per cent do not have access to pipe-borne water. It can be concluded that condition and maintenance of housing is much below the minimum requirement, and on the average 50 per cent of the households find their housing inadequate. The question which is posed by the survey is whether the government's commitment to the Public Housing System is the best use of limited resources and in the best interests of the majority of the low-income group. Despite huge expenditure on public housing there is ample evidence that water supply, drainage, garbage collection and roads are all in an unsatisfactory condition.

Those families on the upper limit of the low-income group, though still a minority, require some assistance in the purchase or rental of housing, such as easier mortgage loans, reasonable interest rates, and help in land acquisition. This group has some ability to pay and some knowledge of the ways in which housing finance works. Indirect forms of government assistance could be extended such as the promotion and development of savings and loan systems and co-operatives through initial capital infusion and the provision of incentives to encourage families to participate and save in these systems.

Those people at the lower limit of the low-income group require a substantial subsidy if they are to be provided with government housing. However, assistance might be better to take the form of technical advice for self-help housing built on land serviced by only the most basic utilities. If assistance is to be given to squatters to better their own housing, this could be done best by legalizing squatter groups' rights to the land they have built on. This can be an incentive to them to improve their housing on an incremental basis over time at their own cost. Where governmental outlays are made they can best be used in providing improved access routes, piped-in water and other basic facilities needed by the community, with neighbourhood families volunteering the physical, unskilled labour needed for these projects.

References

Andrezewski, A. 1967. 'Housing policy and housing system: models in some socialist countries'. In Nevitt, A. (ed.), *The economic problems of housing* (London: Macmillan)

Batchelder, A. 1966. *The economics of poverty* (New York: John Wills and Sons)

Beyer, A.G. 1965 *Housing and society* (New York: Macmillan)

Black and Veatch 1969. *Master plan for a sewerage system for the Manila Metropolitan Area* (Manila)

Buranasirig 1982 'Bangkok's low income housing needs: an overview of the problems and perspectives'. In *Housing as a basic need* (Singapore: RIHED), pp. 69–80.

Burgess, R. 1978. Petty commodity housing or dweller control: a critique of John Turner's views on housing policy, *World Development.*, vol. 6 (9/10), pp. 1105–33.

Galabraith, J. 1969. *The affluent society* (London: Hamish Hamilton)

Hollnsteiner, M. 1975. Metamorphosis: from Tondo squatter to Tondo settler, *Ekistics*, September 1975, pp. 21–32.

IBRD 1975. *Urban Sector Survey*, Vol. II (Washington DC)

ICFTU/IFBWU 1970. *The housing situation of low income groups* (Brussels: International Housing Committee)

Institute of Environmental Planning 1971. *Manila Bay Metropolitan Framework Plan* (Quezon City: University of the Philippines)

Interagency Committee on Metropolitan Manila 1973. *Metropolitan Manila Authority: a development and reform strategy proposal* (Manila: Government Printing Office)

ILO 1976. *Employment, growth and basic needs: a one-world problem*, (Geneva: ILO)

Laquian, A. 1966. *Slums and squatters in six Philippine cities* – a final report (Manila)

Laquian, A. 1972. 'Manila'. In W. Robson and D. Regan (eds) *Great cities of the world: their government, politics and planning*, vol. II (London: George Allen and Unwin Ltd.) pp. 621–4.

Lim, S.W. 1982. 'An alternative development strategy for urban centers in the Third World with special reference to ASEAN countries'. In *Housing as a basic need* (Singapore: RIHED), pp. 211–26.

Liu, T.K. 1975. 'Design for better living conditions'. In S.H.K. Yeh (ed.), *Public housing in Singapore* (Singapore: Singapore University Press)

Marcos, I. 1976. Manila–challenge to the visionary, *The Philippine Quarterly*, vol. 8, no. 1, January 1976, pp. 22–5.

Myrdal, G. 1960. *Beyond welfare state* (London: Methuen)

Nierras, J. 1979. Improving mass transportation in Metropolitan Manila: some short-range, non capital intensive techniques, *The Philippine Planning Journal*, vol. X, no. 2, April 1979, pp. 1–24.

National Housing Authority 1976. *Metro Manila Housing Program*, Interim Report No. 1 (Manila: NHA)

National Census and Statistical Office 1975. *Census* (Manila: NCSO)

Overseas Technical Cooperation Agency 1973. *Urban transportation study for Metro Manila Area* (Manila: DPWTC)

Rein, M. 1969. 'Problems in the definitions and measurement of poverty'. In L.A. Fermen *et al.* (eds) *Poverty in America* (Ann Arbor: University of Michigan Press)

Smith, F.W. 1970, *Housing, the social and economic elements*, (Berkeley, Los Angeles: University of California Press)

Tekie, M. 1981, Coastal land use planning in the Philippines, *Proceedings of the National Conference on Coastal and Foreshore Lands* (Quezon City: National Environmental Protection Council)

Turner, J.F.C. 1976, *Housing by people* (London: Marion Boyess)

Turner, J.F.C. 1978. Housing in three dimensions, *World Development*. vol. 6 (9–10), pp. 1135–45.

United Nations, *Techniques of surveying a country's housing situation, including estimating of current and future housing requirements*, ST/ ECE/HOU/, Sales No. 66.11 E. Mim. 3.

United Nations, *Major long term problems of government housing and related policy*, ST/ECE/HOU/, Sale No. 66, 11 E. Mim. 3.

World Bank 1975. Housing Sector Policy, May, 1975 (Washington: World Bank)

11
Workers, retrenchment and urban-rural linkages in Kano, Nigeria

H.A.C. Main
Department of Geography, Bayero University, Kano, Nigeria.

Migration is in many cases a response to inequality, and urban migration in much of the Third World is arguably a product of inequalities created by the incorporation of the periphery into the world capitalist economy. This being the case, migration cannot be fully understood without analysis at the structural level. Similarly, the spatial dimensions of population movements are more usefully interpreted as manifestations of social process than as independent variables. However, migration and urbanization vary with the particular social formations in which the migrants are located and with the way in which these formations are combined with international capital. This paper specifically examines urban-rural linkages of migrants in Metropolitan Kano, and why those who have lost jobs remain in the city. The starting point for this analysis is the social formation in which these migrants are located, with particular regard to changes in the Nigerian political economy over the past 20 years. Both have influenced the departure of migrants from the rural areas and their subsequent employment in the city. Attention is also drawn to the nature and development of semi-industrial capitalism and proletarianization in Nigeria together with the conditions and 'development' of the rural areas since independence.

Nigeria in the late twentieth century

Prior to the growth of the oil economy during the 1970s, capitalist production in Nigeria was predominantly rural and export-oriented. The major form of appropriation was through the monopoly agricultural marketing boards for exports. During the colonial era, the product of farmers' labour was channelled towards British industry, but from about the time of flag independence in 1960 it went more to the creation of the Nigerian bourgeoisie. The northern Nigerian export crops (mainly groundnuts and cotton) were grown by farming households along with food crops, and not in plantations. The agricultural year was divided into a busy growing rainy season and a slack non-growing dry season, which enabled farmers to undertake non-farming occupations for perhaps five months of the year. Many travelled long distances to sell their labour in the docks, plantations and mines of Lagos, southern Nigeria, southern Ghana and the Plateau: seasonal labour circulation both supplemented the cash income of rural households and conserved their food stocks. Therefore the demand for labour in the extractive peripheral economy with little industrial activity was sufficiently seasonal to restrict towns to slow growth rates based mainly on administrative and commercial functions.[1]

The petroleum boom of the 1970s drastically altered the Nigerian economy and the nature of social relations within the country. Nigeria was already an African giant in population, with about half of the people in West Africa; during the 1970s Nigeria also became an African giant in production. The petroleum boom combined with the effects of the civil war to create an unprecedented centralization of power in the federal government: total federal revenue, including all export earnings, multiplied from US$ 1 billion in 1970 to US$ 23 billion in 1980 (Lubeck 1985). These huge new funds were allocated partly through state budgets (about half of total federal revenue by 1979) and partly through federal contracts, development projects and other expenditures. The volume of imports into Nigeria was approximately 14 times greater at the end of the 1970s than at the beginning. During the same period the value of food imports grew even more rapidly (some 20 times) rising to 11.3 per cent of total imports in 1980 (Andrae and Beckman 1985). Increasing demand for food by non-farmers and the commercialization of food production encouraged a redirection of some crops from export to domestic markets, and an overall shift away from export crops. The agricultural marketing boards found increasing difficulty in competing with local markets for crops like groundnuts and palm oil, and virtually ceased their buying operations (Williams 1981). Thus agricultural exports declined at the same time as agricultural imports were growing dramatically. The latter included huge quantities of wheat (for bread) and rice, especially during the Shagari administration of 1979–83, imposing new staple foods and consumption patterns not only on the urban élites but on a large proportion of Nigeria's population (Andrae and Beckman 1985; Gidado 1984).

Changes in mass food consumption, and a new dependence on agricultural imports which occurred at the same time as a declining agricultural export sector, have had a tremendously disruptive effect on Nigeria's rural economies. The situation has been worsened for many peasant farmers by government policies supposedly designed to improve agriculture. Although the Third National Development Plan (1975–80) emphasized the need for improved food production and marketing, the strategies employed for achieving this aim have failed to build on the existing abilities and strengths of Nigerian farmers (Wallace 1981). Both the River Basin Development Authorities' irrigation projects and the Agricultural Development Projects (funded by the World Bank) are notably capital-intensive: a large proportion of funds is spent on consultants, contractors and engineers, and imported machinery and fertilizers. Their prime aim is greatly to increase the production of food crops (especially rice, wheat, maize and vegetables) for the urban markets. But production costs of wheat, for example, are far greater than those of importing wheat (Williams 1981); farmers are inadequately compensated for fertile land inundated by the reservoirs or taken over by the projects (Beckman 1984); downstream communities of farmers and fishermen lose their livelihoods through the disruption of river régimes (Stock 1978; Adams 1985); conflicts with management range from the crops that should be grown to the provision and cost of necessary seeds, water, tractors and fertilizers (Wallace 1980). These government policies are a function of the former availability of vast petroleum revenues, but the chief effect of both the economic and the political changes on the Nigerian peasantry has been rising prices and the loss of livelihood for many directly affected. Those who have benefited most from these agricultural developments are the 'progressive' farmers chosen by the Agricultural Development Projects and the 'businessman farmers' who have access to bank loans and see agriculture as a good investment. Such projects therefore reinforce existing trends towards inequality both in rural communities and between rural and urban sectors: 'the emergence of a wealthy class of farmer-traders, and ... the impoverishment of poor farmers without access to land or to other opportunities for earning adequate incomes.' (Williams, 1981, p. 92.) The projects' year-round production has reduced the local incidence of seasonal labour circulation (Baba 1980), but they have also caused much additional unemployment in four ways: (a) displacement of people for construction purposes, (b) inadequate compensation of land-deprived farmers, (c) small farmers who cannot afford the high operational costs selling out to richer farmers, and (d) the declared intent of project managements to mechanize fully farm operations (Gidado 1985).

The other side of the coin from declining rural economies has been growth, and at times boom, in the urban sector. Petroleum revenues generated a large increase in demand for consumer goods, and this stimulated rapid industrial expansion in Nigeria during the 1970s – the beginning of semi-industrial capitalism, superseding the mercantile capitalism of export-oriented agricultural production (Lubeck 1982). Industrial production is located in the cities, and huge contracts have been awarded by both federal and state authorities for urban infrastructural projects (roads, industrial estates, offices, universities and other educational institutions, housing, etc.) that have been heavily concentrated in the state capitals. Probably the most spectacular growth has been achieved in the construction industry, with its flexible labour needs (Lubeck 1985).

All of this has created unprecedented demand for wage labour in the state capitals and other major towns. But such has been the undermining of the rural economy that this demand has been more than matched by the number of urbanward migrants. The considerable excess of new urban residents over the job opportunities available to them has greatly extended the size and complexity of the informal sector of urban income-generation. This informal sector, with its lower wages and relative insecurity of employment in most cases, is for most migrants and other urban residents very much a second-best, something to fall back on when jobs in the formal circuit end, or fail to materialize. But studies of the informal sector in Nigerian cities, as elsewhere in the Third World, have emphasized its great flexibility in continuing to absorb newcomers by providing them with some income, however small (Santos 1979).

This shift of population from the agricultural to other sectors contributes to the problems of rural communities. At the very time when food producers have been faced with an annual increase in demand of over 10 per cent, they have seen major losses of labour (the migrants being heavily weighted towards young adult males) which have made labour costs more expensive. However, capitalist farming, with its reliance on wage labour, has not been noticeably successful and continues to rely on government subsidies through projects and other channels.

> *Nigeria is unable to feed herself not because of the backwardness of her agricultural producers or their lack of commercial orientation. Their markets have been undercut by policies which have favoured the importers. Unrestricted imports have encouraged an excessive rate of increase in the non-agricultural population.*
>
> (*Andrae and Beckman 1985*)

The economic boom years of the 1970s in Nigeria came to an end in the early 1980s as a consequence of declining world petroleum market demand. The peak oil export level of 2.1 million barrels per day in 1980 dropped by a third to 1.4 million barrels per day in 1981. The Shagari administration, elected in 1979, was spending public funds at an unprecedented rate so that the import spree reached its peak in 1981 before an attempt at austerity measures in April 1982, and the collapse of confidence among foreign creditors in late 1983, led to a great decline in imports and the downfall of the Shagari government. Austerity measures were strongly reinforced by the Buhari military authorities during 1984: federal and state budgets were slashed, various projects abandoned, public services badly hit (for example, hospitals were without medicines) and manufacturing industry was crippled by a lack of imported inputs such as raw materials and spare parts. It is noteworthy that wheat imports escaped the 1984 cut in 'unessential' imports, and Nigeria remains a major buyer in world wheat markets: 'bread has become the cheapest staple food of our people' (Buhari 1984).[2]

Oil exports levelled out at about 1.2 million barrels per day by 1983, helped by OPEC's reduction in oil prices. Export earnings were roughly halved in real terms between 1979 and 1983, so that Nigeria's income was drastically reduced though she remained much wealthier than most of her neighbours. The economic decline of the early 1980s produced mass retrenchments, first in manufacturing industry and the private sector and then during 1984 in government employment also. Many who were not made redundant suffered from non-payment of wages (for example, teachers in Benue State, and local authority workers in Niger State), or reduced working hours and pay, as well as high inflation.

Development and changing spatial inequalities in Nigeria

Proletarianization in Nigeria began in earnest in the 1970s with the transition to semi-industrial capitalism, which entailed the growth of import-substituting industrialization and urbanization. The separation of ruralites from their rights to land was either forcible, as in the case of peasants whose farms were taken over by agricultural projects, or 'voluntary'; but the choice to leave the land could hardly be declining agricultural economy and few alternative rural opportunities. Either way, the loss of access to land left increasing members of ruralites (except those artisans who could practise their craft in town) dependent on selling their own labour in order to earn a living. Such a living has been generated both directly and indirectly by the rapid increase during the last 15 years in investment in industrial production. Directly, industrialization has provided employment that has been long-term and continuous for the lucky minority but, for many more, short-term prior to the loss of one job and the renewed search for another. Indirectly, industrialization has greatly enlarged the concentrated market, and perhaps also extended some backward linkages, providing the means whereby others can earn a living in the informal sector of the urban economy.

The transition to semi-industrial capitalism has therefore been associated with the rise of three categories of what may be considered the proletariat: (a) the long-term employed in the formal economy, the proletariat proper;[3] (b) the short-term employed, who seek a living in the urban informal sector between jobs; these are defined by some authors as a semi- or proto-proletariat, though others maintain that 'once a worker enters the factory floor then he is 'proletarianised', though he does not, for example, necessarily act similarly to his West European counterpart (Peace 1975, p. 284);[4] (c) those who have not obtained formal-sector employment, remaining dependent on the informal sector; some may remain effectively part of the peasantry, but those who are in wage employment may share a common social identity with formal-sector wage workers, that is they may be considered part of the proto-proletariat (Lubeck 1982).

Among all fractions of the proletariat, the loss of rights in rural farmland has the effect of loosening links with the village and committing one's future to urban wage labour; and the major encouragement in the city to loosening the links is the belief in steady, adequately paid, future employment. Thus the intimate reciprocal association between industrialization and proletarianization and urbanization unfolds under semi-industrial capitalism, each process being dependent on the others for its own furtherance.

The lack of reliable census or other population data in Nigeria during recent decades means that assessing urban populations or growth-rates can only be at best informed guesses. Estimates of industrial employment in Kano are probably more accurate and give a clearer impression of the direct effects of industrial investment there: from about 7,500 in 1966 industrial employment grew during the civil war years to about 11,000 in 1969 before accelerating to approximately 35,000 in 1976 and 45,000 in 1980.[5] The mass retrenchments of the last few years have considerably reduced industrial employment in Kano from its peak in the early 1980s.

The extent to which recent retrenchments have slowed the rate of annual population growth in cities like Kano is debatable. Central government and some state governments have pursued a campaign of encouraging urban residents to go back to farming. But it is unlikely that either the loss of urban employment or the authorities' exhortations have had any great effect in getting urban migrants to return to their villages. The term 'migrants' here refers to those who have made a decision to remain urban residents in the long term, and not to seasonal or short-term movers who have intended to go back home (Prothero 1982). Convincing evidence of recent return-migration on a large scale in northern Nigeria is absent (Main 1985). The point made by Santos (1984), that expected income differences are not the only criterion considered by potential migrants, is pertinent in the Nigerian context as elsewhere.

Employment and urban-rural linkages: Kano survey data

Data are presented here from the Employment, Retrenchment and Occupation in Kano Survey (EROK).[6] These data are analysed below under two subheadings, 'employment' and 'urban-rural linkages'. The information on employment and retrenchment allows us to place the survey's respondents in the overall context of national economic decline in the early 1980s, and to get some indication of how it affected employment in urban Kano. Survey data on urban-rural linkages are analysed with respect to the manifold nature of such linkages, and in particular the question of whether retrenchment is likely to cause much return migration; or, on the other hand, whether Santos' view that urban migrants are most unlikely to re-enter the rural economy, even when short-term economic prospects in the city are gloomy, is tenable here in Kano.

The EROK survey data reported here have been drawn from interviews with 645 respondents between November 1984 and May 1985.[7] All of these individuals had been employed in formal-sector jobs, but were at the time of interview no longer employed in the formal sector. They were all resident in neighbourhoods adjacent to Metropolitan Kano's three purpose-built industrial estates: Bompai, built on the north-eastern edge of Kano during the late 1950s, Sharada on the southern periphery, built in the early 1970s, and Challawa, about 5 kms to the south-west of Sharada, built in the early 1980s (Figure 39). A fourth concentration of industrial employment, located between Bompai and the commercial centre of Kano, the Township (or *Waje*) industrial area also draws labour from the neighbourhoods by Bompai. The 1963 Metropolitan Kano Twenty Year Plan (Trevallion 1963) asserted that the Township site was already overcrowded with residential as well as industrial land, and that Bompai industrial area was filling rapidly. It recommended Sharada, also adjacent to the railway, as the best alternative for future development. Two of the Sharada Industrial Estate phases have now been occupied almost fully, and a third phase is well under way. Plenty of space remains for future development at Challawa, the first of Kano's industrial estates not to have been built next to the railway. Most of the plots on these estates are occupied by manufacturing activities, the remainder being mainly construction companies and distribution warehouses. Several multinational companies are among the major employers, including Raleigh and Lonrho at Bompai, Bata and Union Carbide at Sharada, and Coca-Cola at Challawa.

The construction of these industrial estates entailed some displacement of communities which had been farming and living on the land, and some of these communities were rehoused in the neighbourhoods from which samples were drawn. Some of the neighbourhoods around Bompai have the reputation of being among Kano's main working-class residential areas. The Sharada sample is drawn from a population that is more mixed than Bompai's in terms of class, with a higher proportion of respondents formerly working in government employ-

Fig. 39 Metropolitan Kano 1985: industrial estates and survey neighbourhoods

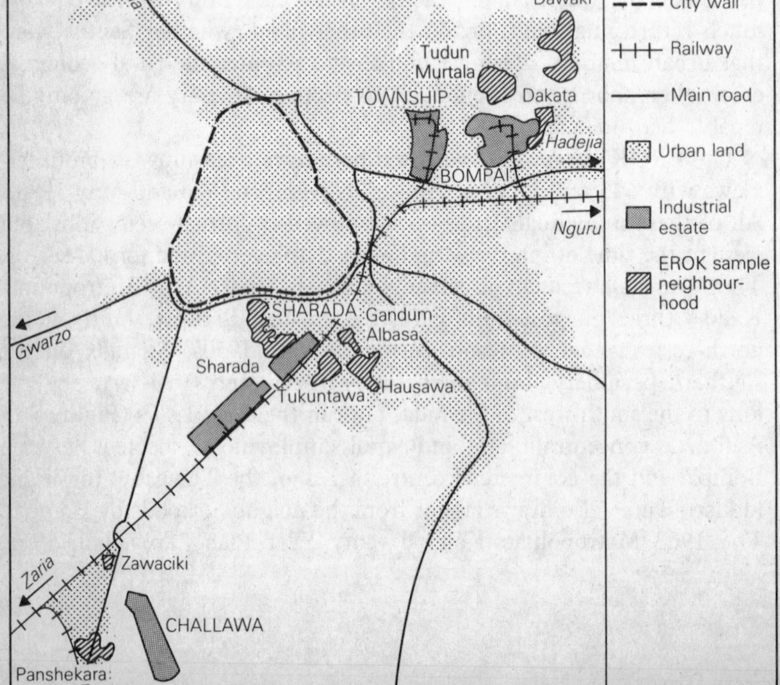

ment (Main 1985). Some of the sampled neighbourhoods near Challawa Industrial Estate retain close links with the rural economy, and most of the active males in one village were away seeking temporary employment in Lagos and elsewhere during the 1984–5 dry season. But in Panshekara village, employment has been provided for over 50 years by the government-run electricity generating station (coal-fired, and now closed) and water-pumping station.

Employment

Of the 645 respondents sampled, 511 reported having worked only in one of the following: industry (259), government (145) and other employment (107, chiefly in construction and transport). A further 121 had worked mainly (but not exclusively) in one of these three sectors (see Table 11.1). Thus almost half of the total sample had worked only or mainly in industry, and about a quarter in each of the other two sectors. The total duration of employment was markedly lower among the industrial workers (almost two-thirds of whom had had less than four years' total employment) than among those with government jobs (about half of whom had had over eight years' service). Each government employment had lasted on average several years longer than each industrial employment.

Table 11.1 Type of employment and duration

Employment	3 years or less	4–7 years	8 years or more	unspecified	Total
Industry only	156	65	25	13	259
%	(60)	(25)	(10)	(5)	(100)
Government only	21	47	64	13	145
%	(14)	(32)	(44)	(9)	(100)
Other only	45	26	25	11	107
%	(42)	(24)	(23)	(10)	(100)
Industry mainly	23	13	7		43
%	(53)	(30)	(16)		(100)
Government mainly	4	15	13		32
%	(13)	(47)	(41)		(100)
Other mainly	14	14	18		46
%	(30)	(30)			(100)
Combinations,			(39)		
durations unspecified				13	13
Total	263	180	152	50	645
%	(41)	(28)	(24)	(8)	(100)

A total of 1,029 job terminations were reported by the 645 respondents between 1937 and 1985 (see Table 11.2). More than two-thirds of them were retrenchments: most respondents described this as 'redundancy' or 'recession', but some gave a more specific reason (lack of sales or raw materials, end of contract, etc.). Other compulsory terminations, accounting for about eight per cent of the total, were for personal reasons (for example, boss's hatred, refusal to pay a bribe) or behaviour (late for work, sleeping on duty, imprisonment and other such candid reasons). About one in six jobs had ended voluntarily,

Table 11.2 Date and cause of job termination

	Retrenchment	Compulsory	Dispute	Health	Voluntary	Total
1985	21	1	2			24
1984	279	14	3	8	24	328
1983	100	9	2	3	22	136
1982	80	2	3	5	13	103
1981	46	6	2	5	11	70
1980	37	9	3	3	12	64
1979	29	5	2	1	20	57
1978	18	4	1	2	11	36
1977	9	5		2	9	25
1976	16	3	3	1	8	31
1975	8	3	1		6	18
1974	10	2		3	5	20
1973	1	1			6	8
1972	6	2	1		7	16
1971	1	2			2	5
1970	3	4			1	8
1969	2		1		4	7
1968	1	1			2	4
1967		2			1	3
1966		2			2	4
1965	4	1			4	9
1964					3	3
1963	3	1	2		2	8
1937–60	4	3		1	9	17
Unspecified	15	4	1		5	25
Total	693	86	27	34	189	1029

mostly for family reasons but some because enough capital had been saved (for example, for trading) or because a better opportunity was available. Formal disputes and health reasons together comprised about six per cent of the job terminations.

It is noteworthy that prior to 1974 almost half of all terminations were for voluntary reasons. Jobs were seemingly taken by many people up until that time as a temporary measure, employment being sought by some only for the dry season before returning to the economic mainstay of farming at home. Retrenchment accounted for only 27 per cent of all terminations before 1974. It was in the same year that the number both of retrenchments and of total terminations rose quite markedly, as the effects of the petroleum boom fed through industrial investment and overall employment. Since 1977 this rise has been continuous. But between 1977 and 1984 the proportion of voluntary job terminations shrank from 36 to 7 per cent, while retrenchments rose steeply from the same level of 36 to 85 per cent. Clearly, jobs are no longer the temporary fill-ins that they used to be for many: in the last decade formal-sector employment has become much more valuable and worth retaining. It can reasonably be inferred from these data that, as retrenchments and other compulsory reasons have grown to comprise 90 per cent of all job terminations, while voluntary and health reasons have strunk to only 10 per cent, competition among the labouring poor in the Kano employment market is now tight. Thousands of urban residents, both long-established and recent migrants, are competing for factory and other jobs at a time when thousands are being made jobless. This urban labour surplus, the industrial reserve army of the proto-proletariat, comprises people who no longer see farming as a viable alternative.

It is patently clear that 1984 was by far the worst year to date for retrenchment, the culmination of a steadily worsening situation since 1977 that became critical after Shagari's government lost the confidence of foreign creditors in late 1983. Nearly three times more retrenchments were reported in the survey during 1984 than in the previous year. But this escalation was not spread evenly across the public and private sectors of employment (see Table 11.3). Whereas the build-up of retrenchment followed a temporal pattern among industrial and other non-government employment that was similar to the overall pattern after 1977, government workers' jobs were not under such a rising threat until after 1982. In 1982, nine per cent of all retrenchment reported in this sample were in government employment; that figure increased to 23 per cent in 1983 and 35 per cent in 1984. The data in Table 11.3 reinforce a point made above: prior to the mid-1970s, these respondents' employment (and therefore retrenchment) was spread more equally between the industrial, governmental and other sectors than has been the case subsequently. Since about 1974, industrial growth in Kano has caused industrial retrenchment to be approximately half of this sample's yearly total retrenchment.[8]

Table 11.3 Retrenchment by year and according to employment sector

Year	Industrial	Governmental	Other	Total
1985	9	7	5	21
1984	115	93	57	265
1983	44	21	28	93
1982	54	7	21	82
1981	22	10	11	43
1980	22	5	11	38
1979	12	8	7	27
1978	8	5	4	17
1977	5	2	3	10
1976	8	6	4	18
1975	5	1	3	9
1974	5	2	3	10
1973		1		1
1972		1	3	4
1971	1	1		2
1970	2	1		3
1960–9	2	7	3	12
1950–9		1	1	2
pre–1950		1	1	2
Unspecified	9	2	2	14
Total	323	183	167	673

Urban-rural linkages

Just over half of all respondents were born in Metropolitan Kano, most of them in the neighbourhoods where they now live (see Table 11.4).[9] This proportion of urban indigenes is much lower around Bompai, where migrants have been attracted to factory employment for almost 30 years, and much higher around Challawa with its short industrial history. Of the remaining 315 migrants, then, 70 per cent were resident around Bompai. The Bompai sample has a high propor-

Table 11.4 Birthplace

Present residential location	Near present residence	Elsewhere in Metropolitan Kano	Local Kano State*	Non-local Kano State	Outside Kano State	Total
Around Bompai	101	36	60	87	76	360
%	(28)	(10)	(17)	(24)	(21)	(100)
Around Sharada	63	21	12	35	15	146
%	(43)	(14)	(8)	(24)	(10)	(100)
Around Challawa	92	14	4	17	9	136
%	(68)	(10)	(3)	(13)	(7)	(100)
Total	256	71	76	139	100	642
%	40	11	12	22	16	100

* 'Local Kano State' is the adjacent LGAs of Minjibir, Gezawa and Dawakin Kudu.

tion of industrial, compared with government and other, retrenchments. Thus the migrant sub-sample has a high proportion of former factory workers, about 55 per cent.

The 315 migrants, about one-third of them born outside Kano State, were asked whether they intended ever to return 'home' to live, and how retrenchment had affected these intentions (see Table 11.5). Over 60 per cent of them said they would never return: some had lost all contact with their birthplaces, owing to their parents' death or because they had left when young, but most retained some sort of contact. Analysing these intentions according to the number of years spent in employment suggests only a slight firming of resolve (never to return 'home') with longer duration of total employment. This may be interpreted as a result of the interplay of many factors pulling in one direction or the other. Two such factors that would tend to have opposite effects are, on the one hand, acculturation to an urban lifestyle so that the passing years tend towards a lower probability of return; on the other hand, the opportunity with longer employment to accumulate more capital so that it becomes increasingly feasible to go back to the village as a man of substance, someone who has succeeded in the city and has something to show for it. A structural interpretation would point to the constraints placed on the decision whether to return to the village by the process of proletarianization, which would not be expected to be noticeably further advanced among migrants who had lived longer in the city than among short-term migrants. The nature of their former employment appears to have remarkably little significance for the scale of the preponderance of those declaring no intention to return. As for those who did express the possibility of returning, only about one in five of them indicated a strong commitment. The most common response was 'if it is the will of Allah, I shall return', but the occasional respondent backed up his strong resolve with the building of a house in the village, affection for farming or for the home community, or disaffection with Kano.

Table 11.5 Migrants' response to questions about their intention to return 'home' to live?

Q1 Do you intend to return home to live?

Former employment (only or mainly)	answer	total years employed 3 years or less	4–7 years	8 years or more	total
Industrial	sometime	39	17	4	60
	never	59	27	9	95
Governmental	sometime	4	10	8	22
	never	7	11	18	36
Other	sometime	11	7	6	24
	never	21	10	12	43
All migrants	sometime	54	34	18	106
	never	87	48	39	174
	Total	141	82	57	280

27 migrants' durations of employment were not properly established. Of these, 20 (74%) said they would never return home.

Q2 Did retrenchment make you think of returning home sooner?

Former employment (only or mainly)	answer	Total years employed 3 years or less	4–7 years	8 years or more	total
Industrial	yes	29	15	5	49
	no	55	23	7	85
Governmental	yes	3	3	3	9
	no	7	14	20	41
Other	yes	9	6	6	21
	no	20	10	8	38
All migrants	yes	41	24	14	79
	no	82	47	35	164
	Total	123	71	49	243

25 migrants' durations of employment were not properly established. Of these, 17 (68%) said retrenchment had no such effect.

Q3 Do you know of others in this neighbourhood who have moved home since retrenchment?

Former employment (only or mainly)	answer	Total years employed 3 years or less	4–7 years	8 years or more	total
Industrial	yes	17	6	1	24
	no	83	37	12	132
Governmental	yes	1	0	1	2
	no	10	20	25	55
Other	yes	8	4	2	14
	no	24	14	17	55
All migrants	yes	26	10	4	40
	no	117	71	54	242
	Total	143	81	58	282

26 migrants' durations of employment were not properly established. Of these, 24 (92%) said they knew of no such people.

A second question on the subject of return sought the effects of retrenchment. One-third of respondents said that retrenchment had made them think of returning home sooner, but only about half of these actually intended to move. The other half must have rejected the idea after due consideration. Thus only about one in six sampled migrants both expressed some intention to return home and felt that retrenchment had encouraged this intention. Retrenchment appears to have had a weaker impact on ex-government employees' intentions than on the other groups; this may be partly because of the longer duration of government work, and the fact that long-term employed seem to be less affected in this respect by retrenchment.

Clearly this sample is totally biased against those who have already moved home, because they would no longer be among the population sampled. But a third question was asked regarding other migrants formerly in the neighbourhood who had in fact moved home since retrenchment. Only one respondent in seven knew of such movers. Slight differences between the results for former industrial, government and other employees suggest the possibility that social groups are beginning to be more work- or occupation-oriented than previously. Again, those with longer employment durations knew of fewer movers.

Migrants were also asked about other forms of contact with their birthplaces: their visits, letters and messages sent, money and goods remitted. They were asked to estimate the frequency of these various contacts (a) when employed and (b) after retrenchment.[10] Sub-samples based on present residential location, and on employment sector, produce little evident difference; however, birthplace location offers much greater variability in contact frequency. A clear distance-decay function is evident in the frequency of visits: more than half of the sampled migrants from nearby areas of Kano State (that is the Local Government Areas of Minjibir, Gezawa and Dawakin Kudu) visit home weekly or fortnightly whether employed or not, while a majority of migrants from outside Kano State visit home yearly at most. This effect of distance on migrants' home contacts is much less marked in the case of messages, and appears to make little or no difference to the frequency of remittances. It seems that only eight per cent or fewer of migrants have cut off all links with their birthplace: this figure rises slightly from five per cent for local Kano people to nine per cent for those from outside the state.[11]

As for the effects of being in or out of employment on contact frequency, these appear to be marginal for both visits and messages. In either case, loss of a formal-sector job slightly delays contacts. But money and goods are remitted far less often after retrenchment. More than half of all employed migrants in this sample make monthly or quarterly remittances – whereas three-quarters of them remit rarely or never once employment has ended. The monthly pay-day of the formal sector clearly is of great significance to many of the migrants' home communities.[12] Mass urban retrenchment then has a major effect in reducing the amount of money circulating in rural economies, at a time when the worsening national economy is directly weakening rural economies through cutbacks on funds for rural services and projects. Under these circumstances, it is understandable that national economic slump does little to encourage either more return migration from the cities or less migration to the cities. These are however circumstances under which the informal urban economy is under pressure from both the increased number of people striving to generate an income within it, and the reduced funds available for input from the formal sector.

Conclusion

The debate among geographers on the nature of space and location concerns the degree of autonomy of space and spatial organization: whether emphasis should be laid on space as an explanatory or as a dependent variable. One of the debates on how best to understand the transformation process of development is broadly on the question of whether to start analysis from the overall social context or from the details of communities and individuals. Light is cast on both debates by the materialist interpretation of society with its emphasis on the mode of production. The form and function of space are an expression of the structure of the social formation within which the space is located, and this spatial structure changes with development as one mode of production declines and another mode becomes dominant. This is not to deny the complex operation of multivariate behavioural components in either spatial inequalities or development, but to argue that behavioural components cannot be understood unless they are interpreted within the overall social context.

This paper has taken a materialist view of inequalities in contemporary Kano by starting from some of the features of the expansion of semi-industrial capitalism in Nigeria in recent years. Social changes in both rural and urban Nigeria have greatly encouraged the proletarianization process, undermining the rural economy while industrialization creates some jobs in the cities. The reluctance of most urban migrants sampled in Kano to return to their rural origins, even after they have lost their jobs in the formal employment sector, can be best understood in the context of the changes introduced by peripheral capitalism. Retrenchment's main effect on their rural links appears to be a great reduction in remittances, on which the rural economy is becoming increasingly dependent. Thus, far from encouraging return migration or discouraging urbanward migration, retrenchment (and the wide fluctuations in the economy that are so characteristic of peripheral capitalist societies like Nigeria) actually has the opposite effect. Retrenchment tends to reinforce the existing process whereby rural societies are becoming more dependent on the urban economy and decisions made far away. It extends proletarianization and urbanization, and thereby contributes to the creation of an urban labour surplus which both expands the informal sector of the urban economy and feeds the demands of capitalist industrialization.

Notes

1 On rural production, see Williams (1981). On *cin rani* labour circulation from and within northern Nigeria, see Prothero (1957); Swindell (1984). On urbanization, see Mabogunje (1968).

2 Quoted by Andrae and Beckman (1985, p. 2) from which this paragraph borrows heavily.

3 Arrighi and Saul's (1973) 'labour aristocracy' are the small upper stratum within the wage-earning class whose wages are high enough to justify a

total break of links with the village. See also Riddell (1981).

4 Peace (1975), writing on the Lagos proletariat, disputes such a division among the working class. Arrighi and Saul's 'marginally or partially proletarianized class' are the much larger lower stratum within the wage-earning class who obtain most of their income from outside the wage economy. This proto-proletariat (McGee 1976) or semi-proletariat therefore retains close links with the peasantry, or may indeed be part of the peasantry much of the time.

5 Source for first three figures is Lubeck (1982); the last figure is derived from Kano State (1980).

6 The survey has been partly supported by a research grant from Bayero University. Arrangements for interviews were made through the ward heads and neighbourhood heads, and I am grateful for their help. Research assistants Mal. Muhtari Sadique and Mal. Muhammad Bashir have interviewed respondents and processed results.

7 The results of the EROK survey are preliminary, the survey is continuing with interviews of individuals presently in formal employment, and individuals never employed in the formal sector. A further survey is planned, entailing in-depth discussion with a small number of respondents.

8 The fact that the populations sampled by the EROK survey were resident in neighbourhoods adjacent to the industrial estates obviously precludes extrapolation of the precise percentages to a wider population, in Kano or elsewhere. But it appears likely that in relation to the structural determinants the trends hold good in broader contexts than the industrial suburbs of Kano.

9 The reduction in total sample to 642 is because three respondents did not answer questions in this part of the interview. Numbers answering subsequent questions also vary.

10 Details of the amount of money remitted were not sought; to do so would create suspicion and responses of questionable accuracy. Sikhitbis (1983, p. 20) reports that in a Plateau State survey all attempts to quantify remittances were abortive.

11 These figures are the smallest number of 'never' responses by each subsample for any contact.

12 Okafor (1985) estimates that 31 per cent of village income in a part of Anambra State is provided by urban migrants. On the importance of migrants' remittances to village economies elsewhere in Nigeria, see Sikhitbis (1983) on Plateau State and Raza *et alia* (1983) on Kaduna State.

References

Adams, W.M. 1985. The downstream impact of dam construction; a case study from the Sokoto valley in Nigeria, *Transactions Institute of British Geographers* (new series), vol. 10 : pp. 292–302.

Andrae, G. and Beckman, B. 1985. *The wheat trap : bread and underdevelopment in Nigeria* (London: Zed Press)

Arrighi, G. and Saul, J.S. 1973. *Essays on the political economy of Africa* (London : Monthly Review Press)

Baba, J.M. 1980. 'Trends in farm labour mobilization and population mobility in a modern irrigation project : the case of the Kano River Project' (Paper presented at the seminar on Change in rural Hausaland, Kano).

Beckman, B. 1984. 'Bakolori : peasants versus state and capital' (Seminar paper, Dept. of Political Science, Ahmadu Bello University).

Buhari, M. 1984. *Budget Speech by the Head of State*, 7 May 1984. (London: Arnold)

Gidado, S.I. 1984. 'Nigeria's agricultural development in perspective : a study of the contradictions of dependent development' (Seminar paper, Faculty of Social and Management Sciences, Bayero University).

Kano State 1980. *Directory of industrial and commercial establishments for Kano State* (Kano: Statistics Division, Dept. of Budget)

Lubeck, P.M. 1978. Labour in Kano since the petroleum boom, *Review of African Political Economy* vol. 13.

Lubeck, P.M. 1982. 'Industrial labour in Kano : historical origins, social characteristics and sources of differentiation' (Seminar paper, Depts. of Geography and Sociology, Bayero University).

Lubeck, P.M. 1985. Islamic protest under semi-industrial capitalism : *'yan Tatsine* explained, *Africa* vol. 55, (4), pp. 369–89.

Mabogunje, A. 1968. *Urbanization in Nigeria* (London: University of London Press)

Main, H.A.C. 1985. 'Employment, retrenchment and occupation in Metropolitan Kano : urban-rural linkages' (Paper presented at the Nigerian Geographical Association conference, Lagos).

Okafor, F.C. 1985. 'Survival strategies in a depressed economy : occupational multiplicity in rural southeastern Nigeria' (Paper presented at the Nigerian Geographical Association conference, Lagos).

Peace, A. 1975. 'The Lagos proletariat: labour aristocrats or populist militants?' In R. Sandbrook and R. Cohen (eds), *The development of an African working class: studies in class formation and action* (London: Longman)

Prothero, R.M. 1957. Migratory labour from north-western Nigeria, *Africa* vol. 27.

Prothero, R.M. 1982. 'Perspectives on studies of population distribution and redistribution.' In J.I. Clarke and L.A. Kosinski (eds), *Redistribution of population in Africa* (London: Heinemann)

Raza, M.R., Voh, J.P. and Kazzah, B.T.S. 1983. 'Rural linkage of urban migrants: a case study of return migrants in Samaru-Kataf village of Kaduna State', (Paper presented at seminar on Nigeria's population dynamics, Ahmadu Bello University).

Riddell, J.B. 1981. Beyond the description of spatial pattern: the process of

proletarianization as a factor in population migration in West Africa, *Progress in Human Geography* vol. 5, p. 3.
Santos, M. 1979. *The shared space : the two circuits of the urban economy in underdeveloped countries*
Santos, M. 1984. Geography in the late twentieth century: new roles for a threatened discipline, *International Social Science Journal* vol. 36, (4), pp. 657–72.
Sikhitbis, J.A. 1983. 'Migration Process and rural transformation : a case-study of Chip and Mupun rural communities of Plateau State' (Paper presented at seminar on rural transformation in Nigeria, Jos University).
Stock, R.F. 1978. 'The impact of the decline of the Hadejia river floods in Hadejia Emirate.' In G.J. Van Apeldoorn (ed.) *The aftermath of the 1972–74 drought in Nigeria*' (Centre for Social and Economic Research, Ahmadu Bello University).
Swindell, K. 1984. Farmers, traders and labourers, *Africa* vol. 54, 1, pp. 3–19.
Trevallion, B.A.W. 1963. *Metropolitan Kano : report on the twenty year development plan, 1963–1983* (Oxford: Pergamon)
Wallace, T. 1980. Agricultural Projects and land in northern Nigeria, *Review of African Political Economy* vol. 17, pp. 59–70.
Wallace, T. 1981. The challenge of food : Nigeria's approach to agriculture, *Canadian Journal of African Studies* vol. 15, 2, pp. 239–258.
Williams, G. 1981. Inequalities in rural Nigeria. *Development Studies Occasional Paper No. 16* (University of East Anglia).

12
Inequality and Domestic Energy in Kano, Nigeria and Freetown, Sierra Leone

R. Akindele Cline-Cole
Department of Geography, Bayero University, Kano, Nigeria

Introduction

The practice of using per capita commercial energy consumption as an index of development or modernization is well established. Variations in this index are generally interpreted as indicating the differential progress of towns, regions and countries along the industrialization continuum. Therefore it may be considered part of the normal development process that Freetown accounts for some 80 per cent of the Sierra Leone national electricity consumption, as it did between 1945 and 1964 (Cline-Cole 1984a). Similarly, that the domestic electricity consumption per capita in rural Kano represents no more than two per cent of the corresponding consumption rate for Metropolitan Kano, as was the case in 1981 (Kano Statistical Year Book 1981).[1] However, these 'skewed' distributions raise questions about the equitable access to resources, and how discrepancies between one area and another have arisen. The use of per capita indices may permit the identification of inequalities, but they stop short of providing adequate explanations of the patterns described.

The assumption that large-scale spontaneous shifts in energy use occur with modernization is also open to question. Changes from the use of traditional non-commercial sources to modern commercial fuels as societies progress towards industrialization have not been universally realized. This is true even in urban centres such as Kano and Freetown, which have attracted most of the growth-generating investments and modern energy supplies (Falola *et al.* 1984; Cline-Cole 1984a). Traditional energy-based habits (in particular cooking) have held very firm, although in varying degrees among different categories of domestic consumers, and between different sections of these cities.

Variations in the use of different types of energy within cities have received much less attention than have discrepancies between urban and rural areas. Therefore this paper has two aims: first to identify the significant elements of the production, distribution and consumption of energy for domestic cooking and lighting in Freetown and Kano; and second, to examine the patterns within an explanatory framework which emphasizes unequal access to scarce societal resources. It is argued that while irregularities in energy distribution and consumption have a spatial expression, they are ultimately structural in origin. The paper begins with a brief overview of inequality and the links between social process and spatial form in the city as a means of understanding inequalities in domestic energy consumption and distribution. This is followed by a discussion of data from Freetown and Kano demonstrating who does what, where, how and why in domestic energy terms.

Inequality and domestic energy in the city

Understanding inequality implies a comprehension of the processes through which some individuals, neighbourhoods, regions and countries succeed in increasing their command over scarce societal resources to the detriment of others, who consequently find themselves increasingly disadvantaged (Mabogunje 1975). Numerous explanatory theories have been addressed to this question of who gets what, where, and how; these have recently been summarized by Akeredolu-Ale (1975) who suggests four categories or types. First **necessity theory** which is largely functionalist and evolutionary (survival of the fittest). Second, **natural-circumstantial theory**, where inequalities are put down to factors such as geographical location and natural environmental endowment. Third, **individual attributes theory**, which espouses differentials in the 'need for achievement' of individuals. Fourth, **power theory** which presents the structure of political power as the most important determinant of inequality. Power theory highlights the establishment and maintenance of an exploitative property system as a channel for the allocation of opportunities, income and wealth by the ruling classes to the detriment of subordinate classes; the development of inequality is thus seen as a historical process, and is neither spontaneous nor irreversible. Certainly, this line of analysis holds promise for explaining, among other things, the gross inequality in electricity consumption between the rural and urban areas already mentioned. In the case of inequalities in domestic energy consumption within the city itself, a good starting point is Harvey's analysis of social process, spatial form, and inequality (Harvey 1975).

Within the localized resource system comprising the city, the availability of non-ubiquitous resources such as energy depend on accessibility and proximity; there are thus several ways in which an individual's access to such resources can change. For present purposes such a change can be deemed to occur through a change in the quantity of free unpriced energy, a change in the price of energy, or a modification in the cost of access to energy. It is in this latter respect that the 'price' of accessibility and 'cost' of proximity achieve their true significance for households as consumers.

However, as a result of the interrelated nature of the city-system, the process of commanding resources produces both wanted and unwanted by-products which affects people's welfare indirectly and directly. These 'externality effects' are conceived as costs (or benefits, depending on who is affected – producer or consumer) and the nature of the effect; externalities can simultaneously be positive and negative. The energy-consuming household can therefore be proximate to a fuelwood or charcoal market representing a source of noise, traffic and vermin, thus implying costs. But it can also experience, as a result of its location, an improvement in accessibility to energy in the form of preferential rates or even free supplies, thereby offsetting the need for overcoming distance using time, effort and money to gain access to a more distant source. Therefore, 'location' is an 'impure' public resource whose availability is non-homogenous for different sectors of the urban population. It assumes central importance in any understanding of externality effects, and in this case in relation to the consumption and distribution of domestic energy.

The location of sales outlets in energy distribution networks is determined partly through public action such as town planning restrictions, location of state- or municipal-controlled wood plantations and charcoal making units. Also location is determined through enterpreneurs' perceptions of the business potential of different areas of the city, operating within – and often in spite of – broad planning constraints which determine the locations of filling stations, gas retail shops, firewood and charcoal piles. In either case location is largely without considerations of externality or third party effects; consequently, the pattern of costs and benefits imposed by proximity to energy supplies varies considerably from noise emission and traffic congestion at one end of the scale, to the provision of jobs and free supplies at the other. Since energy represents a good which provides both benefits and losses, and the consumer does not enjoy a qualitatively and quantitatively homogeneous supply, then the energy resource can be considered an impure public good, even if its distribution is largely privately controlled. As with other impure public goods, the associated externality effects can be conceived as a 'spatial field' of varying intensity and extent characterized by distance-decay. Therefore in a system where the maximization of profits by producers or distributors does not necessarily coincide with maximum benefits for consumers, it is to be expected that considerable inequalities in energy availability and accessibility will exist; these operate under normal cicumstances to the advantage of higher or more powerful income groups and to the detriment of the lower-income earners.

However not everyone will rank energy alternatives equally (particularly for cooking) and this has already been alluded to; the explanation lies in an observable heterogeneity in social and cultural values. People value alternative energy sources differently and thereby render them 'Pareto non-comparable', a fact which has far-reaching implications for income redistribution as it affects those energy consumers who can least afford to lose an external benefit, or incur an external cost.[2] An examination of the technological and cultural characteristics of an energy resource should clarify this point further. Cooking with 'modern' energy implies the possession of technological equipment (cooker, stove) and the cognitive skills necessary for their use; but even more fundamental is a consumer's value system motivating him or her to use gas or electricity in conjunction with, or in place of wood or charcoal. Indeed, for a good many urban residents in Kano and Freetown neither the gas or electric grill nor the microwave oven can impart the 'correct' flavour to a whole range of foodstuffs of which kebabs ('suya' in Hausa and 'rosbif' in Krio) represent a common example.

None the less, cultural appraisals and cognitive skills change over time, as well as in space. In the first place cognitive skills are unequally distributed throughout a population and in domestic energy consumption terms, high density and low density residential areas represent completely different environments. This is demonstrated by the wide contrast between the shanty town dweller, who has no electricity, or uses illegal electrical connections, street lighting and woodfuel, versus the high-income suburbanite for whom gas and electricity (in Kano very often self-generated) may be taken for granted. Secondly, cognitive skills are learnt through education, innate intelligence, and experience with environments; 'cross-cultural' transitions from one set of energy alternatives to another (traditional to modern or vice versa) are thus possible given the requisite changes in accessibility and proximity of the fuels concerned to the consumer.[3]

An extension of this line of analysis is that government decisions affecting domestic energy use such as a subsidy on fossil fuels, but not on traditional energy, or the price control of gas and kerosene but not of wood and coal, creates or reinforces heterogeneity in energy use, and erects barriers which often prevent the energy transition already referred to. References to the transfer of rural habits of domestic energy use to urban centres and a consequent diluting effect on the modernizing role of these centres in the spread of 'modern' cooking methods and appliances (see for instance Vennetier 1980) would seem in need of qualification (Cline-Cole 1981). To the extent that such heterogeneity would be reflected in patterns of residential differentiation, the spatial inequalities in domestic energy use and supply would appear essentially structural. Such inequalities would represent products of particular configurations of social, psychological, economic, political stimuli existing in the different urban contexts concerned.

Variations in urban domestic energy needs and demands do not only render value comparisons of, say, fuelwood depots or kerosene dumps between different parts of the city difficult; they also possess significant policy implications. There is a need for familiarity with energy utility scales for different sectors of the population, when making decisions about the location and allocation of urban energy resources. The activities associated with the production, distribution and consumption of domestic energy are arranged in a given spatial form; large-scale redistributive effects operating through externalities associated with major locational changes are bound to result from significant modifications to this spatial form. Given that large-scale changes of the type envisaged here are invariably the product of decisions taken within the public sector on behalf of the entire urban system, the operation of an income inequality-generating mechanism of this type could be linked via the power theory to political processes in the city. It is thus particularly relevant that the externality effects associated with the production and consumption of domestic fuels should be thoroughly investigated to ensure that changes being advocated do not inflict heavier energy costs on the lower income classes than they already have to bear.

The structure of domestic energy consumption in Kano and Freetown

The two cities selected for testing some of the theoretical constructs outlined in the preceding section are Freetown and Kano.[4] A combination of historical, socio-economic and political circumstances have generated and perpetrated structural inequalities among the various sectors of Sierra Leone and Nigeria. And while the two cities represent islands of privilege and 'development' surrounded by their respective seas of deprivation, they are themselves characterized by significant internal inequalities (Table 12.1).

Table 12.1 Structural and situational variables: Freetown and Kano

Index	Freetown	Kano	Notes
(1) Lowest income as ratio of highest	1:23	1:12	Figures for Kano refer to State Government employees; Freetown data covers both formal and informal employment categories.
(2) Unemployment	22.8%	29%	Unemployed as percentage of economically active population (Freetown); registered unemployed as percentage of State Government establishment (Kano).
(3) Annual rate of inflation	11.3%	17.1%	Freetown: 1970–9; Kano: national figure for Nigeria (1970–83)
(4) Highest income earners as per cent of population	>10	>2	

Source: Cline-Cole (1984a); Kano State Statistical Yearbook (1981); Freetown Yearbook of Labour Statistics (1984).

Structural and situational differences make it difficult not to yield to the temptation of pursuing a line of analysis which sees patterns in domestic energy production, distribution and consumption as 'adaptive' responses by individuals and groups occupying different structural positions within the urban political economy to varying 'environmental' stimuli (cf. Remy 1976). The domestic energy economy consequently becomes directed first towards the goals of household income and resource augmentation and/or maximization; second, to household expenditure minimization.[5] Socio-economic data collected in both study cities would seem to suggest that an examination of these activities within the context of the urban occupational structure, and the implications of such a stratification for the command of societal resources, might well be a logical starting point for examining who

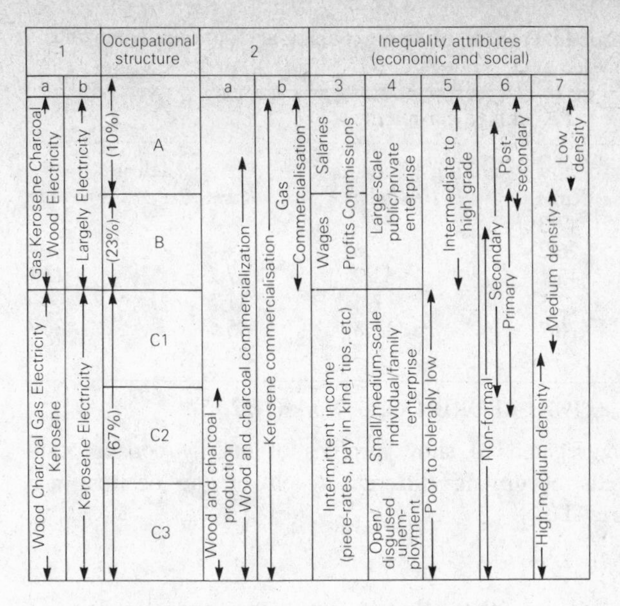

A Senior government officials, business managers, university professors and professionals

B Middle-level officials and supervisors, owner entrepreneurs

C1 Skilled constructions and factory workers, trade and service workers

C2 Handicraft workers, street and market traders, domestic workers

C3 Unemployed

1 Energy end-use mix
  (a) cooking
  (b) lighting
2 Energy supply network
  (a) Woodfuel
  (b) Fossil fuel
3 Income type
4 Employment status
5 Housing quality
6 Education
7 Residential differentiation

Fig. 40 Production, consumption and supply of domestic energy within the socio-economic system of Kano

does what, where, how and why within the domestic energy economy (Figure 40). Location within this occupational structure implies not just differences in monetary income, but also variable access to a whole range of other resources which collectively 'condition' the household's specific energy needs and demands, and equally importantly, its ability to satisfy these wants. This 'structural environment' constitutes an essential element of the household energy equation, as it does for everything touching on the welfare of the household.

When the data for Freetown and Kano are taken together, there emerges a clear indication of the overall importance of wood and charcoal in the satisfaction of energy needs for cooking. The full range of five available fuels is exploited in both cities (Table 12.2). Of more immediate relevance is, however, the pattern which emerges when the

Table 12.2 Domestic fuel consumption for cooking and lighting: Kano and Freetown

Fuel	Percentage consumers			
Fuel	Cooking		Lighting	
	Kano	*Freetown*	*Kano*	*Freetown*
Wood	47.3	73	—	—
Coal	16.2	37.6	—	—
Kerosene	45.1	32.2	47.2	13.6
Gas	32.5	7.4	11.5	—
Electricity	6.2	11.8	95.6	86.4
Oil	—	—	30	—

Source: Cline-Cole (1984a); RUREN Field Work (1982–5)

results are disaggregated to show profiles of energy consumption among households occupying different levels of the occupational hierarchy (Figure 41).

Cooking

With respect to cooking, three fuels – wood, gas and electricity –

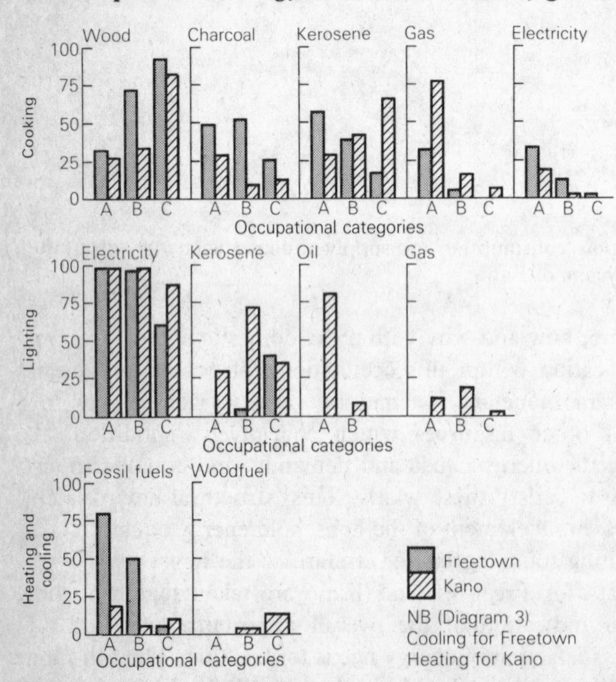

Fig. 41 The structure of domestic energy consumption by occupational categories, Kano and Freetown

play perfectly predictable roles. Wood represents the most widely accessible fuel technologically, socially, cognitively and economically; it is thus the most widely used of all the cooking fuels. None the less, upward social mobility would appear inconsistent with continued dependence on wood because of increased access to fuel alternatives. Such improved access to alternatives like gas and electricity by A and B households is in part the product of policies which encourage the provision of modern cooking appliances in subsidized part-furnished accommodation or free energy supplies and housing improvement loans (Figure 40). The gas and electricity profiles not surprisingly therefore are the reverse of the firewood profile. However, Pareto non-comparability militates against the complete disappearance of wood even at the summit of the hierarchy. For example in a well-placed large household (in Kano not infrequently in excess of twenty people), a selectively changing cultural appraisal of energy sources is observable. Certain dishes still have to be prepared over a wood fire, while there is a lack of appropriate cognitive skills permitting the use of modern cooking appliances which itself is largely a reflection of the inequality between sexes. All of these factors contribute in varying degrees to the maintenance of a 'wood culture'.

The profiles for kerosene and charcoal demand special explanation. For the first of these, the profiles of Kano and Freetown represent the reverse of each other. This is a reflection of kerosene's cost relative to other fuel alternatives in the two cities. In oil-rich Nigeria, its low price has made it economically accessible to the lower-income earners, who constitute the single largest group of Kano consumers. In oil-importing Sierra Leone, on the other hand, government price subsidies have operated in favour of the better-off. In effect, the economic inaccessibility of kerosene to some 75–80 per cent of the lower and middle-income Freetown groups have facilitated the emergence of charcoal as a substitute to both wood and kerosene, particularly for the upwardly mobile B-category households. An initial capital outlay on a *kolpot* (brazier) and its perceived higher price when compared to wood are among the explanations for a percentage utilization rate which is twice as high for category B-type as for category C-type consumers. Finally, the case of charcoal for category A-type households in Freetown as well as Kano (where its overall importance as a cooking fuel is negligible) rests very largely on its appropriateness for barbecuing.

Lighting

The dominant energy source for this purpose is electricity. Official responsibility for its generation rests with public corporations: the Sierra Leone Electricity Corporation National Power Authority (NPA) in Sierra Leone and National Energy and Power Authority (NEPA). However, a significant 82 per cent of category A-type Kano households reported the consumption of privately generated electricity in response to the legendary unreliability of the NEPA supply; for some of these households, self-generated power has almost replaced publicly supplied electricity. The lesser categories of B- and C-type households supplement unreliable public supply through the use of kerosene, and to a lesser extent, butane gas lamps. Presumably, then, decisions affecting the survival and functioning of NEPA taken in the public interest are done so by the category of people who are most insulated from the worst effects of the corporation's poor public performance.

Households without electricity do of course exist, and in both cities they are made up exclusively of category C consumers; some of them have had supplies disconnected for failure or inability to pay their bills, while others occupy various categories of substandard accommodation which does not conform to safety standards required for official connection. Household access to electricity in Kano is in reality much more restricted than Figure 41 would suggest, because illegal connections represent a widespread means of electric power acquisition. An indirect idea of the extent and magnitude of this device as a means of improving household accessibility to this impure public good can be obtained via an extrapolation from responses indicating that some households have no idea of their monthly electricity expenditure. If it is assumed that a large proportion of the 26 per cent category A households affected either have their electricity payments deducted at source, or benefit from free employer-funded supplies, the practice would then become a significant resource redistribution device for one-third and one-quarter of category C and category B households respectively. As Mabogunje (1975) puts it:

> *In terms of access, the informational capacity of individuals becomes a factor in their ability to identify resources in their environment to appreciate how these can be commanded, to be mindful of the need to maximize its positive whilst minimizing its negative externalities and to realize the importance of institutionalizing this advantage over the long run. (p. 75)*

The periodic official mass-disconnection drives against illegal electricity consumers have rarely, if ever, been extended to the suppression of illegally generated electricity. To the extent that they both represent variants of the same 'crime' this provides further proof of how inequality-generating and reinforcing mechanisms could be linked via power to political processes in the city.

Heating and cooling

The evidence provided by Figure 41 suggests that consumption profiles here are largely 'normal' with the percentage number of woodfuel consumers decreasing and that for fossil fuel increasing as one moves up the 'pecking order'. While some 80 per cent of Freetown's category A households are cooled by fans and air conditioners at the height of the hot season, some 90 per cent of their less fortunate co-inhabitants have to make do with manual fans and frequent cold baths; similarly, while category C Kano consumers burn wood and coal to provide warmth against the harmattan chill, their more fortunate neighbours depend on electric blow-heaters. It is worth pointing out that Figure 41 underplays the significance of the wood or coal fire during the harmattan months for the survival of Kano's 'floating' population – the temporarily or permanently urban unhoused, the peripatetic *almajirai*, the seasonal or periodic labour migrant – against whom a household-based energy survey is inevitably biased. It may thus be instructive that it is this group of shelter- and warmth-seeking 'pyromaniacs' who have been consistently blamed for the frequent fire outbreaks at the Sabon Gari market.[6]

It has already been pointed out that as people's conditions of existence change, and their accessibility (in all senses) to energy becomes modified, the indications are that the 'energy shifts' which result are neither unidirectional nor do they proceed at a uniform rate for all categories of consumers. For instance, between 1966/8 and 1981, the Freetown woodburning population declined by 8.9 per cent; the change in percentage utilization of the other fuels in use for cooking purposes over the same period is given in Table 12.3.

This trend is confirmed by data collected in Kano, where 25 per

Table 12.3 Changes in percentage utilization of cooking fuels 1966/8 – 1981: Freetown

Fuel	Percentage
Kerosene	+ 19.7
Charcoal	– 30.1
Gas	+ 2.3
Electricity	+ 6.1
Wood	– 8.9

Source: Cline-Cole: 1984a, p. 205

cent of wood-consuming households interviewed said they would prefer to replace wood with electricity, an equal percentage gas, and an overwhelming 75 per cent, kerosene. At the other end of the spectrum which demonstrates a 'reverse' energy shift are fossil fuel-burning households with a preference for increased wood consumption at the expense of kerosene (45%), gas (25%) and electricity (25%); for 20 per cent of these households wood would complement fossil fuels whose consumption would be maintained at existing levels. These figures would, in fact, suggest that the greatest movement is actually taking place at the bottom of the hierarchy (wood to charcoal; charcoal to kerosene; wood to kerosene) where there is room for improved accessibility leading to *qualitative* modifications in energy use rather than at the very top, where improvements in energy accessibility are largely diverted to *quantitative* energy adjustments.

For all but a very select few in society energy shifts would appear to imply either the maintenance of a household's energy range at a constant level through a straight swopping of individual fuels, or a contraction in existing household energy ranges resulting from a reduction in the total number of fuels used.

Stratification in energy distribution and commercialization

The domestic energy distribution and commercialization system in both cities is the product of public and private initiatives. The distinction thus needs to be made between the official public and private non-governmental subsectors of the distribution network. Public participation is direct in the production and sales of fuelwood in both cities, but in charcoal sales in Freetown only. Through the activities of the Nigerian National Petroleum Corporation and the Sierra Leone Oil Refinery, the official public sector is responsible for the production of fossil fuels, while their commercial distribution to the domestic consumer rests largely in the hands of private entrepreneurs (the major oil and gas companies) as well as small-owner concerns (Figure 40, columns 1 and 2). Indirect public participation at the level of commercialization to the household finds expression in devices such as selective recommended, but not necessarily enforceable, retail prices.

One important characteristic of potential inequality-generation and reinforcement in public sector participation is its built-in aversion – for reasons of organization and cost – to participation in the commercialization of energy products in small quantities. Official sector sales of firewood by the cord of approximately 2 cu.m (in both Freetown and Kano), of charcoal in 30–40 kg bags (in Freetown), of kerosene by the gallon (both Freetown and Kano) effectively exclude the majority of category C households from sharing the benefits of what are in reality subsidized goods. This state of affairs runs counter to officially voiced intentions, such as providing a social service to the whole community through the rational exploitation of a common good – the forest resources.[7] The publicly owned forest resources are in fact being managed and exploited for the benefit of a small minority who can afford to buy wood and coal in a wholesale market at preferential rates. It has to be a very perverse logic indeed which would justify the exclusion from a specialized commodity market of that commodity's largest single category of consumers. Such logic might, however, be found in the official Freetown charcoal markets where 20 per cent of the total charcoal production for the period 21 May 1979–20 January 1981 was unofficially supplied to category A government officials. 'To him that hath . . .'!

The private energy market has, over the years, capitalized on the formal market's two biggest shortcomings, especially from the point of view of category C consumers. First, through their extremely limited economic accessibility to wholesale quantities, and second, through their equally limited physical accessibility to extra-neighbourhood supply points. The private sector offers a wide range of retail units and wood bundles of different sizes, charcoal measures of varying sizes, and kerosene in various quantities, and offers mobile retail facilities such as barrow boys in Kano, wood lorries and mobile charcoal sellers in Freetown.

There exists, of course, the unmistakably unequal distribution of impure public goods. Cursory examination reveals that the relatively close spacing of filling stations (for petrol and kerosene) in the medium- to low-density residential Aminu Kano Way – Kofar Kabuga – Bayero University area contrasts with the extremely sparse distribution in the high-density area covering much of Kano Old City (*birni*). In Freetown filling stations are completely absent from slum areas like Susan's Bay and Kru Bay. But physical accessibility, as has been pointed out, does not necessarily imply economic accessibility – for one thing category C households do not generally buy kerosene by the gallon, while for another, petrol and not kerosene accounts for the large part of the sales, proceeds and profits of filling stations. For the same reasons, fuelwood markets, depots and piles are located away from high-class residential areas where demand for wood is low and from where they are, in any case, banned by planning restrictions which are more rigidly enforced in such areas than anywhere else. Such spatial inequality in the distribution of modern and traditional energy retail outlets can only have any real meaning in the context of the specific conditions of their accessibility and proximity to the various categories of consumers for 'agents and the "objects" of production are combined in a specific structure of the distribution of relations, places and functions' (Ay 1980).

The domestic energy market is very complex in its organization, and rigidly hierarchical in structure. This is hardly surprising as the necessary capital investment for participation in this market varies from a few to several tens of thousands of Leones or Naira depending partly on the fuel to be sold or produced, and partly on the proposed point of entry into the market hierarchy. The greatest outlays are demanded by gas bottling plants and filling stations followed by gas retail outlets and wood transporting lorries. Participation at this highest level of the market hierarchy with its monetary and organizational demands is predictably restricted to investors or their representatives in occupational categories A and B (Figure 40). Immediately below this first level come the kerosene, wood and coal redistributors whose investment demands are considerably more modest – a few hundred Leones or Naira. Although these include some B-level participants, the majority are actually recruited from the ranks of the levels C1 and C2 urbanites.

At the lowest level of the hierarchy operate the labourers who offload, split, bundle and sell wood on piece rates for the group 2 investors (Kano), or who work as apprentices on wood lorries in exchange for food and accommodation (Freetown). Also belonging to this category are the temporarily or permanently unemployed and 'second occupation' woodcutters who exploit the Peninsula forests in the immediate vicinity of Freetown. Returns to investment strongly mirror the market hierarchy elaborated above with the greatest total profits accruing to the biggest investors. However, when profits are measured as a percentage of investment the preceding order is inverted and the 'smaller' participants emerge as the biggest recipients (Cline-Cole 1984a). In the Freetown fuelwood market, of the total number of stationary woodsellers, less than 10 per cent occupy the topmost level of the trade hierarchy and in an activity numerically dominated by women (a ratio of 2.3:1), they only constitute one-third of the sellers at the apex of the trade pyramid. This pattern of inequality is repeated at the largest firewood depot in Kano (Yanawaki) where on a normal working day one would expect to find somewhere between 120 and 200 mostly rural-based labourers offloading, splitting, bundling and selling wood for about 30–50 wood pile owner-operators. A quick calculation premised on an average daily labourer population of 160 suggests a monthly labourer turnover of 4,800 individuals. In the last 12–15 years only about *six* labourers have managed to narrow their personal inequality range to the point of owning and operating their own wood piles. It took Malam Madaki, the most recent of these 'success stories', 12 years to make the transition. As Althusser explains, 'this determines the places and functions occupied and adopted by the agents of production'.

Table 12.4 gives a comparison of the prices of some domestic fuels in the official and non-governmental subsectors of the energy market in the two study cities. The differences in price between the recommended official prices and the actual open market prices can be considered the cost or negative externality effect of the official market's decision to deal only in 'wholesale' quantities. This cost is borne by the consumers who are excluded from the official market; these have been identified as the poorer urban inhabitants who 'survive' from one day to the next on intermittent, fluctuating and generally low incomes.

Supplies at this lower level of the consumer hierarchy are, of necessity, obtained in small individual quantities. In this way official management of a public resource can be seen as initiating a process of inequality which subsequently becomes reinforced by the operation of the non-official market. Consider the range of prices in the private sector market in the two cities, in particular their upper limits. Firewood in Kano, for instance, costs twice as much when bought as a 65 k bundle than when bought as a N1 bundle. The same relationship holds for all the other fuels: price per unit weight or volume increases as the unit of sale decreases in size. The better-off households who can afford to buy their energy in larger units are thus paying much less for the energy they consume than their less favoured co-citizens who, constrained by a lack of funds, buy in smaller and ultimately more expensive units.

Intra-fuel price inequality of this type is replicated on the inter-fuel price level as Table 12.5 shows. Gas consumers are getting the greatest value for money spent on domestic cooking energy of any group of consumers. Reference to Figure 41a indicates that gas consumers are overwhelmingly category A households. At the other end of the price scale is electricity which, as the most expensive fuel in Kano, costs three times as much as gas. This explains its unpopularity as a cooking fuel among all categories of consumers although category A households represent the single largest consumer category. Firewood is only marginally cheaper than electricity, an observation which throws into sharp relief once again the extremely unfavourable situation of the urban poor who depend so heavily on it for cooking. It is worth

Table 12.4 Fuel price comparisons in Kano and Freetown

Freetown		Kano	
Official/recommended price	*Actual price*	*Official/recommended price*	*Actual price*
Lell. 79/cu.m [1] (wood)	Le20-Le100/cu.m	1.3 k/kg [5] (wood)	4.5–91 k/kg [2]
5.7 c/kg [1] (charcoal)	6.3c–44.4 c/kg	13 k/litre [3] (kerosene)	13.3–33.3 k/litre [3]
		17.7 k/litre–18.9k/litre (gas)	18.2–25.3k/litre [4]

100 cents (c) = 1 Leone (Le); 1981 prices
Sources: (1) Forestry Division, Ministry of Agriculture

100 kobo (k) = 1 Naira (N); 1985 prices
(2) Yanawaki fuelwood depot
(3) Open market prices at Yakasai Ward (Kano Old City)
(4) Eagle Gas bottled by the National Oil and Chemical Marketing Co., Kano
(5) Parks and Gardens Division of Kano State Forestry Department

Table 12.5 Inter-fuel cost inequalities in Kano, 1985

Fuel	Unit of Measurement	Price (kobo)*	Energy content (kilocalories)	Kcals of energy 1 kobo will buy
Gas	litre	21.8	11,500[1]	527.5
Firewood	kg	8.6	3,200[2]	372.1
Kerosene	litre	23.3	10,100[1]	433.5
Electricity	kwh	6	860.5[3]	143.5

* Mean of private market price ranges in Table 12.4
Sources: (1) Schatzl 1980; (2) Ay 1980; (3) Smil and Knowland 1980

reiterating the point made earlier that where producer maximum profit and consumer maximum benefit do not coincide, considerable inequalities in availability and accessibility will exist and these will operate to the advantage of the higher income groups.

Domestic energy, inequality and space

Inequalities in domestic energy production, distribution and consumption do not just happen in space; they are created and maintained by a complex interplay of factors. Some of the most significant of these operate outside the control of the individual. This is however neither to advocate determinism nor to overlook the tremendous range of individual energy 'environments' within which participants in the energy economy operate.

Household energy environments constitute part of a wider socio-economic and political system in which everything affects everything else and within which energy inequalities are explicable in terms of social processes. These processes as well as the energy inequalities which they foster can and do have an expression in the space occupied by the energy producer, distributor and consumer. The emergence of distinctly similar domestic energy profiles in say, Nassarawa (Kano) and Hill station (Freetown) is of course tightly tied to the evolution of the differentiation between the former Senior Service and non-Senior Service government workers (thus a structural differentiation) being transformed into residential segregation. The colonial Senior Service was long ago replaced by an indigenous Senior staff, and residence in such areas can be still correlated with subsidized energy bills.

The method of analysis proposed here involves, at an initial stage, the consideration of domestic energy production, distribution and consumption units as existing in one-dimensional space (up-down/along the occupational and status hierarchy). This location in structural space is then extended to location in actual physical space where participation in domestic energy activities actually takes place. Thus activities associated with participation in the domestic energy economy are arranged in various spatial configurations: the distribution of fuelwood piles and markets in Kano, the distribution of filling stations in Freetown, the distribution of predominantly woodfuel burning or fossil fuel consuming neighbourhoods in both towns – any or all of these take on identifiable forms in space. Adjustments to the structural environment are translated into modifications in the spatial expressions which have resulted directly from such an environment's existence in a particular form or manner. The evolution of Kano's firewood delivery and distribution system over the last two decades serves as a case in point (Falola *et al.* 1984).

The traditional rural-based Kano fuelwood distribution network was focused on small semi-permanent supply nodes in the *birni* and linked to rural producers via short-distance donkey delivery. This network has declined in the last two decades to be replaced by a lorry and pick-up long-distance delivery system, focused on large permanent supply points whose range of operations is greatly extended by the activities of rural-based seasonal and periodic cart-pushing labourers. Urban bias in development and its attendant population explosion has implied a continuous absolute and relative increase in the numbers of category C households. These structural changes and their spatial responses have ultimately created a situation which has gone against the rural-based donkey delivery system and benefited urban-based lorry-owning or operating entrepreneurs; former rural-based wood producers have become labourers who now migrate to Kano to work at the preparation and commercialization of wood while they now neither own nor produce.

Figure 42 shows the distribution of firewood and charcoal-consuming households by electoral zones in Freetown. It has already been shown that firewood is used by all categories of households. Thus it is hardly surprising that the distribution in Figure 42a averages out at around the citywide mean. In addition technological and cognitive skills (even

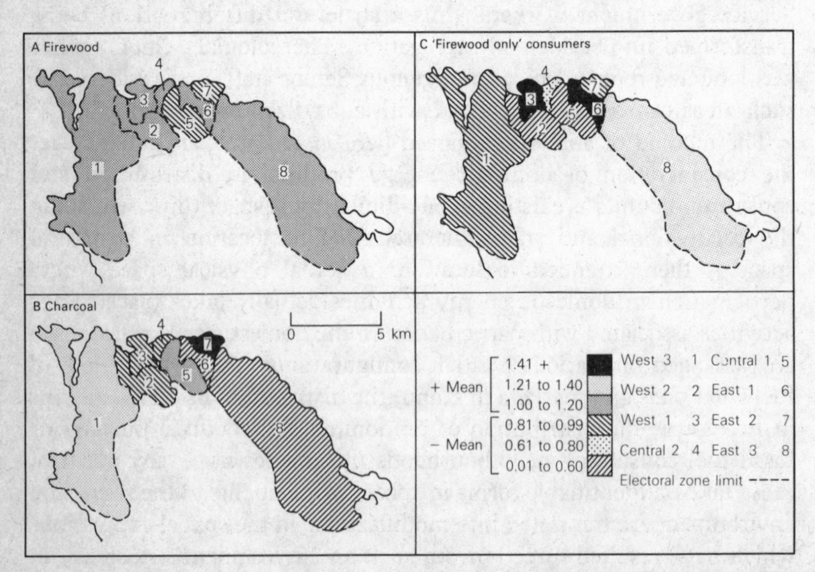

Fig. 42 Indices of woodfuel consumption by electoral zones, Freetown

if not economic access) are very evenly distributed throughout the population. The spatial distribution of inequalities in firewood use is actually suppressed as a result of the widespread use of the fuel by all groups. Yet the poorest consumers have to use wood even though the costs in monetary and physical terms may be considerable. A much better idea of spatial inequality in energy consumption here is provided by the mapped distribution in Figure 42c of households for whom firewood represents the only fuel.

The situation presented in Figure 42b for charcoal consumption is very different from that in Figure 42a. Charcoal represents a fuel with a more limited physical and economic accessibility. Its use also entails cognitive and technological skills which are characterized by a more restricted distribution than those needed for wood use. Finally, for people at the bottom end of the urban hierarchy it does not represent a 'bottom-line' fuel – there is always firewood as a last resort. Charcoal seems, then, eminently more suitable for demonstrating spatial inequalities in energy use than firewood. Indeed Figure 42b demonstrates a more differentiated spatial pattern in energy utilization than does Figure 42a. Significantly, and in contrast to firewood, the percentage distribution of charcoal consumers by electoral zone proved to be positively correlated with consumer access to the fuel as measured by the ratio of households to charcoal retail points in each constituency. This, together with the inverse relationship observable between charcoal and 'firewood only' consumption, suggests that the utilization and distribution of energy resources characterized by increasingly restricted physical and economic access for the consumer might in fact provide increasingly useful insights into inequalities in domestic energy use.

Energy policy formulation and implementation

The socio-spatial field of externality effects has already been defined and its characteristics identified. With reference to domestic energy activities it is the negative externalities making up this field which have traditionally preoccupied officialdom: the accident hazards represented by wood-selling carts (*amalankes*) and poorly maintained wood lorries, traffic congestion, deforestation, etc. are all synonymous in official minds with the location and functioning of wood and charcoal production and commercialization units in both Freetown and Kano. Positive externality effects such as creation of employment and improved consumer access to fuels, etc. are more often than not completely ignored or poorly understood, creating the potential for well-meaning but ill-informed regional and urban planning policies which exacerbate rather than reduce social and economic inequality, as the following examples from an ongoing study in Kano shows.

The Yanawaki fuelwood depot was established at least 30 years ago in its present location at the eastern edge of the *birni* in the Kofar Wambai-Fagge area; it is reportedly the first permanent fuelwood market in urban Kano. Together, the wholesale and retail sections make Yanawaki by far the biggest firewood market in urban Kano with a labour demand of about 4,800 man-days per month – from some 30–50 wood pile operators. Task specialization prevails, encouraging a wide distribution of income-earning possibilities and preventing the accumulation of such inequality-ameliorating opportunities by a small number of labourers.[8] Labourers are recruited mostly from among the ranks of daily and periodic seasonal migrants originating outside metropolitan Kano, the nearby Local Government Areas (LGAs) of Dawakin Tofa, Bichi and Gezawa being better represented as source areas than the more distant Dambatta, Ringim and Gumel. Extreme seasonality in the availability of labour is reported, with shortages in the agricultural season alternating with often excessive dry season peaks.

A random sample of 15 labourers revealed that about two-thirds were occupied in agriculture before taking up urban wage labour; an equal proportion cited agriculture as their second occupation. Only a quarter of the sample were 'proletarianized' in the sense that wage labour represented their only economic activity and money earning source. Of the total sample one-third had been involved in firewood labouring for two years or less while more than half indicated participation of five years or longer. The mean participation length for the 'proletarianized' sub-sample is six years. No firm conclusions can be drawn regarding the link between proletarianization and length of time in wage labour – both the longest-serving labourers (12 years) and the newest (one week) maintain farms in their area of origin. Links with migrant source areas remain largely intact, raising questions concerning the significance of urban wage-earning opportunities of this type for the complex processes of social and economic change and rural differentiation taking place in the urban peripheries of towns such as Kano (Swindell 1985); in one instance recorded, two brothers from Dakata at the eastern edge of Kano, who work full-time at firewood labouring during the dry season, alternate this with farm work at weekly or fortnightly intervals during the agricultural season. The field of externality effects here would appear to stretch all the way from Yanawaki to the surrounding rural areas with the intensity of the effect being characterized by a very gentle distance-decay function.

Although the preceding examples ought not to make one lose sight of the contradictions inherent in the type of 'development' being pursued by the country,[9] it is unquestionable that wage-earning opportunities which directly ameliorate inequality do exist in the firewood economy even if these give rise in turn to new types of inequality such as proletarianization, labour exploitation, etc.[10] Positive externalities operate through indirect employment also, as demonstrated by the activities of water-carrying and cooked-food selling which have developed to service the depot; these female-dominated income-generating activities assume tremendous importance in interpersonal inequality reduction in a society where gender inequality operates overwhelmingly against women. With this second set of positive externalities the intensity of the socio-spatial field of effects decays at a very rapid rate with increasing distance from Yanawaki; all the people involved in the activities identified come from the immediate vicinity of the depot.

The cost of proximity or negative effects (traffic congestion, noise, vermin, poor sanitation) evidently weigh heaviest on individuals and households in the immediate vicinity; it is however this same category of urbanites for whom the price of physical and economic accessibility to wood is lowest, as 'waste' (wood chips or *dauso*) and defective products (wood pieces too short in length or too small in diameter to be used in bundles) can be obtained free or at one-quarter to one-third of the price of good quality bundled wood. The depot thus attracts a daily foraging population of two or three hundred children of both sexes and middle-aged/old women who collect such products for both domestic consumption and sale.[11] Furthermore, community projects such as the construction of a new bridge in the vicinity of the depot are financed in part through voluntary contributions by the Kano State Firewood Sellers Development Association, comprising firewood sellers from different parts of Kano and based at Yanawaki where the Association's President has his firewood pile.

Externality effects associated with domestic energy activities are thus extremely complex in nature requiring careful and detailed examination, particularly as planning/policy decisions based on their incomplete understanding often have effects detrimental to people, expressed in socio-spatial inequalities. This is of particular relevance to recent public sector proposals for the large-scale spatial reorganization of Kano's firewood trade. The Environmental Sanitation Campaign operating through the Petty Trading (Control) Edict 1984, the Petty Trading Control (Amendment) Edict 1985 and the Petty Trading (Exclusion of Roads) Order 1985 threatens to exacerbate already parlous conditions of inequality by making it illegal to:

(a) erect or place any temporary structure in, near or adjacent to any road,
(b) carry on any trade or business in any temporary structures in, near or adjacent to any road,
(c) hawk any goods in, near or adjacent to any road, or
(d) sell any goods or offer any goods for sale in, near or adjacent to any road.

But it is the neighbourhood effect, easy consumer accessibility to the non-formal domestic energy market, which has enabled it to supplant the official domestic energy delivery system: 91 per cent of the Kano wood-consuming sample obtain their supplies within the Kano urban area and 12.5 per cent outside the Kano metropolis; of the consumers who buy wood within the Kano urban area, 26 per cent obtain supplies regularly from cart-pushers, and 73 per cent, direct from their neighbourhood wood pile operator. Thus the proposed twin measures of forced relocation of fuelwood piles at Yammata and the total ban on *amalanke* trade have the potential for setting in motion a whole range of income-redistribution effects which will not favour the lower-income households whose physical and economic accessibility to their most important cooking fuel will be drastically reduced. On the supply side the concensus at Yanawaki is that more than two-thirds of the existing contingent of wood pile 'enterprises' will not survive the combined move to the sparsely populated and peripherally located Yammata area and the loss of revenue from a discontinued *amalanke* trade; small, newly established businesses such as Mallam Madaki's (he is still paying off the loan acquired as part of his starting capital) are those most at risk, while the three or four wood pile owners who are also transport operators are most commonly cited as those best suited to survive these proposed changes.

Conditions external to the Kano State economy complicated matters even further. The unprecedented national wealth generated by the 1970s petroleum boom financed wide-ranging energy subsidies, which even though overwhelmingly favourable to higher-income earners still permits the widespread use of kerosene among the lower-income earners.[12] The recent downturn in the country's economic fortunes due to a glut in the international oil market and economic mismanagement at the national level has seen the initiation of loan negotiations with the International Monetary Fund, one of whose standard conditions for the successful negotiation of loan agreements is the withdrawal of energy subsidies: a move which would result in (a) reverse energy shifts (kerosene to wood) at the lower end of the income hierarchy and (b) an increase in the price of wood to the final consumer resulting from increased wood transportation costs. If this is compounded by the 'centralization' of fuelwood activities at Yammata, the negative externality effects which would be borne by the lower-income urban residents become cumulative. The intention here is not to suggest that *only* low-income earners are subject to the adverse effects of the changing economic climate in the country but rather to reiterate that 'the poor can less afford to lose an external benefit or incur an external cost' (Harvey, 1975 p. 81).

Conclusion

This paper started with the observation that the widely expected traditional to modern shift in domestic energy consumption has not taken place in newly industrializing countries. It has attempted to show, using a structuralist framework of analysis which emphasizes unequal access to scarce societal resources, why this is the case in Freetown and Kano. But the brand of structuralism employed in the paper leaves room for the input derived from behavioural analysis in the explanation of differentiations in domestic energy use within the urban environment. How are specific energy end-use patterns developed? What conditions (social, economic, political) lead to identifiable differentiations or inequalities in domestic energy production and consumption? Questions of this nature justify the need for a line of analysis which situates such patterns within society's opportunity hierarchy, and the positions occupied by individual consumers and producers within the structure which is ultimately the product of major social processes. These are, in the final analysis, responsible for explaining who does what, where, how and why in terms of domestic energy.

Notes

1 In any case, only 46 per cent of the Local Government Areas – mostly Headquarter towns – were electrified in 1981.

2 People value different things in different ways, rendering the measurement of 'intensity of preference' among individuals extremely difficult. The 'unanimity rule' offers a possible solution to this problem through its assumption that everybody in a given population would rank preferences over a set of alternatives in the same way; such alternatives are said to be 'Pareto-comparable' when this rule holds and 'Pareto-non-comparable' where it does not (see Harvey 1975).

3 Rural–urban migrants who earn a living as domestic servants in middle- to high-income households make, almost routinely, the transition from the

so-called non-commercial energy to 'modern' energy. The question thus arises of what effects a more equitable distribution of resources between 'environments' (intra-urban, rural-urban, inter-rural) would have on domestic energy end-use patterns.

4 The Freetown research was carried out in 1981 and involved a total of 599 households. Grateful acknowledgement is made here for a Government of France Postgraduate Grant which covered fieldwork expenses. The Kano data (involving information collected from 86 households) represents preliminary results of on-going research as part of the United Nations University-funded Kano Rural Energy Research Project. I am grateful to the other members of the project for permission to use data collected as part of the project. Research Assistants Aminu Shehu and Muhtari Sadique were particularly helpful and deserve a special mention of appreciation. The ideas expressed in this paper are, of course, not binding on any other member of the group.

5 This does not in any way discount the significance of 'Pareto non-comparability' which becomes subsumed in resource maximization.

6 The newly rebuilt Sabon Gari market is now out of bounds to 'night watchmen' and this 'floating population' is truly floating once again. For discussions of the origins and internal dynamics of this population see Main (Chapter 11 of this book).

7 Personal communication from the Divisional Forest Officer, Western Area, Freetown, April 1981.

8 Newly recruited and 'unskilled' labourers offload lorries; three categories of 'skilled' labourers work at splitting (producing wood pieces of appropriate length and diameter from delivered logs), bundling (involving the preparation of bundles of different sizes and prices) and mobile retailing (cart pushers are responsible for establishing numerous long-term customer-seller relationships).

9 Both rural–urban migration and informal sector participation can be considered responses to inequality, the former on the regional scale (Riddell 1970; Main see chapter 11) and the latter on the intra-urban scale (Fowler, 1976).

10 Sada identifies the three principal employment functions of the urban informal sector as (a) providing employment for unskilled labour, (b) representing an avenue for transitional employment and (c) playing the role of a source of supplementary income.

11 Two teenagers who started secondary school during the 1984/5 academic session were able to save enough money from selling *dauso* to buy bicycles; at least one household near the depot has not spent any money on the satisfaction of its firewood needs in the last three years, depending solely on free *dauso* and offcuts collected at the depot.

12 The 1970s petroleum boom was a direct product of the formation and functioning of OPEC, a move which had been prompted by the need to counter inequality on the global scale, that is unequal terms of trade between the oil-producing developing countries and the large-scale industrial oil consumers.

References

Aboyade, O. 1975. 'On the need for an operational specification of poverty in the Nigerian economy'. In Teriba, O., Phillip, O., and Akeredolu-Ale, E.O. (eds) *Poverty in Nigeria*, Proceedings of the 1975 Annual Conference of the Nigerian Economic Society.
Akeredolu-Ale, E.O. 1975. 'Poverty as a social issue: a theoretic note'. In Teriba, O. *et al.* (eds) *Poverty in Nigeria*.
Ay, P. 1980. 'Fuelwood and charcoal in the West African forest: field research in Western Nigeria'. In Morgan, W.B., Moss, R.P. and Ojo, G.J.A. (eds) *Rural energy systems in the humid tropics*, Proceedings of the First Workshop of the United Nations University Rural Energy Systems Project, Tokyo.
Cline-Cole, R.A. 1981. Perspectives on energo-politics: implications for 'energy crisis' considerations in the Third World, *Africana Research Bulletin*, vol. XI (1 & 2), pp. 50–80.
Cline-Cole, R.A. 1984a. 'Les energies traditionnelles en Afrique tropicale : les bois de chauffage et le charbon de bois à Freetown (Unpublished doctoral thesis, Université de Bordeaux)
Cline-Cole, R.A. 1984b. Towards an understanding of man-firewood relations in Freetown (Sierra Leone), *Geoforum*, vol. 15, no. 4, pp. 583–94.
Coates, B.E., Johnston, R.J. and Knox, P.L. 1977. *Geography and inequality* (Oxford: Oxford University Press)
Falola, J.A., Cline-Cole, R., Main, H.A.C., Mortimore, M., Nichol, J.E., Patrick, S. and O'Reilly, F.D. 1984. 'Fuelwood in contemporary Kano', Paper presented at 27th Annual Conference of the Nigerian Geographical Association, Nsuka.
Fowler, D. 1976. The urban-informal sector in Sierra Leone, *Africana Research Bulletin*, vol VI (3), p. 40–30.
Harvey, D. 1975. *Social justice and the city* (London: Edward Arnold)
International Labour Office 1984. *Yearbook of Labour Statistics* (Geneva: ILO)
Kano State Yearbook 1981.
Mabogunje, A.L. 1975. 'Prolegomenon to urban poverty in Nigeria'. In Teriba *et al.* (eds) *Poverty in Nigeria*, Proceedings of the 1975 Annual Conference of the Nigerian Society.
Remy, D. 1976. 'Underdevelopment and the experience of women: a Nigerian case study'. In Williams, G. (ed.) *Nigeria: economy and society* (London: Rex Collings)
Riddell, J.B. 1970. *Spatial dynamics of modernisation in Sierra Leone: structure, diffusion and response* (Evanston: Northwestern University Press)
Schatzl, L. 1980. *'Structure and development of Nigeria's energy sector: a macro-analysis'*. In Morgan, W.B. *et al.* (eds.) *Rural energy systems in the humid tropics*, Proceedings of the First Workshop of the United Nations University Rural Energy Systems Project, Tokyo.
Smil, V. and Knowland, W.E., *Energy in the Developing World* (Oxford: Oxford University Press)
Swindell, K. 1985. *Farm Labour* (Cambridge: Cambridge University Press)
Vennetier, P. 1980. 'Les problèmes du bois de feu et du charbon de bois en

Afrique Tropicale' in *L'energie dans les communautés rurales des pays du tiers monde*.
Williams, G. 1976. 'Nigeria: a political economy' in Williams, G. (ed.) *Nigeria, economy and society* (London: Collins)

Section Four: Time, Policy & Development

13
An evaluation of the differential impact of public policy on spatial inequalities in Sri Lanka since 1977

Vidyamali Samarasinghe
Department of Geography, University of Peradeniya, Sri Lanka

Introduction

Spatial inequality reflects the differential impact of socio-economic development on geographic space. Although spatial inequalities exist both in advanced countries (ACs) and in less developed countries (LDCs) 'planning only for the upliftment of the backward region so as to bring it to the national growth level' (Estall 1982) as practised in the ACs is almost a luxury that the LDCs can ill-afford. A major dilemma with which the latter group is confronted is how to activate a mechanism to stimulate economic productivity to achieve higher growth rates while redressing obvious spatial imbalances. In the short run the two processes could compete with each other for the limited quantum of investment available. This may also lead to a situation against which Alonso (1968) cautioned, where he argued that the dispersal of investment on a wider spatial basis in order to achieve both equity and efficiency may not deliver the desired overall economic growth. Nevertheless, the political reality in LDCs is such that government interventionist policies are expected within a relatively short period of time not only to steer economic development but also to stimulate its spatial dispersion in order to eliminate and/or redress spatial inequalities.

The island of Sri Lanka falls into the LDC category with a per capita income of $340 in 1984. It is 65,610 sq km in size with an estimated population of 15.6 million in 1984. It has a multi-ethnic society where 74 per cent of the population are Sinhalese, 12.6 per cent are Sri Lankan Tamils, 7.1 per cent are Moors and 5.5 per cent are defined as Indian Tamils;[1] 79 per cent of the population are rural and agrarian. The country is divided into 24 administrative districts

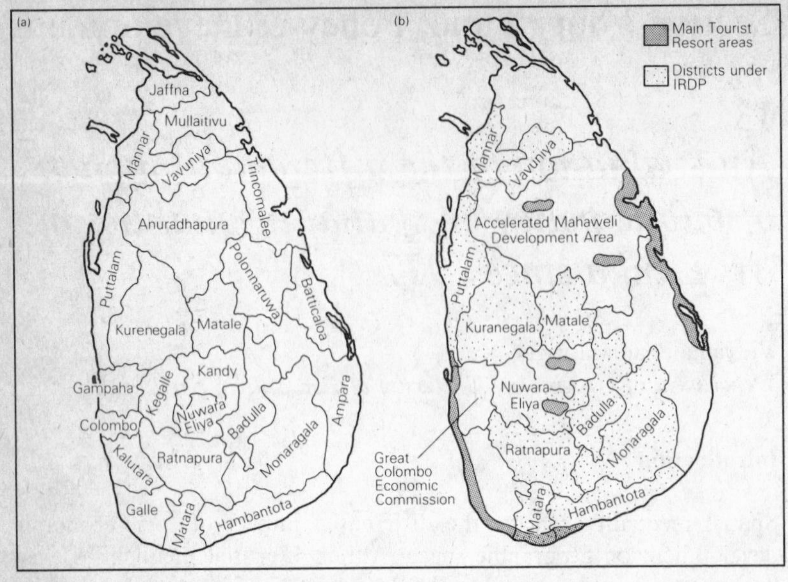

Fig. 43 (a) Districts of Sri Lanka
(b) Areas benefited by the IRDP, AMDP, GCE and tourism

(See Fig. 43a) The small size of the country and a fairly well-established road and railway network have facilitated inter-regional accessibility. However, a combination of factors, mainly historical and structural in relation to changing socio-economic priorities, has resulted in the incidence of spatial inequalities (Samarasinghe 1980).

The present study attempts to review and analyse the spatial impact of public policy on economic development in Sri Lanka since 1977.[2] The Sri Lankan economy came under increasing state control over the period 1950–77, but in 1977 the government changed its policy-orientation somewhat by liberalizing the economy and reducing state control. Market forces were allowed greater play to induce growth and consequently, the gross domestic product (GDP) grew at an average rate of six per cent per annum. This recovery is significant in that there was a near slump condition in growth in the immediate pre-1977 phase at only 2.9 per cent per annum. The growth rate of the GDP per capita recovered to 4.3 per cent between 1977 and 1984 from 1.3 per cent during 1971–7. However the political reality in Sri Lanka is such that overwhelming emphasis on productivity via an open economy with scant regard to equity both in terms of income distribution and regional balance is not possible. Hence public policy has had to strike a balance between promoting productivity mainly through the private sector, while at the same time implementing state-sponsored sectoral and/or area development programmes. Such policies could turn out to be competing forces and result in a differential impact on geographic space. Productivity-oriented free market forces may benefit the already rich regions since profit motivation would certainly induce investors to locate economic ventures where markets, skills and other facilities are already available. State-sponsored development policies on the other hand may not contain the quick dynamic growth content and they may also be expected to operate in poor backward areas where quick returns to investments would not be forthcoming. Depending on the success of the two different aspects of public policy, rich regions may become richer while poor regions may become poorer; or alternatively while rich regions may get richer the poorer regions may become less poor.

Spatial inequalities before 1977

The sharp polarization of Colombo through its links with the commercial agricultural estate or plantation sector, and the colonial power, was a significant feature of the spatial pattern during the late colonial period (see Samarasinghe 1980; 1982). This was reduced with the implementation of the state-sponsored dry zone irrigated agricultural schemes[3] which were conceived and put into initial operation during the latter part of the colonial period and continued with vigour after independence. Thus a neglected backward region of the country was given a new lease of life, primarily in the hope of achieving self-sufficiency in rice, the staple food crop. Confronted with the deteriorating terms of trade and falling foreign exchange earnings the government of 1956 launched a programme of industrialization on the lines of import substitution. A general policy of locational dispersal was followed in relation to large-scale government-owned industries. An incentive package was offered to private investors in order to promote a limited range of small-scale consumer industries mainly for the local market. In the absence of specific locational policy for such private industry, by the early 1970s 85 per cent were located in the district of Colombo itself. Until the Land Reform Acts of 1972 and 1975, commercial plantation agriculture, popularly known as the estate sector, was allowed to function with the minimum of interventionist policies on management. Although the plantations generated a sizeable share of the GDP, the vast army of resident labour, mostly of Indian Tamil origin, received low wages and lived under insanitary conditions. Moreover, it was also reported that the worst pockets of poverty were found in the hill country in the Kandyan districts among the rural communities which are surrounded by plantations (Gunatilake 1978). Heavy taxes were levied on the profits of the plantation sector and most of the income was syphoned off towards investment in the dry zone agricultural settlement schemes and expenditure on national welfare programmes. Consequently, the distinct geographic space encompassing the plantations in the central hilly regions of the country remained backward in terms of economic and social benefits. The western coastal districts, benefiting from their proximity to the metropolitan area of Colombo and the advantages of better transport, health care and education, fared better. Jaffna in the north, with its concentration of Sri Lanka Tamils, also enjoyed better status especially due to superior educational and welfare facilities (Samarasinghe 1980).

The 'sectoral' orientation of public policy was somewhat changed by the implementation of the Divisional Development Council (DDC) programme of 1972. This was an attempt to stimulate development incorporating community participation at a regional level. However reviews on the operation of DDCs reveal that they did not live up to expectations and were virtually abandoned by 1976 (Karunatilake 1978; Peiris 1972).

Economic policies after 1977

Public policy on productivity-related activities since 1977 could be classified into four groups. They are (a) agriculture, (b) manufacturing industry, (c) service sector industry and (d) rural development. The first three are mainly sectoral while the fourth has an overriding regional component. In analysing the spatial manifestations of these policy measures an attempt will be made to discern the impact of present policy on the incidence of regional inequalities in Sri Lanka.

Agriculture

The Accelerated Mahaweli Development Project (AMDP) constitutes the biggest investment decision of the government of 1977 (Figure 43b). It is mainly an agriculturally oriented policy designed to expand irrigated farmland and new settlements in the Dry Zone of Sri Lanka. In the original Dry Zone Colonization Schemes conceived during the latter part of the British colonial rule, the main thrust was food production in the face of a growing crisis in relation to food imports (Farmer 1957). Nevertheless, the desire to develop the Dry Zone so that it could sustain a prosperous, self-supporting and self-respecting multitude of peasant proprietors (Clifford 1927) was also given much prominence. Furthermore, the necessity of developing a backward region has been a prime motivating factor behind the Dry Zone colonization scheme strategy. All these factors continue to be important in the context of the AMDP today. It plans to:

1 divert the excess water from the upper reaches of the river Mahaweli to the dry zone, in order to irrigate, according to current projections, approximately 350,000 acres of land (mostly new land);
2 open planned settlement schemes for peasant farmers while strengthening the economic viability of existing *purana* (old) land;
3 provide water for double cropping; and
4 provide approximately 700 Mwhs of additional hydro-electric power to the national grid by constructing five dams across various points of the river.

The lull in government spending on irrigation seen during the period 1965–75 has been shattered with the massive investment on the AMDP. It amounts to 25 per cent of the annual capital expenditure of the government.

On a spatial basis the main beneficiaries of irrigation and settlement schemes are the districts of Anuradhapura and Polonnaruwa in the North Central Province and Trincomalee district in the Eastern Province. These two provinces have been the main beneficiaries of previous colonization schemes as well. The Dry Zone colonization programme has resulted in tangible development of these regions. The period between 1946 and 1963 saw a massive flow of internal migrants into the area (Vamathevan 1960). The intercensal migration statistics for the following period, 1963–73, also indicate that the North Central Province recorded the highest rate of migrant flows into the region (ESCAP 1976). The AMDP in its entirety constitutes a new planning region based on the multifaceted development of a river basin. The success of regional development lies in the capacity of the region to sustain and keep the population and also to attract migrants. This depends on the viability of the economic base of the region.

Industry

In the sphere of industrialization, the pace of growth has been slow since agriculture has always been given precedence in formulating development strategy. Industrialization is normally identified with urbanization. Urbanization in Sri Lanka has not only been slow, but the major urban areas are identified more with services or administrative functions than with manufacturing industry. The limited programme of industrialization after 1956 had an inward-looking orientation and the spatial location pattern revealed a dispersal of government industries away from the main metropolis of Colombo while the smaller scale private industries preferred the locational advantages offered by Colombo. The dispersal of public industry meant an implied acceptance by the government of regional locations. In 1978, by an Act of Parliament the Greater Colombo Economic Commission (GCEC) was established to promote industrialization within or near the capital (Figure 43b). By this policy decision the government made a decisive and a conscious move to locate industries in the two urbanized districts of Colombo and Gampaha. The main objectives of the GCEC were to promote foreign investments in industrial ventures, increase export earnings from industrial goods and create employment opportunities for the local population. It planned to develop an export-oriented structure of industries through the use of mainly foreign capital. The main component of the GCEC is the Investment Promotion Zone (IPZ) located 20 miles north of the city of Colombo in Katunayake. An attractive incentive package was offered to the industrial investors and by the end of 1984 there were 62 industries located in the IPZ, most of which were foreign-owned. Local direct employment amounted to approximately 29,000 people. Indeed, the major impact on regional development is in the creation of employment opportunities in the areas in relation to the production of construction material, and for other service activities which the IPZ generates. The available evidence suggests that a sizeable proportion of the labour force comes from the districts of Colombo and Gampaha.

The viability of this economic system of industries depends on the strength of its structure to act as a basis for the expansion and growth of new industries. The majority (54 per cent) of IPZ industries are garment industries. The bulk of raw material and intermediate inputs for the industry are imported and the product is exported; there are no incentives to forge inter-industry linkages or to foster feeder industries. However, the immediate tangible impact on the local scene, apart from direct employment in the IPZ factories is in the expansion of service activities, especially in relation to bulk haulage container traffic and commuter transport.

The guiding principle of spatial development in the post-war period in Sri Lanka was the location of economic activity away from the main metropolitan area and frequent references to the 'Congested South-west' and the 'Neglected Dry Zone' reflect this attitude. The metropolitan area of Colombo stood to gain only when market forces were allowed free play. The location of the IPZ and the development envisaged of the GCEC area as the industrial base reflects a certain degree of change in such a policy. Although such a policy seems to be inspired purely by the need to stimulate sectoral growth by stimulating market forces, regions like Colombo stand to gain due to the momentum it already has in relation to urban industrial growth.

Tertiary sector

In the tertiary sector of economic activity, the tourist industry in Sri Lanka was an important area of income generation until 1983. It was classified as one of the fastest growing industries. Public policy in relation to tourism has been geared towards offering attractive incentives to private enterprise in order to encourage foreign tourist travel.

Tourist arrivals steadily increased from 28,272 in 1968 to 103,204 in 1975 and 380,000 in 1982. The spatial implications of tourism in Sri Lanka is felt mainly in four areas. They are (a) Colombo city and district, (b) the coastal region – mainly the south coast and east coast, (c) the high country resort region, and (d) the historic cities region. In terms of accommodation capacity in graded hotels the Colombo region claims the largest share (Ceylon Tourist Board 1983). However, the nature of the industry is such that it is highly dependent on 'whims' and 'choices' of people who come as tourists. Tourism as an industry is also more vulnerable to external forces such as recession and internal factors such as ethno-political conflicts, and since the ethnic riots of 1983 income from tourism has declined very sharply.

Integrated Rural Development Programme (IRDP)

A sizeable section of Sri Lanka running from north to south with a slight curve in the middle does not fall within any of these basically productivity-oriented categories discussed in the foregoing analysis. The Integrated Rural Development Programme (IRDP) which is the only overtly regional planning policy scheme of the government of 1977 embraces the bulk of this residual region (Fig. 43b) The Districts of Mannar, Vavuniya, Puttalam, Kurunegala, Matale, Kegalle, Nuwaraeliya, Badulla, Monaragala, Hambantota, Matara Batticaloa and Ratnapura had IRD programmes either at the initial stage of planning or at the implementation stage.

The IRDP of Sri Lanka is basically a programme designed to stimulate productivity in the rural sector and uplift the quality of life of the population. The IRD programmes for selected districts in Sri Lanka are either country-sponsored (NORAD – Norwegian; SIDA – Swedish and Dutch) or supported by World Bank loans. The monitoring and evaluation undertaken on certain IRD schemes show that investment per capita is generally low, and that even this modest scale seems to come up against certain institutional constraints of implementation (Rao, *et al.* 1983). The target areas and groups in this programme are the most backward. Hence even if the limited quantum of investment is properly utilized, the ultimate goals of productivity would be hard to achieve. The key themes underlying the IRDP in Sri Lanka appear to be: (a) 'small is beautiful and appropriate' and (b) 'rehabilitation'. While there is nothing inherently wrong in either of these it is debatable whether such a limited vision would stimulate growth of the region so that it will not fall behind the other regions which have more productivity-oriented programmes.[4]

Income distribution

Let us examine the pattern of income distribution in order to gain some insight into the effectiveness of productivity-oriented public policy on the population. Clearly the income disparity among different income classes has increased since 1973 (See Table 13.1) This is particularly significant since there has been a reduction in the levels of income disparity during the preceding period, that is, 1963–73 (Central Bank 1976; Jayawardena 1974; Karunatilake 1974).

Table 13.1 Percentage of income received by ranked income receivers 1963, 1973, 1978/9 and 1981/2

	1963	1973	1978/9	1981/2
Lowest 10 per cent	1.2	1.8	1.2	1.21
Lowest 40 per cent	12.0	16.1	12.1	11.78
Highest 40 per cent	39.2	30.0	39.0	41.70
Gini coefficient	0.49	0.41	0.49	0.52

Source: *Report on consumer finance and socio-economic survey*, 1973–1978/9, Central Bank of Ceylon: 1976, 1982, 1984.

Income distribution data is also available on a geographical basis. The island is divided into five zones and the boundaries coincide with the district administrative boundaries.[5] Although the relative real incomes of each group had increased by 1978/9 the share of the total real income of the richest 40 per cent had increased substantially from 30 per cent to 39 per cent, while the share of the other categories had declined. In attributing reasons for the increase in income inequality *The consumer finance survey of the Central Bank of 1978/9* argued that given the economic reforms of 1977 and massive increase in investment it is likely that the higher-income groups would receive substantial gains in the short run and that benefits from major economic reforms do not percolate down in such a short time (*Central Bank 1982*). The results of the *Consumer finance survey of 1978/9* cannot be expected to show a comprehensive or final picture of the manifestations of public policy of 1977; the period is too short. However, it may very well reveal certain important trends which are continued during the subsequent period up to 1981/2 (Table 13.2). The real income of all groups and zones has increased but there is a steady fall in the ratio of mean to median income indicating a worsening of income distribution among the different categories. The income receivers are also divided into three groups – urban, rural and estate. The estate sector (plantation sector) showed a significant increase in real mean incomes between 1973 and 1978/9, which is attributed to a rise in wages after nationalization.[6]

The median income levels of every geographical zone (See Figures 44a and 44b) have increased over time (Table 13.2). Among the five zones, Zone V (Metropolitan Colombo) records the highest median incomes, and the sharpest rates of increase especially since 1978/9. With the increase in commercial activity stimulated by liberal import policies adopted since 1977, it is not surprising that the Colombo Metropolitan area, which is the urban hinterland of the main port of

Table 13.2 Median income (one month) received (according to geographical zones) in rupees (at current prices) 1973, 1978/9, 1981/2

Geographical Zones	1973	1978/9	% increase 1973–79	1981/2	% increase 1979–82	% increase 1973–82
Zone I (western and southern coastal districts)	202	451	123%	721	59.86%	256%
Zone II (Dry Zone interior colonization districts)	223	401	79%	641	59.85%	187%
Zone III northern and eastern districts)	236	451	91%	752	66.74%	218%
Zone IV (Central Highlands Plantation districts)	137	301	119%	534	77.4%	289%
Zone V Colombo Metropolitan	224	501	123%	966	92.8%	331%

Source: *Consumer finance and socio-economic surveys*, 1973, 1978/9, 1981/2, Central Bank of Ceylon: 1976, 1982, 1984.

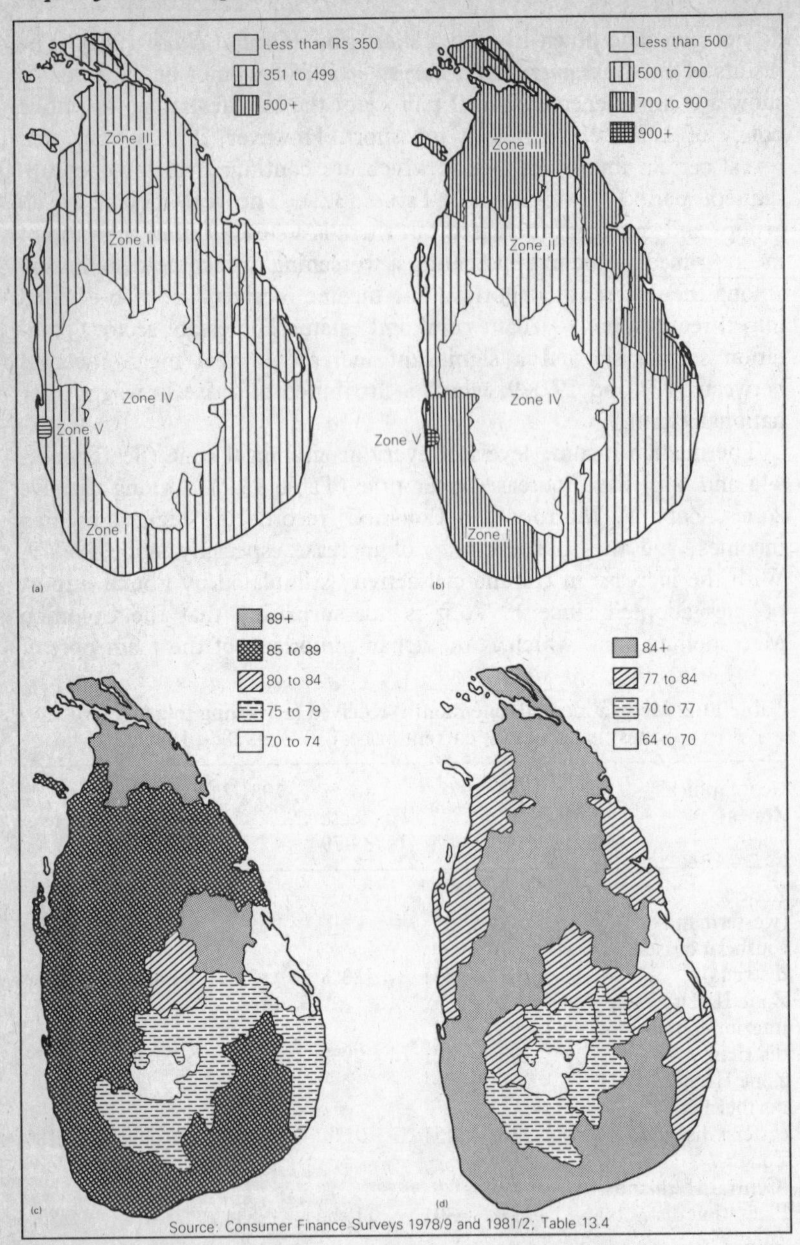

Fig. 44 (a) Median income levels (rupees per month) 1978–9
(b) Median income levels (rupees per month) 1981–2
(c) Physical Quality of Life Index (PQLI) 1971
(d) Physical Quality of Life Index (PQLI) 1979–81

Sri Lanka, recorded increased median incomes. Furthermore the service facilities necessary to attract foreign industrial investors to the New Export Promotion Zones were mostly located in Metropolitan Colombo.

At the other end of the scale, low median incomes are recorded for Zone IV which is formed by the districts in the Central Highlands and which includes the tea and rubber plantation areas. This zone has not gained any major benefits from either the industrial, commercial or service activities inspired by the private sector, or the state-sponsored high investment programme of the AMDP. It should be noted, however, that Zone IV has continuously recorded the lowest median income levels. Most of the districts in this zone are included in the IRD programmes. However they do not seem to have the capacity to inject the required stimulus for development.

The Dry Zone districts of the interior lowlands fall within the Income Zone II. Most of the newly settled areas under irrigated Colonization Schemes fall within this category. Between 1973 and 1981/2 its rate of increase has slowed down considerably in comparison to Zones I, III and V. The Dry Zone farms are small family units not exceeding an average of five acres per family. Although massive government-sponsored investment schemes by way of providing irrigation and land settlement facilities have been undertaken, individual median incomes continue to be low, mainly due to the low scale of operations.

Zone I (western and southern coastal districts) and Zone III (northern and eastern districts) have increased their lead in median incomes over Zone IV over the period 1973–1981/2. With its proximity to Metropolitan Colombo, Zone I would be a beneficiary of the increase in commercial, industrial and service activity. Zone III (northern and eastern districts) have in fact recorded better median incomes than Zone I from 1978/9 to 1981/2. The performance of Zone III is more difficult to explain in terms of one specific policy measure, as it is geographically more remote from Metropolitan Colombo. Industrial activities are relatively low, but this zone includes districts which have benefited from older state-sponsored colonization schemes (Amparai and Trincomalee). The northern districts have benefited also from open economic policies since 1977, which stimulated service-oriented small business enterprises. Liberal import policies since 1977 adversely affected the cultivation of substitute food crops such as cassava, maize and sweet potatoes in the southern districts of Sri Lanka. Such policies did not slow down production of subsidiary crops as red onions, chillies and potatoes which the northern districts traditionally produced. In fact production of the main subsidiary food crops in the northern districts, that is red onion, had increased since 1977 (Samarasinghe 1985). The northern and eastern districts are also important fish-producing areas.[7]

An examination of unemployment data by zones (Table 13.3) indicates that Zone III has the lowest percentage of unemployment measured in relation to the labour force.

Zone III has a high percentage of a minority ethnic group, that is, the Sri Lanka Tamils, which as an ethnic group has the second lowest rate of employment in Sri Lanka in 1981/2. The lowest rate recorded is for the Indian Tamil group, which is concentrated geographically in Zone IV. High employment in the plantation sector where they predominate is limited to estate employment at very low wages.

Table 13.3 Unemployment by zones

Zone	1978/9	1981/2
Zone I	6.8%	5.6%
Zone II	3.3%	2.4%
Zone III	2.6%	1.7%
Zone IV	5.8%	4.0%
Zone V	7.2%	4.0%

Source: *Consumer finance and socio-economic survey* 1981/2, Central Bank 1984.

Levels of welfare

The levels of distribution of social welfare facilities are an important component of spatial inequalities. The historical experience of the ACs suggests that social indicators generally reflect economic levels attained. State intervention in spreading social welfare facilities was considered a positive result of high economic growth. However, it is clear that the pattern seen in Sri Lanka does not conform to this concept. The physical quality of life index[8] (PQLI) of Sri Lanka has been rising steadily over the years (Sumansekera 1983). It had reached the level of a middle-income country by the early 1970s without a corresponding increase in the GNP. The average PQLI for Sri Lanka was 78.9 in 1971 and 84.2 in 1979/80 (see Table 13.4). Morris and McAlpine, making an interesting comparison between Taiwan and Sri Lanka, observe that Taiwan has achieved high rates of economic growth with an accompanying increase in the PQLI, a pattern which corresponds well with the historical experience of the ACs, while in

Sri Lanka the increase in PQLI has not been a result of such economic growth (Morris and McAlpine 1982). Thus the high levels of the PQLI in Sri Lanka has to be explained not in terms of high income per capita but probably in terms *inter alia* of the establishment of a relatively sophisticated social infrastructure and effective delivery system of social welfare benefits to all income groups and regions as part of a public policy. Free education and health services, and subsidies on food and transport, formed the important components of the welfare package which has continued to operate with minor changes. However, it is evident that there is a distinct inter-regional variation of welfare levels (see Figures 44c and 44d).

Table 13.4 Distribution of PQLI Scores by district 1971, 1979/81

District	1971	1979/81
Colombo	85.30	86.00
Kalutara	87.30	88.40
Kandy	75.10	78.20
Nuwaraeliya	64.00	71.60
Matale	78.00	83.00
Galle	86.60	86.80
Matara	85.60	85.59
Hambantota	84.60	87.40
Jaffna	88.10	91.20
Mannar	79.80	86.70
Vavuniya	84.20	86.25
Mullaitivy		89.26
Batticaloa	68.10	72.50
Amparai	79.10	78.50
Trincomalee	79.00	85.10
Kurunegala	85.40	86.80
Puttalam	85.60	88.40
Anuradhapura	80.20	86.40
Polonnaruwa	86.20	89.60
Badulla	72.40	75.40
Monaragala	80.40	86.20
Ratnapura	76.60	79.50
Kegalle	81.60	87.30
Sri Lanka	78.90	84.20

Source: *Literacy rates*, 1971, 1981, *Infant mortality rates*, 1971, 1981, Computed from the *Report of Census of Population, 1971, 1981*, Department of Census and Statistics 1973, 1983, Ministry of Plan Implementation.
Life-expectancy rates, 1971, *Bulletin on vital statistics*, 1979 Registrar General's Office 1981, Life-expectancy rates 1979/80, Unpublished data, Dept of Census and Statistics 1983, Ministry of Plan Implementation

The PQLI scores computed for 1971 and 1979/80 reveal that individual scores for each district had improved with the minima pushed from 64 in 1971 to 71.3 in the subsequent period. However, the hierarchy of levels among the districts remains more or less constant over the period. Nuwaraeliya, the main plantation district in the central hill country, with a large Indian Tamil population, had the lowest score in both periods. Generally scores are relatively low in most plantation districts in the central zone and most of these districts also fall into Zone IV of the income zones, where the median incomes were the lowest. In the high score category with PQLI of over 77, there were 17 in 1971 and 20 in the subsequent period. In 1971, the top cluster of the PQLI scores is occupied by Jaffna, Kalutara and Polonnaruwa, with values over 86. In the 1979/81 period Jaffna continues to have the best score, followed by Mullaitivu. Mullaitivu, which lies adjacent to the Jaffna district, was a part of Vavuniya district until 1978. Its high illiteracy rate (20.7 per cent among the Muslim community, compared with a national average of 9.5 per cent), has also contributed towards the poor overall performance of Batticaloa. The cluster with the lowest PQLI score is probably explained in terms of its adjacency to Jaffna and the presence of an efficient delivery system of social welfare facilities. Vavuniya also shows a score of 84. (It is also possible that Gampaha which was separated from Colombo in 1978 would also show a high PQLI score, since its literacy rates are high and infant mortality rates are low. But life-expectancy data was only available for the two districts together and it was not possible to compute a separate index for Gampaha.) Polonnaruwa, a major agricultural colonization scheme situated in the Dry Zone, continues to have a high PQLI score.

When regional clusters are identified the highest scores are in the Dry Zone – two in the Northern Province, and one in the North Central Province. It is significant that all three have identical and very low infant mortality rates (18 per 1000) and very high literacy rates (above 86 per cent). The predominantly Sri Lanka Tamil population clusters in the north score more than 86. However, Batticaloa, which also has a high percentage of Sri Lankan Tamils, in the Eastern Province shows a very low score at 72.5 and it has consistently been in the low-score group. Its literacy and life-expectancy rates are below the national average. Apart from the fact that Sri Lanka Tamils in Batticaloa have not received educational opportunities as have the Northern Province, its sizeable Muslim population (24 per cent of the total for the district) which as a community have high rates of literacy is concentrated in the central plantation regions. The PQLI scores are depressed mainly because of the relatively high concentration of Indian Tamils, who as a community have very high infant mortality rates and low life-expectancy and literacy levels. The western and southern coastal districts have high PQLI cores and so has the Dry Zone colonization zone – they correspond roughly to income zones I and II. In general the PQLI scores have a direct relation to income zones. The exception is Zone II, corresponding to the Dry Zone colonization area where the income levels are comparatively low but PQLI comparatively high. It may be speculated here that the delivery system of welfare facilities which formed a part of the colonization scheme strategy may have been more effective.

Moore (1984) argues that in Sri Lanka it is the population density and its aggregate need and demand for service per square kilometre that has contributed towards the higher PQLI. Indeed, the population density factor is very much associated with the political process in operation in Sri Lanka. However, the delimitation of electorates was made in such a way that areas with lesser population but which encompass large land areas were also well-represented in Parliament. Hence in a system of electoral politics where each member of Parliament strives to deliver a reasonable flow of welfare measures in order to maintain his or her popularity, economically backward areas also stood to gain from social welfare benefits. In general the high PQLI scores of the upper cluster of the high order group may be explained by the better delivery system facilitated by the advantages of early development, population density and more effective political accessibility. The relatively new economic package programme of 'Peasant Colonization' which benefited the Dry Zone also had a positive effect on the PQLI scores. At the other end of the scale lie those regions with lesser PQLI scores which were obviously influenced by a less effective social welfare delivery system, lesser density of population, difficult terrain, and distance from the core area of Colombo. Lack of political accountability, as in the Indian Tamil plantation workers until recent times, would undoubtedly have had a decisive impact on the level of the PQLI. It is significant that four out of the five districts which form the low-score category have sizeable Indian Tamil estate populations.

In the sphere of social welfare, government policy on health and education remained basically unchanged since 1977. However, a new programme of food subsidies was implemented. The free or subsidized issue of rice which had been operative since World War II was replaced by a selective means-tested food stamp scheme. Although it was estimated that it reached nearly 50 per cent of the population, it has been acknowledged by the policy-makers that there are weaknesses in the programme, especially due to the decline in the purchasing power of the stamps and poor targeting (Ministry of Plan Implementation 1985).

Internal migration

It would be appropriate at this point to turn our attention to a brief survey of internal migration in Sri Lanka as migration flows are generally sensitive to the changing regional development levels of a country. The pattern in Sri Lanka during the period 1946–71 suggests that those areas which received large-scale public investments, such as the Dry Zone colonization districts, accounted for the highest percentage increase in net migration flows. The relatively strong administrative, service and industrial base of Colombo was largely responsible for attracting the greatest number of net migrants although its percentage increase for the district was lower than that recorded for the Dry Zone districts of Anuradhapura and Polonnaruwa (see Vamathevan 1960; Samarasinghe 1980). Among the net in-migration districts in 1971, Colombo claimed 34.10 per cent of the total migrant flow, while the two colonization districts of Anuradhapura and Polonnaruwa claimed 35.17 per cent of the total. The latter increased to 41.06 per cent when Trincomalee was included in the Dry Zone colonization group. The districts of Kandy, Nuwara Eliya, Badulla, Kegalle and Kurunegala, which form a central regional zone; the Wet Zone coastal districts of Kalutara, Galle and Matara; and Jaffna in the north constituted the major out-migration districts. Group 1 in this category accounted for as much as 50.9 per cent of the flow from all out-migration districts. Group 2 claimed 32.83 per cent while Jaffna accounted for 12.19 per cent of the total flow from the major out-migration districts.

The pattern of internal migration during the subsequent period, 1971–81, has not changed basically (Table 13.5, Figure 45). It may be mentioned at this point that there is no way of differentiating between the pre-1977 and post-1977 periods, as the migration numbers consist of the cumulative aggregate of a specific district over a 10 year period. The market forces released with the open liberal economic policies would no doubt act as an impetus towards the continued location of service industries, manufacturing and trade in areas with better locational advantages as the metropolitan districts of Colombo and Gampaha. These two districts have increased in-migration flows during the period between 1971 and 1981.

Table 13.5 Internal Migration of Sri Lanka, 1971–81

District	Net in-migration	Percentage change over 1971
Colombo	+ 78,043	+ 4.59
Gampaha	+ 114,871	+ 10.39
Hambantota	+ 2,505	+ 0.59
Mannar	+ 19,074	+ 17.85
Vavuniya	+ 31,171	+ 32.5
Mullativu	+ 31,433	+ 40.43
Amparai	+ 53,114	+ 13.73
Trincomalee	+ 49,904	+ 18.26
Puttalam	+ 40,643	+ 8.23
Anuradhapura	+ 128,014	+ 21.77
Polonnaruwa	+ 121,761	+ 46.34
Monaragala	+ 53,387	+ 19.08
Ratnapura	+ 22,897	+ 2.87

District	Net out-migration	Percentage change over 1971
Kalutara	– 29,572	– 3.57
Kandy	– 60,147	– 5.34
Matale	– 15,709	– 4.33
Nuwara Eliya	– 18,501	– 3.54
Galle	– 116,683	– 14.32
Matara	– 138,093	– 21.45
Jaffna	– 55,344	– 6.65
Batticaloa	– 2,713	– .84
Kurunegala	– 20,547	– 1.69
Badulla	– 29,246	– 4.54
Kegalle	– 101,745	– 14.90

Source: Computed from *Population Tables – Census of Population and Housing* 1973, 1981, Department of Census and Statistics, 1983.

The Dry Zone colonization districts of Anuradhapura, Polonnaruwa and Trincomalee display increases in net in-migration both in numbers and in the percentage share of the total. Anuradhapura, Polonnaruwa and Trincomalee have increased their percentage share of the total flow among all in-migration districts from 41.6 per cent in 1971 to 42.9 per cent in 1981. The largest streams of migrants that flow into the districts of Colombo and Gampaha are mainly from the major out-migration districts of Galle, Matara and Kalutara and to a lesser extent from the central zone. The Dry Zone colonization districts of Anuradhapura and Polonnaruwa receive the largest flow from the

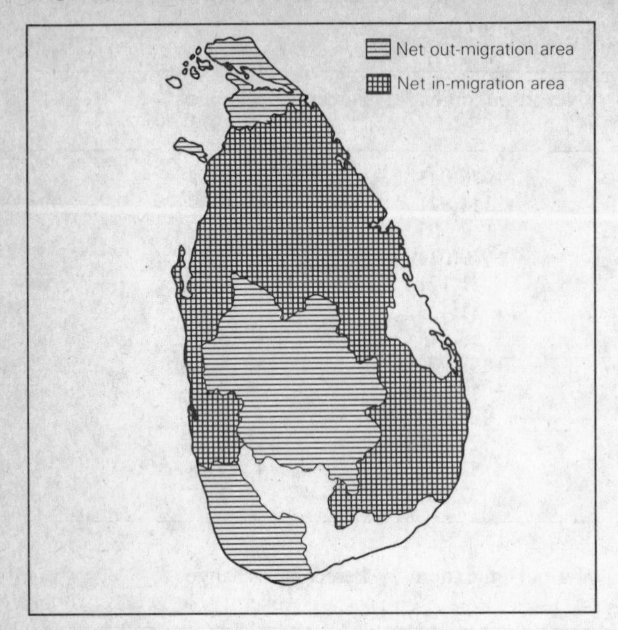

Fig. 45 Internal migration in Sri Lanka, 1971–81

central zone. It is significant to note that the latter zone belongs to Zone IV of the *Consumer finance survey* and records the lowest median income for the island.

In general the pattern of internal migration reveals the relative attraction of regions mainly in terms of economic opportunities available. The two main axes of attraction in Sri Lanka are: (a) The urban industrial region of Colombo and Gampaha and (b) The Dry Zone districts of Anuradapura and Polonnaruwa. The first region combines relatively high-income zones, mainly stimulated by market forces, and good state-sponsored welfare facilities. The second region exemplifies the government interventionist policy geared towards the uplifting of a region via the implementation of state-sponsored investment packages which include land settlement and sponsored migration.

The two major clusters of out-migrant districts are (a) the Central Highland region and (b) the south-western and southern coastal zone. None of these districts fall into any lead projects either state-sponsored or market-oriented. Most of the districts of these two regions have IRD programmes. However as noted earlier the IRDP does not carry significant investments and is geared towards providing certain basic infrastructural facilities and a few low-investment income-generating projects. The locational advantages or the momentum necessary for the attraction of economic/service activities through the newly released market forces are also lacking in both regions.

Conclusions

The most spectacular achievement in distributative justice across income groups and regions in Sri Lanka is seen not in any economic development policy but in the sphere of social welfare benefits. The food subsidy scheme and controlled prices of food in the pre-1977 era were an important 'leveller' of incomes because they were distributed among all income groups. The replacement of these by a means-tested food stamps scheme has certainly depressed real incomes more drastically for those who are outside the new scheme but whose incomes are just above the cut-off point on the income scale. This appears to have contributed towards the reported sharpening inequality among income groups, within all sectors and zones (Central Bank 1984).

The spatial manifestation of productivity-oriented public policy also suggests that the income inequality between high-income areas and lower-income areas has increased. It was argued that in the preceding phase the decrease in the incidence of spatial polarization of Colombo was mainly due to the uplift of peripheral regions – notably the Dry Zone (Samarasinghe 1982). After 1977 that trend towards sharpening the polarity of Colombo is supported mainly by the increasing industrial/service/commercial activity which resulted from the liberalizing policy of an open economy. Moreover, urban incomes have risen faster (see Central Bank 1984) and, although the rate of urbanization in Sri Lanka is low (21 per cent of the population was urbanized in 1981), the bulk of the urbanized population live in the district of Colombo and income levels in the region, it may be argued, are accordingly high.

The performance of the Central Zone has been consistently poor. All the districts of this zone save Kandy have ongoing IRD programmes; however, the effectiveness of the IRD programmes in stimulating growth seems unimpressive. There is a distinct possibility that they may slip back further, thus increasing the gaps in spatial inequality. The IRDP could be restructured to function as the principal agent of improving accessibility by developing an efficient road system, of improving the marketing system by strengthening the existing periodic markets known as *polas* and by expanding the credit scheme in order to help small farmers. Thus a firm foundation could be laid on which to build a more growth-oriented sectoral plan such as the Export Promotion Village Scheme (EPVS), whereby small-scale industrial ventures are located in selected villages with initial state aid. A few such schemes have already been started on an experimental basis. The yet untapped land resources of the northern districts in Mullaitivu and Vavuniya will also have to be brought into a viable development strategy.

It has been acknowledged that 'there is some evidence that social groups at the lower end of the income distribution scale have experienced the worsening of their position in relative and in some cases absolute terms' (Ministry of Plan Implementation 1985). Furthermore the same report states that there exist 'certain regional disparities which calls for corrective action'. The foregoing analysis seems to suggest that public policy adopted in the period 1977–84, while triggering overall growth, has made rich areas richer, and poor areas poorer. Indeed one could argue about the inevitability of such an outcome in the short run, where regions with high-investment state-sponsored development programmes generally take longer for benefits to accrue, while those areas benefiting from the market-oriented private sector would show quicker results. However, given the growing aspirations of the population for better living standards and their demand for an equitable share of social and economic opportunities, articulated mainly through the political process, public policy-makers are faced with the unenviable task of simultaneously achieving sectoral growth and regional equity with the minimum dislocation of society in general.

Notes

1 The Indian Tamil population of Sri Lanka was originally brought to the country during the second half of the nineteenth century by the British Colonial rulers to work as labourers in the newly created coffee and tea plantation located mainly in the Central Highlands.

2 The analysis uses the administrative districts as the basic spatial units. There were 22 districts in 1971 which were increased to 24 in 1981 (Figure 44a). The districts which were divided into two units each in 1981 were Colombo and Vavuniya.

3 The country is divided into two main agro-climatological areas – the Wet Zone and Dry Zone. The Wet Zone is limited to approximately one quarter of the land area in the south-western quarter of the country, and includes a lowland coastal area and the western section of the central hilly region. The Dry Zone which is mainly a lowland, encompasses the North, North Central, Eastern and parts of North-Western, Central and Southern Provinces, and accounts for three-quarters of the land area.

4 The present housing policy known as the 'Gam Udawa' (Village Reawakening) policy, though more than just a housing programme, will not be considered as it is not directly related to economic productivity.

5 The 24 Administrative Districts excluding the area covered by the Colombo Municipality are divided into five zones.
Zone I: Colombo (excluding the municipality), Gampaha, (western coastal) Kalutara, Galle, and Matara.
Zone II: Hambantota, Monaragala, Ampara, Polonnaruwa (Dry Zone) Anuradhapura and Puttalam.
Zone III: Jaffna, Mannar, Vavuniya, Mullaitivu, (northern and eastern) Trincomalee and Batticaloa.
Zone IV: (Central Estate): Kandy, Matale, Nuwara Eliya, Badulla, Ratnapura, Kegalle and Kurunegala.
Zone V: Colombo Municipality.
6 The estate sector/plantation sector is defined as the category where the cash crops, mainly tea and rubber cultivations predominate.
7 Fish production in the northern and eastern districts fell sharply since 1983 due to the ethnic conflict between the majority Sinhalese group and the minority Sri Lankan Tamil group.
8 The PQLI developed at the Overseas Development Council under the direction of Morris D. Morris is a composite index of three simple indicators (equally weighted). Life expectancy at age one is converted into an index using the formula:

$$\frac{\text{life expectancy at age one} - 38}{.39}$$

Infant mortality rate is converted to an index number using the formula:

$$\frac{229 - \text{infant mortality rate per 1000}}{2.22}$$

Literacy index corresponds to the actual percentage data. (Morris D. Morris 1979)

References

Central Bank of Ceylon 1976. *Report on consumer finance and socio-economic survey 1973, Sri Lanka*. (Colombo:)
Central Bank of Ceylon 1982. *Report on consumer finance and socio-economic survey, 1978/9, Sri Lanka* (Colombo:)
Central Bank of Ceylon 1984. *Report on consumer finance and socio-economic survey, 1981/2, Part I*, (Colombo:)
Ceylon Tourist Board 1983. *Annual Report*, 1982 (Colombo:)
Clifford, H. 1927. Some reflections on the Ceylon Land Question, *Tropical Agriculturist, Ceylon*, vol. 67, pp 283–301.
Department of Census and Statistics, 1973, 1983. *Report of the census of population*, 1971, 1981 (Colombo:)
Economic and Social Commission for Asia and the Pacific – (ESCAP) 1976. *Population Monograph*, no. 4 (Bangkok:)
Estall, R. 1982. Planning Appalachia: an examination of the Appalachian Regional Development Programme and its implication for the future of the American Regional Planning Commission, *Transactions of the Institute of British Geographers*, New Series, vol. 7, no. 1, (London), pp. 15–35.
Farmer, B.H. 1957. *Pioneer peasant colonization* (London: Oxford University Press)
Gunatilake, G. 1978. Participatory development and dependence – The case of Sri Lanka, *Marga 5 (3) Special Issue*, pp. 38–172 (Colombo)
Jayawardena, L. 1974. 'Country report on Sri Lanka'. In Holis B. Chenery *et al.* (eds) *Redistribution with Growth* (London: Oxford University Press), pp. 273–80.
Karunatilake, H.N.S. 1974. Changes in income distribution in Sri Lanka, *Central Bank Staff Studies*, vol. 4 no. 1 (Colombo), pp 87–109.
Karunatilake, H.N.S. 1978. An evaluation of the development programme under Divisional District Councils in Sri Lanka, *Sri Lanka Journal of Social Sciences*, vol. 1, no. 1 (Colombo), pp 1–26.
Moore, M. 1984. Categorising space: urban-rural or core-periphery in Sri Lanka, in *Journal of Development Studies*, vol. 20, no. 3, April (London), pp 102–23.
Morris, M.D. 1979. *Measuring the condition of the world's poor: The physical quality of life index* (New York: Pergamon)
Morris, M.D. and McAlpine, M.B. 1982. *Measuring the condition of India's poor* (India: Promilla Publisher)
Ministry of Mahaweli Development 1979. *Mahaweli: projects and programmes*, (Colombo:)
Ministry of Plan Implementation 1985. *Public investment 1985–1989* (Colombo:)
Peiris, G.H. 1972. Agricultural growth through decentralization and popular participation: a survey of the DDC Farm Projects in Kandy District 1971–1973, *Modern Ceylon Studies*, Peradeniya, vol. 3 no. 1, pp. 60–90.
Rao, V.K, Peiris G.H. and Tilakaratne, M. 1983. *Planning for rural development*: a *study of the District Integrated Rural Development Programme of Sri Lanka* (Bangkok ARTEP/ILO, mimeographed)
Samarasinghe, V. 1980. The impact of government policy on regional devel-

opment, *Conference on Post-war economic development of Sri Lanka, Ceylon Studies Seminar* (Mimeo)

Samarasinghe, V. 1982. Spatial polarization of Colombo: a study of regional inequality, *Sri Lanka Journal of Social Sciences*, vol. 5, no. 1 (Colombo), pp. 75–95.

Samarasinghe, V. 1985. 'Spatial inequalities and the ethnic conflict in Sri Lanka'. Paper presented at the *National Workshop on the Economic Dimensions of the Ethnic Conflict in Sri Lanka*, August 1985. (Kandy, Sri Lanka International Centre for Ethnic Studies – mimeo)

Sumansekera, H.D. 1983. Measuring the regional variation of the quality of life in Sri Lanka, *Sri Lanka Journal of Agrarian Studies*, vol. 2, no. 1 (Colombo), pp. 27–40.

Vamathevan, S. 1960. *Internal migration in Ceylon*, Monograph, no. 13, Department of Census and Statistics, Colombo.

14
Urbanization and Urban Policy in East Africa

R.A. Obudho
Associate Professor of African and Afro-American Studies, Geography, and Regional Planning at State University of New York, Albany, U.S.A. and Lecturer in Geography, University of Nairobi.

Introduction

East African countries, comprising Kenya, Uganda and Tanzania, cover a diverse region in the central portion of Eastern Africa.[1] The three states have had varied historical, economic, political and socio-cultural developments which must always be taken into account when one is discussing the urbanization and planning policies of these countries.[2] (See Table 14.1 and Figure 46).

East Africa is predominantly rural with a low level of urbanization relative to the continent as a whole, to the average of Less Developed Countries (LDCs), and to the world. Moreover, within East Africa, the three countries under study are somewhat less urbanized than the rest of the region. At present, Kenya is more urbanized than Uganda and Tanzania. Even by the end of the century, only about one-quarter of the populations of these three countries will live in urban areas.

These data support the hypothesis that the less urbanized countries experience the higher urban growth rates. In the last two decades the urban populations of Kenya, Uganda and Tanzania have been growing nearly twice as fast as the average for developing countries. Moreover, whereas urban growth rates have been falling secularly both in the world as a whole and in LDCs in general, this is not yet the case in these three countries. This combination of low levels of urbanization and high rates of urban growth make the formulation and implementation of sound national urban policies very critical to the economic and social development of these countries. The policy decisions are made more complicated by high rates of rural–urban migration

Table 14.1 Comparative demographic data for Kenya, Tanzania, Uganda, East Africa and Africa, 1985

	Kenya	Tanzania	Uganda	East Africa	Africa
1 Population estimate (mid-1985 in millions)	20.2	21.7	14.7	159.0	557.0
2 Rate of natural increase (annual %)	4.1	3.5	3.5	3.1	2.9
3 Population projection for the year 2000	37.3	37.3	24.5	258.0	869.0
4 Total fertility rate	8.0	7.1	6.9	6.8	6.3
5 Percentage of population under 15 years of age	52.0	46.0	43.0	47.0	45.0
6 Life expectancy at birth	53.0	50.0	52.0	49.0	50.0
7 Urban population percentage	16.0	14.0	14.0	17.0	31.0
8 Per capita gross national product in U.S.$	340.0	240.0	220.0	2,454.0	11,711.0

Source: Population Reference Bureau, 1985 World Population Data Sheet (Washington, D.C. 1985), p. 1.

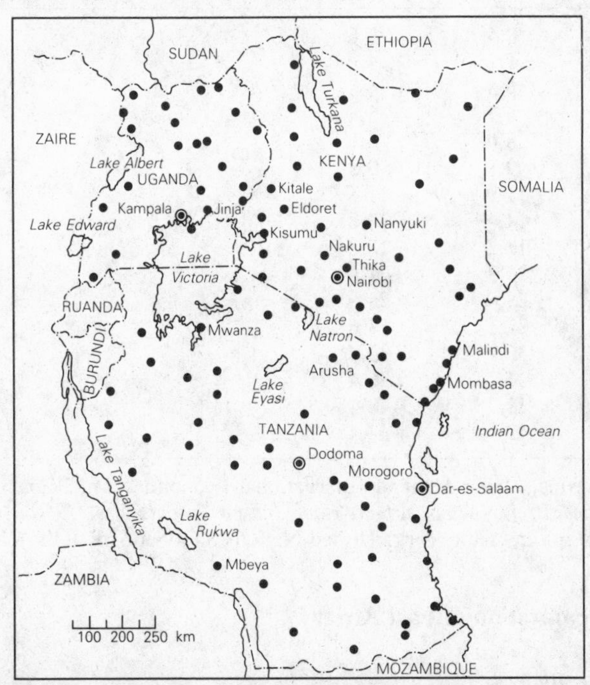

Fig. 46 Selected urban centres in East Africa

(in the period 1970–5, net migration accounted for 64 per cent of Tanzania's urban population growth, 52 per cent of Uganda's and 44 per cent of Kenya's). These high rates of rural–urban migration offer, at least, the potential for moulding the pattern of urbanization by influencing migrant behaviour. Although approximately half of the combined urban populations of the three countries live in primate cities, a sizeable number of their urban centres are intermediate cities which have considerable potential for future growth. Despite the fact that East Africa shows the lowest percentage of urbanization compared to all African regions, the region has the highest urban growth rate. For example, between 1960 and 2025 the urban annual growth rate is estimated to be the highest for all regions of Africa (Table 13.2). The other region of similarly high growth rates in Africa was Central Africa. Like Central Africa and West Africa, East Africa will probably double her urban population by the end of the century.

Table 14.2 Estimates of urban population share in Kenya, Uganda and Tanzania, 1950–2025.

Year	Kenya	Uganda	Tanzania
1950	5.6	3.4	3.6
1955	6.4	4.2	4.2
1960	7.4	5.3	4.8
1965	8.5	6.5	5.6
1970	10.2	8.0	6.9
1975	12.0	9.8	9.2
1980	14.2	11.9	11.8
1985	16.7	14.4	14.8
1990	19.2	17.2	18.2
1995	22.7	20.3	21.6
2000	26.2	23.5	24.9
2005	29.9	27.1	28.6
2010	33.8	30.8	32.4
2015	37.8	34.7	36.4
2020	41.8	38.7	40.4
2025	45.7	42.7	44.4

Source: United Nations, Department of International Economics and Social Affairs. *Estimates and Projections of urban, rural and city populations, 1950–2025: The 1980 Assessment*, (New York: United Nations ST/ESA/SER.R145), p. 28–9.

The phases of urbanization in East Africa

Pre-colonial urbanization

Western urbanization of inland East Africa is almost entirely a twentieth-century phenomenon and is mainly a product of German and British colonization of the region. Despite the fact that the region has a long historical contact with Western and Eastern countries urbanization was, and still appears to be, superimposed on the East African socio-cultural landscape.

In order to analyse the development of pre-colonial towns, villages or hamlets in East Africa as central places, we will adopt Richard Hull's definition of a traditional, pre-colonial African town as 'a collective body of inhabitants under the jurisdiction of an élite with political, economic or religious authority ... a centre not only of population, but of religion, the arts, government, the military, industry or commerce' (Hull 1976). This definition is very appropriate to East African pre-colonial towns since all of them have been centres of commerce, culture, and government. These same pre-colonial central places have been termed by Taylor 'invisible towns', which he defines 'as locations where many of the functions of a town are carried on but where there are fewer, if any, permanent structures associated with these functions than observers, used to a western concept of a town, might expect' (Taylor 1978). These invisible traditional centres formed the original nuclei in rural East Africa on which long distance trade was based. Although trading centres were established along the coast of what are now Kenya and Tanzania as early as the first or second century AD, the coastal urbanization did not have any impact in the interior until the mid-nineteenth century when the interior towns were established. These towns were founded next to the invisible towns. In Uganda, there were towns in the pre-colonial kingdoms of Buganda, Bunyoro-Kitara, and Ankole.

Colonial urbanization

The location, size and distribution of the modern urban centres in East Africa are almost entirely decisions of British and German colonizers who started to control the region effectively as from the 1880s. Through the siting of administrative centres, the routeing of transport lines, and the identification of areas of strategic and economic importance to their interest, a whole new system of urban centres was superimposed on the East African landscape. The first colonial centres to emerge were the major ports, which were used as basing points for colonial penetration of the interior and as the centres for the export of commercial products from the interior. The growth of these ports contributed to the decline of once bustling pre-colonial centres. With the penetration of inland East Africa by the British and German colonizers, a fifth layer of urban centres emerged, distributed in such a way as to tap accessible resources and link the East African interior with international markets. These urban centres were sited close to, but not in the same place as, pre-existing invisible towns. These urban centres in one way or another merged with the caravan towns of the pre-colonial era. The next layer was created through the development of a network of administrative centres.

The siting of these administrative centres was primarily influenced by health factors, accessibility to the invisible centres, areas of high ground and good drainage systems. The seventh layer of the spatial system was missionary schools and hospitals which were sited far away from the urban centres. Through the process of consolidation of the pre-and post-colonial era layers have merged in such a way that one can now identify four broad layers of central places. In the process of establishing these centres, the colonial governments ignored the pre-colonial spatial systems, the principal manifestations of which were the invisible towns. The colonial administrators did, however, realize the importance of invisible towns in the spatial systems of East Africa and, as a result, created new invisible towns in concurrence with administrative centres, thus developing a dual system of urban centre subsystems in the region. Although these two subsystems overlapped to some extent, they have never been fully integrated. The modern system was initially dominated by the colonial administration, while

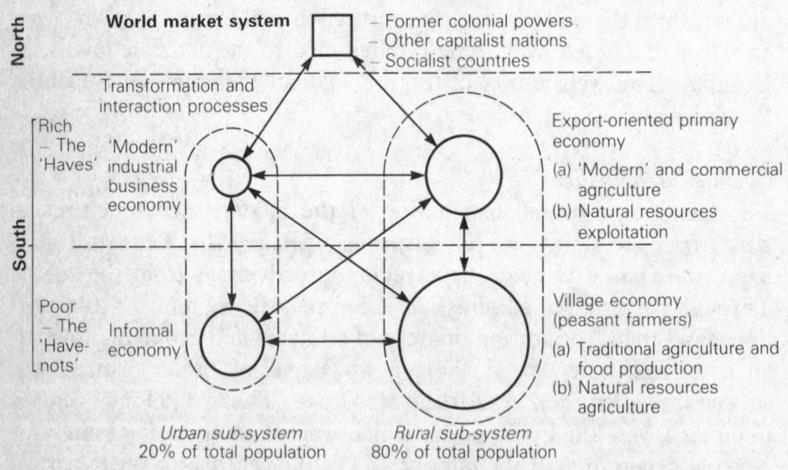

Source: adapted from D.R.F. Taylor, 'Spatial organization and rural development in Africa', paper presented at the Second Annual Kenya Students Conference, York University, Toronto, Canada, 2–4 January 1981, p. 14; and R.A. Obudho and D.R.F. Taylor (eds), *Spatial structure of development: a study of Kenya* (Boulder, Colorado: Westview Press, 1979)

Fig. 47 A dynamic basic macro-model for East Africa

the periodic market systems have been dominated by the Africans. Taylor (1979) has thus identified a six-sector model (urban-formal, urban-informal, rural-formal, rural-informal, North and South) as shown in Figure 47.

The dispersed nature of rural settlements and the unbalanced socio-economic nature of East Africa are the basis for the diverse national urban policies currently being pursued by the three countries (Soja and Weaver 1976). Current urban policies in the three countries are based on promoting components of the middle-layer settlement (Obudho 1984) The post-colonial urbanization process is briefly considered here on a country-by-country basis.

Post-colonial urbanization: Kenya

The overall rate of population growth in Kenya has been increasing since 1962, but this has been matched by an even faster acceleration of urban growth, increasing from 8.7 per cent in 1962 to 15 per cent in 1986. The rate of population growth, on the other hand, was about 3.4 per cent per annum during 1948–79, and increasing to 4.1 per cent per annum in the period 1979–86 to become one of the highest in the world. The rapid rate of urbanization in Kenya is primarily the result of accelerating rural–urban migration and also of natural increase.

The growth of urban population can also be visualized by looking into the number of urban centres in groups of different size over space and time. At the time of the first Kenya population census in 1948, there were 17 towns with an aggregate population of 276,240 (Table 14.3). The urban population was proportionately small (5.2 per cent of the total) and disproportionately concentrated in Nairobi and Mombasa (83 per cent of the total urban population) with the majority of urban dwellers being non-Africans. In the 1962 population census, however, the number of towns doubled to 34 and the urban population increased to 670,950 people with an annual urban growth of 6.6 per cent per annum. This represented an urbanization level of 7.7 per cent. During 1948–62, the intermediate urban centres recorded the highest increase. The growth of towns both in number and population accelerated after independence when the Africans were allowed to migrate to the urban areas without any legal and administrative restrictions. According to the 1969 and 1979 population censuses, there were 48 and 90 urban centres respectively in those years. During the 1962–69 intercensal period, the urban population doubled. The urban population grew from 670,950 in 1962 to 1,082,437 in 1969;

growing at the rate of 7.1 per cent per annum. In 1969 this represented 9.9 per cent of the total population.

The 1979 population census indicated 90 urban centres with an urban population of 2,238,800. The level of urbanization had risen to 14.6 per cent, representing more than a doubling of one total urban population in about 10 years. The urban population grew at the rate of 7.9 per cent per annum during the 1969–79 intercensal period. During the 1962–79 censal period, the increase in the number of towns took place in all size-groups but the highest increase of 13.9 per cent per annum was for the size-group 20,000 to 99,999. The size-groups of towns with population over 100,000 people and those between 2,000 to 4,999 inhabitants grew almost at the same rates of 5.6 and 5.7 per cent per annum, respectively, showing both the slowing down of the growth of primacy in Kenya and also the increasing importance of the small urban centres.

Table 14.3 Kenya: Distribution of towns and population by size-groups, 1948, 1962, 1969 and 1979 (population in thousands)

Size-group	1948		1962		1969		1979		Growth rate of population in size-group
	No.	*Pop.*	*No.*	*Pop.*	*No.*	*Pop.*	*No.*	*Pop.*	
Over 100,000	1	119	2	523	2	756	3	1,322	5.6
20,000–99,999	1	85	2	62	2	80	13	568	13.9
10,000–19,999	2	29	3	44	7	91	10	140	7.1
5,000–9,000	3	20	11	70	11	72	27	154	4.8
2,000–4,999	10	23	16	49	26	83	37	123	4.7
Total	17	276	34	670	48	1,082	90	2,307	6.9

Source: Based on data from Republic of Kenya, *Kenya Publication Census 1948, 1962, 1969 and 1979* (Nairobi: Government Printers).

The two urban centres of Nairobi and Mombasa together accounted for between 70 and 74 per cent of urban population during the 1948, 1962 and 1969 censuses but only about 50.7 per cent in the 1979 census. The rate of annual increase of all urban centres during 1969–79 was over 10 per cent per annum except for Nairobi, Mombasa, Nakuru, Thika, Malindi, and Nanyuki. These urban centres, whose annual increases were below 10 per cent, are the ones whose percentage share of urban population over the year has been the highest. The population of other towns grew by 15.6 per cent per annum while their share of urban population increased from 5.3 per

Table 14.4 Kenya's urban population growth for the years 1948, 1962, 1969 and 1979 for selected urban centres

Urban Centres	1948	1962	1948–62 Annual growth rate	1969	1962–69 Annual growth rate	1979	1969 Annual rate
Nairobi	118,976	266,974	5.9	509,286	9.7	827,775	5.1
Mombasa	84,746	179,575	5.5	247,073	4.5	341,148	3.3
Kisumu	10,899	23,526	5.6	32,431	4.7	152,643	16.7
Nakuru	17,625	38,181	5.7	47,151	3.1	92,851	7.0
Thika	4,435	13,952	8.7	18,387	4.1	41,324	8.4
Elderet	8,193	19,605	6.4	18,196	(1.1)	50,503	10.7
Nanyuki	4,090	10,448	6.9	11,624	1.6		5.1
Kitale	6,338	9,432	2.8	11,573	3.2	28,327	9.3
Malindi	3,292	5,818	N/A	10,757	9.3	23,275	7.8
Kericho	3,218	7,692	6.5	10,144	4.0	29,603	11.5
Nyeri	2,705	7,857	8.0	10,004	3.4	35,753	13.7
Other towns			13.7		76.6		15.7
Total urban	285,545	670,934	6.6	1,082,437	7.1	2,307	7.9
Total rural	5,120,421	5,965,329	3.2	9,860,258	3.1		2.8
Total Kenya, pop.	5,405,966	8,636,263	3.1	10,942,705	3.3		3.4
Secondary towns (excluding Nairobi and Mombasa as % of urban Population)	17.0	33.4	–	30.0	–	49.3	–
Urban pop. as % of total population	5.1	7.8		9.9		15.1	

Source: Based on data from Republic of Kenya, Central Bureau of Statistics, *Kenya Population Census 1948, 1962, 1969 and 1979*, (Nairobi: Government Printer).

cent in 1948 to 28.9 per cent in 1979, doubling in the last decade (Table 14.4).

Post-colonial urbanization: Uganda

The striking feature of Uganda's population is the smallness of the urban population (Obudho and Musyoki 1987). Uganda's urban population has doubled over a decade from 302,646 or 4.5 per cent of total population in 1959, to 675,520 or 7.0 per cent of the total population in 1969. This increase represented an urban growth rate of 7.5 per cent per annum, compared to the national average growth of 3.6 per cent annually during the same period (Republic of Uganda 1972). Although comparison of the two censuses is not easy because the boundaries of the majority of the urban centres have been increased since the 1959 census, an analysis of Uganda's urban population by size-group is very important for understanding the nature of the country's urbanization process (Table 14.5).

Table 14.5 Uganda: Distribution of towns and urban population by size-groups, 1959 and 1969 (population in thousands)

Size-group	1959 Number	Population	1969 Number	Population	Annual growth rates
Over 100,000	1	159	1	331	7.8
20,000–99,999	1	56	3	144	9.8
10,000–19,999	3	35	8	111	12.1
5,000– 9,000	3	21	7	446	7.9
2,000– 4,999	9	32	13	39	2.1
Total	17	302	32	670	8.3
Urban population as % total population		4.6		7.0	4.3

Source: Based on data from Government of Uganda, Uganda *Population Census(es) 1959 and 1969* (Entebbe: Government Printer, 1959–1969).

Although the proportion of urban population has doubled, the proportion of those living in the urban area is very small. Also, although the urban population is small, the primacy of Kampala is very evident. Like Kenya, the highest increase was recorded by the intermediate urban centres (Table 14.5). According to the 1969 population census the concentration of Uganda's urbanization is in the southern part of the country since the region accounted for 76 per cent of total urban population, while 10 per cent is found in the west. The northern and eastern regions both accounted for seven per cent each of total urban population.

Service centres which are located between the dispersed settlements and urban centres are often too small to be defined as urban centres and too large to be called rural settlements. These centres are the focal points in which the majority of the rural population have contact with the outside world. In studying the urban hierarchy in Uganda, Funnel (1976) has demonstrated the significance of the service centres in the overall pattern of urbanization and space economy from the viewpoint of city rank-size distribution. According to the 1959 and 1969 censuses, there were 17 and 22 service centres, respectively. These service centres acted as integral nodes on either main or feeder transportation systems and as centres for rural-urban exchange of goods and services.

Post-colonial urbanization: Tanzania

Despite its initially low urban population during the colonial era, Tanzania is one of the most rapidly urbanizing countries in Africa. The urban population of Tanzania was 183,862 people or 2.3 per cent of total population in 1948. By 1967, the urban population had risen to 685,547, or 5.7 per cent of total population. The latest population census in 1978 gave the country a total population of 17.5 million of which 2,173,816, or 12.7 per cent lived in the urban areas. The percentage share of the country's urban population has more than doubled in the decade 1967 to 1978. Between 1948 and 1957 the total urban population of Tanzania increased at an annual rate of 7.1 per cent while the rural population increased annually by 1.5 per cent. The rural population of mainland Tanzania grew at an average annual compound rate of 2.3 per cent compared to an urban rate of 6.8 per cent. The urban sector in Tanzania has been growing in population at almost three times the rate of rural areas. This high rate of urbanization is however only limited to a few towns which offer employment opportunities.

The urban areas accounted for about 12.7 per cent of the country's population with the population of Dar-es-Salaam reaching a total of 850,700 people in 1978. Over the 1957–67 and 1967–78 intercensal periods, the urban population grew at the average rate of 6.0 per cent and 11.1 per cent, respectively, with some intermediate towns growing at the average rate of between 10 and 14 per cent per annum. As a matter of fact the rate of urbanization is faster than the growth rate of the country's total population. The intermediate urban centres are growing at higher rates than has ever been witnessed in the history of urbanization in Tanzania. As in the case of Uganda and Kenya, most of the urban growth in Tanzania is due more to rural–urban migration than to urban natural increase.

National urban policies

The main aim of the current national planning policy in East Africa is to strengthen the growth of medium-sized urban centres as a means of increasing urbanization which is a necessary prelude to industrial growth and modernization of the region's economy. We shall, again, highlight this point with a brief country-by-country survey of policies.

Kenya

The urbanization policies for Kenya started in a rudimentary form between 1900 and the 1950s when decisions were made by the colonial governments to locate periodic markets, trading centres and towns in various parts of the colony. These original plans required that a two-level system of centres of periodic markets and trading centres was added to the country's spatial structure.

In the 1950s, two plans were introduced that altered the cultural and economic landscape of the nation. The first major policy formulation was the Troupe Report, which focused on the problems of farming in the White Highlands and its major recommendation was to increase European immigration and settlement (Colony and Protectorate of Kenya 1953). The second report, by Carpenter, was primarily concerned with urban wages, although there was a section on rural wages. It proposed the policy of stabilization of urban labour through increased wages and collective bargaining as the best means to achieve stabilization (Carpenter 1953). The third report was the Swynnerton Plan which dealt with the problems of agriculture in African areas, especially the introduction of individual tenure and the cultivation of export crops hitherto prohibited to Africans (Swynnerton 1954). The other major report which attempted to set a national urban policy for the three East African countries was the Royal East African Commission whose aim was to identify the causes, conditions and trends of over-population in the urban areas and to suggest measures for the economic development of East Africa. One of its most important recommendations was the abolition of racial distinctions in landholdings. Michael Salier summarized the national urban policy well when he said that:

> *The initial concerns of town planning in East Africa were in health and hygiene and the laying out of well demarcated areas of differential land use; these concerns are still found enshrined in a large portion of the existing planning legislation. . . . The properly planned areas, well*

laid out and serviced to a high standard, were and are the main administration, commercial, and industrial quarters, and restricted . . . residential zones . . . all of which are closely allied with the predominantly externally oriented modern urban sector.

(*Salier 1972*)

Prior to the post-colonial era, most of the physical planning in Kenya was carried out within the statutory boundaries of the towns and most of it was *ad hoc* with the plans usually taking the form of fully developed land-use maps. Comprehensive national and regional development planning which took account of the strategic elements for promoting urban growth was not adopted until 1964. But even after this period, the spatial development plans were focused on the most obvious target – the export enclave. Practically all of the studies on urbanization processes in Kenya were mainly concerned with social surveys until 1962, when Fair proposed his regional approach to the economic development of Kenya, in which he stressed that:

it is thus necessary to establish regional as well as sectoral targets, for co-ordinated national planning which involves the provision not only of individual but also of the development of more than one natural resource in a variety of areas of wide differing character. In all economic planning, therefore, sector analysis should be supplemented by regional analysis so that comparative development possibilities, problems and priorities can be assessed region by region as well as sector by sector.

(*Fair, 1962*)

This high growth rate put pressure on the government to deal with the country's housing problem (ILO 1979). The government invited a United Nations team of experts who recommended the establishment of a National Housing Corporation to build houses for the low-income households and the Housing Finance Company of Kenya to finance houses for the middle- and upper-income Africans. The first four-year development plan of post-colonial Kenya, from 1964 to 1970, did not present any urban and regional planning strategy different from colonial development strategy of the 1950s and early 1960s. The first serious attempt to bring urban and regional planning techniques to bear on the development of Kenya was a study carried out by the Deutsches Institute für Entwicklungs-politik in 1966 (Obudho and Walter 1976). As a result of their study, the government of Kenya prepared a complete planning survey for the Central Province. This was the beginning of physical planning at national, regional and local levels in Kenya, and since then physical plans have been prepared for each and every province as well as urban centres in Kenya.

The Development Plan, 1970–4, recognized the need to focus development on plans which included the creation of inexpensive urban housing for the low-income groups as well as the allocation of site and service plots as a means of combating the growing slum and squatter settlements, and that the urban growth must be decentralized among the intermediate growth centres. With this policy of building an alternative housing before the slum settlements were erased, the government extended the urban policy to include regional policy of improving rural living conditions as a means of retarding rural–urban migration. Every four years since the first four year plan in 1964, the government has published four-year development plans as a basis for national urban policy. In addition to the Provincial Physical Development Plans and the four-year development plans, the government also prepared short- and long-term physical development plans for each major urban centre in the nation.

The other type of post-colonial development plan was the Special Rural Development Program (SRDP) which was created by the Kenyan Government as a series of experimental, externally financed, pilot programmes in a number of smaller districts in which an integrated approach to rural development might be designed and tested (Republic of Kenya 1974). The major aim of SRDP was to raise the standard of living in the rural areas by creating jobs and increasing income.

The second National Development Plan, 1970–4, contained a formal commitment to rural development in which 'the key . . . is to direct an increasing share of local resources available to the nation towards the rural areas' (Republic of Kenya 1969). This was when the strategy of 'selective concentration' as opposed to 'concentrated development' was adopted by the government. This strategy was continued, and indeed reaffirmed, in the Third Development Plan of 1974–8. The Development Plan 1979–83 continued with the emphasis of rural development. The main theme of the plan was to alleviate poverty throughout the nation by creating income-earning opportunities and providing for basic needs such as nutrition, water, health, education and housing.

The 1984–8 plan emphasized that rural development cannot be a self-contained process. The rural areas must be knit closely to urban markets for supplies of both farm inputs and consumer goods. The spatial development strategy for Kenya is, therefore, directed towards the small and medium urban centres because they would

relieve the population pressure in the countryside, provide less congested and populated urban living in the primate city, . . . increase the modernisation spin-off which urban centres provide to the surrounding rural areas, and provide a better integration with the economy of the rural hinterland.

(Republic of Kenya, 1978)

Because of the economics of concentration which could accrue from the policy of encouraging the development of Nairobi and Mombasa with very limited investment of other designated 'growth centres', the government has encouraged their development and at the same time emphasized rural development. The policy of the country is to bridge the rural-urban gap by decentralization downwards, thus creating an urban hierarchy to spread the benefits of modernization to the rural hinterlands.

The District Focus Policy (DFP) contained in the 1984–8 Development Plan is the latest and perhaps the most articulate documentation of decentralized planning in Kenya (Republic of Kenya 1974; Cohen and Cook 1985). In essence the DFP strategy asserts that district-based projects implemented by the government should be identified, planned and implemented at the district level. The rationale for the DFP strategy was summed up by the President in his speech of 6 June 1985, in which he said that:

First, the people will be directly involved in the identification, design, implementation, and management of the projects and programmes. This will make development more consistent with the needs and aspirations of the Wananchi. Secondly, the decision-making structure will centre around the districts themselves. This will minimize delays that often characterise centralised decision-making systems. Thirdly, it is being directed to areas of most needs.

The DFP strategy has, therefore, emphasized (a) strengthening planning capacity at the district level; (b) improving horizontal integration among operating ministries' field agents; and (c) expanding the authority to district officers for managing financial and procurement aspects of local project implementation. But it is still too early to assess the successes or failures of the DFP strategy as a concept of planning from below based on the intermediate urban centres.

Uganda

The national urbanization policy of Uganda was essentially the same as that of Kenya up to the period of the East African Royal Commission Report except that, unlike Kenya, Uganda had a National Development Plan as early as 1946. This plan was subsequently followed by other national urban policy plans which were nothing more than projects that the colonial government deemed it desirable to undertake. Eventually some attempts were made to introduce a three-year annual expenditure forecast. The first Five Year Plan was launched in 1961 and it analysed the problems, needs and potentialities of the whole national economy before the plan formation. Despite the fact that the overall targets for many sectors were set and appropriate government policies and other measures drawn up, the First Five Year Plan of 1961 had still a great deal of room for improvement in the overall planning process.

Urban planning in Uganda dates back to 1913 when the government employed planners to advise on the development of a number of towns following the establishment of the Protectorate in Uganda. In the 1930s the developments of Kampala and Jinja were prepared with the idea of studying the possible extension of the township boundaries. As a result of this study, the Department of Town Planning was established in 1953 but during the period up to independence in 1962 its role was restricted to advising on urban areas. This policy ignored the fact that rapid settlement was taking place on the periphery of the administrative urban areas in which no control was exercised. At the same time no attention was given to the planning of the rural areas of Uganda. By 1962, when the country attained political independence, the Department of Town and Regional Planning was established to co-ordinate urban and rural planning policies. Since 1962, there have been four United Nations Regional Planning Missions to Uganda (Seaff *et al.* 1964). The first mission worked on the development problems of the Mengo Municipality in 1963. The second United Nations Mission was on Kampala-Mengo as well as the other areas of Uganda in 1964/6. The second mission analysed the growth trends of many centres in the country to the year 2000. This study then formed the basis for the co-ordination of physical and economic planning of the subsequent five year plans. The second Mission also resulted in the establishment of Kampala Metropolis containing the four separate local urban authorities of Kampala City Council, Mengo Municipality, Nakawa Township Authority, and Kawempe Town Board. The third United Nations Planning Mission of 1967/9 also carried similar studies for other urban centres and regions of Uganda, but they recommended the decentralizing of the urbanization process in the country. The planning machinery was decentralized at District level with the idea of integrating the urban and rural planning process. Since then rural-urban planning projects have been used by government to address such issues as water supply, low-cost housing sewage system, urban mass-transportation and the creation of urban employment opportunities. Political instability has adversely affected the implementation of urban policies in Uganda.

Tanzania

Both Kenya and Uganda, having been colonized in the late nineteenth century by Britain, developed similar urban development policies up to the time of independence. Tanzania's colonial urban development policy was different before World War I, but afterwards followed a similar path of development until the 1969–74 Development Plan. It was the urban centres created during the German colonial rule and expanded during British rule which established the pattern and trend of urbanization in Tanzania. The residential zoning policy in Tanzania, like the other East African countries, therefore, followed the residential segregation based on race and income. Zoning of residential land provided for low density areas for Africans. This policy was reinforced first through the Town Development Control Ordinance of 1936 and later perpetuated by the Town and Country Planning Ordinance of 1956.

In 1961 the law was heavily revised and the responsibility for physical planning was also integrated into the national plan. The government also created the National Housing Corporation in 1962 in order to improve poor housing as well as to build and administer new and old houses in the urban areas. In the first Five Year Plan, higher proportion of capital resources for new development went for urban projects. This policy of concentrating development efforts in nine growth poles in the Development Plan of 1969–74 was declared unsuccessful in the Development Plan of 1976–81 and was replaced by a more balanced policy in which all 22 regional headquarters were to be promoted. In order to check the disproportionate growth of urbanization and to control the form and quality of development within the urban centres, Tanzania has evolved a set of urban policies consistent with its broad economic and political strategies. These strategies were basically the result of the Arusha Declaration of 1967 which was argued on economic and political principles. These policies include the *Ujamaa* policy (creation of self-reliant communal villages) and the policy of decentralization of government machinery as well as the introduction of ten growth centres in mainland Tanzania. The Arusha Declaration argued that the burden of services and development in urban areas was borne largely by the rural peasants (Nyerere 1967; 1973). The Arusha Declaration warned against the concentration of development in urban areas at the expense of rural areas (United Republic of Tanzania, 1967).

Until the Arusha Declaration in 1967, Tanzania had pursued two main strategies to alleviate the pressure on housing and urban community services: a building strategy, and a land control strategy. The building strategy started with the formation of the National Housing Corporation in 1962, while the control and allocation of land through the Lands Division started in 1963 (Stren 1979). For the first time in 1967, a clear distinction was made at the national level that in the future the development of rural areas would be given priority over that of urban areas. The Arusha Declaration, therefore, influenced the formulation of urban policy in the Second Five Year Plan.

A major policy goal was to decentralize certain government functions and to locate new industries away from Dar-es-Salaam. Thus, in order to solve the problem of concentrating development in only a few centres, the plan formulated a strategy of nine growth centres, to reduce the industrial concentration in Dar-es-Salaam. In principle, the application of the nine-growth-centre approach was the best urban and regional policy for Tanzania, but in practice the strategy has had only a limited success in Tanga, Morogoro, Mbeya, Arusha, Mwanza and Dodoma. The rest of the nine growth centres did not attract investment because of a lack of enough economic infrastructure, appropriate criteria for selection of the centres, clear and enforced industrial policy, sound implementation strategy, and because Dar-es-Salaam had already acquired enough momentum to grow.

The second Five Year Development Plan proposed a decentralization plan whose major aim was to give each region freedom to propose and implement projects according to their own priorities. Every region, therefore, prepared a Regional Integrated Development Plan (RIDEP). Despite a few drawbacks because of lack of manpower, several medium-sized towns have grown due to this decentralization policy.

The National Housing Corporation aimed to increase the rate of house construction, and the government was committed to provide at least 5,000 site and service plots annually. In 1971, the government acquired rented properties and began to charge rent for all government and parastatal employees who occupied such public housing. All these new moves were justified on the ground that it was a logical outcome of Tanzania's commitment to socialism. This change of urban policy did not mean that the urban areas would be neglected. The policy of rural development continued with the regrouping of widely scattered peasants into organized village communities called *Ujamaa*. The *Ujamaa* policy and the creation of *Ujamaa* villages is one of the national development strategies which focuses on rural development through modernization of agricultural production. Under the villagization policy, *Ujamaa* villages were started with the aim of rediverting the disparity in standard of living between the urban and rural areas. The villagization economic goals were to create viable economic units, control and plan land-use, give the unemployed and under-employed a chance to engage in farming, and encourage commercial agriculture. While the social objective of the *Ujamaa* policy was to guarantee a better provision of public facilities and service, resettle villagers from remote areas in villages with better accessibility to main transport systems, and decrease the disparity in income-distribution and, hence, living standards between urban and rural areas, the main aim of these social and economic objectives was to reduce the high rate of rural-urban migration and thus control the rate of urbanization in the country. But since force was used in the villagization programmes, and because of lack of manpower, funds and arable land, the economic aims of the modernization of agriculture and the introduction of socialist elements in the process of production were not achieved.

In order to reinforce the 1972 decentralization policy in 1973, a decision was made to move the capital from Dar-es-Salaam to Dodoma. According to the resolution of the National Executive Committee of the Tanganyika African National Union (TANU), the transfer was to take place gradually over ten years. According to the National Master Plan, the moving of the capital to Dodoma would: (a) increase administrative effectiveness since Dodoma was centrally located at a junction of transportation as opposed to Dar-es-Salaam which is peripherally located; (b) reduce the congestion of people and activities in Dar-es-Salaam; and (c) act as a growth pole that would stimulate development in the surrounding backward areas. By 1975, Dodoma had already been established and the population was estimated to be 45,000. The physical planning of Dodoma was carried out under the National Capital Master Plan. The Plan emphasized the use of locally produced, low-cost materials, the building of an efficient transport system and the planning of the town around a series of small connecting communities which can be spatially integrated with the future development of Dodoma (United Republic of Tanzania 1974).

Notwithstanding the plan to move to Dodoma, the primacy of Dar-es-Salaam has continued until now because of the poor infrastructural sources and poor facilities in Dodoma. The continued concentration of industry in Dar-es-Salaam despite the growth-centre and the decentralization and relocation policies, led the government to introduce a new decentralization of industrial strategy, aimed at the development of regional towns, in the Third Five Year Development Plan (1976–81).

The new strategy's aim was to distribute industries not only in the nine growth-pole areas but also in the rural areas.

A comparison of national urban policies

As analysed above, the urban policies and performance of the three East African countries have some broad similarities as well as major differences. Because of common historical and geographical experiences, the divergence of urban policies started during the post-colonial era, due mainly to the different social and political parameters. While initially Kenya pursued a capitalist, top-down growth model, Tanzania drifted away from the growth-pole approach to development and adopted radical policies emphasizing an agropolitan approach, which advocates bottom-up development and endorses the supremacy of territorial integration and endogenous development within a system of 'selective spatial closures'. Uganda, on the other hand, has taken an intermediate path between the Kenyan and Tanzanian models since independence.

In comparing the urban policies of the three countries, it is safe to conclude that Tanzania, more than Kenya and Uganda, has had an

> *active development of national site-and-service programmes; (evident from) the* de facto *recognition of existing squatter settlements, coupled with the intention to gradually improve services to them; a new rental policy with regard to civil servants; the establishment of Tanzania Housing Bank; and the decision to move the capital from Dar-es-Salaam to one of the least-developed regions.*
>
> (United Republic of Tanzania 1976)

Although Kenya and Uganda created a National Housing Corporation and a Housing Finance Bank, they have not implemented the urban policies they were supposed to perform. Kenya is now in the process of decentralizing her urban policy programmes to the District Development Committee as the main focus of rural development. The local or district councils in Kenya and Uganda are stronger than their Tanzanian counterparts and as a result they have been able to implement the urban policies delegated to them by the central government.

Tanzania's planning approach was influenced by the Marxist paradigm, which calls for more radical analysis of spatial problems of development and dismisses development paradigms based on 'capitalist ideology' (Lundquist 1981). In Kenya and Uganda, on the other hand, the spatial development model which is still 'centre-down', urban-based, and outward-looking, continues to dominate the economic landscape of the two countries. In the three countries, urban planning policies are still oriented towards the rural and urban formal sectors, although the rural informal sectors are now receiving more spatial planning. These urban planning ideologies are based on the different political structures and attitudes of the respective countries. The political differences between the three countries have also developed contrasting class structures which require different urban policies. Comparing Kenyan and Tanzanian urban policies Richard Stren stressed that

> *the greater proportion of middle- and upper-income earners in Kenya put considerable pressure on both local and central government to provide high standard services and facilities ... in the Tanzania environment, any policy which does not at least attempt to benefit lower-income groups will alienate the government from the overwhelming majority of the urban population.*
>
> *(Stren 1979.)*

Summary and conclusions

This study has shown that there has been a significant shift in the pattern of urban growth from the primate urban centres to the small and intermediate urban centres in East Africa. The small and medium centres have grown in importance since the first population census in 1948. The factors contributing to this new trend of rapid urbanization of small and intermediate centres are the improvement in income-gap between the urban and rural areas; increased cost of living in the major urban areas; the creation of income-earning opportunities such as food-processing and agro-based industries in the secondary towns; and the growing importance of the economic and social base of the invisible towns and trading centres. The ensuing period up to the eve of independence saw a doubling in the number of urban centres, and a sharp increase in the importance of secondary towns in the urban system, resulting from the growth and diversification of the economy and administrative system following World War II. Ironically, in the period immediately following independence, the reverse happened – a modest increase in the urban population shares of Nairobi, Dar-es-Salaam and Kampala as a result of rural–urban migration by Africans. However, in the most recent period another resurgence of small and secondary towns has occurred so that they now account for nearly half of the urban population in each of the three countries.

The increasing importance of small and secondary towns over the last three decades is consistent with cross-sectional data from other nations suggesting an inverse relationship between economic development and primacy. Some argue that in the earliest stages of development, urban concentration increases because development does not occur fast enough, or evenly enough, to support many large secondary towns. The nature of the colonial experience, the lack of a tradition of urbanism, the economics of industrial location, and a small national area are some factors that may lead to high levels of primacy. As levels of economic activity continue to increase, and political conflicts between the largest city and its periphery are resolved in favour of the periphery, intermediate towns become more economically viable and begin receiving a larger proportion of public resources (Obudho 1985; Westcott and Obudho 1982). It is true that the centralization of urban activities in the primate cities of East Africa is partly historic and partly economic. There is, and will continue to be, a tendency of human activities to agglomerate in the primate cities to take advantage of the economies of scale. Increasing urban size generates increasing economies of scale which in most cases will be very efficient. But in Kenya, Tanzania and Uganda, large primate cities would reinforce the dualistic character of the national economy and create an even wider gap between the primate cities and the rural areas. The role of the small and intermediate centres is to bridge the gap in this development process. Life in urban centres of East Africa at any level is evidently viewed as preferable to rural poverty, and many studies document the fact that by far the largest numbers of absolute poor live in rural areas. However, any strategy to alleviate poverty in East Africa cannot ignore urban centres. Urban wage-earners make important contributions to rural welfare through remittance payments. Thus secondary towns are becoming increasingly important centres of opportunity for rural–urban migrants, and catalytic nodes for more effective linking of rural areas to the national economy. It is to these intermediate urban centres that the urban policy of East African governments should be redirected as a means of lessening the rural–urban migration. Secondary towns have played an increasingly important role in East Africa during the last few decades and will probably continue to do so in the foreseeable future. The most obvious symbol of their importance is their rapid rates of population growth, paralleled by corresponding increase in formal and informal employment. The East African governments have to play an important role in stimulating the growth of these towns and their resultant impact on rural hinterlands by promoting industrial dispersion and administrative decentralization. However, many of the expressed intentions of these programmes have yet to be realized. The only way to realize these objectives is to have a sound national urban policy which recognizes the growing importance of the intermediate urban centres in East Africa.

Notes

1 For a detailed study of urbanization in East Africa see J. Hutton, *Urban challenge in East Africa*, (Nairobi: East African Publishing House, 1972); G.W. Kanyeihamba and J.P.W.B. McAuslan (eds), *Urban legal problems in Eastern Africa*, (Uppsala: Scandanavian Institute of African Studies, 1978); and R.A. Obudho, National Urban Policy for East Africa, *Regional Development Dialogue*, vol. 4, no. 2 (1982), pp. 87–177. See also, S.H. Ominde: *The population of Kenya, Uganda and Tanzania* (Nairobi: Heinemann, 1974) and S.H. Ominde, *Population change and socio-economic development in East Africa* (Nairobi: University of Nairobi, Population Structure and Research Institute, 1980).

2 For a bibliographical survey of East African urbanization See R.A. Obudho, *Demography, urbanization and spatial planning in Kenya: a bibliography* (Westport, Conn: Greenwood, 1985), and R.A. Obudho and Agnes K. Musyoki, *Demography, urbanization and regional planning in Uganda and Tanzania* (Westport Connecticut: Greenwood Press, 1987).

References

Carpenter, F.W. 1953. *Report of the Committee on African Wages* (Nairobi: Government Printer)

Cohen, J.M. and Cook, R.M. 1985. *District development planning in Kenya* (Cambridge, Massachusetts: Harvard University, Harvard Institute for International Development)

Colony and Protectorate of Kenya 1953. *Report of the Inquiry into the general economy of farming in the Highlands* (Nairobi: Government Printer)

Fair, T.J.D. 1962. Regional approach to economic development of Kenya, *South Africa Geographical Journal*, vol. 42.

Funnel, D.C. 1976. 'The role of small service centres in regional and rural development; with special reference to East Africa'. In A. Gilbert (ed.) *Development planning and spatial structure* (New York: Wiley), p. 79.

Hull, R. 1976. *African cities and towns before conquest* (New York: New York University Press), p. xiii.

Hutton, J. 1972. *Urban challenge in East Africa* (Nairobi: East African Publishing House)

Kampala Mengo Regional Planning Studies 1966. (Entebbe: Government Printer)

Kenyeihamba, G.W. and McAuslan, J.P.W.B. (eds) 1978. *Urban legal problems in Eastern Africa* (Upsala: Scandinavian Institute of African Studies)

Lundquist, J. 1981. 'Tanzania: Socialist ideology, bureaucratic reality and development from below'. In W.B. Stohr and D.R.F. Taylor (eds), *Development from above or below: the dialectics of regional planning in developing countries* (New York: Wiley)

Nyerere, Julius K. 1967. *Socialism and rural development* (Dar-es-Salaam: Government Printer)

Nyerere, J.K. 1973: *Freedom and development* (Dar-es-Salaam: Oxford University Press)

Obudho, R.A. 1982. National urban policy for East Africa, *Regional Development Dialogue*, vol. 4, no. 2, pp. 87–177.

Obudho, R.A. 1984. National, urban and regional planning policy in Kenya, *Third World Planning Review*, vol. 6, no. 4, pp. 363–87.

Obudho, R.A. 1985. *Demography, urbanization and spatial planning in Kenya: a bibliography* (Westport, Connecticut: Greenwood)

Obudho, R.A. and Musyoki, A.K. 1987. *Demography, urbanization and regional planning in Uganda and Tanzania* (Westport, Connecticut: Greenwood Press)

Obudho, R.A. and Waller, P.P. 1976. *Periodic markets, urbanization and regional planning: a case study from Western Kenya* (Westport, Connecticut: Greenwood Press)

S.H. Ominde 1974. *The population of Kenya, Uganda and Tanzania* (Nairobi: Heinemann)

Ominde, S.H. 1980. *Population change and socio-economic development in East Africa* (Nairobi: University of Nairobi, Population and Research Institute)

Republic of Kenya 1969. *Development Plan 1970–1974* (Nairobi: Government Printer), pp. 85–6.

Republic of Kenya 1974. *Development Plan 1974–1978* (Nairobi: Government Printer), p. 66.

Republic of Kenya 1978. *Human settlement in Kenya: a strategy for urban and rural development* (Nairobi: Government Printer)

Salier, M. 1972. 'Urban problems, planning possibilities and housing policies'. In J. Hutton (ed.), *Urban challenges in East Africa* (Nairobi: East African Publishing House)

Seaff, A.H. *et al.* 1964. *Recommendation for urban development in Kampala and Mengo* (New York: United Nations TAO/Uganda)

Soja, E.W. and Weaver, C.E. 1976. 'Urbanisation and underdevelopment in East Africa'. In B.J.L. Berry (ed.), *Urbanisation and counter urbanisation* (Beverly Hills, USA: Sage), pp. 233–66.

Stren, R.E. 1979. 'Urban policy'. In J.D. Barkan and J.J. Okumu (eds), *Policies and public policy in Kenya and Tanzania* (New York: Praeger)

Swynnerton, R.T.M. 1954. *A plan to intensify the development of agriculture in Kenya* (Nairobi: Government Printer)

Taylor, D.R.F. 1978. The concept of invisible town and spatial organisation in East Africa, *Comparative Urban Research*, vol. 5, no. 213, p.44.

Taylor D.R.F. 1979a. *Employment income and equality: a strategy for increased production employment in Kenya* (Geneva: ILO)

Taylor D.R.F. 1979b. 'Spatial aspect of development process'. In R.A. Obudho and D.R.F. Taylor (eds), *Spatial structure of development: a study of Kenya* (Boulder, Colorado: Westview)

Republic of Uganda 1972. *Third Five Year Development Plan 1971/2, 1975/6* (Entebbe: Government Printer), p. 69.

United Republic of Tanzania 1967. *The Arusha Declaration and self-reliance* (Dar-es-Salaam: Government Printer)

United Republic of Tanzania 1974. *Tanzania: Second Five Year Plan for Economic and Social Development, 1st July, 1969 – 30th June 1974* (Dar-es-Salaam: Government Printer)

United Republic of Tanzania 1976. *National capital master plan, Dodoma, Tanzania* (Toronto: Project Planning Associates), pp. 89–90.

Clay, Wescott and Obudho, R.A. 1982. Between farm and city: secondary towns in Kenya to the year 2000, *African Urban Studies, no. 13* (Spring 1982), pp. 32–53.

15
Regional Disparity, Central Development Banking and Manufacturing in Nigeria: Emerging Patterns and Issues

J.O. Akintola-Arikawe
Department of Geography, University of Lagos, Nigeria

Introduction

The issue of highly disproportionate regional distribution of income within national economies has engaged the attention of regional scientists and planners for about four decades now. Regional income disparity is itself linked to regional differences in economic activity structures and related employment opportunities. Therefore public policies aimed at inducing convergence have been fundamentally directed at influencing employment-generating conditions in the economy such that the income-earning capacities of relatively backward regions would be improved. The ultimate aim in a national context is a more equitable distribution of income and welfare among the regional units comprising the economy. Contrary to the confusing arguments of Marxist analysts, the interest thus shown in regional matters is not directed at empty spatial or regional units *per se*, but rather at enhancing the welfare of the inhabitants that live in, and give meaning to, such regional units (Soja 1980).

The public policy problem of influencing the regional welfare structure in any economy so as to induce convergence is not limited to any particular sector of the economy. Analysis of regional disparity and policies which induce convergence are therefore preferably based on income indices as general or aggregate reflectors of welfare (Higgins 1972). However, in circumstances (particularly in a developing country such as Nigeria) where regionally structured data on income (no matter how rough) are unavailable, data on economic activity structures and related transactions could be used, either on an economy-wide basis or on a sector-specific basis.

This paper takes the sector-specific approach, examining the regional structure of Nigerian manufacturing with a view to eliciting how much, and in what direction, an important element of direct public policy has influenced it. The choice of the sector-specific approach and the manufacturing sector has to do with such considerations as the prominent attention given to industrial development matters in the public policy of contemporary Nigeria; the greater visibility of industrial establishments in the modern sector and the close association of public anti-disparity pronouncements with the sector; the limited space prescribed for this contribution; and the insurmountable data problems that an economy-wide analysis would create.

The specific objective of the paper is thus to examine the regional structure of Nigerian manufacturing at appropriate points in time (1974 and 1980) and to relate to that structure one prominent tool of public policy which is endowed with great potential for inducing convergence. The tool consists of the financing activities of development banks owned by federal government. The expectation is that the functioning of this instrument of public policy in an economy where the anti-disparity stance has been rather militant would, over time, propel the regional structure towards convergence. The analysis here tries to reveal how much this has been the case. The paper concludes with an evaluation regarding the convergence-induction issue and the other realities of the environment in which the two financing institutions involved function as a policy instrument.

Nigerian anti-disparity policy in perspective

Along with such notable problems as structural imbalance, contextually stunted, erratic and unimpressive growth rates, and its fundamentally dependent status in terms of basic inputs of technology and raw materials, the problem of spatial imbalance (regional/state distribution of manufacturing enterprises) has received unprecedented attention in Nigeria's planning philosophy and public policy since the early 1970s. The evolution of the convergence-induction policy (alternatively described as the equity principle) has been traced at length elsewhere (Akintola-Arikawe 1981; and a forthcoming volume). Some of the relevant policy statements are recalled here for purposes of documentation.

A clear statement of the policy came in the *Second National Development Plan, 1970–74* which was launched just after the Civil War:

An important element of social justice for national integration is the worthy objective of balanced development as between different geo-

graphical areas of the country. The reduction of existing disparities must be pursued openly, although this cannot be accomplished at the cost of stagnation in areas which are presumed to be relatively more developed .... The objective is to move rapidly to the achievement of minimum economic and social standard for every part of the country.
(*Federal Republic of Nigeria, 1970:34*)

When the Third Plan (1975–80) appeared, the statement of policy was even stronger, indicating that 'a situation where some parts of the country are experiencing rapid economic growth while other parts are lagging behind can no longer be tolerated' (Federal Republic of Nigeria 1975, p. 30).

This policy has been variously re-stated not only in the *Fourth National Development Plan, 1981–1985* but also in numerous other public documents. For instance, the booklet *Nigerian Industrial Policy and Strategy: Guidelines to Investors*, published in 1980, features a section on the dispersal of industries in which the active promotion of the 'policy of fostering even development of all parts of the country' is re-emphasized (Federal Republic of Nigeria 1980, pp. 19–20). Indeed, the conception of the equity principle in Nigeria extends beyond the state units to the local government units within each state. That is, just as central government policy advocates even development among the states, the states are also expected to maintain an anti-disparity policy in respect of the local government units constituting them (Federal Republic of Nigeria 1976, p. 9). The convergence-induction principle has thus become an important all-embracing element of development planning philosophy in Nigeria.

The policy tool and data considerations

Governmental influences on economic activity structures, whether sectorally or spatio-regionally, are so pervasive that one might not be able to disentangle and measure them in all their ramifications. The attempt here has been to identify, juxtapose and analyse the influence of one type of policy tool which, if decisively used, could (along with others), significantly alter the regional pattern of Nigerian manufacturing within a relatively short period of time. The institutional tool involves the financing activities of the two central development banks which function in the area of manufacturing in Nigeria: the Nigerian Industrial Development Bank Limited (NIDB) and the Nigerian Bank for Commerce and Industry (NBCI). The two banks may be introduced briefly.

NIBD, the older of the two, is Nigeria's industrial finance institution *par excellence*. Established in 1964, NIDB has undergone various forms of change which reflect responsiveness to changes in the Nigerian economic environment. Only 25.0 per cent of it was owned by Federal Government in 1964 but by 1979, it had become 99.6 per cent owned by the Federal Government and the Central Bank. Also, since 1970, the Bank has had to ensure not only that the enterprises it finances are mostly Nigerian-controlled but also that they are financed in ways consistent with the central government policy of even development. A normal feature of the 'Chairman's Statement' in NIDB's *Annual Report* has therefore been the inclusion of statements reflecting adherence to a policy of 'more even geographical distribution of its investments' (NIDB 1980). As a result of these characteristics, NIDB could now be described as a public industrial finance institution which, with a keen eye on encouraging convergence in the regional distribution of manufacturing, provides medium- and long-term finance (in the form of loan and equity investments) to both new and expanding medium- and large-scale enterprises registered in Nigeria as limited liability companies, are wholly Nigerian-owned or have substantial Nigerian equity contents, and is involved in manufacturing, non-petroleum mining or tourism (essentially large hotels).

The Nigerian Bank for Commerce and Industry (NBCI) on the other hand, was established by the NBCI *Decree No. 22* of 1973 and its ownership capital has been, from the beginning, contributed by the Federal Government of Nigeria (60 per cent) and the Central Bank (40 per cent). Its principal function is to provide equity capital and loans to indigenous persons, institutions and organizations for medium- and long-term investment in industry and commerce (Federal Republic of Nigeria, NBCI Decree, 1973, section 2). The Bank is also empowered to engage in merchant banking, related stocks, shares and debentures, as well as the provision of guarantees and some other financial functions. Like NIDB, NBCI has it as a policy 'to ensure even geographical spread of its investments all over the Federal Republic of Nigeria' (NBCI 1981, p. 8).

The sanctions data (involving both equity and loans) for NIDB and NBCI have been used for this study. On the basis of experience with NIDB data, it is established that data on sanctions and disbursements are strongly correlated. With time the values should be identical but while sanctions data are more organized, disbursement data, by their nature, occur in lumpy streams and are therefore more tardy and disjointed (Akintola-Arikawe forthcoming, Table 9).

On the whole, the main analysis covers data for the period 1974 to

1980, using those two specific years as critical points in time in respect of:

1 manufacturing establishments employing at least ten people; and
2 loans and equity sanctions (total financing) by NIDB (cumulated from 1975 to 1980) and by NBCI (cumulated from 1974 to 1980).

The initial data year of 1974 corresponds to the early 1970s when the convergence-induction policy became pronounced in Nigeria. The two sets of data were, for the most part, gradually assembled over the last six months and it is apparent that an attempt has been made to establish a temporal mesh between them.

Analysis

The incidence of regional convergence, or lack of it, could be elicited by various methods: simple correlation analysis in which the directions of the coefficients (positive or negative) are more important than their strengths or significance ratings, X^2 procedures, cumulative percentage curves of certain characteristics and rank difference analysis (Akintola-Arikawe 1981, pp. 13–18 and 1984, pp. 83–7). Using and comparatively interpreting the results of all these procedures would be ideal. However, the constraints of space preclude this. In the circumstances, the procedure considered most inherently explicit – the rank difference procedure – has been used for the analysis. Its logic will be clear in context.

The existing regional pattern of manufacturing in Nigeria at the time when the convergence-induction policy gained ascendency is represented by the data for 1974 shown on Table 15.1. Any of the measures on the table (number of establishments, employment and gross production) could be used to indicate the existing levels of industrial development since they are strongly correlated positively. However, Gross Production Value (GPV) has been favoured not only because it is particularly compatible with an analysis which emphasizes financial investments but also because it reflects industrial output and activities better than the other two measures. Similarly, Table 15.2 shows the combined totals of loan and equity financing as well as the number of establishments financed by the two central development banks, NIDB and NBCI. The last column of each of the tables shows the ranks of the regional/state units in terms of their percentage shares of manufacturing GPV (Table 15.1) and financing by the two development banks (Table 15.2).

Analysing the ranked proportions in the two tables provides the desired insights into the expected relative 'downward levelling' of

Table 15.1 Regional (state) pattern of Nigerian manufacturing, 1974

S/N	States	Establishments		Persons employed		Gross Prod. Value		
		No	%	No	%	Amount (N'00)	%	Rank
1	Anambra	98	9.9	4,851	2.9	46,103	3.4	5
2	Bauchi	4	0.4	348	0.2	576	0.04	19
3	Bendel	55	5.6	13,436	8.1	43,838	3.3	6
4	Benue	8	0.8	112	0.1	1061	0.1	16
5	Borno	8	0.8	678	0.4	7265	0.5	13
6	Cross River	48	4.9	8,844	5.3	13,476	1.0	12
7	Gongola	14	1.4	231	0.1	748	0.1	18
8	Imo	54	5.5	2,329	1.4	20,084	1.5	9
9	Kaduna	48	4.9	20,725	12.4	105,966	7.9	3
10	Kano	83	8.4	12,854	7.7	114,986	8.6	2
11	Kwara	23	2.3	2,534	1.5	18,511	1.4	10
12	Lagos	282	28.5	79,607	47.8	843,862	63.0	1
13	Niger	8	0.8	183	0.1	777	0.1	17
14	Ogun	42	4.3	2,939	1.8	22,398	1.8	8
15	Ondo	33	3.3	2,742	1.6	2487	0.2	15
16	Oyo	98	9.9	5,980	3.6	23,623	1.8	7
17	Plateau	45	4.6	3,618	2.2	53,818	4.0	4
18	Rivers	15	1.5	2,185	1.3	14,604	1.1	11
19	Sokoto	22	2.2	2,344	1.4	5,772	0.4	14
	Total	988	100.0	166,540	100.0	1,339,966	100.0	

Source: Computed by author from the returns of the 1974 industrial survey conducted by the Industrial Survey Division of the Federal Office of Statistics in Lagos.

states with comparatively high levels of existing industrial activity, and the relative 'upward levelling' of those with initially low levels. The rank values have been arranged systematically and extended in Table 15.3, using GPV (manufacturing) rankings as the organizing variable. With respect to the existing (1974) levels of manufacturing, it is clear that Lagos State ranks first and Bauchi State ranks nineteenth or last; other states occupy various positions in-between.

The *hypothetical-financing rank* in Table 15.3 derives from the inverse relationship expectation postulated above: that is, if institutional financing allocations had been made with the convergence-induction policy strictly in mind (with the desire to 'level up' less developed states and 'level down' more developed states), the more industrially developed states at the time the even-development policy gained ground (1974) should receive the least financing, and the less industrially

Table 15.2 Regional (state) pattern of combined financing (sanctions) by NIDB and NBCI. Cumulative (1974–1980)*

S/N.	States	Projects/Establishments *No.*	*%*	Combined Financing *Value (N'000)*	*%*	*Rank*
1	Anambra	30	7.9	31,194.0	5.93	6
2	Bauchi	10	2.6	39,039.4	7.42	4
3	Bendel	30	7.9	36,605.5	6.96	5
4	Benue	5	1.3	30,300.0	5.76	7
5	Borno	13	3.4	16,950.0	3.22	13
6	Cross River	15	3.9	27,965.0	5.31	8
7	Gongola	7	1.8	11,815.5	2.25	16
8	Imo	26	6.8	19,976.8	3.78	11
9	Kaduna	19	5.0	22,950.8	4.36	10
10	Kano	19	5.0	24,471.0	4.64	9
11	Kwara	20	5.3	13,914.4	2.64	15
12	Lagos	76	20.0	101,790.2	19.34	1
13	Niger	10	2.6	17,058.2	3.24	12
14	Ogun	33	8.7	52,426.0	9.96	2
15	Ondo	9	2.4	11,539.5	2.19	17
16	Oyo	31	8.2	40,640.0	7.72	3
17	Plateau	4	1.1	1,470.0	0.28	19
18	Rivers	12	3.2	15,349.0	2.92	14
19	Sokoto	11	2.9	10,928.8	2.08	18
	Total	380	100.0	526,284.1	100.00	

* Note: NIDB data are cumulated from 1975 to 1980 while NBCI data are cumulations from 1974 to 1980.
Source: Enquiries at NIDB and NBCI Headquarters in Lagos.

developed states greater financing, commensurate with the extent of their backwardness in this connection. Thus, Lagos State should have received the least institutional financing by 1980 (with rank 19) while Bauchi should have received the largest (with rank 1). However, as the last two columns of Table 15.3 reveal, the actual ranks deriving from the financing patterns of the two central institutions differ from the hypothetical ranks derived on the basis of convergence-induction considerations.
The extent of the differences or *derivations* appears in the last column of Table 15.3.

For clarity, it should be stated that the smaller the numerical value of a state's rank the higher is the rank of that state. Therefore, in calculating deviations, if a state's actual financing rank value is lower than its hypothetical financing rank value, that state is regarded as having a positive deviation (denoted by the plus sign), indicating that

Table 15.3 Ranking of states on manufacturing (GPV) in 1974 and combined institutional financing by NIDB and NBCI 1974–1980.

S/N	States	State rank on 1974 Manufacturing (GPV)	State rank on combined institutional financing. 1974–80		
			Hypothetical	*Actual*	*Deviation*
1	Lagos	1	19	1	+18
2	Kano	2	18	9	+9
3	Kaduna	3	17	10	+7
4	Plateau	4	16	19	−3
5	Anambra	5	15	6	+9
6	Bendel	6	14	5	+9
7	Oyo	7	13	3	+10
8	Ogun	8	12	2	+10
9	Imo	9	11	11	0
10	Kwara	10	10	15	−5
11	Rivers	11	9	14	−5
12	Cross River	12	8	8	0
13	Borno	13	7	13	−6
14	Sokoto	14	6	18	−12
15	Ondo	15	5	17	−12
16	Benue	16	4	7	−3
17	Niger	17	3	12	−9
18	Gongola	18	2	16	−14
19	Bauchi	19	1	14	−3

Note: The mean value of all deviations in the last column is 7.6.
Source: Derived from Tables 15.1 and 15.2.

the state did not experience sufficient 'downward levelling' in the distribution of financing. Conversely, where a state's actual financing rank value is higher than the hypothetical, the deviation is negative, indicating that the state did not enjoy enough 'upward levelling' with respect to its acquisition of financing.

The real values of the deviations are not as critically important as their directions (that is, whether they are positive or negative) except in so far as the deviation values reflect the extent of departure from hypothetical expectations. What the analysis of central institutional financing (*vis-á-vis* the initial (i.e. 1974) regional pattern of manufacturing) thus reveals could be summed up as follows.

First, only two states – Imo and Cross River – conform perfectly to the hypothetical expectations of the equity principle underlying the convergence-induction policy. The two states are expected to rank eleventh (Imo) and eighth (Cross River) and they do; they therefore have deviation values of zero.

Secondly, of the remaining 17 states, seven do not experience sufficient 'downward levelling', as their positive deviations indicate, while ten did not have enough 'upward levelling', as denoted by their negative signs. However, the wide-ranging deviation values could be fairly neatly interpreted by reference to the mean value of all deviations which turns out to be 7.6 (disregarding the sign in the averaging process). States with deviation values below the mean could be regarded as having 'tolerably' conformed to the expected outcome of the convergence-induction process, and those with deviations above the mean value as having had 'unacceptably' high financing.

Thus, the third point revealed is that the seven states with deviations less than the mean – Kaduna (+7), Plateau (−3), Kwara (−5), Rivers (−5), Borno (−6), Benue (−3), and Bauchi (−3) – exhibit 'tolerable' levels of conformity. However, while one of these could be said to have positive tolerability (since its deviation is positive), the other six, for the opposite reason, exhibit negative tolerability.

On the other hand, ten states reflect unacceptably high levels of deviation from the mean. While six of the states (Lagos, Kano, Anambra, Bendel, Oyo and Ogun) have positive unacceptability, the remaining four (Sokoto, Ondo, Niger and Gongola) exhibit negative unacceptability.

The strength and, therefore, the degree of acceptability of the relationship between the actual and hypothetical financing rankings of the 19 states could be even more succinctly elicited by statistical testing. For this purpose, Spearman's rank-difference correlation, (**rho**), is particularly appropriate (Blalock, 1972: 416–418), the aim being to ascertain whether the rankings of the states, on actual institutional financing (1974–80), correlate significantly with their hypothetical financing rankings (derived from levels of manufacturing activity in 1974). This is done by applying the formula

$$P = 1 - \frac{6 - D^2}{N\,(N^2 - 1)}$$

where D^2 = the sum of the squared differences between the ranks and

N = number of pairs of measurements. Computing with the values in the 'hypothetical' and 'actual' columns in Table 3,

$$P = 1 - \frac{6 \times 1494}{19\,(19^2 - 1)} = \frac{8964}{6840}$$

$$= 1 - 1.3105263 \text{ or } - 0.3105.$$

It turns out that the obtained negative coefficient (P = −0.3105) is less than the critical value for significance even at the 0.05 level of confidence. The hypothesis of no correlation is therefore upheld. The conclusion is thus simple: there is no significant relationship or correlation between the rankings of the 19 states with respect to actual and hypothetical (or expected) financing by the two financial institutions. That is, in spite of the wide publicity enjoyed by the convergence-induction policy of government and the avowed acceptance of the policy by NIDB and NBCI, the distribution of these institutions' investments (financing) among the state units has not been carried out in proportions that, to any important extent, take cognizance of existing levels of manufacturing activities and the related societal philosophy that urges convergence-induction.

Departures from expectations could hardly ever disappear completely from this type of analysis. This is so for several reasons. First, the financing process is based on sanctioning one project at a time as the promoters come forward, apply and see the transaction to a conclusion. There is no way of knowing, *a priori*, how many enterprises would come from a state in the course of a year or any given period of time. Thus, while the financial institutions might strive to accommodate the few applications from 'disadvantaged' states, they could not always withold assistance to good projects from less disadvantaged states.

Secondly, the above implies an individual-initiative basis (on the part of client enterprises) for coming forward to apply for financing. The problem has not been lack of funds but lack of sufficient patronage especially from states with low levels of industrial activity. One is tempted to view this as confirming the capital-shortage illusion thesis: that the problem in many less developed countries is not so much lack of capital but the absence or paucity of viable projects in which to invest available capital (Schatz 1974, pp. 89–101). What might help the situation is aggressive and diversified promotional activities on the part of the development banks, especially in low-activity states. Since each of the two institutions have branch offices in all the 19 state capitals, they seem to be potentially favoured to engage in extensive promotion.

That raises the third point: since the financing opportunities of the central credit institutions are available to all establishments (new and existing/expanding), an element of circular and cumulative causation is bound to pervade the aggregate financial structures that result. That is, areas with more industrial establishments would produce more applicants for, and recipients of, the banks' funds. The overall effect would be ever-increasing levels of activity in already 'favoured' areas and relative backward sliding for low-activity areas. And that may be in spite of the readiness of the institutions to accommodate all the financeable projects from such areas and even to assist poorly conceived projects to achieve financeable status.

Fourthly, it is possible that the development banks merely subscribe to the convergence-prone policy without being able to operationalize and implement it meaningfully. Such institutions obviously need alert and competent research departments to collate and analyse data, and to co-ordinate their activities with the statistical agencies of government and other relevant bodies. But even if this were so, the situation may not be very different for the regional convergence issue, except under conditions where funds are short and consequently financing is rationed in favour of 'disadvantaged' states.

It is instructive to recall an earlier paper in which this writer examined the regional convergence issue in relation to Nigerian manufacturing and allocations by central government to industrial projects in the Third National Development Plan, using the same analytical procedure as in this paper, the results were not very different: the allocations bore no significant relationship to the existing levels of manufacturing in the component states (Akintola-Arikawe 1981).

Perhaps it was in the realization of how slippery the convergence-induction problem was, that the Shagari administration went beyond traditional incentives to introduce (from 1980) an administrative process of locational approval for new private industrial enterprises, the ostensible hope being to favour disadvantaged areas in an approval-based locational diversion process. However, there is neither enough data nor space to probe the implications and results of that revolutionary experiment here.

The persistence of polarization

In the meantime, the regional pattern of industrial activity in Nigeria continues to be polarized (Table 15.4). This is underlined by a comparison of the patterns for 1974 and 1980 in Table 15.5. A quick verification has been done by devising a tabular version of the cumulative percentage curves which have been found useful elsewhere (Akintola-Arikawe 1984, pp. 85–6). The table shows the number of states accounting for 90 per cent of the country's manufacturing (GPV) in both 1974 and 1980. The value of 90 per cent has been arbitrarily set simply to represent a clearly high proportion of the country's manufacturing.

If there had been convergence in the whole regional (state) system, the number of states accounting for the 90 per cent proportion would be more numerous for 1980 than for 1974. The reverse would hold if divergence or polarization had been occurring.

Table 15.4 Regional (state) pattern of Nigerian manufacturing, 1980

S/N	States	Establishments		Persons employed		Gross production value	
		No.	%	*No.*	%	*(N'000)*	%
1	Anambra	113	9.1	12,256	4.2	153,276	2.2
2	Bauchi	13	1.0	1,103	0.4	36,716	0.6
3	Bendel	82	6.6	13,129	4.5	146,853	2.1
4	Benue	43	3.5	1,811	0.6	10,189	0.1
5	Borno	15	1.2	1,580	0.5	15,306	0.2
6	Cross River	34	2.7	14,993	5.2	78,253	1.1
7	Gongola	69	5.6	4,401	1.5	16,109	0.2
8	Imo	36	2.9	4,390	1.5	66,985	1.0
9	Kaduna	43	3.5	28,144	9.7	562,570	8.1
10	Kano	150	12.1	22,785	7.8	474,110	6.8
11	Kwara	23	1.9	1,675	0.6	20,134	0.3
12	Lagos	303	24.4	152,646	52.5	4,857,262	70.2
13	Niger	18	1.5	523	0.2	3,426	0.1
14	Ogun	63	5.1	5,166	1.8	79,013	1.1
15	Ondo	66	5.3	2,823	1.0	13,610	0.2
16	Oyo	80	6.4	5,996	2.1	107,796	1.6
17	Plateau	30	2.4	4,458	1.5	65,362	0.9
18	Rivers	38	3.1	9,490	3.3	169,454	2.4
19	Sokoto	24	1.9	3,321	1.1	55,975	0.6
	Total	1,243	100.0	290,693	100.0	6,921,399	100.0

Source: The Federal Office of Statistics, Industrial Survey Division, Ikoyi, Lagos.

Table 15.5 Number of states accounting for 90 per cent of national manufacturing (GPV) in 1974 and 1980

Year	Number of states contributing	Contributing states (in rank-order sequence)
1974	6 (90.2%)	Lagos, Kano, Kaduna, Plateau, Anambra and Bendel.
1980	5 (89.7%)	Lagos, Kaduna, Kano, Rivers, Anambra.

Source: Derived from Tables 15.1 and 15.4 above.

The slight change noticeable in the number of contributing states is in the direction of polarization: Six states accounted for the 90 per cent proportion in 1974 while the same proportion was concentrated in only five states in 1980 – a revelation which reinforces the result of the rank-difference analysis. And, except for the inclusion of Rivers State, the five contributing states of 1980 were among the six of 1974. The implication is that there had been no major regional shifts in the distribution of Nigerian manufacturing during the study period, a fact visibly apparent from the almost identical distribution structures depicted in Figure 48.

Conclusion

The conclusion to the 1981 allocation study referred to briefly above also applies very well here. A societal objective such as the equity principle may never be completely achieved. It is to be hoped, however, that each successive period will mark some progress toward the ultimate objective of reducing regional disparity in the location of growth-inducing and employment-generating economic activities. On the other hand, in view of spatially varying resource endowments and the concomitant opportunities for evolving a dynamic system of nationally complementary production structures based on regional specialization, the analysis of only one sector of the economy in terms of a fundamental philosophy such as the equity principle could produce only an incomplete picture. This is because various areas of the country have unequal potentials in respect of any one area of activity chosen for analysis. Thus only an analysis covering all aspects of the economy (agriculture and related activities, power, transport and communications, as well as other areas not often viewed by planners as belonging in the 'economic sector') could give a complete picture of the extent to which the equity principle has been applied in the Nigerian developmental process.

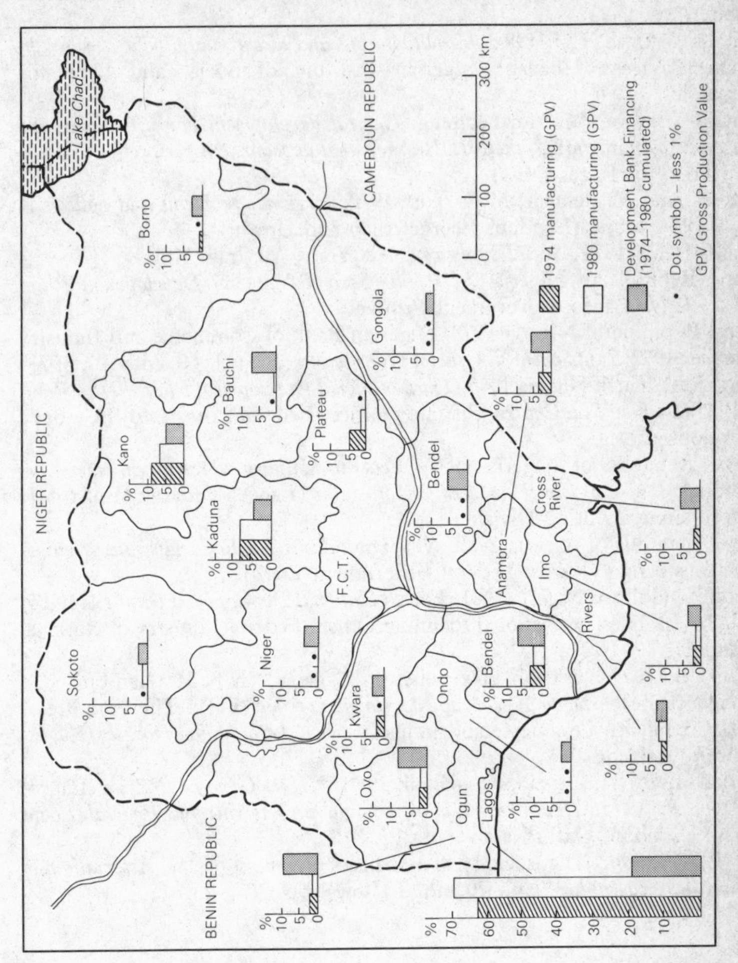

Fig. 48 The patterns of Nigerian manufacturing (GPV) and Central Development Bank financing (1974–1980)

References

Akintola-Arikawe, J.O. 1981. The equity principle and central plan allocation in the manufacturing sector: the Nigerian Third National Development Plan, *The Nigerian Journal of Economic and Social Studies*, vol. 23, no. 1 (March), p. 1–22.

Akintola-Arikawe, J.O. 1984. *Manufacturing and direct public policy in South-Western Nigeria* (Ibadan: Nigerian Institute of Social and Economic Research)

Akintola-Arikawe, J.O. forthcoming. *Central development bank financing and Nigerian manufacturing: the NIDB in regional development perspective* (Lagos: University of Lagos Press)

Allen, K. and Maclennan, M.C. (eds) 1970. *Regional problems and policies in Italy and France*, (London: George Allen and Unwin)

Blalock, H.M. 1972. *Social statistics* (New York: McGraw Hill)

Federal Republic of Nigeria 1970. *The Second National Development Plan, 1970–1974* (Lagos: Government Printer)

Federal Republic of Nigeria 1973. Nigerian Bank of Commerce and Industry Decree, 1973 *Supplement to Official Gazette No. 26*, vol. 60, May 10, 1973.

Federal Republic of Nigeria 1975. *Third National Development Plan, 1975–1980*, vol. 1. (Lagos: The Central Planning Office, Federal Ministry of Economic Development)

Federal Republic of Nigeria 1976. *Federal Military Government views on the Report of the Panel on creation of states* (Lagos: Federal Ministry of Information, Printing Division)

Federal Republic of Nigeria 1980. *Nigerian industrial policy and strategy: guidelines to investors* (Lagos: Federal Government Press)

Federal Republic of Nigeria 1981. *Fourth National Development Plan 1981–85*, vol. 1. (Lagos: The National Planning Office, Federal Ministry of National Planning)

Higgins, B. 1972. 'Growth pole policy in Canada'. In N.M. Hanson (ed.), *Growth centres in regional economic development* (New York: The Free Press)

Nigerian Bank for Commerce and Industry 1981. *Information Booklet* (Lagos: Tower Fernandez)

Nigerian Industrial Development Bank 1980. *NIDB General Policies* (Lagos)

Schatz, S.P. 1974. *Development bank lending in Nigeria: the Federal Loans Board* (London: Oxford University Press)

Soja, E.W. 1980. The socio-spatial dialectic, *Annals of the Association of American Geographers*, vol. 70, no. 2 (June), pp. 207–25.

16
Trade and Inequality in Borno, North-east Nigeria

G. Porter
Honorary Fellow, Department of Geography, University of Durham, England

It is now generally accepted that a historical perspective is an important dimension in studies of inequality.[1] But frequently the emphasis has been on the development of those regions associated with major export crops, with little analysis of the changes which have occurred in more peripheral areas. This paper is concerned with one of the remoter parts of Nigeria, that of Borno in the north-east. Borno is a dry largely Sudan savanna region whose economy is overwhelmingly rural-based and which has been bypassed by many of the major developments within Nigeria during the present century. Today it is one of Nigeria's poorest and least developed regions.

Two themes are pursued in this study of spatio-temporal patterns of inequality in Borno. First, the development of inequalities within the region (both inter-rural and rural-urban), which can be traced back to the pre-colonial period; second, the inter-regional inequality between Borno and other parts of Nigeria. The role of trade is considered crucial to both themes and in this context an attempt is made to draw comparisons with other regions, particularly neighbouring Hausaland, and to assess the varying impact of colonial rule thereon.

During this century Borno's peripheral position in relation to the economy of Nigeria as a whole has become increasingly marked; it experienced only latterly, and to a limited extent, the sort of cash-cropping developments which occurred in neighbouring Hausaland during the colonial period. Since independence there has been no major change in its position relative to the rest of the country. However, the region has seen important internal changes in the patterning of inequality over a long period; some rural areas are richer than they were in the past, others have declined; some urban centres have grown and prospered, others have disappeared. Spatial inequality is not a new feature of the Borno scene.

In this paper an attempt is made to assess the effect of changes in the pre-colonial and colonial trading relationships on the development of Borno, the extent to which new internal inequalities have been created, and Borno's external relationships altered. This involves some consideration of the changing structure of political power and administration which has remoulded and redefined trading relationships. Since the genesis of certain features of the present patterning of inequality in Borno antedates the colonial era, the period from 1800 is examined.

The nineteenth century: patterns of taxation and trade in a pre-colonial society

It is possible to put together a fairly clear, general picture of Borno society and the pattern of wealth distribution in the nineteenth century, from the reports of European expeditions and the anthropological and historical research of Cohen and Brenner, although a detailed economic history of the region (comparable to the work of Lovejoy and others on Hausaland) remains to be written. Additional material on the history of rural market centres was collected during a field survey of contemporary markets in the late 1970s. The focus here, as in subsequent sections, is on the core region of Borno emirate, though some attention is also given to the surrounding areas which were, from time to time, in positions of vassalage to the Borno state.[2].

In nineteenth century Borno there were various potential sources of income: payment in cash or kind, extracted through tribute and taxation; gifts; production from agriculture or craft industry; and trade, both internal and foreign. An attempt is made, in this section, to analyse – from albeit limited information – the flow of goods and cash in the Borno economy, and the principal beneficiaries of those flows. The century can be discussed as a whole since, despite changes in the ruling dynasty of Borno, many features of the economy and society prevailed until at least the late 1880s.

Wealth obtained through taxation was closely concentrated in the hands of the Borno royalty, courtiers (*kogonas*) and court-based *mallams* and *furma*[3] through the nineteenth century until the 1890s. The organization of the nineteenth century state was probably little different under the al-Kanemi dynasty (who ruled Borno from the 1820s) than it was under the preceding Saifawa dynasty.[4] Borno was administered and taxed mainly through a system of fiefs, some territorial, some ethnic or clan-based, which were in the hands of the monarch's clients. Under both the Saifawa and al-Kanemi dynasties all fiefholders (*chima kura*) lived permanently in the capital city, supported by a basic income in money, goods and food, obtained from the *binumram* tax on the harvest, and other more minor taxes.[5]

The change in rulers in Borno during the nineteenth century made for changes in both the group of nobility who benefited from the ruler's largesse, and the spatial allocation of that wealth. When the al-Kanemi dynasty replaced the Saifawa dynasty, there was an almost complete change in the ruling class of Borno as the clients of al-Kanemi replaced those of the Saifawa Mai. The new court was composed largely of Kanembu and Shuwa Arabs who had assisted al-Kanemi in his rise to power, and fiefs was reassigned to these followers. By 1846 the takeover was complete. The domination of the ruling classes thus continued under the al-Kanemis and, according to Brenner (1973), there was, in general, very little mobility between the ruling class and the commoners, despite the widespread use of client-patron relationships to promote advancement.[6] When the capital city of Birni Gazargamu was abandoned after the Fulani wars in 1809 the establishment of a new capital Kukawa (near Lake Chad) shifted the focus of the Borno empire eastwards together with the major concentration of wealth generated by taxation (Figure 49). Permanent residence at court was essential for the nobility, in order to keep in the favour of the ruler.[7] Revenue from taxation thus remained largely directed towards the capital city. A very small portion was kept by the *chima-kura's* local representative (*chima gana*) and local headmen who resided in the fief.[8]

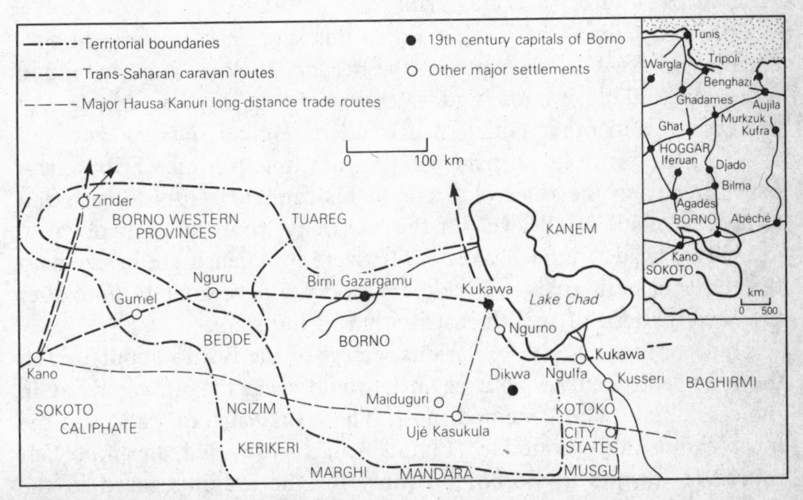

Fig. 49 Borno in the nineteenth century

The extraction of wealth from the *tala'a* (commoners) by taxation was not uniform. Under al-Kanemi and his descendants the Shuwa Arabs and Kanembu, located, in particular, south of Lake Chad, seem to have fared better than others. Brenner (1973) states that the Shuwa Arabs are remembered as having paid *jangali* (cattle tax) only once during the reign of the al-Kanemis, in 1865. The Kanembu also benefited from tax exemptions.[9] The extent to which *chima-kuras* levied taxation varied and some were particularly notorious for their extortion and greed. However, the spatial impact of this variation would have been diminished somewhat, since the fiefholdings were not in contiguous units but generally fragmented and dispersed over the entire kingdom, with fiefholders possessing rights of taxation over up to 20 or more separate pieces of land.[10]

At the end of the nineteenth century, the successful invasion of a Sudanese adventurer, Rabeh fadl Allah, brought about a further redistribution of wealth in Borno. Eighteen major fiefholders were selected from among Rabeh's followers. This time the fiefs seem to have consisted of discrete areas of land. Again, however, the fiefholders were based in the capital city (this time in Dikwa), and fiefs were administered for the absentee landlords through *wakils*, some of whom were also Rabeh's followers. According to Hallam (1977) the latter group grossly abused their positions. The concentration of wealth in Dikwa emanating from taxation was probably limited, however, since the severity of Rabeh's rule caused large-scale temporary population movements out of Borno. To some extent this was compensated by raids to pagan areas and Baghirmi.[11]

Gifts and tribute were other important sources of income in precolonial Borno. Various states on the borders of Borno paid tribute in order to avoid slave raids, and, perhaps, to acquire some measure of protection from other potential marauders. Gumel, Damagaram and Logone, for example, all paid tribute from time to time. Tribute was paid directly to the ruler of Borno at his capital.[12] Gifts in cash and kind were made at all levels of the hierarchy from the ruler down to the village head. Obviously these gifts were commensurate in size with the status of both giver and recipient, and can have done little to alter the basic pattern of wealth distribution in the state.[13]

Trade brought wealth to various sectors of the Borno population in the nineteenth century, but again it would seem that it was those in the capital city who benefited most. The trans-Saharan trade was the most exotic and profitable (Figure 49). It provided an important source of income in Borno, but only for the nobility based in the capital city and for North African traders. It was an enclave development which had little connection with domestic economy. As Brenner points out, the *kogonas* received their basic income from their fiefs and slave farms, but derived surplus wealth from commercial ventures. For the first two-thirds of the nineteenth century this meant, above all, the slave trade, which dominated the Borno–Fezzan–Tripoli route until the close of the 1860s. Slaves were derived from tribute and periodic raids into the pagan areas to the south and south-west of Borno. They were a commodity over which the ruling class had a near monopoly and the income from their sale reaped by North African traders represented almost pure profit.[14] The Tripolitans, also capital-city based, made considerable profit from the slave trade and return trade in North African and European goods to Borno.[15] With the decline of the slave trade, other trade goods had to be found in Borno. Ostrich feathers and ivory became the major substitutes; both, according to Nachtigal (1881), obtained largely from the border districts of Borno, and thus neither product involving the state directly in production. Again, it is likely that the ruling class dominated trade.[16]

Trade fluctuated in the latter part of the nineteenth century, but continued even after Rabeh's accession. In this latter period trade was probably based even more on plunder from surrounding areas than in previous decades. The main beneficiaries were those with the means to carry out such raids – the ruling class – and the Tripolitans who organized the trade northwards.[17]

In addition to the trans-Saharan trade, Borno was involved in long-distance trade within West Africa. One of the principal long-distance trades involved salt and potash, produced mainly north of the river Yo and on the borders of Lake Chad.[18] This region produced an annual output of salt of perhaps 3,500 to 5,000 metric tons (calculated from Lovejoy's estimates) and involved perhaps 25,000 workers. The trade was handled mainly by Kanuri and Hausa commoner merchants who took salt westwards to Hausaland (whence it was distributed as far as the Volta Basin by Hausa traders) and southwards towards the Benue. In return kola nuts, tobacco, cotton cloth and clothing were brought from Hausaland. Some of this trade went further east, across to Baghirmi and Wadai, where a number of Hausa and Kanuri traders had established themselves along the pilgrim routes to Mecca in the nineteenth century.[19]

The salt works in Borno were owned by members of the old Saifawa aristocracy who seem to have lived permanently in the salt camps area. Before the fall of Birni Gazargamu in 1808 they were city-based. The majority of workers were free migrant labourers who moved northwards in the dry season and established temporary camps at the salt workings. The workers, élite owners and merchants involved in distribution of the salt must all have benefited to some degree from the trade, thus bringing some wealth to this north-western region of Borno, even after the destruction of Birni Gazargamu. The salt works themselves generated local demand for foodstuffs and other produce. However, the destruction of Birni Gazargamu and the abandonment of many towns in western Borno in the early nineteenth century meant that western Borno as a whole was much less wealthy than it had been in the previous century. The once famous Borno textile industry, which had probably been centred in the Birni Gazargamu area before 1808, apparently collapsed after the Fulani invasion and, in the nineteenth century, textiles from Kano and northern Zaria supplanted Borno production. Borno thus lost ground to the fast-growing commercial attraction of Kano city and its environs, and Hausa traders became increasingly involved in the commerce of Borno. A number of enterprising Kanuri had moved westwards around the beginning of the nineteenth century, just before the *jihad*, to Hausa country, perhaps encouraged by somewhat better climatic conditions to the west. Some of them ultimately established a trading network based on a trade in kola from the Volta Basin, which they brought to Hausaland and Borno, taking potash as a return load westwards. These traders, the Kambarin Beriberi, were urban-based and their urban orientation 'stood in marked contrast to the rural concentration and origins of the Agalawa and Tokarawa' (Lovejoy 1973; the latter being other important Hausa trading groups). They did not trade in rural areas. This reflects the urban character of Borno trade in general.[20]

The region of western Borno was thus seen to be an area of diminishing opportunity; the advantage lay with Hausaland and much wealth from the salt and kola trade, which had gone previously to merchants resident in Borno, was now syphoned off to the west. Lovejoy (1978b) describes Borno as an 'economic satellite' of the central Hausa country by the end of the nineteenth century and suggests, as a major cause of this decline, the Great Drought of 1738–56 and continued climatic degradation.[21] Borno probably also suffered because of its relatively low population density (which can be attributed to deteriorating climatic conditions but also to the Fulani wars and consequent migration and enslavement of population). Slaves obtained from outside Borno provided some assistance for the Borno economy, but compared to Hausaland – which was expanding territorially in the nineteenth century – Borno was at a disadvantage. The establishment of the Fulani emirates of Adamawa, Bauchi and Gombe cut off Borno from its major sources of supply. Moreover, the indigenous population available to obtain and direct the slaves was limited, and slaves, when obtained, were often not used productively. Many slaves lived luxuriously at court, while others formed the basis of Borno's military forces. Thus Borno never developed an economy comparable to that of Hausaland where cheap slave labour was used in rural areas to produce trade goods, such as cloth, and to grow food to support a productive non-farming population.[22]

The Borno *tala'a* probably benefited little from long distance trade in the nineteenth century. The salt trade was in all likelihood dominated by merchants based in Hausaland, while the cloth industry of western Borno collapsed at the beginning of the century. In the important trade in horses from the Shuwa areas, the Hausa were also the principal traders. The Borno élite and North African traders alone benefited from the trans-Saharan trade. What indigenous wealthy traders and craft specialists there were in Borno were generally located in the capital, in close proximity to the ruling class for which they catered. Some of these rich commoners had slave farms in order to support their households in the capital but there seems to be no evidence, as yet, to suggest that the farming was aimed at anything more than small-scale household production.[23]

There was some purely local trade, based on agricultural and craft production by the *tala'a* throughout the nineteenth century. Many rural periodic markets which exist today in Borno date back to the mid-nineteenth century or even earlier. In Auno, Mafa, Maiduguri and Konduga districts, 15 markets date back to the mid-nineteenth century. This was, however, probably one of the richer parts of Borno, after the decline of the western region in the early part of the century. Barth observed that every large place in the area had a market. Despite the somewhat arbitrary demands of a predatory state, agricultural producers must, therefore, have been left a certain surplus with which to trade. Even during Rabeh's short reign, new markets were founded in Borno. However, it is clear that these rural markets, like their counterparts in Hausaland, were generally small and involved mainly local foodstuffs.[24]

To summarize, wealth in nineteenth century Borno was, above all, urban-based, indeed concentrated in one urban centre, the capital city. There must have been very considerable inequalities – though we cannot measure them – between the capital and the rest of the state. Polly Hill (1975) has suggested that Hausa rural communities would have been far more inegalitarian than they are today, given the greater opportunities of large-scale farming and the profitability of rural-based long-distance trade and craftwork. In Borno the situation was quite different because of the deeply embedded urban tradition, which made it essential for any person with pretensions to social status to be city-based; and the lower density of population in the rural areas which was inadequate to support a thriving rural economy with resources for an extensive export trade.[25]

There would have been even less wealth, however, in the pagan areas on the southern and south-western borders of Borno where economic production was continually disrupted by the depradations of the Moslem slavers and internecine warfare between local groups. The unsettled conditions often forced these people into defensible remote hill sites, or swamp settlements like Gashua and other Bedde towns, where agricultural potential was limited, the development of trade inhibited, and the concentration of population presumably increased the incidence of disease. The difference in conditions of life between these people and the nobility of Borno have been enormous.[26]

The colonial era: trade, administration and taxation in a new context

The British expeditionary force which arrived in Borno in the dry season of 1902 described the country as 'flat, stale and unprofitable'. They were welcomed in Borno, however, which had suffered considerably under Rabeh's administration. Soon a new administration was established and Borno was gradually brought into a new set of relationships which altered both patterns of wealth within the region, and the position of the area relative to surrounding regions.[27]

Internal changes in the spatial distribution of wealth and privilege date from circa 1904, when the pre-Rabeh fiefdoms were enlarged and consolidated into discrete administrative units, and leaders (*ajias*) selected by the Shehu were sent out to reside in the districts they controlled. Meanwhile, the Shehu, who had resided at Monguno and Kukawa, was persuaded to move south. He set up his court in Uje fief close to the British fort of Mafoni in 1907. The new decentralized political organization meant that wealth from the fiefs was no longer transferred directly to the centre. District capitals grew up because of the residence there of the district heads and, after some reorganization in the early years, tended to remain at the same town. Markets at these centres expanded since the *ajia* and his retinue had urban lifestyles and consumption habits which they could support in the rural locations by continuing the collection of pre-colonial feudal tributes from the *tala'a* – despite British administration directives to the contrary. They were subsequently joined by Native Administration officials of similar status and income and together formed 'a class of urban cosmopolitans on the rural scene' (Cohen 1967). Roads were built connecting the district capitals with Maiduguri (the new capital of Borno Province), thus expanding the potentialities for trade in the district headquarters and encouraging a movement of population into those centres.[28] For the *tala'a* the new situation of heavy taxation and tribute cannot have been easy; although following on, as it did, from Rabeh's depradations, it was acceptable. The district heads had to obtain more resources from the fiefs than before because, in addition to their own requirements, they had to satisfy the new demands of office under the colonial régime. They could not survive in their new positions – as Cohen has stressed – without their retinues because of the need for assistants to round up cattle nomads to collect tax; if they did not obtain the tax they would be demoted by the British for inefficiency.[29]

The relocation of the Shehu and his court also affected the spatial distribution of wealth in the state since Kukawa and Dikwa rapidly diminished in size, and Maiduguri as base of the traditional and colonial leadership became the centre of the region's wealth. As early as 1904, Maiduguri probably possessed the largest market of Borno.[30] The growth of Maiduguri and decline of Kukawa was also assisted by the reorientation of the foreign trade of the province. The trans-Saharan trade suffered a double blow under the British administration: firstly, the slave trade was very rapidly brought to an almost total conclusion leaving only ostrich feathers and ivory as major exports; secondly, the British pursued a policy of re-orienting trade to the southern coast of Nigeria, whence trade could be directed straight to Britain.[31] With the extension of the railway to Kano the demise of the trans-Saharan trade was assured. By 1911 there had been no direct caravan from Borno to Tripoli for some time (and very little trade via Kano). In 1912, large quantities of ostrich feathers and skins were being sold at the Niger Company's Nafada station (on the river Gongola) and the Borno Annual Report of that year therefore concluded that the majority of Tripoli trade now went westwards.[32]

The reorientation of trading patterns was soon to disadvantage Borno relative to other areas – notably Hausaland – which had been brought under British rule. In the trans-Saharan trade, Borno had an equal advantage, locationally, with Hausaland in terms of distance to the Mediterranean coast. In the context of the new British acquisitions, this was no longer the case. It was much further from the coast and the major port of Lagos than Southern Nigeria, the Middle Belt, or Hausaland. Borno's peripheral position was confirmed when the rail-

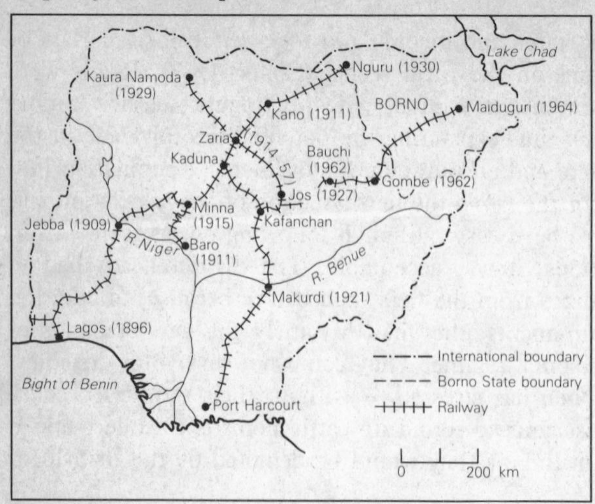

Fig. 50 Extension of the Nigerian railway system towards Borno

way line was built to Kano in 1911. Central Borno did not obtain a rail link with the rest of Nigeria until after independence and, throughout the colonial period, much of this region remained somewhat remote and inaccessible, despite the development of road links and the construction of a railway to Nguru on its western border (Figure 50). Thus, in the twentieth century, the pre-colonial labour constraint which had retarded development was joined by an increasingly apparent second constraint, the transport problem.[33]

Colonial trade

Despite Borno's distance from the coast, there was a very early colonial interest in export trade development in the province, based (almost wholly) on peasant production.[34] In the early decades the emphasis was on hides and skins which were more valuable in relation to weight than groundnuts, and could thus be profitably carried over much greater distances. In 1908, the Borno annual report noted that a considerable industry in tanned skins was developing, sold through the Niger Company store at Nafada, and in 1916 hides were 'almost the sole article bought by European and all alien traders'.[35]

A number of companies moved into Borno fairly soon after the British occupation, to take advantage of this – and other – potential trade. The London and Kano Trading Company (established in Kano in 1905) arrived first in British Borno in 1912, but by 1915 there were seven non-African firms. Representatives of Patterson Zochonis and John Holt arrived in 1916 and 1917 respectively. By 1934 European companies held permanent trading plots at Maiduguri, Nguru and

Geidam and temporary plots in a much larger number of centres. Fellmongering plots were occupied at Maiduguri (20 in number); Nguru (28); Potiskum (1); Damaturu (1) and Geidam (1). In Maiduguri these were all in European hands, (with Patterson Zochonis, London and Kano, UAC, GBO, John Holt, CFAO and L. Ambrosini all represented) but in Nguru ownership was more diverse, and in addition to the main European companies, there were about 12 owners of Lebanese nationality and certainly one indigenous firm, Dantata (which was also very important in the Kano groundnut trade).[36] This invasion of European companies into Borno was small, however, compared with Hausaland. In Kano there were 18 expatriate trading companies operating by the end of 1913 (compared to, at most, two Lebanese firms in Maiduguri) and expansion from that time was rapid. Much of the trade in skins and livestock from western and northern Borno went direct to Kano and it is not possible, therefore, to make an accurate estimate of the Borno trade in hides and skins. The trade in hides and skins continued to grow in Borno, however, and in the early 1950s UAC in Nigeria purchased 36 per cent of its hides from the north-east (Borno and Adamawa).[37]

The groundnut trade in Borno developed much more slowly than in Hausaland, although as early as 1911 'fair quantities' were being taken from the western districts to Nafada for sale, and there was some export of groundnuts to Kano from Allaguerno district from 1919. The construction of the railway extension to Nguru, opened in 1930, brought a local boom in groundnuts at Nguru railhead, however. All over the province, for a distance of up to 250 miles from the railway, farmers grew and transported groundnuts to Nguru. UAC purchased groundnuts at Maiduguri for the first time in 1932 and Potiskum, on the Jos road, developed as an important centre for the trade. The majority of nuts at this time were reportedly handled by Kanuri, with the emphasis on marketing by the producer or his direct agent.[38]

By 1937 it was recognized that groundnuts were, in much of Borno, a gamble, due to the heavy freight costs and fluctuations in groundnut prices. Nonetheless, the trade continued with considerable fluctuations in purchases from year to year.[39] The groundnut boom did not cause such widespread problems in Borno as in Hausaland, but it did result in shortages of grain in the Nguru area, from time to time, as farmers enlarged their groundnut acreage at the expense of food crops. The lack of an overwhelming conversion to groundnut cultivation was to the advantage of the pastoralists in Borno, since the expansion of their herds could continue without constant competition from cultivators.[40]

Another export crop which eventually made some inroads in Borno

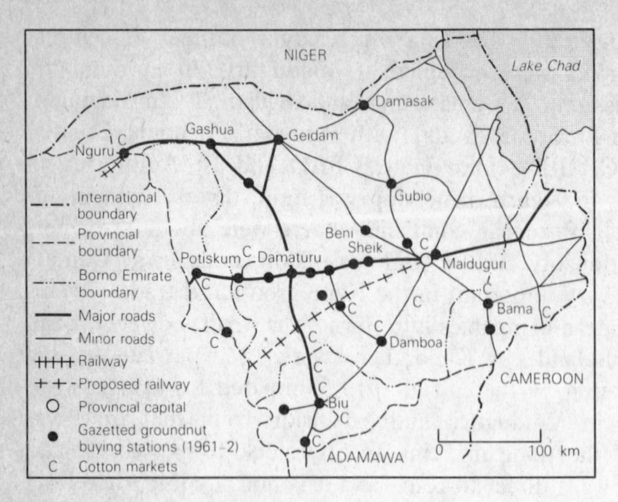

Fig. 51 Borno circa 1960

was cotton, which had been grown in pre-colonial times to supply a limited local textile industry. Due to the introduction of European textiles and the effects of the 1913 famine, the local industry declined in some areas and, consequently, so did cotton-growing, as in Allaguerno and Machena districts, for example. Sporadic attempts were made to encourage cotton production and a cotton market was eventually opened for the 1934 season, in Nguru. However, there seems to have been little real development of cotton-growing until the 1950s, when cotton markets were established over a wide area in the higher rainfall districts of southern Borno (Figure 51). Even then, no ginneries were established within the province; the crop was evacuated to Misau and Gombe.[41]

Borno was perhaps more importantly involved in the production of foodstuffs for the expanding urban markets within Nigeria, particularly in the plateau and southern coastal towns. A large live-cattle trade developed (though it had its beginnings in the pre-colonial era). As early as 1908 many cattle were being sent to Kano, Bauchi and as far as Lokoja and Ilorin, and despite the Rinderpest plague and the increasingly efficient collection of *jangali* (cattle tax), the cattle business boomed. It was based, to some extent, on imports from *jangali*-evading cattle keepers who had moved to French territory. A dried-fish trade also grew rapidly, particularly from the 1930s, as southern demand grew and long-distance transport improved. The major fishing areas were Lake Chad and the Gashua-Bedde area where migrant Hausa fisherman contributed considerably to the catch.[42]

Which people and areas then benefited from the various aspects of colonial trade in Borno? The trade in hides and skins brought some income to many parts of Borno, not only to the Fulani and Shuwa, but also to the settled Kanuri, many of whom kept livestock. The cash was used to buy salt, kola, new imported goods – and to pay increased taxes. Much of the profit from the trade, however, went to the long chain of middlemen involved in the purchasing network. Groundnut and cotton receipts similarly went to (settled) *tala'a* over a wide area, from time to time, after the Nguru extension in 1930, but only in limited areas, notably the railhead region and, to some extent, the Potiskum area on the Jos road, can the impact have been very considerable. Before the Second World War a good portion of groundnut and cotton profits went to the trading companies and their Lebanese factors, who bought the crops and profited from the advance purchase system, and – through the high level of taxation in Northern Nigeria (which had stimulated cash crop production in the first place) – to the government. The subsequent establishment of marketing boards for groundnuts and cotton, with their monopolistic pricing and marketing arrangements, did not greatly assist rural producers, since crops were purchased at well below world prices, the revenue diverted to the state's coffers and used to finance projects which were largely urban-based. The Licensed Buying Agents of the boards (at first urban-based foreign companies; subsequently influential indigenous traders) also benefited; there were many allegations from farmers of cheating by the LBAs and, in addition, crop-pledging was common everywhere.[43]

The Borno *tala'a* probably did not benefit greatly from the expanded West African long-distance trade either. The cattle trade was handled, above all, by the Hausa. Within Borno there were early reports that the Fulani were being exploited by Kano-based Syrian traders (who purchased cattle at very low prices). Hausa traders were later widely in evidence in the major Borno cattle markets and seem to have dominated the trade, particularly in western Borno. In the fish trade, southern Nigerians have played an important role since before the Second World War. The fish trade, by the late 1930s, was largely in the hands of Yoruba and Hausa traders based in Nguru and Maiduguri, who acted as agents for buyers based in cities with substantial southern populations. The trade came increasingly under the control of southerners after the Second World War. Obviously, some profit accrued to local producers but the major profits would seem to have gone to traders originating outside Borno, many of whom were non-resident.[44] Finally, much of the traditional West African long-distance trade of Borno – particularly the Manga salt and potash trade –

continued as before. All the main features of pre-colonial commercial organization – landlords, brokers, credit and the family firm – survived in Borno as elsewhere in West Africa. Indeed, the improvements in transport encouraged the expansion of this trade. Again, however, the major traders involved in the distribution of salt and potash beyond Borno were outsiders; in this trade the Hausa traders of pre-colonial times were joined by the new Yoruba entrepreneurs.[45]

Plange (1984), in an examination of the effects of colonial rule on northern Ghana, has suggested that European capital sought to wrest the control of trade and resources from the hands of local traders and reduce them to producers, wage earners or both. In some respects Borno was not dissimilar in its position to northern Ghana, since that region was also peripheral to the export economy of the country concerned (though Borno played a more limited role than northern Ghana as a recruiting ground for labour for the mining enclaves). However, the foregoing analysis of the beneficiaries of colonial trade in Borno indicates that an interpretation in this vein is not entirely adequate, for here local traders had already been ousted, to some extent, by Hausa competition. Hausa traders had played an increasingly important role in Borno trade from the early nineteenth century and the Tripolitan traders were a very powerful foreign group. The interests of southern Nigerians in Borno trade, however, followed very closely the northward movement of the British in the early years of the twentieth century, and were probably encouraged by the appointment of southern clerks in the British administration. Southerners soon saw the opportunities open to them in Borno and the advantages of their contacts in southern towns. Thus a Yoruba trader had established a canteen at Potiskum by 1927, just after the opening of the all-season route to Jos, and others bought lorries and plied the route from Potiskum to Jos, supplying the mining areas of the plateau with corn and other foodstuffs. By 1945, the dried-fish trade from Lake Chad was in southern hands, as was a greater part of the dried-meat trade from Nguru and Gashua.[46]

In later years the expansion of hide- and skin-buying stations and groundnut and cotton production perhaps stifled local entrepreneurship, as Lebanese and European companies established themselves more widely in Borno and set up small trading stations where produce was purchased and merchandise sold (Figure 51). The colonial administration in Borno provided some assistance to these foreign companies, but on occasions made recommendations directly counter to the interests of overseas companies; perhaps a sort of benevolent paternalism. The trading stations never supplanted rural periodic markets which continued to thrive. There was, indeed, some integration between the two systems, traders hawking wares obtained from the urban canteens, and purchasing produce in the markets for sale back to the canteens. The penetration of mercantile capital had occurred at a later date and less intensively than in Hausaland, and this delay, in some respects, probably benefited the Borno rural *tala'a*; it did not, however, necessarily benefit the city-based indigenous trading community.[47]

Other aspects of colonial administration were perhaps more damaging than their limited direct interference in trade; in particular, the fact that despite Borno's reliance on agriculture and pastoralism, these activities gained little attention, or investment, from the colonial administration who were preoccupied with export crop production. The loss of labour in southern Borno to the tin mines was perhaps also significant, in a region where labour was an important constraint on agricultural development. The fact that rural women in Borno did not go into household seclusion in this period (unlike their counterparts in Hausaland) is probably a reflection of the low density of population and the shortage of labour. The contribution of women to agricultural production continued (and has continued up to the present) to be essential to the vast majority of rural households.[48]

There is also some evidence to suggest that the vulnerability of the population in times of drought was increased, as in Hausaland, by the impact of the colonial state. Cohen has suggested that food shortages were more serious in Borno in the colonial era because the large stores associated with the pre-1900 taxation system were no longer kept and the traditional tax exemptions which were temporarily applicable, in times of drought or disaster, to allow communities to recover, were no longer made. The British taxation system was characterized by its rigidity.[49] Certainly, Borno suffered considerably in the 1913 drought. The population of Borno emirate as a whole was estimated to have fallen by 29 per cent in 1914, due mainly to a massive temporary migration (involving men particularly). Deaths directly from starvation in Borno Province were reported only from Bedde, where it was estimated that 2.18 per cent of males and 14 per cent of females died. Corn, when available here, rose from 2 or 3 shillings per 25 lb to 8 shillings per 25 lb. Taxation remained high. It is possible that Bedde suffered so much, partly because drought was slightly more intense in this region. Another contributory factor may, however, have been the location of the region closer to the centres of export production, in Kano province and the Bauchi tin areas, than the rest of Borno, and the fact that it was supplying both with corn at this time. Whether the social network of reciprocity and redistribution, which functioned to ameliorate conditions at times of crisis, disintegrated as rapidly in Bedde and Borno emirates as it apparently did in Hausaland on the introduction of colonial rule is not clear, but by the 1970s such a breakdown had certainly occurred.[50]

Colonial trade and spatial inequality

With the decentralization of administration and the spread of trading posts colonial rule brought what might superficially appear to be an amelioration of the spatial inequalities – notably the great gulf between capital city and rural areas. However, such developments represented urban enclaves and did little to bring genuine rural transformation. There were some opportunities for the settled rural *tala'a* to produce goods for trade – in the context of increased taxation this was necessary – and rural periodic markets continued to thrive. The cattle nomads, some of whom had benefited under the al-Kanemis, once more benefited – at least in the short term – as a result of increased demand for cattle hides and skins. On the other hand nomads were faced with an enormous increase in taxation and reduced opportunities for evasion. The opportunities for making money were, as before, greater in the towns (especially the capital) than the rural areas. In these centres benefits of increased trade accrued to a somewhat larger group than in the pre-colonial era: the old aristocracy (some of whom were involved in trade), and the old-established wealthy Kanuri and Hausa traders (who still benefited through their important connections), but also the new traders: Yoruba, Ibo, Lebanese, Syrian and European, all of whom favoured urban residence. In the context of urban-biased colonial expenditure on health, education, markets and other facilities, this preference is understandable. Wealth thus remained primarily a feature of the urban centres, not just the capital city, but also to a greater extent than in pre-colonial times, other important towns such as Nguru.

Throughout the rural areas the period saw some adjustment, notably the growing advantages of the already comparatively rich Maiduguri central region, and the rapid expansion of the Nguru region and the Potiskum area (previously in the no-man's-land between Borno and the Sokoto Caliphate, and which in the colonial period became more productive by a borehole sinking programme). In the latter areas, advantages in increased income from groundnuts and grain were to some extent offset by increasing vulnerability to external fluctuations in demand and intervention by outsiders in the local economy. The Kukawa area meanwhile declined relative to other rural areas, disadvantaged by the loss of Kukawa's status as capital city, the disappearance of the trans-Saharan trade and its remoteness from Maiduguri and the rest of Nigeria. Perhaps the greatest beneficiaries of the colonial régime were the inhabitants of the old pagan areas on Borno's borders. The 'pax brittanica' for these people meant an end to slave raiding, an opportunity to expand out of their difficult defensive sites, and a considerable growth of local trade and markets. Even here, however, the picture is not clear-cut since these areas faced new demands and impositions: the introduction of Muslim chiefs and, for some areas, the introduction of taxation for the first time. In western districts this necessitated, for many, withdrawal from agriculture for periods of temporary labour in the tin mines of the plateau, or elsewhere labour in road construction gangs. The expansion of trade itself, according to the Northern Nigerian medical reports, led to the spread of disease in pagan areas.[51]

Overall, it may be concluded that the expansion and redefinition of trade in the colonial era brought a much greater internal variation in patterns of wealth distribution than had been current in the nineteenth century, greater variation between rural areas and the reduced dominance of the capital city; but the most notable feature remained the overwhelming urban concentration of income and other benefits. There was no withdrawal from the countryside in Borno, such as Hill (1982) describes as occurring in Hausaland in the colonial era. It had taken place long before 1800.[52]

At the inter-regional level, meanwhile, Borno lost ground because of its peripheral position in the new state of Nigeria. By the end of the colonial period it was clearly one of the least developed parts of the country. The beginnings of this decline, however, were already evident in the nineteenth century. It was not wholly attributable to locational disadvantages or colonial rule. It is, none the less, interesting to speculate how different Borno might be today had the proposals of 1903, for a railway to Lake Chad, been implemented.[53]

Continuity in the post-independence period

Many of the inequalities evident in Borno prior to independence have continued to exist in the period since 1960. Indeed, the distinctions in wealth between urban and rural areas are probably sharper than ever before. The Nigerian oil boom of the 'seventies brought increasing income from trade and government salaries to some urban dwellers, who have also benefited from the rapid expansion in government-spending on health, education and other services and facilities in the major centres. Political power has remained urban-based in Borno, and the extension of government investment in rural areas consequently limited and often strongly biased, when it does occur, to district headquarters which had already achieved importance in the colonial era.[54]

Usoro's (1978) survey of Nigerian rural poverty identifies the Kukawa region as one of Nigeria's poverty areas. It has been one of the poorer rural regions of Borno since the early colonial period. By contrast, farmers in the vicinity of Maiduguri (a region which has been consistently one of the more fortunate in Borno for perhaps 130 years or more) have benefited from the expanding local market for foodstuffs in the capital. The railway, opened in 1964, and subsequent improvement of the road links between Maiduguri and the west in the 'seventies also provided some additional advantages to central Borno, though the groundnut trade declined sharply after the drought of the early 1970s, and there is nowadays more advantage to be gained in supplying foodstuffs to local markets.

In the Maiduguri region and elsewhere, the rural periodic markets continue to function and assist in the supply of foodstuffs to the capital. New markets are still being established. In the remoter bush areas of this region, however, there is evidence that many markets are declining; in the six years 1978–84 seven markets (already in decline in the late 1970s) have totally collapsed. Some of those remaining are very small indeed and the limited range of products on sale reflects the poverty of the surrounding villages. Rich traders do not visit because incomes in these remote areas are inadequate to purchase luxury items. Many villages and hamlets moved with their markets to the roadside, in the 1960s and 1970s, where there is greater opportunity for trade of all kinds. A modification of the distribution of wealth, such as there is, has evidently occurred in rural Borno associated with the major road construction programme and increased vehicle ownership since independence. The availability of land in many parts of Borno makes such a reorganization of settlement still feasible. It has allowed the traditional system of rural periodic markets to continue where in other parts of Africa they may be in decline.

Villagers have responded rapidly to the new opportunities open to them, exhibiting a degree of flexibility which has been characteristic of the region for many years. But the fact that they have been able to move so easily reflects the poverty and lack of infrastructural development of the villages concerned. Despite the spatial reorganization of local marketing, there is a clear pattern of movement up-hierarchy from small bush-markets to larger bush-markets, to roadside centres and from there to Maiduguri. The biggest traders are located in the capital; only the part-time petty traders are based in bush hamlets and even these travel to Maiduguri periodically to purchase trade goods.[55]

Recent developments in modern agriculture in Borno are unlikely to have a major impact on rural inequalities, at least in the near future. Large-scale non-irrigated commercial farming by local entrepreneurs has not expanded as rapidly in Borno as elsewhere in Nigeria in recent years, perhaps because of the high risk of crop failure and low levels of productivity in agriculture in an area of low and variable rainfall. Some development has occurred but is unlikely to have altered the basic pattern of urban wealth concentration. There does not seem to be much evidence, as yet, of a significant class of wealthy farmer-traders emerging in the rural areas of Borno, such as has been described by Clough (1981) in Hausaland, associated with modern commercial farming. Indeed, it is probable that in Borno, entrants into large-scale commercial farming will retain their urban residential status. As Cohen (1967) has pointed out, 'many Kanuri are not rooted in the land emotionally'. Moreover, there is no tradition of long-distance trade based in rural areas, as there was in Hausaland.[56]

The development of the major irrigation scheme at Lake Chad and smaller schemes elsewhere has probably improved the lot of some farmers, though the impact of such schemes on rural communities in Borno awaits detailed assessment. The widespread extension of irrigation may have serious long-term implications for the pastoralist population of Borno who have been competing increasingly with farmers for access to water in recent years. The seemingly advantageous development of boreholes, in the late colonial and post-independence years has exacerbated problems of overstocking, overgrazing and land degradation (particularly in north-east Borno, an already disadvantaged region) and pastoralists may well suffer further difficulties as the irrigated acreage expands.[57]

Conclusion

Relative to the rest of Nigeria, Borno remains a disadvantaged peripheral region, despite the completion of the railway and the road building programme of the 'seventies. In 1975 it contained only 10 modern industrial establishments and although its share of Nigeria's industrial employment subsequently expanded slightly (from 0.2 to 0.8 per cent between 1975 and 1980) the proportion remains remarkably low. While investment by large multinationals may not be the answer to Borno's problems, the lack of industrial development is indicative of the unattractiveness of the region. Borno contains today about four per cent of Nigeria's population, but the proportion is declining, due to a combination of out-migration and lower rates of natural increase than other parts of Nigeria. This can, again, be related to the disadvantaged position of Borno. Asiwaju (1984) in a study of the problems of Nigeria's borderlands, has recommended compensatory investment in borderland LGAs in the form of a special development fund from the federal government, but the likelihood of an early introduction of such measures appears remote. Only perhaps in the context of a major oil industry development in the Chad Basin can one see Borno's position changing radically.[58]

To conclude, Borno has experienced considerable change in its administration and trading relationships over the 185 years considered in this survey; the impact of the colonial period was particularly great. At the inter-regional level Borno has declined relative to other areas of Nigeria which has benefited perhaps more from Borno trade than has Borno itself. Internally, inter-rural variations in wealth have increased but remain secondary to the major urban-rural distinctions which have been evident since 1800. The roots of current patterns and problems – particularly the urban emphasis – thus extend far back in Borno history. It is only by considering the historical perspective that present inequalities can be understood.

Notes

1 For example, Hill (1982); Berry (1975); O'Brien (1979); Watts (1983).
2 Brenner (1971, 1973); Cohen (1964, 1966, 1967, 1971a, 1971b); Cohen and Brenner (1974); Lovejoy (1978a, 1980).
3 *Furma*–mounted clients of *kogonas* and other men of relatively high status (Brenner 1973, pp. 94–5).
4 Cohen and Brenner (1974, p. 128).
5 Detailed information on pre-colonial taxation in Borno is presented in Cohen (1971), in Brenner (1973), and in Cohen and Brenner (1974). A second major annual tax, the *Sadaga*, or royal tithe, collected primarily in grain, belonged formally to the ruler, but permission to collect the tax was given to courtiers who obtained, for the service, a portion of the tax in payment (Brenner 1973, pp. 109, 110). It too, therefore, benefited the court-based aristocracy. The establishment of slave villages (Kaliyari) in the countryside represented another potential income source. They were established by courtiers in their own or other fiefs and were not taxed. Virtually all surplus farm produce from these villages went directly to the owner. There has been considerable research on slave production in Hausaland (eg. Lovejoy 1978) but no detailed work on Borno slavery.
6 Brenner (1973, pp. 63, 94, 102, 113); Cohen and Brenner (1974).
7 The only exception to the norm of capital-city residence among the nobility

was the Galadima, an official allowed to maintain a separate residence in the Nguru area to defend the western border and approaches to Birni Gazargamu under the Saifawas. The position and power of this office declined in the nineteenth century (Cohen and Brenner 1974, p. 188).

8 Cohen (1970, p. 237); Brenner (1973, pp. 60, 62, 94–5); Cohen and Brenner (1974, p. 126–7). Various local fees (Kaskaram) were paid to local headmen and some village heads apparently became moderately wealthy on the portions of tax they retained. All kept a few clients and owned some slaves (Cohen 1970).

9 Brenner (1973, pp. 20, 110). More widely scattered (and therefore with presumably no major spatial impact) were the tax-exempt holdings of koranic scholars who farmed and studied together in priest settlements established by the court all over Borno.

10 Cohen (1966); Cohen (1967, p. 26). According to Temple (1919/1965, p. 437) the Magira, the Shehu's official mother, had 48 villages in her fiefdom scattered over 12 districts. Among the *kogonas* the largest owner had 12 villages in eight districts.

11 Hogben and Kirk-Greene (1965, p. 348); Johnston (1967, p. 203); Hodgkin (1960, pp. 320–1 citing Gentil); Brenner (1973, pp. 19–20); Hallam (1977, pp. 83–4, 159, 160–1).

12 Karnak Logone, the prosperous centre of a small state and vassal of Borno from circa 1830, paid an annual tribute of 100 slaves and 100 gowns (Hallam 1977, pp. 121–2).

13 Brenner (1973, pp. 109, 141); Denham, Clapperton and Oudney (1826, vol. 1, p. 261).

14 Brenner (1973, pp. 112, 114–5); Hopkins (1973, pp. 113, 122); Nachtigal (1980, vol. 2, p. 233). The Borno-Fezzan-Tripoli route was one of three major trans-Saharan routes in the first half of the nineteenth century, and perhaps the most active of all until the 1820s (Boahen 1964), after which it was disrupted by political disturbances. It became increasingly unsafe, resulting in a growing emphasis on the Kano-Ghadames route. The Sokoto Caliphate, unlike Borno, was able to control the desert tribes along the latter route (Johnston 1967, pp. 160–1). In the 1850s it was necessary to make amendments to the British commercial treaty with Borno, organized by Barth, because the Bornoans were unable to warrant the security of the road between Borno and Fezzan (Benton 1968 vol. 1, pp. 198–203). For references to the importance of the slave trade on the Borno route see, for example: Proceedings of the Association ... (1810, p. 160); Denham, Clapperton and Oudney (1826, vol. 2, p. 190); Nachtigal (1980, vol. 2, p. 233).

15 Brenner (1971, pp. 142, 150); Proceedings of the Association ... (1810, p. 181). In Denham's day some traders returned to North Africa with 15–20,000 dollars (Johnston and Muffett, 1973, p. 93). According to Nachtigal (1980, vol. 2, p. 235) profits of 200–300% were usual on the return trade southwards.

16 Nachtigal (1980, vol. 2, p. 234); Lovejoy and Baier (1975). Baier (1980, p. 65) suggests, however, that in Hausa areas the peasantry obtained some benefit from the ostrich trade, as large-scale producers enjoyed no real advantage over small-scale operations. Kanuri village heads in Damergu thus acted as entrepreneurs in the trade, selling directly to Ghadamasi

merchants (though one of two dominant Tuareg groups in the area taxed them and took half the value of their trade).

17 In the 1860s, Borno experienced a depression in trade, but in the 'seventies the value of Sudan products entering Tripoli had increased nearly six-fold. Although much of this increase was probably due to the trade from Hausaland it seems likely that Borno also profited. There was further trade depression in the early 'eighties and the severe *Kumoreji* tax was instituted (Brenner 1973, p. 87) which involved collecting half the possessions of the populace through court agents. After 1888 the depression deepened, probably due to syphoning of trade along the Wadai route further east. Rabeh's invasion precluded the trade recovery that occurred on the Kano route in the 1980s. After Rabeh's accession, caravans certainly travelled from Tripoli and Benghazi to Borno in 1899 (PRO, CO446/5 no. 28632 and 658/23 no. 23571). Despite the exodus of Tripolitans to Kano and Sokoto at the beginning of Rabeh's occupation, there were still approximately 100 Tripolitan traders in the town when it was occupied by the French. Trade cannot have been great, however. In 1897 the British consul in Tripoli estimated that 84 per cent of Tripoli's exports towards the Sudan were destined for the Kano route. Hallam (1977, pp. 132, 168); Baier (1980, p. 39); Nachtigal (1980, vol. 2, pp. 234, 238); Smalldone (1971, p. 161).

18 The desert salt trade from Bilma was already out of Borno hands. See Lovejoy (1978b); Proceedings of the Association ... (1810, pp. 158, 169); Brenner (1973, p. 24).

19 Lovejoy (1978b); Brenner (1971, p. 140); Adamu (1978, pp. 92, 185); Works (1976, p. 183). Large shipments of kola reached Abeche and even Khartoum in the late nineteenth century.

20 Lovejoy (1978b); Denham, Clapperton and Oudney (1826, vol. 1, p. 211); Adamu (1978, pp. 92, 185); Baier (1980, p. 31); Lovejoy (1973, 1978a).

21 Lovejoy (1978b); Nicholson (1978, p. 10). Barth notes in Kano the transit of natron from Borno to Nupe which 'always passes into other hands' at Kano and 'in so doing leaves a considerable profit in the place' (Barth cited in Hodgkin, 1960, p. 261). Elsewhere he records that Borno people very rarely carried natron beyond Gumel and passes many Hausa traders not only on the Borno roads but in Baghirmi. Earlier in the century, Denham wrote 'Bornu is scarcely anything more than a mart of rendezvous of caravans from Hausaland ... The Tripoli and Fezzan traders ... are waiting with their northern produce to tempt the cupidity of the Hausa slave merchants.' (Denham cited in Johnston and Muffett 1973, pp. 95–6.)

22 Fisher and Fisher (1970, p. 125); Denham in Johnston and Muffett (1973, p. 95) Migration of one sort or another seems to have continued throughout the nineteenth century. Vogel in a letter to Barth observed, 'countless emigrants to the Bauchi hills, carrying their little property, bear witness to the bad government in Borno; the same is proved by the large ruined and deserted towns that one passes on the road'.

23 Law (1980, pp. 55, 56); Cohen (1970, p. 238).

24 Barth (1857, vol. 5, p. 93); Hill (1975).

25 According to Brenner the exploitation of the peasantry was widespread in Borno, particularly in the second half of the nineteenth century. In view of the lack of bonds between the new, mainly immigrant Shuwa and Kanembu ruling class of the al-Kanemi dynasty and the Kanuri peasantry,

this state of affairs was not perhaps surprising. (Brenner 1973, pp. 109, 114.)

26 Gleave and Prothero (1971).

27 Nigerian national archives, Kaduna (henceforth NAK) SNP 10, 286 p/1913 Borno Emirate Assessment Report, 1912.

28 Cohen (1964, pp. 505, 508); Cohen (1967, p. 102), Cohen (1971b, p. 71). A new market thus appeared at Damaturu (NAK, SNP 10, 426 p/1919, Allaguerno district assessment report) while the Dapchi market increased greatly in importance, again as a result of the *ajia's* residence (NAK, SNP17, K2041, Borsari district assessment report 1918).

29 Cohen (1971b, p. 563) The official taxation alone for Bedde emirate in 1913 was based on roughly 10 per cent of a man's wealth. (NAK, SNP 10, 242, Bedde 1914) The tax per adult male was £0.05 (still considerably lower than the Kano emirate tax of £0.17 – Hogendorn, 1978, p. 65). When the local officials had taken their unofficial cut this must have represented a considerable burden to the area, particularly in such times of drought.

30 Boyd Alexander (1907, vol. 1, p. 267).

31 Slave trading continued in Borno from time to time. There is a report as late as 1935 from Kanembu District that slaves were being brought from the south and taken on through Mobber to French territory. (NAK, MAIPROF 3300 Kanembu district touring reports and district affairs 20 Feb. 1935.) Lady Lugard indicates the significance of trade reorientation:

> *since the superiority of the road from Lagos to Kano has been demonstrated over the desert route to Tripoli, it is to be hoped that* English goods *(my emphasis) will before long take the place in the market of Kano which has hitherto been held by other European goods imported through the Mediterranean coast.*
>
> (Shaw 1905, p. 496).

32 PRO, CO 446/98, 1911 Borno Niger Co Trade; NAK, SNP, 182 p., 1913 Borno annual report, 1912. It would be naive to suggest that Borno's trans-Saharan trade would have continued long after the turn of the century, even if there had been no European assumption of authority in the Central Sudan. The slave trade was being choked in the Mediterranean by European intervention which culminated in the Italian occupation of Cyrenaica in 1911. Moreover, less hazardous, cheaper routes to the Central Sudan were being developed. 'The camel was obviously no match for the steam vessel.' (Bovill quoted in Markovitz 1977, pp. 36–7).

33 An all-season road between Jos and Potiskum was not opened until 1925–6 and at that time the Kano-Maiduguri route was still at best a dry-season route only. It took three days to get from Kano to Maiduguri 'barring accidents' (Migeod 1924). Trade was thus much more restricted than in Hausaland. Lady Lugard presents an impression of the prevailing attitude towards Borno. She recommends the building of a light railway from the Niger to Kano:

> *This [the Kano-Niger route] is the caravan route which traverses some of the richest and most populous districts of the country.* When the markets of this district have been worked, *it would be time enough to extend a similar cheap service from Kano to the capital of Borno*
>
> (Shaw 1905, p. 499).

34 The only attempt by Europeans in Borno to produce directly for export was the ill-fated Allaguerno ranch venture. See Dunbar (1970).
35 NAK, SNP7, 1894/1909, Borno annual report, 1908; NAK, SNP7, 145p/1917, Borno annual report, 1916.
36 NAK, SNP7, 169p/1915, Borno annual report, 1914; NAK, SNP7, 471p/1915, Borno half yearly report, June 1915; NAK, SNP7, 152p/1916, Borno half yearly report, Dec. 1915; NAK, SNP7, 398p/1917, Borno half yearly report, June 1917; NAK, MAIPROF 2180 schedule of trading stations, Northern Provinces, 1934–50; NAK, MAIPROF 771 Temporary trading plots, 1928–42. The firm of Pagenstecher & Co had a representative over the border in German Borno at Dikwa in 1905 (Wirz 1974, pp. 169ff).
37 Hogendorn (1978, pp. 58–60). NAK SNP7, K102 vol III, Borno annual report, 1926. Gazeteers of Borno Province (1929, p. 70): 'the bulk of the trade in Borno is ... untouched by Maiduguri firms. The people ... prefer to travel to the bigger markets of Kano and the Benue with salt, stock and skins for sale'. See also U.A.C (1951).
38 NAK, SNP7, 904/1912 Borno annual report, 1911; NAK, SNP10, 426p/1919 Allaguerno, 1919; NAK, SNP7, K102 vol. III, Borno annual report, 1926; NAK, SNP7, 19187, vol. I, Borno annual report, 1932.
39 NAK, SNP7, 29641 Borno annual report, 1937 etc. Purchases fluctuated for example from 26,000 tons in 1945/6 to 41,141 in 1946/7.
40 Hogendorn (1978, pp. 97, 125); NAK, MAIPROF 11 36/S1, 5, 6, 8, cotton industry and marketing. The problem of grain shortages was put forward as a reason for not encouraging cotton in the Nguru area.
41 NAK, SNP10, 426p/1919, Allaguerno district assessment report, 1919; NAK, SNP17, 12168, Machena district assessment report – here there had been 335 industrial households in 1912, only 44 remained in 1917. NAK, SNP7, 10160 Shari district, Biu Division Assessment report 1928. Here, however, the reduction in cotton growing was attributed to the loss of labour to the tin mines. NAK, SNP7, 23596 Borno annual report 1934; NAK MAIPROF, 1136/s.8, cotton markets, Borno Province 1956/7.
42 NAK, SNP7, 1271/1909 Borno annual report, 1909. Borno's *jangali* in 1910–11 was £6,800, representing over 85,000 cattle and 76,000 sheep and goats. Many of course evaded assessment. NAK, SNP7, Borno annual reports 1907 onwards. NAK, MAIPROF 3181, fishing industry 1927–51. The fish tonnage railed from Nguru increased by 400 per cent between 1936 and 1938.
43 Williams (1981, pp. 4, 10, 12); Bates (1981, pp. 12–20); Forrest (1981, pp. 231–2). Nigerian farmers in the 1950s and early 1960s received only about one-fifth of the international (f.o.b.) price for their cotton and about half for their groundnuts. (Onitiri and Olatunbosun 1974). Vigo's survey of agricultural credit in 1956 (cited by Watts 1983, pp. 247–251) indicates the extent of rural indebtedness in Borno. In the 10 Borno villages surveyed 65 per cent of informants were in debt, 42 per cent of all credit coming from traders and 67 per cent of all loans being used to buy food.
44 NAK MAIPROF 200/1922 Allaguerno district general, 1922; NAK MAIPROF 3, Acc 21 Marte district notebook; NAK MAIFPROF 3, Acc 20 Gujba district notebook; NAK MAIPROF 2569, trade relations with

French territory; NAK SNP7, 40235, Borno annual report, 1945; NAK MAIPROF 3181, fishing industry, 1927–51.

45 NAK MAIPROF 2569, trade relations with French territory; Hopkins (1973, p. 250).

46 NAK, SNP7, 6808 vol. I, Borno annual report, 1927; NAK MAIPROF 3181, fishing industry – Nguru's 'foreigners' trading union' seems to have been wholly Yoruba in composition in 1938. NAK MAIPROF 3300 Kanembu touring report and district affairs.

47 In northern Ghana there was apparently considerable intervention by the colonial administration in local markets; in Borno emirate the colonial records suggest that the British very rarely intervened directly in local market development; though administrative rearrangements did result in the growth of new markets at district headquarters and the decline of other markets elsewhere, as in northern Ghana (Porter 1986).

48 Freund (1981).

49 The situation in Hausaland was not dissimilar. See Shenton and Watts (1979, p. 57); Apeldoorn (1981, p. 92); Watts (1983).

50 The *jangali* rose by 200 per cent between 1912 and 1914 (Mshelia 1977, cited in Watts 1983, p. 293). See note 29 *re* Borno taxation in 1913. 353 mm of rainfall were recorded in Western Borno, 355 mm at Maiduguri in 1913 (Grove 1973); Apeldoorn (1981, pp. 58, 62). See also NAK, SNP7 285p/1913, Borno quarterly report, March (grain exports); NAK, SNP7, 63p/1915, Borno quarterly report, December 1914; NAK, SNP7, 152p/1916, Borno half yearly report, December 1915.

51 Freund (1981); NAK, SNP7, 10160 Shani district, Bui division assessment report, 1928; NAK, SNP7, 16187, vol. I, Borno annual report 1931, Dikwa division; NAK 1035 C, D. Hill districts (Dikwa emirate); Kuczynski (1948, p. 684).

52 Hill (1982, Ch. 12).

53 PRO, CO 6596 Feb. 1903.

54 Ijere (1983).

55 Porter (1984). A new market at Leje in Mafa district was established in 1981 as a result of road construction.

56 In Auno, west of Maiduguri, according to the district head, migrants who live in Maiduguri are returning home to farm at weekends because of the escalating cost of foodstuffs in the city market. (Field visit, 1984.)

57 Elsewhere in northern Nigeria such multi-million naira schemes have not benefited ordinary farmers (see for example Wallace 1980); Grove (1970); de Leeuw, Lesslie and Tuley (1972). Increases of 77–129 per cent in cattle-tax figures are reported by James (1973) from the mid-1950s to mid- or late-1960s in parts of north-east Borno. See also NAK, BORNUNA 296/sl for reports of overgrazing problems in the artesian area, 1962.

58 Ayeni (1981); Adegbola (1982); Asiwaju (1984).

References

Adamu, M. 1978. *The Hausa factor in West African history* (Zaria: Ahmadu Bello University Press)

Adegbola, O. 1982. 'The regional impact of federal policies' (Unpublished Ms, N.G.A. Conference, Ibadan)

Alexander, B. 1907. *From the Niger to the Nile*, 2 vols. (London)

Asiwaju, A.I. 1984. 'Local governments in border regions: The special functional requirements of Nigerian states' (Unpublished Ms, Lagos)

Ayeni, B. 1981. 'Spatial aspects of urbanization and effects on the distribution of income in Nigeria.' In H. Bienen and V.P. Diejomaoh (eds), *The political economy of income distribution in Nigeria*' (New York), pp. 237–268.

Barbour, K.M. *et al.* 1982. *Nigeria in maps* (London: Hodder and Stoughton)

Baier, S. 1980. *An economic history of central Niger* (Oxford: Clarendon Press)

Barth, H. 1857. *Travels and discoveries in Northern and Central Africa* (London)

Bates, R.H. 1981. *Markets and states in tropical Africa* (Berkeley)

Benton, P.A. 1968. *The languages and people of Bornu*, 2nd edition, 2 vols. (London)

Berry, S.S. 1975. 'Export growth entrepreneurship and class formation in rural western Nigeria'. In R.E. Dumett and L. Brainard (eds), *Problems of rural development* (Leiden)

Boahen, A.A. 1964. *Britain, the Sahara and the Western Sudan 1788–1861 (Oxford)*

Brenner, L. 1971. 'The North African trading community in the 19th century central Sudan'. In D.F. McCall and N.R. Bennett (eds), *Aspects of West African Islam* (Boston) pp. 137–50.

Brenner, L. 1973. *The shehus of Kukawa* (Oxford: The Clarendon Press)

Clough, P. 1981. Farmers and traders in Hausaland, *Development and Change*, vol. 12, pp. 273–292.

Cohen, R. 1964. 'Conflict and social change in a Northern Nigerian emirate'. In G. Zollschan and W. Hirsch (eds) *Explorations in Social Change* (Boston.)

Cohen, R. 1966. 'The dynamics of feudalism in Bornu'. In J. Butler (ed.), *Boston University Papers on Africa*, vol. II (Boston)

Cohen, R. 1967. *The Kanuri of Bornu* (New York)

Cohen, R. 1970. 'Social stratification in Bornu'. In A. Tuden and L. Plotnicov (eds), *Class and status in sub-Saharan Africa* (New York: Holt, Rinehart and Winston)

Cohen, R. 1971a. 'Bornu and Nigeria: political kingdom in a troubled nation'. In R. Melson and H. Wolpe (eds), *Nigeria, modernization and the politics of communalism 557–580* (East Lansing)

Cohen, R. 1971b. 'From empire to colony: Bornu in the nineteenth and twentieth centuries'. In V. Turner (ed.), *Colonialism in Africa 1870–1960*, vol. 3 (Cambridge)

Cohen, R. and Brenner, L. 1974. 'Borno in the nineteenth century'. In J.F.A. Ajayi and M. Crowder (eds), *History of West Africa*, vol. 2 (London)

Denham, D., Clapperton, H. and Oudney, W. 1826. *Narrative of travels and discoveries in Northern and Central Africa* (London: John Murray)

Dunbar, R. 1970. African ranches Ltd., 1914–1931, *Annals, Association of American Geographers* vol. 60, pp. 102–23.
Fisher, A.G.B. and H.J. 1970. *Slavery and Muslim society in Africa* (London)
Forrest, T. 1981. 'Agricultural policies in Nigeria, 1900–78. In J. Heyer *et al.*, *Rural development in tropical Africa* (New York)
Freund, W.M. 1981. Labour migration to the northern Nigerian tin mines, 1903–45, *Journal of African History* vol. 22, 73–84.
Gleave, M.B. and Prothero R.M. 1971. Population density and slave raiding – a comment, *J.A.H.* vol. 12, 2, pp. 319–24.
Grove, A.T. 1970. *Africa south of the Sahara* (Oxford: O.U.P.)
Grove, A.T. 1973. A note on the remarkably low rainfall of the Sudan zone in 1913, *Savanna* vol. 2, 2, pp. 136/7
Hallam, W.K.R. 1977. *The life and times of Rabih Fadl Allah* (Ilfracombe)
Hill, P. 1975. The relationship between cities and countryside in Kano Emirate in 1900, *West African Journal of Sociology and Political Science*, vol.1, pp. 3–19.
Hill, P. 1982. *Dry grain farming families* (Cambridge: C.U.P.)
Hodgkin, T. 1960. *Nigerian perspectives: an historical anthology* (Oxford: O.U.P.)
Hogben, S.J. and Kirk Greene, A.H.M. 1965. *The emirates of Northern Nigeria* (Oxford: O.U.P.)
Hogendorn, J.S. 1978. *Nigerian groundnut exports: origin and early development* (Zaria: Ahmadu Bello University Press)
Hopkins, A.G. 1973. *An economic history of West Africa* (London: Longman)
Ijere, J.A. 1983. 'Local organizations as mechanisms for rural development in Borno State, Nigeria: analysis of spatial processes and patterns' (Unpublished Ph.D. thesis, Michigan State University)
James, R. 1973. 'Drought conditions – a note on the response of farmers and livestock owners to the dry 1972/3 season in the sandy plains and dunefields and the clay plains of the pressure water zone, N.E. Nigeria'. (Unpublished paper, Symposium on drought in Africa, School of Oriental and African Studies)
Johnston, H.A.S. 1967. *The Fulani empire of Sokoto* (Oxford: O.U.P.)
Johnston, H.A.S. and Muffett, D.J.M. 1973, *Denham in Bornu* (Pittsburgh)
Kuczynski, R.R. 1948. *Demographic survey of the British Colonial Empire*, vol. 1 (London)
Law, R. 1980. *The horse in West African history* (London)
Leeuw, P.N. de, Lesslie, A. and Tulley, P. 1972. *The land resources of north-east Nigeria, Vol. 4 Present and potential land use*, Land Resource Study no. 9 (Tolworth: Land Resources Centre)
Lovejoy, P.E. 1973. The Kambarin Beriberi: the formation of a specialized group of Hausa Kola traders in the nineteenth century, *J.A.H.* vol. 14, 4, pp. 633–51.
Lovejoy, P.E. 1978a. Plantations in the economy of the Sokoto Caliphate, *J.A.H.* vol. 19, 3, pp. 341–68.
Lovejoy, P.E. 1978b. The Borno salt industry, *International Journal of African Historical Studies* vol. 11, 4, pp. 629–8.
Lovejoy, P.E. 1980. *Caravans of Kola* (Zaria: Ahmadu Bello University Press)
Lovejoy, P.E. and Baier, S. 1975. The desert-side economy of the central Sudan, *Int. J. of African Historical Studies* vol. 8, 4, pp. 551–81.

Markovitz, I.L. 1977. *Power and class in Africa* (New Jersey: Englewood Cliffs)
Migeod, F.W.H. 1924. *Through Nigeria to Lake Chad* (London)
Nachtigal G. 1881, trans. 1980. *Sahara and Sudan*, vol. 2, A.G.B. and H.J. Fisher (London)
Nicholson, S.E. 1978, Climatic variations in the Sahel and other African regions during the past five centuries, *Journal of Arid Environments* vol. 1, pp. 3–24.
O'Brien, D.B. Cruise 1979. *Political economy of underdevelopment: Dependence in Senegal* (Beverley Hills)
Onitiri, H.M.A. and Olatunbosun, D. 1974. *The Marketing Board system* (Ibadan)
Palmer, H.R., revised Welman, J.B. 1929. *Gazeteer of Bornu Province* (Lagos: Government Printer).
Plange, N. 1979. Underdevelopment in northern Ghana: natural causes or colonial capitalism?, *Review of African Political Economy* vol. 15/16, pp. 4–13.
Plange, N. 1984. The colonial state in northern Ghana: the political economy of participation, *Rev. Afr. Polit. Econ.* vol. 31, pp. 29–43.
Porter, R.E. 1984. Traders' travel patterns: the case of part-time trade among the Kanuri of Borno, *Nigerian Geographic Journal*, vol. 27.
Porter, R.E. 1986. Periodic rural markets and rural development in Borno, north-east Nigeria, *Annals of Borno* vol. 3, pp. 107–26.
Proceedings of the Association for promoting the discovery of the interior parts of Africa, 1810 (London)
Shaw, F. 1905. *A tropical dependency* (London)
Shenton, B. and Watts M. 1979. Capitalism and hunger in Northern Nigeria, *Rev. Afr. Polit. Econ.* vol. 15/16, pp. 53–62.
Smalldone, J.P. 1971. 'The firearms trade in the central Sudan in the nineteenth century'. In D.F. McCall and N.R. Bennett, *Aspects of West African Islam* (Boston), pp. 151–171.
Temple, O. 1965. *Notes on the tribes of northern Nigeria*, 2nd edition. (London Frank Cass)
U.A.C. 1951. Produce goes to market: The hides and skins trade of Nigeria, *U.A.C. Economic and Statistical Review*, September 1951. pp. 27–48.
Usoro, E.J. 1978. 'Observed disparity in Nigerian rural poverty'. In Nigerian Economic Society Annual Conf. Proceedings of 1975: *Poverty in Nigeria* (Ibadan)
Van Apeldoorn, G.J. 1981. *Perspective on drought and famine in Nigeria* (London)
Wallace, T. 1980 Agricultural projects and land in northern Nigeria, *Rev. Afr. Polit. Econ.* vol. 17, pp. 59–70.
Watts, M. 1983. *Silent Violence* (Berkeley University of California Press)
Williams, G. 1981. 'Inequalities in rural Nigeria', Development Studies occasional paper no. 16. (Norwich: University of East Anglia)
Wirz, A. 1974. *Vom Skalvenhandel zum kolonialen Handel: Wirtschaftraume in Kamerun vor 1914* (Freiburg)
Works, J.A. 1976. *Pilgrims in a strange land: Hausa communities in Chad* (New York)

17
Ecology, Time and Development in Kano State, Nigeria

J.A. Binns and M.J. Mortimore

School of African Studies, University of Sussex and Centre of West African Studies, University of Birmingham

Introduction

Development has a poor track record in tropical Africa. Initiatives begun with enthusiasm in the high noon of independence have stagnated and even led to identifiably harmful effects on vulnerable societies and ecologies. Evaluations of the benefits of development tend to be ambiguous. Notwithstanding the evidence for economic progress in some areas, it would be naive to ignore the frustration that has resulted from the failure of developmental impulses to diffuse through the bulk of the population with measurable benefits.

What are we trying to measure?

The search for a meaningful definition of development continues *ad infinitum*. Theorists and practitioners debate whether development has occurred or is occurring in a variety of spatial and societal contexts, and frequently there is precious little agreement. The truth is that 'development' means very different things to different people – it is shrouded in value judgements and infused with subjective viewpoints.

For the economist, development might focus on increasing yields and productivity in relation to inputs. For the technologist, development may be about machines and fertilizers. For others, development is more to do with the quality of life and the fulfilment, or non-fulfilment of what are widely regarded as basic human needs – food, water, health and literacy. For the African farmer or herder, development, in more concrete terms, is likely to be concerned with the adequacy of family food supplies, the ability to pay taxes, school fees and medical bills and having the means to get through one year into the next.

Whilst confusion about the 'goals to be achieved' in promoting development remains, recent newspaper headlines inform us of widespread famine and starvation in rural Africa, suggesting that very little progress has actually emerged from the interminable discussions and considerable expenditure in financial and human terms. In particular, it seems that inequality, one of the key measures of development used by Seers (1969), may have increased, in spite of, or, as some would firmly believe, because of so-called 'development' programmes. Such programmes may actually be promoting a retrogressive process of underdevelopment.

Development in time and space

Development (or underdevelopment) is a process that operates through time as well as in space. The choice of time scale therefore has as much significance as the level of spatial resolution in any empirical study of the process. The penetration of market forces into areas where a subsistence priority has previously characterized farming and livestock production operates on a longer time scale than a government intervention in the form of an irrigation scheme. Indeed, economic change in rural Africa is a composite of events and processes having widely different temporal amplitudes. In the same way, ecological variables – especially the key production parameter of rainfall – may be discerned at several temporal scales varying from the diurnal patterns at one extreme to secular trends at the other.

Development (or underdevelopment) processes also have a characteristic of spatial discrimination; that is, not all areas are affected equally. Such differentiation is too often ignored because it adds to the complexities of analysis and requires simplistic conclusions to be qualified. However this problem is not satisfied merely by measuring and mapping selected parameters of development in chosen spatial units at a point in time, or even sequentially. The spatial dynamics of such patterns are not constant, and reflect underlying structural relationships whose explanation must be sought beyond the patterns themselves.

Combining the spatial and temporal dimensions of the processes of development (or underdevelopment) with ecological variables creates a very complex conceptual matrix in which the question of inequality is embedded. Inequality is encountered both socially (in differences between individuals, families or larger groups) and spatially (in the differences between populations inhabiting defined areas). Usually, in the developmental context, it is *economic* inequality that is the subject of interest. Given that economic inequality is an accepted social goal (a liberal assumption which is not shared by all), trends in inequality are valid measures of the effectiveness of development policies.

This chapter explores two case studies of the interactions of time, ecology and inequality in northern Nigeria. The first study assesses the impact of a rural development project in transforming the rural landscape, exacerbating tensions between communities and increasing inequality, spatially and socially, over a time span of about a decade. In the second, the longer-term impact of 'development' on social inequality will be traced among farming families faced with a major subsistence crisis. The two studies together illuminate aspects of inter- and intra-community inequality over different periods of time.

The setting

Nigeria in the 1980s is in the aftermath of an oil boom which, between 1970 (the end of the Civil War) and 1978 (the beginning of 'austerity') multiplied national income, supporting a manifold increase in public expenditures on infrastructure, development projects, and social services. Euphoria soon gave way to disillusionment as the economy lurched into oil-dependency and other sectors, notably agriculture, stagnated. Many critical studies have emphasized that the windfall gains in national wealth increased rather than diminished social inequalities in its distribution (for example, Williams 1981; Collier 1983; Bienen 1984, Watts 1987).

Kano State, with over 10 million people, is Nigeria's most populous state. Though predominantly rural and agricultural, the State's economy is dominated by the ancient and burgeoning metropolis of Kano City with a population approaching two millions. A striking feature in the so-called Kano Close-Settled Zone (KCSZ), radiating up to 100 kms from Kano City, is the intensity of land use with a population density of around 200 persons per square kilometre, unusually high by African standards. Around Kano some 85 per cent of the land has long been under cultivation making reserves of uncultivated land very scarce (Mortimore 1967).

That part of Kano State in which the case studies were carried out is semi-arid with a mean annual rainfall of about 800 mm, falling mainly during the short growing season from May until September. Evapotranspiration exceeds rainfall in all months except between June and September. Soils are mainly brown or reddish-brown sands, though in low-lying depressions alluvial and colluvial *fadama* soils are to be found.

Cultivation in the Kano Close-Settled Zone

Cultivated land may be divided into two main categories according to soil type and the level of the underlying water table. Upland, comprising 80 per cent of the area, provides the basis of the agricultural economy, growing guinea corn (sorghum), millet, maize, and a variety of leguminous crops such as beans and cowpeas. Seasonally waterlogged or flooded *fadamas* represent only four per cent of the cultivated area, yet their importance greatly outweighs their area, enabling cultivation of rice, tomatoes and vegetables well into, and in some places throughout, the dry season. In addition to supplying the growing urban areas with large quantities of vegetables, *fadamas* may also be utilized for grazing livestock and fishing.

With the great competition for land it has become a marketable commodity with increasingly frequent cash sales. Prices are escalating rapidly, Morris (1981) quoting compensation rates (generally much lower than real market prices) for compulsorily purchased land of ₦625 (about £550) per hectare in 1978, whilst *fadamas* can fetch three or four times more than upland (Turner 1984). There is considerable variation in access to land, with a generally positive correlation between holding size and economic well-being. Average holding size is under three hectares, declining to around 1.5 hectares closer to Kano. The long-established feature of individualized land tenure is reflected in fixed, and often rectilinear, field boundaries and repeated cultivation with little or no fallow. Many farmers keep some small livestock and soil fertility is maintained by the application of manure, compost and even urban refuse. On the outskirts of Kano, where every scrap of cultivable land is under crops, pickup trucks have largely replaced donkeys in carrying this refuse to surrounding farms, where farmers painstakingly separate organic material from the products of a modern 'throwaway society' such as tin cans, plastic bottles and polythene bags. Economic trees such as locust bean, mahogany, tamarind, mango, *Acacia albida* and baobab, are an important and protected feature of the landscape in this 'farmed parkland'.

Links between town and countryside are strong, and though many would give farming as their main occupation, a large proportion of the rural population supplement their farm income with a variety of off-farm activities, particularly during the dry season when farm work is slack. As Morris comments, 'the opportunity to pursue employment off the family farm has been a decisive factor in sustaining population growth'.

Pastoralism in Kano State

The other main component in the traditional rural landscape of Kano

State, as indeed across much of northern Nigeria, is the Fulani pastoralist with his herds of cattle, sheep and goats. During the lengthy period since the Fulani migrated into Nigeria in the early fourteenth century, a growing interdependence has developed between pastoralists and sedentary, predominantly Hausa, farmers, a relationship which is frequently termed 'symbiotic'. The basis of this symbiosis is the exchange of dairy produce for farmers' grain and root crops, together with the grazing of Fulani livestock on farmland after harvest, when animals can eat crop residues whilst breaking up old cultivation ridges and depositing valuable manure. Farmers have traditionally ensured maintenance of dry season access to farms and water by means of cattle tracks, and passing groups of herders might be invited to make camps and even find stalk huts erected for them (Van Raay 1974).

Fulani herders have a detailed understanding of their natural environment, including the quality and availability of pasture and water, the presence of insects and disease and the movements of other Fulani whose herds may compete for pasture and water or bring disease. In addition a Fulani herdsman 'must be aware of the sedentary populations through which he passes, the extent of their farmland, the suitability of their markets, the friendship or animosity of their chiefs' (Stenning 1957, p. 67). The Fulani calendar is closely related to all these factors and six eco-periods are recognized, each associated with particular climatic features and the quantity and quality of grazing resources.

The most stressful period is from February to June, coinciding with the end of the dry season, the retreat of the cool and dusty Harmattan and a marked deterioration in grazing conditions. Towards the latter part of the dry season most movement is necessary. Morale is at a low ebb, milk yields decline, the household diet may have to be supplemented with berries and wild plants, stock may be sold to buy much-needed grain, and, if the dry season is protracted, as it was in 1983, animals may suffer from nutritional stress and may die.

The life-style of the Fulani pastoralist is not easy and recent evidence suggests that it is becoming more difficult. For example, the symbiotic relationship between farmers and herders is not always as harmonious as it is portrayed and tensions frequently occur. A common cause of disagreement is occasioned when animals stray onto land under crops, particularly during the planting season in June, when animals are desperately short of grazing and farmers are eager to sow their seed and reap the benefits of the oncoming rains. With increasing population pressure and competition for farmland in Kano State, the pastoral free-range concept of land no longer meets with the approval it once enjoyed. In the face of a growing obsession with squeezing as much out of the land as possible, Fulani herders are having increasing difficulty finding pasture and water. Farmers are sensitive about animals damaging standing crops, and *fadamas*, which could once be relied upon to provide vital dry season grazing and water, are now often fenced off. Even the crop residues seem to be fewer, as sorghum stalks are gathered up and fetch a good price in Kano as fuel or construction material. But the Fulani in recent years have been facing even greater difficulties in Kano State. The much-publicized droughts of 1968–73 and the early 1980s have depleted herds and created severe water and fodder shortages. In the last few years rinderpest has returned to northern Nigeria killing many animals as the hard-pressed veterinary service has been unable to maintain an effective immunization programme.

Fulani pastoralists, always a rather marginal group in northern Nigeria, have become even more marginalized in recent years through dwindling grazing and water reserves due to drought and agricultural intensification. Furthermore, national and state government policies have done much to enhance this process with large-scale irrigation projects generating further pressures both within and between communities of farmers and herders.

Farmers and herders on the Kano River Project

The Project

At a time of growing interest in development literature about village-level, small-scale projects utilizing intermediate technology, Nigeria was embarking in the 1970s on a number of ambitious large-scale irrigation schemes in its northern states. In the Third National Development Plan (1975–80), river basin development, 'had become accepted by the federal government as a medium of regional planning and resource allocation as well as for achieving development at the grassroots of Nigerian society' (Baba, in this volume). By Decree No. 25 of 1976, the country was divided into 11 River Basin Development Authorities, including the Hadejia Jama'are River Basin Development Authority (HJRBDA) covering the whole of Kano State and half of neighbouring Bauchi State. In Kano State a huge proportion of the budget was earmarked for the development of irrigation, yet this covers only a small fraction of the State and involves relatively few farmers.

A report, commissioned by the Nigerian government from an

American team, recommended in June 1968 the damming of the Kano River at a point near Tiga (73kms south of Kano), the water being used for drinking, power and irrigating some 24,000 hectares of land within the loop formed by the Kano River south of Kano. Feasibility studies for the so-called Kano River Project were undertaken in 1969 by NEDECO (Netherlands Engineering Consultants) and in the dry season of 1970/1 construction started on the Kadawa Pilot Scheme and the Tiga Dam. The former was completed at the end of the 1972/3 dry season, whilst Tiga Dam, with a capacity of 1,963 million cubic metres of water was finally completed in 1974.

By 1976 Tiga Dam was irrigating land on the Kano River Project, growing a variety of crops, but principally wheat, tomatoes and rice. Some 22,000 hectares are being developed around Kadawa south of Kano, and Phase II of the project will irrigate a further 40,000 hectares around Wudil, using water from both Tiga and the Chalawa Gorge Dam (931 million cubic metres). East of Kano, in the downstream Hadejia valley, a further irrigation scheme will eventually cover 25,000 hectares associated with a barrage across the river near Hadejia.

The Kano River Project has already received much criticism from social scientists. The scheme bears all the hallmarks of 'top-down' development designed to transform rural landscape, economy and society: 'the key role in the scheme is allocated to the management, the farmer is just there to be persuaded or coerced into transforming his role in agriculture . . . at no point is much attention paid to understanding the farmer, his farming system, his needs, his knowledge' (Wallace 1978, p. 12).

The unequal land distribution which existed before the project has actually been exacerbated. Baba has shown that in 1971 the top 10 per cent of population held 19.6 per cent of total farmland, whereas by 1979 the figure had increased to 33.2 per cent. Possibly those who have benefited most from the scheme are the so-called 'big men', local traditional leaders, influential people such as project officials and wealthy absentee landlords, many of them living in nearby Kano City (Wallace 1978).

The costs of irrigated farming were often beyond the resources of the small farmer, with payments for seed, tractor use, fertilizer and water due before the dry-season harvest. Some farmers resorted to expensive project credit or paid high interest rates charged by local moneylenders. Dry-season labour was both difficult and expensive to hire, since NEDECO overlooked the fact that virtually every adult male has some non-farm job, mainly undertaken in the dry season.

The project has transformed the landscape of the area with the uprooting of many shade trees and the destruction of valuable henna hedges. The new cropping system introduced by the project represents a major departure from traditional farming systems. Two crops can now be grown each year: in the dry season wheat, tomatoes and vegetables, whilst in the rainy season maize, rice, millet and vegetables. Farmers are discouraged from growing the staple food, guinea corn, on irrigated land because it is not harvested until November, by which time the dry-season wheat crop should already be planted. Many important cropping decisions are now taken by the authorities rather than the farmers. Crops are grown primarily for sale, tomatoes being carried to urban markets or tomato paste factories, whilst wheat is an import substitution crop and sent to urban markets and flour mills. This emphasis on cash crop production means that project farmers often have to buy their basic foodstuffs, which in a drought-prone area with widely fluctuating food prices, might be seen as undermining their self-reliance.

Some farmers have increased their incomes considerably as a result of irrigation, and tomato production has at times been particularly profitable. Baba has shown that mean farm incomes increased by about 338 per cent between 1971 and 1978, but the distribution of these incomes has become much more unequal.

The effects of the Kano River Project have been felt much more widely within Kano State, not least in the downstream areas to the east of Kano. Prior to impoundment in 1974, the flood plain was the most important rice and cotton producing area of Kano State, dry-season vegetable and wheat cultivation was locally important, and the uncropped area provided abundant dry-season pasture and water supplies for Fulani herds migrating into the area. Furthermore, the Hadejia River system between Hadejia and Nguru was Kano State's most important fish producing area.

Between 1972 and 1977, a combination of drought and the inauguration of the Tiga Dam transformed this once productive area, such that rice production, pastoral and fishing activities suffered greatly. Stock (1978) estimated that some 260,000 people may have been adversely affected in Hadejia Emirate. People unanimously blamed the Dam for the poor floods and subsequent economic difficulties. Instead of an annual flood, the river régime is now controlled by the Dam in such a way that the channel has become incised and narrower (Olofin 1984). *Fadama* land may now be left high and dry above the annual flood and deposition of silt. Valuable dry-season grazing has disappeared. Inhabitants of downstream areas also point to a marked decline in fishing. On the other hand, the perennial flow now assured in the main channel supports increasing numbers of small pump-irrigated enterprises, and attempts are being made by channel modifications to reactivate rice cultivation in some of the formerly flooded areas.

Pressures on pastoralism

In the various studies of the establishment and impact of the Kano River Project only brief reference has been made to the implications for Fulani pastoralists. There is a need for much greater understanding here. The establishment of a large irrigation scheme across traditional grazing areas and migratory routes, together with a decline in *fadama* grazing in downstream areas has made the position of pastoralists even more tenuous in an already difficult situation. In their report of 1976 NEDECO recognized the profound implications of the project for pastoralists, albeit only in the project area itself,

> *the implementation of the Kano River Project, although essentially an agricultural scheme, will have an enormous influence on the livestock situation in the Kano Project Area. In the future many traditional management methods will have outlasted their practicability. They will either be prohibited, or be impossible, because the old facilities will no longer exist. On the other hand many new possibilities will be created. To take full advantage of the new situation, livestock owners will have to reorientate themselves completely.*
>
> (NEDECO 1976, p. 91.)

NEDECO estimated that out of a total resident population of 121,000 in the project area, some 6,000 were Fulani who were the principal owners of the estimated 10,000 cattle, 35,000 sheep and 55,000 goats. In addition, some 30,000 head of non-resident livestock passed through the project area each year, moving south in the dry season and returning north after the rains have set in. The consultants' report also referred to some 100,000 trade cattle passing through the area each year on their way to the slaughterhouses of the south, following special routes to prevent contact with resident and nomadic herds, since they are notorious carriers of disease. These routes have declined considerably in recent years with better road transport and the improvement of slaughtering facilities in Kano (NEDECO 1976, p. 94).

Several measures have been taken to control the movement of livestock within the project area. The aim seems to be to improve the quality of resident cattle at the expense of nomadic and trade cattle whose tracks have been rerouted around the irrigation scheme, thus, in theory at least, excluding them altogether from the developed areas. For resident livestock, NEDECO recommended that grazing be restricted to designated areas, located close to settlements and with good water and pasture. Wasteland areas near the cattle sites may also be used for grazing, but they are inadequate for the resident cattle population and any upgrading would require them to be fenced off, goats and nomadic cattle excluded, and management committees established to improve pasture and prevent erosion.

In short, the presence of wandering livestock is incompatible with the organization and objectives of an irrigation scheme. NEDECO recognized that care would have to be taken to avoid damage to irrigation canals and drains and prevent overgrazing and erosion. They were concerned that resident livestock numbers might increase with more crop residues from double cropping and better water supplies, and with farmers earning higher incomes there might be a desire to invest in more cattle (NEDECO 1976). Throughout their report there is an expressed desire to exclude nomadic livestock and settle resident livestock on fixed grazing sites where pasture, water and livestock quality can be maintained, with associated veterinary, extension and milk collection facilities. Nomadic pastoralism is thus, to all intents and purposes, being gradually replaced by settled grazing.

In an attempt to assess the impact of the irrigation scheme on pastoralists, a survey was undertaken by one of the authors in February and March 1984, during which a total of 127, predominantly semi-settled, Fulani herdsmen were interviewed in three areas: the irrigated area of the Kano River Project at Kadawa, 50kms south of Kano; the downstream area of the Hadejia valley around Ringim, to the east of Kano; and a third, control area with no irrigation or major rivers, centred on Rimin Gado, west of Kano (Binns 1984). The timing of the interviews was significant; firstly because the three rainy seasons prior to 1984 had rainfall totals well below average and pastoralists were experiencing some long-term difficulties. For many, the meagre harvest of 1983 was already severely depleted or even exhausted and crop residues were in short supply. Secondly, the months of February and March are, even in average rainfall years, difficult times as grazing and water reserves are gradually exhausted and many herders are forced to move further afield, usually southwards.

Cattle, sheep, goats and chickens were the main livestock owned by respondents, whilst a few had donkeys and other poultry such as guinea fowl. There was some reluctance to give numbers of livestock, possibly because they genuinely did not know, or perhaps more likely because they were suspicious about the reintroduction of the cattle tax, known as *jangali*. Virtually all the Fulani interviewed grew crops close to their main settlement. Maize, millet and guinea corn were the main crops, with some vegetables, together with groundnuts and, to a lesser extent, cotton, for sale. Cultivation was undertaken by older men, whilst youths tended the livestock. Major sources of income were from sales of crops and dairy produce and sometimes from selling male animals. Some herders actually received payment from farmers in return for manuring their farms. Main items of expenditure were female animals, household items, clothes, marriages, food, and salt and potash for the cattle.

Although some of those interviewed in the project area actually lived in the vicinity, many had moved from the north in search of dry-season grazing. In the downstream and control areas, migration was more on a daily basis, with young men taking herds away from the settlement during the day, whilst evening supervision of animals was undertaken by older men with milking and milk sales performed by the women. A common practice is for grazing to take place close to the settlement in the rainy season, and then in the dry season the herd splits up with young animals and lactating females remaining near the settlement whilst the rest of the herd moves south.

Herds comprising 20–40 cattle, with up to 20 sheep and 20 goats, were most common. Many Fulani spoke of smaller herds than five years earlier, due to shortages of pasture and water and animal diseases, notably an outbreak of rinderpest. Some had been forced to sell cattle to buy food, and numbers of goats and sheep had often increased relative to cattle. In downstream areas the shortage of pasture and water had necessitated a decline in the average size of cattle herds, resulting in a reduction in milk production and a decline in income from dairy sales. One herdsman complained there were fewer youths available to take care of the animals due to the attraction of nearby towns and Kano City.

When asked about changes in grazing and water resources, pastoralists in the downstream area lamented the reduction in dry-season *fadama* grazing, due to the absence of an annual flood since the completion of Tiga Dam. At Ringim the river channel is incised and former *fadama* pastures are now rarely flooded. Fulani in this area complained bitterly about the effects of Tiga Dam thus: 'the dam has denied us water in the *fadamas* and has compelled us to reduce the size of our herds to a size manageable by well water.' The water and pasture situation was particularly difficult in the Rimin Gado control area, where villagers were dependent on rainwater remaining in pits dug by the builders of the Kano-Gwarzo road. But they had to travel some distance and water delivered to villages was expensive. Pastoralists in that area also complained about the shortage of water, but a major concern was the intensification of cultivation on both upland and *fadama* particularly since the upgrading of the road. One herdsman complained that it was even difficult finding a suitable track through the cultivated areas without fear of upsetting neighbouring farmers.

In the project area herders told how the grazing situation had changed since construction of Tiga Dam, lamenting the loss of large tracts of land over which their herds could wander. They recalled how the area was once well-wooded with good grazing and plentiful supplies of leaves from mahogany trees which could be fed to cattle in the dry season. Though the project area nowadays had a reliable water supply, herders spoke of restricted grazing and common conflicts with cultivators. Movements of livestock are constrained and Fulani were aware that an overconcentration of animals could lead to deterioration of pasture and erosion. *Fadama* land, once used for dry-season grazing was now under crops, and fertilizers used on the project were sometimes detrimental to both pasture and animals.

Pastoralists seemed to be well aware of the environmental changes brought about by the dam and irrigation projects, and the majority of those interviewed felt these changes had been for the worse. They complained about food shortages, the decline in dairy produce and the problem of rinderpest, all compounded by the recent drought years. Some expressed a desire for government help in establishing storehouses for food and animal fodder to overcome seasonal shortages, whilst others wanted legitimate rights to their own grazing land. Many, whilst expressing pride in their herds and life-style, gave the impression that they were gradually succumbing to the pressures to settle and adopt a mixed farming economy.

The patterns and processes associated with the general intensification of agriculture in Kano State, together with the effects of government intervention in the form of the Tiga Dam and Kano River Project have severely constrained the life-style of the Fulani pastoralists. The recent drought years have brought further suffering to all except the most wealthy families. It is likely that pastoralists have suffered more than any other group, since their long-established ability to cope with shortages of water and pasture, through migration, has been progressively restricted.

Development for whom?

The rural landscape and traditional livelihood systems of Kano State have been transformed over the last two decades. The effects of these developments on Fulani pastoralists gives particular cause for concern, since although an accepted feature of the northern Nigerian landscape, they have always been neglected and somewhat peripheral to development efforts. Whilst the Kano River Project may have had some positive effects on project farmers, though there are those who would doubt it, cultivators in downstream areas, together with livestock herders have undoubtedly suffered. Tomato and wheat production may well have increased for a small proportion of Kano State's population, but for a much larger majority there have been few, if any, benefits from the considerable financial and human investment. Inter-community inequality has undoubtedly increased. Can it therefore be stated confidently that 'development' has occurred when so many farmers and pastoralists have evidently become less equal and more marginalized in rural society? 'Development' continues to mean different things to different people!

Adaptive capability in northern Kano State

The hypothesis

The second study takes a longer-term view and inevitably it becomes impossible to distinguish between 'development' and the transformations brought about by colonial and post-colonial agents of change. In particular, Nigerian groundnut exports, which began on a significant scale after the railway reached Kano in 1911, reached an all-time peak of over a million tons in the season of 1966–7. With growing monetization came urbanization and intensified inter-regional and rural-urban interaction as transport infrastructures improved. Early studies of the Sahelian drought (Copans 1975; Derrienic, *et al.* 1975) drew attention to weaknesses in subsistence production which had been brought about by the growing emphasis on export agriculture. Writing of the Sahel, Raynaut (1977) has argued that the pre-colonial subsistence system has been disrupted profoundly in its social aspects – a disorganization of the principles of storage and redistribution within social groups, and of reciprocity and solidarity within such groups; the splitting of productive social groups and the emergence of wage labour, and of land selling. Watts (1983), writing specifically of Nigerian Hausaland, argued the gradual erosion of a 'moral economy', as distributive networks, patronage, and storage systems disintegrated, commodity production penetrated the rural economy and the population became increasingly subject to indebtedness, exploitation by grain traders, taxation and social expenses.

By 'adaptive capability' is meant the ability of individuals, families or larger groups to respond to the consequences of meteorological drought. Such response may be made at three levels (which are not mutually exclusive): to agricultural drought, to poverty, and to hunger. The first level consists of a repertoire of adaptations within the farming system. Such adaptations are flexible, sequential and innovative in nature. The second level consists of seeking alternative sources of income with which to buy food, usually through the market. The third level consists of a range of alternative foods obtained by labour-intensive exploitation of ecological resources, both in the bush and on farm trees. The present discussion is confined to the second level of response (the first and third are explored elsewhere: Mortimore, forthcoming).

Adaptive response has been investigated in a number of African rural communities in the context of famines that occurred in the 'seventies and 'eighties. In northern Nigeria (Hill 1972), it has been shown that it is related to social differentiation, the poorest always being the weakest; indeed, social inequality can be defined in terms of adaptive capability in times of hunger. The Hausa term *masu dan hali*, used to denote better-off members of the rural community, may be translated 'masters of circumstances', or 'those who can cope'.

If adaptive capability depends on social differentiation, then it follows that changes through time in the relative capabilities of economic groups are tantamount to changes in social relations. It also follows that low capability in the poorest groups may accelerate the adoption of irreversible responses – such as selling land – which further weakens their capability and widens inequality within the community. This hypothesis has generated a controversy which focuses initially on the question of whether adaptive capability has significantly diminished for a majority of the rural population since the imposition of colonial rule at the beginning of the present century (Kates, *et al.* 1981). Or, as expressed by Wisner (1977), whether enlarged choice for the few has been countered by narrowing options for the many.

The data

Direct testing of this hypothesis would only be possible by means of medium-term longitudinal studies of family and individual incomes, an objective almost impossible to achieve under the usual constraints of field research. This approach is an indirect one, drawing on data from extensive studies in northern Kano State during the period 1973–86. In 1973–4, some 631 village heads in 20 administrative districts, and 125 family heads in five villages, were interviewed on various aspects of the impact of the Sahelian drought. This period of subnormal rainfäll culminated in harvest failures of up to 70 per cent in 1972, and more than 75 per cent in 1973. In the succeeding years, a longitudinal profile of one village was built up from multiple visits from 1974 to 1986, to evaluate the impact of drought and famine, the responses they invoked, and their aftermath.

Adaptive response to poverty in the subsistence crisis of 1972–4 may be considered under four headings: social networks, asset liquidation, alternative sources of income, and mobility.

Social networks

The first group of responses, having the strongest continuity with the past, consisted in mobilizing social networks. Normally, some redistribution of wealth takes place via the kinship system, or clientage, or on the basis of Islamic injunctions to help the needy, or as alms given to scholars and clerics. In 1974, of the 631 village heads, 95 per cent said that the *masu dan hali* (in which class they probably included themselves) had insufficient food even for their own families and could not help the poor (*talakawa*). In this respect the times compared unfavourably with the past. Nevertheless, many of the family heads interviewed in the five villages had received gifts of food, and of money, in both years of famine. Personal borrowing was also widespread (Table 17.1). But indebtedness is not freely admitted in northern Nigeria since usury is proscribed by Islam, so it may have been more extensive. Begging, finally, was unknown previously in the five villages, except for the

Table 17.1 Frequency of responses to poverty cited by 125 family heads in both the years 1973 and 1974 (per cent)

A	*Social networks*	
1	Gifts of food	27
2	Gifts of money	10
3	Loans	29
4	Begging	10
B	*Liquidating assets*	
5	Selling livestock	almost universal
6	Selling personal possessions	9 (20)
7	Selling manure	19
8	Selling or pledging land	10
C	*Alternative income*	
9	Labouring	68
10	Mat and rope making	55
11	Wood cutting and selling	33

() Response in one year only

socially approved practice of almsgiving to scholars and clerics; it is quite striking that one family head in ten admitted to it in 1973 and 1974.

Of course, there is no way of knowing whether this level of mobilization of social networks represents a decrease in quantitative terms from the levels obtaining in former famines (the major ones remembered were in 1913–14, 1926–7 and 1942–3). The view, often expressed – that in former times there was food, but if you had none, a friend or relative could give you some, but nowadays you do things on your own – could be wishful thinking. A consensus, apparent in 1974, that 'the rich no longer help the poor' suggests the disintegration of clientage rather than kinship or religious networks. Certainly kinship networks retained major significance.

Asset liquidation

The second category of response consisted in liquidating assets. Normally livestock are disposed of when cash is needed urgently, but the bottom had fallen out of the livestock market. So other assets had to be sold. Nearly every village head reported that people were selling items of personal property, such as clothing. Rather fewer admitted to it in the five villages, which are poor and remote. Compulsion to sell productive resources, however – manure, transport animals, land – had more serious implications in the longer term: especially land. Land may be either pledged or actually sold. In 80 per cent of the villages, pledging or selling land was reported, representing a transfer of productive resources from the poor to the better-off either temporarily (when later redeemed) or permanently. The occurrence of land (and other) sales was found to be significantly correlated with out-migration and indebtedness. But in the five villages, fewer than 10 per cent admitted to selling or pledging land. There is little evidence that urban interests were buying up farmland in the region as a whole, though this occurs in some places (see Van Apeldoorn 1981: 57–61). There is no evidence that a landless class has emerged, although studies of land distribution point to the existence of a substrata of smallholders, especially in densely populated districts (Mortimore 1967; Baba 1975; Orogun 1986).

Alternative sources of income

Under the third heading, the least commonly cited incomes were the broad range of normal secondary occupations, such as trade, barbing, weaving, and donkey hire, which tended to be confined to village specialists, since rural demand was extremely depressed. The most important was labouring, used personally by 68 per cent of the family heads interviewed, in both years of famine. Labouring for others on farm work or other tasks is the constant resort of the poorer members of the community, but times of hardship broaden recruitment. Indeed, a convenient way of dividing the village on economic criteria is by segregating labour-hiring from labour-selling households. Clearly the monetization of rural production lies behind this. The second most frequently cited alternative source of income was the manufacture of ropes and mats from the leaves of the dum palm (*Hyphaene thebaica*), for sale to urban traders in periodic markets, and the third was cutting and selling firewood – locally or, more commonly, in urban centres or along inter-city highways.

The second and third groups are directly, and the first indirectly, dependent on the rural periodic market system and rural-urban trading linkages, themselves fuelled by urbanization and the nationwide diffusion of oil revenues. Obviously, recourse to such alternatives could not be had on anything like this scale in the past. The same market system delivered small quantities of food to famine-stricken areas, at a very high price. Village heads were asked to evaluate the famine of 1972–4 in comparison with previous famines. Only a minority gave optimistic evaluations. But it is notable that many of those who did cited transport improvements and 'more food' or 'more money' as their reasons.

Mobility

Resort to spatial mobility further emphasizes integration into the market system. Mobility is not strictly a separate category of response, because it merely amounts to a shift of location while pursuing alternative sources of income. For most people, it meant short-term circulation for periods up to seven months (the length of the non-farming season). Such circulation is an ancient practice – pre-colonial as well as colonial – and deeply embedded in the economy of semi-arid northern Nigeria (see Prothero 1959; Goddard 1974; Swindell 1984; Mortimore 1982). Its incidence rises dramatically when the harvest fails. Such fluctuations have been traced over 13 years in one village, Dagaceri, in north-eastern Kano State. In this village, with a population of about 750, the proportion of family heads absent at any one time might be as high as 44 per cent (and the proportion of junior male adults, higher). Yet permanent migration is uncommon.

One family, which is fairly representative, may suffice to illustrate some of the dimensions of spatial mobility. Born in the village around 1921, *A* departed with a donkey on pilgrimage to Mecca when he was

16, in a party of seven from the village. He spent the next 14 years in the Sudan, mostly working on the Gezira cotton scheme. After returning, around 1951, he embarked on regular dry-season circulation (*cin rani*) to nearby destinations: clearing rice farms in the flood plain of the Yobe River at Gashua, and making mats in the Hadejia valley. Other Dagaceri men at that time were involved in trading natron to Kano, and in trading groundnuts. Meanwhile, he acquired farms, grew groundnuts for the market and foodstuffs for consumption.

When his son, *K* (who was married at his father's expense) was old enough to go in his place, *A* retired from *cin rani* and now makes mats at home. *K* tried trading vegetables in southern Borno (without success) and then travelled all the way to Lagos in the season of 1972–3, to retail goats from the livestock market. On learning that the crops at home had failed a second time in 1973, he brought financial help to his father and then returned. Making several trips each year, by 1980 *K* was borrowing capital in the village to purchase his own goats, but still returned without fail each year for the farm work. He had financed his second and third serial marriages. Others had invested their profits in purchasing plough bulls. The Lagos goat trade attracted a widening spectrum of Dagaceri men, and the numbers rarely fell below 20.

Such flexibility was a response to the collapse not only of the subsistence sector but also of the groundnut economy. In 1975 this crop was demolished by rosette disease, never to recover; Nigeria has exported none since (though production continues further south, for the internal market). In Dagaceri, the longitudinal profile of labour allocations from 1974 to 1986 shows an annual struggle against drought, pests and adverse economic circumstances with only occasional respites. Yet in 1986, the consensus in the village was that conditions were better than during the early 'seventies for most families, while being far below expectations. Resilience was the most noticeable characteristic of the village economy.

Summary

This evidence is not consistent with the thesis that adaptive capability is declining in the longer term. Social networks still have a role to play – time-honoured patterns of social relations have not disintegrated. Alternative sources of income have been amplified, both through the penetration of the market system and by means of circulation. Such responses are available to the poor as well as to the better-off. Asset liquidation, on the other hand, probably accomplishes a transfer of resources in times of crisis which impoverishes the poor in relative terms.

The amplification of adaptive response, involving mobility in particular, has been achieved through intensified integration with the urban-based market system of an oil producing economy. Some would call such integration dependency, the antithesis of meaningful 'development'. Certainly the terms of participation are extremely unfavourable to the part-time farmer who is marginalized economically as well as spatially. It may not be meaningful to compare his welfare under such conditions with what we suppose was the position of his precolonial forbears. But as a window on long-term trends in rural inequality, the subsistence crises of the 'seventies and 'eighties – while demonstrating its existence – do not offer a view of declining adaptive capability among the poor.

Conclusion

The two case studies presented here differ on several parameters of the spatio-temporal matrix suggested earlier. Changes affected by the Kano River Irrigation Project have been confined to about a decade and can be traced to a single intervention in the form of a government development project. On the other hand, the adaptive capability of farmers in northern Kano State to subsistence crises has been affected by a range of external factors over a period of nearly 80 years. In the first example, the evidence for increased inter-community inequality (herders *vis à vis* farmers) is unambiguous. In the second, the evidence for increased intra-community inequality (the poorer *vis à vis* the better-off) is inconclusive. But both examples suggest the relative marginalization of communities that find themselves located on the periphery of the urban, and market-based, economy in northern Nigeria.

One important conclusion arising from this discussion is that the characteristic distribution and trends in economic inequality are much more complex than is often recognized. To view inequality in terms of a sectoral or rural-urban model is a misleading simplification. What actually is the 'agricultural' or 'rural' sector? Who is disadvantaged, relative to whom? Two development policy implications follow from this. First, much better data are urgently needed on income levels and trends, if policies are to be designed to promote further equity and ameliorate inequality. Second, the complexities of inequality call for a corresponding subtlety in such policies which should be formulated on the basis of detailed appreciation of the changing character of rural communities and their associated livelihood systems and a familiarity with local aspirations, knowledge and expertise which could provide the essential catalyst for success.

References

Amin, S. (ed.) 1974. *Modern migrations in West Africa* (Oxford University Press for the International African Institute)

Baba, J.M. 1975. 'Induced agricultural change in a densely populated district: a study of the existing agricultural system in Kura District and the projected impact of the Kano River Irrigation Project, Kano State, Nigeria', (Unpublished Ph.D. thesis, Ahmadu Bello University, Zaria)

Bienen, H. (ed.) 1984. *The political economy of Nigeria* (New York: Praeger)

Binns, J.A. 1984. People of the six seasons, *Geographical Magazine*, pp. 640–4.

Collier, P. 1983. 'Oil and inequality in rural Nigeria'. In D. Ghai and S. Radwan (eds), *Agrarian policies and rural poverty in Africa* (Geneva: I.L.O.)

Copans, J. (ed.) 1975. *Sécheresses et famines du Sahel*, 2 vols. (Paris: Maspero)

Derrienic, H. *et al.* 1976. *Famines et dominations en Afrique. Paysans et éleveurs du Sahel sous le joug* (Rennes: Université de Haute-Bretagne)

Goddard, A.D. 1974. 'Population movements and land shortages in the Sokoto close-settled zone, Nigeria'. In S. Amin (ed.) *op. cit.*, pp. 258–80.

Hill, P. 1972. *Rural Hausa. A village and a setting* (Cambridge University Press)

Kates, R.W. *et al.* 1981. *Drought impact in the Sahelian-Sudanic Zone of West Africa: a comparative analysis of 1910–15 and 1968–74* (Worcester, Massachusetts: Centre for Technology, Environment and Development, Clark University)

Morris, J. 1981. Agrarian structure implications for development. A Kano (Nigeria) case study, *Oxford Agrarian Studies*, vol. 10, pp. 44–69.

Mortimore, M.J. 1967. Land and population pressure in the Kano close-settled zone, northern Nigeria, *Advancement of Science*, vol. 23, pp. 677–86.

Mortimore, M.J. 1982. 'Framework for population mobility: the perception of opportunities in Nigeria'. In J.I. Clarke and L. Kosinski (eds), *Redistribution of population in Africa*, (London: Heinemann), pp. 50–7.

Mortimore, M.J. (forthcoming) *Adapting to drought: farmers, famines and desertification in semi-arid West Africa* (Cambridge University Press)

NEDECO 1976. *Kano River Project, part VI Rural Development*, vol. 2.

Olofin E.A. 1984. Some effects of the Tiga Dam on valleyside erosion in downstream reaches of the River Kano, *Applied Geography*, vol. 4 (4), pp. 321–32.

Orogun, E. 1986. 'Land administration on the Kano River Project' (unpublished M.Sc. Thesis, Bayero University, Kano)

Prothero, R.M. 1959. *Migrant labour from Sokoto Province, Northern Nigeria* (Kaduna: Government Printer)

Raynaut, C. 1977. 'Lessons of a crisis'. In D. Dalby, R.J. Harrison-Church and F. Bezzaz (eds), *Drought in Africa 2*, (African Environment Special Report 6, International African Institute, London), pp. 17–29.

Seers, D. 1969. The meaning of development, *International Development Review*, vol 11(4). Reprinted in D. Lehmann (ed.) 1979. *Development theory: four critical studies* (Cass)

Stenning, D.J. 1957. Transhumance, migratory drift, migration; patterns of pastoral Fulani nomadism, *Journal of the Royal Anthropological Institute*, vol. 87, pp. 57–73.

Stock, R.F. 1978. 'The impact of the decline of the Hadejia River floods in Hadejia Emirate, Kano State'. In G.J. Van Apeldoorn (ed.), *The aftermath of the 1972–1974 drought in Nigeria* (Zaria: Centre for Social and Economic Research, Ahmadu Bello University), pp. 141–6.

Swindell, K. 1984. Farmers, traders and labourers: dry season migration from north-west Nigeria, 1900-33, *Africa*, vol. 54, pp. 3–19.

Turner, B. 1984. 'Changing land-use patterns in the fadamas of northern Nigeria'. In E. Scott (ed.), *Life before the drought* (Allen & Unwin) pp. 149–70.

Van Apeldoorn, G.J. 1981. *Perspectives on drought and famine in Nigeria* (London: Allen & Unwin)

Van Raay, J.G.T. 1974. *Rural planning in a savanna region – the case of Fulani pastoralists in the North Central State of Nigeria* (University Press, Rotterdam)

Wallace, T. 1978. *Rural development through irrigation: studies in a town on the Kano River Project* (Zaria: Centre for Social and Economic Research, Ahmadu Bello University – mimeo)

Watts, M. 1983. *Silent violence. Food, famine and peasantry in northern Nigeria* (University of California Press)

Watts, M. 1987. (ed.) *State, oil and agriculture in Nigeria* (Institute of International Studies, University of California)

Williams, G. 1981. *Inequalities in rural Nigeria* (University of East Anglia)

Wisner, B. 1977. 'Man-made famine in eastern Kenya: the interrelationship of environment and development'. In P.O'Keefe and B. Wisner (eds) *Land use and development* (African Environment Special Report 5, Institute of African Studies, London), pp. 194–215.

Index

Notes are indexed in the form: page number, *n* note number.